For Victor Friedmann, who spells it the way we used to.

Our Friedman Families

A Memoir of German Jews Who Escaped from the
Nazis to Achieve International Success

Wally Friedman

by
Wally Friedman

Bloomington, IN   authorHOUSE®   Milton Keynes, UK

AuthorHouse™
1663 Liberty Drive, Suite 200
Bloomington, IN 47403
www.authorhouse.com
Phone: 1-800-839-8640

AuthorHouse™ UK Ltd.
500 Avebury Boulevard
Central Milton Keynes, MK9 2BE
www.authorhouse.co.uk
Phone: 08001974150

This book is a work of non-fiction. Unless otherwise noted, the author and the publisher make no explicit guarantees as to the accuracy of the information contained in this book and in some cases, names of people and places have been altered to protect their privacy.

First published by AuthorHouse 11/6/2006

ISBN: 1-4259-3825-6 (sc)

Printed in the United States of America
Bloomington, Indiana

This book is printed on acid-free paper.

Library of Congress Control Number: 2006905059

This book is dedicated to my late wife
Babette Klein (Betty) Friedman
and for our grandchildren
Sarah Tamar Friedman,
Rachel Eliana Friedman, and
Alexander Henry Friedman.

Front Cover Photographs

Upper left: left to right, my Oma, Johanna Friedmann, nee Berman, and my father's father, Aron Friedmann. Upper right: left to right, my mother's parents, Johanna and Franz Friedmann, her brothers Karl (on the poney) and Paul, my mother Lotte, and her maternal grandmother, Anna Friedmann, nee Stoller. Middle left: Betty's mother, Frieda Klein, nee Zwickler. Middle right: my parents, Lotte and Hans Friedmann, behind me at our home in Boston, September, 1947. Lower left: the Altmanns; in the rear from left to right: Sophie, Sam, Lina, Siegfried, and Marie; in the middle, Dora, in front, Else, David, and my mother's mother, Johanna. Lower right: Betty's father, Alexander Klein in 1923.

Back Cover Photographs

Above: left to right, in front, Rachel and Sarah; in the rear, Mary, Wally, Michael, Deborah, David, John, and Karen holding Alexander -- all Friedmans. Below: seated, Walter E. (Wally) Friedman and his late wife, Babette Klein (Betty) Friedman.

Acknowledgments

I thank Inge Friedman for her lengthy interviews and for lending me her *Shoah* testimony; Diane Zilka for her mother's *Shoah* videotapes; Sal Marshall for some family letters, my son John for his recordings; and my son David who kept so many family documents, established and still maintains contacts with various relatives and creates awesome descendancy charts. I thank Rita Berman for her help with the manuscript. And my special thanks go to Nicole Friedman for her professional editing, careful proofreading, and unique insight.

Preface

These family memoirs are not the stories of all the members of our families who escaped Nazism and their descendants. But I am covering both sides of my family because both my mother's and father's family names are Friedman. My wife and I, our three sons, and their families are also Friedmans. I include not just first cousins, but distant cousins I feel close to. And many family members not named Friedman.

Concentrating on the past, not the present, I include people who are not family, plus friends, places, events, and a little history to explain our family's history. There are only a few stories about my wife's family because I know only a little about them. There is more about me than anyone else, forgive me, but that's someone I know a lot about.

Our families' stories cover World Wars I and II and the Cold War. I include much about Germany before, during, and after Hitler. The most significant event in all our families' lives -- with ramifications for generations to come -- was the Holocaust. I try to explain the inexplicable. I hope to make the people as relevant and understandable as I can. Yet this is an incomplete story.

To my knowledge only two members of our families have given their recorded testimony to Steven Spielberg's *Survivors of the Shoah* and the *Shoah* Visual History Foundation. (*Shoah* is Hebrew for Holocaust.) I have used both as valuable resources. Plus other sources. Anyone's words I put in quotation marks are their exact words, or my translation, taken from source materials, mostly letters and family documents. These are personal memoirs based on research plus tales told through my filter, only as true as my memory allows. What is missing is as much my fault as what is included.

Although I have traveled to 67 countries and spent a total of 20 years outside the U.S.A., this is not about those trips. Nor is there enough about St. Barth's. It will take another book to do justice to that magical island I love. I'll call it *St. Barth's Stories*.

Some family lore should not be forgotten; tales which may be lost if I don't tell them, stories my grandchildren might not otherwise know. Here you will meet some fascinating people who, genetically, culturally, and emotionally make our Friedman families who they were, what they are, and whatever they will become.

Contents

1. Who I Am

My mother was riding -- all alone -- in the London Underground which the British call the Tube. A stranger in England, her thoughts were not of her home and husband in Germany. Instead, she was thinking of Paris where, last summer, in the ultra-luxurious Ritz Hotel, her baby had been conceived. She wondered if it would be a boy or a girl.

Lotte Rosalie Friedmann's reverie was interrupted when the subway stopped. She felt a twinge, a sudden pain, and decided to get off the train although it was not her stop. She stepped carefully onto the platform. Although she heard a voice say, "mind the gap," she didn't understand because she didn't speak or comprehend much English. She moved gingerly because she carried heavy shopping bags and she was very pregnant.

The baby was not due yet, it was too early. It couldn't be a contraction.

She had almost convinced herself when she felt another stabbing pain -- already! It must be a contraction. What else could it be? What should she do? She was far from her husband in her German homeland, and not near her temporary London home, where she was living with her husband's brother and his wife, Paul and Thea Friedmann.

It was in mid-March 1934 that my father had the idea of sending my pregnant mother to his brother in London so that the baby would be born with dual citizenship: a British subject, being born there, and a German citizen since both parents were German. He thought dual citizenship might come in handy in the future, since Adolf Hitler had come to power in 1933. My father had planned to join my mother in London well before the baby was born.

Now, slowly, 29-year-old Lotte Friedmann followed the crowd to the exit. The station, like most in London, was considerably below the surface and a long, torturous stairway faced her. Today there are escalators at most Underground stations, some of which are dramatically steep. But at that time there were only stairs. Many stairs. Her shopping bags held heavy English woolens bought for the cold German winters. So she proceeded slowly upward and onward, climbing carefully up one steep step at a time. She kept to the right side as faster folks hurried past her on the left.

Lotte trudged up slowly, for the stairs seemed an almost insurmountable obstacle, extending ever higher, practically getting steeper as she climbed, ever upward. She had been thin with a regal bearing but now her pregnancy bulge was in her way. Suddenly, the baby kicked, causing her to become short of breath as she climbed slowly upward.

Taking her time, letting the others pass her, Lotte Friedmann was the last one to make her way, slowly up to the surface. It was exhausting and her heavy shopping bags were a real burden. She stopped, truly afraid, actually frightened. For she felt the contractions, but even more, she felt lonely -- indeed she really was all alone.

Just then her water broke! The baby was coming! It was much too early! It wasn't due yet! Her 40-year-old husband wasn't here! And now she was wet! Cold and wet and tired of climbing. She stood still a while, catching her breath.

Then she continued onward and upward, forcing herself to climb the steep stairwell; embarrassed, exhausted, frightened, a stranger in a strange land. She felt really angry at her husband for sending her away from her home -- without him -- to this foreign place in her condition.

Nevertheless she kept slowly mounting the long staircase. She absolutely had to proceed at her own slow pace, carefully, painstakingly.

Finally, she reached daylight at street level. It was a bitter cold day in London in March, 1934. Wind whistled down the strange streets. There is nothing as lonely as a dreary day in foggy London town.

She had arrived in the Stepney sector of East London. The area was then, as it had been for a long time, one of the worst sections of that great city. It was where Jack the Ripper had terrorized London. He was a serial killer, murdering only women who were alone! And she was truly alone herself! Now she was terribly frightened. She was fearfully aware of just how very lonely and homesick she was.

He had only killed prostitutes who plied their trade in that part of town. The thought frightened her because she knew he had never been captured!

This was London's worst slum section, one of its oldest areas, the rundown district where the poor and the homeless, the sleazy and the criminal, lined the cold streets and sidewalks; it was London's highest crime area. There were many other criminals out there now. They still preyed on women who were by themselves. Lotte Friedmann shivered in the cold March air.

Luckily there was a taxi there to take her to a hospital. The driver said that Jewish Memorial Hospital was not far away. "Jewish" sounded good to her ... but the area didn't look good.

People from that area are called cockneys and they have a very distinct accent, different from all the rest of England, but certainly not distinguished. It was Eliza Doolittle's awful cockney accent that Henry Higgins corrected. Cockneys also speak in a unique way, with an unusual rhyming slang. They famously substitute rhymed phrases for certain words, saying, "trouble and strife" instead of "wife," substituting "box of toys" for "noise," and "dickory dock" for "clock."

The traditional definition of a cockney is anyone born within the sound of Bow Bells. And I was born in the closest hospital to London's famed Church of St. Mary-le-Bow in Cheapside, whose steeple houses the tall campanile or bell tower which contains Bow Bells. They rang that day. They still ring every day.

I was born there on March 28, 1934. But I don't have an English accent and I don't speak cockney rhyming slang because I left England when I was only 28 days old. My parents took me home to Germany.

My father arrived in London before my mother and I were discharged from the hospital. They had a hard time coming up with a name for me. They wanted a name that was both German and English, as well as one that, as is Jewish custom, is a reference to a deceased relative. One idea was to name me after one of my father's two little brothers who had died in infancy, years before he was born. They were named Walter and Ludwig. My parents both preferred the name Walter. It was a German name, as in Walter von der Vogelweide. But was it English?

"Oh, yes, definitely," my father's brother Paul's son Herbert Friedmann told my parents, "Think of Sir Walter Raleigh -- that's as English as you can get!" So I was named Walter after him.

And then there had been the deceased rich uncle on my mother's side, Uncle Erich. I got my middle name from him. So I came into the world as an Englishman and German named Walter Erich Friedmann.

When I was born everyone agreed that I had my mother's hairline, forehead and especially her eyes. They're greenish blue and what they call *schlitzaugen* or slit-eyes -- giving her (and me) a slightly oriental appearance, albeit with blue eyes! And people said that I looked like my father from the nose on down. All the way down!

The fact is, both sides of the family thought I was indeed a real Friedman, with a double "n," at that time. A real Friedmann, they all agreed, because not only was Friedmann my father's surname and now mine, but my mother's maiden name as well! (They were not related until they got married; there are lots of Friedmans in this world, most of whom are not related to us.)

With a double dose of Friedman, I'm a real Friedman, all Friedman and nothing but Friedman. And I am an only child. Therefore, while we are almost all Friedmans in this memoir of my many Friedman families, I am the most Friedman of Friedmans!

I. MY FATHER'S FAMILY
(1880's - 1930's)

2. Schlomo of Schaki

My father's side of the family, with its obviously German-Jewish name, did not come from Germany but rather from tiny Lithuania, the southernmost of the Baltic states.

Lithuania had once been part of the largest country in Europe, the Polish-Lithuanian Commonwealth. Prussia ruled the area from 1795 to 1807 when Poland was partitioned and Lithuania passed to Russia. After the Russian revolution, Lithuania became part of the Union of Soviet Socialist Republics, in its time the largest country.

Today Lithuania is among the smallest of nations, slightly larger than West Virginia. Its present population is about 3½ million people. Lithuania is now in the U.N., a member of NATO, and in the E.U., the European Union.

The capital of Lithuania was and still is, Vilnius. At the time we start our family saga, in the mid-1880's, Vilnius was an international center of Jewish learning and culture, famous as "the new Jerusalem." Its thriving Jewish community was an important part of that metropolis' life.

The most famous Jew of Vilnius in the second half of the 18th century was Solomon Zahnan, known as "the Goan of Vilna." He had messianic visions. It was written that he determined the character of Lithuanian Jewry for several generations.

Our Friedmann family saga starts far from the capital city in a tiny *shtetl* or village that was, and still is, named Schaki (pronounced "sha-kee") but it has been spelled Szaki or, in Lithuanian, Sakiai. I think of Schaki like Anatevka, the village in *Fiddler on the Roof,* but under the strong influence of the Goan of Vilna, about 100 miles away. My father wrote that Schaki was "a couple of miles from the German border town Eidkuhnen, the end stop of the daily express train from Berlin," so he probably visited it.

Schaki was one of the oldest settlements in Lithuania, mentioned in documents dated 1352. By 1405 German crusaders had built a wooden fortress there. The town was granted the rights of a city in 1776. In 1800, there were 574 inhabitants in Schaki, most of them Jews, in 65 houses. In 1807, the town became part of "The Great Dukedom of Warsaw," which made everyone equal before the law -- except for Jews, who were not granted any civil rights.

In Schlomo Friedmann's time, 1850 -- five years before the birth of his first child, Aron -- there were about 2,600 Jews in Schaki, or 55% of its population. By 1856, a year after Aron's birth, 83% of the population was Jewish! Most of them were artisans and greengrocers. They sold their wares on market days, Tuesdays and Fridays. One third of Lithuanian Jews earned their livelihood in crafts. By 1868, when Aron had his *bar mitzvah,* Jews were merchants, shop owners, small peddlers, carters, horse traders; and there was one blacksmith, two tailors, and one watchmaker in town.

For all those Jews in Schaki, however, there was only one synagogue. Judah Reisel, the son of Jacob, was the rabbi and my great-grandfather Schlomo Friedmann was the cantor. Years later, in Berlin around 1905-1908, Schlomo's son Aron taught Wolf Reisel who was also from Schaki. Wolf became the chief cantor of the NeiShul in Amsterdam from 1908 to World War I. There was also a rabbi in Schaki named Aharon Fridman from 1926 to 1934, who was probably not related to us.

Schlomo Friedmann led the prayers on *Rosh Hashanah* and *Yom Kippur,* the High Holidays, in what was called the German synagogue.

And it is for that reason, his eldest son's autobiography tells us, that Schlomo was nicknamed "the German."

Schlomo was born in Schaki and died there in 1886. The name Schlomo isn't German or Lithuanian, but Hebrew. In English it would be Solomon. My father once spelled it "Schelomoh."

Schlomo's wife was Esther Bergmann, a German name meaning "mountain man." My father wrote that "the family had a bakery but Schlomo never baked, he studied scripture. The wife had to do the work."

Esther's sister married a Minkowski. Their children, Oskar and Hermann, both became famous. Oskar (1858 - 1931) was the co-discoverer (with Mehring) that the pancreas is the site of diabetes. Hermann (1864 - 1909) was the first scientist to recognize the 4th dimension and taught Albert Einstein math and physics. Sociology professor Martin Oppenheimer is related to us through the Hermann Minkowski line (See chapter 58).

Schlomo and Esther Friedmann were very religious; today they would be called orthodox. They saw to it that their children, especially the boys, got a solid Jewish education. They had seven children, four boys and three girls. One of their sons became a rabbi, another a cantor. A famous cantor and composer. And my father's father.

3. The Exodus

The last fifty years of the 19th century saw a great exodus from Schaki. By 1896 the number of Jews in town had diminished to 1,600 -- yet they were 80% of the population! There were pogroms in Russia when the Cossacks drove the Jews out. But not in Lithuania. Only a deep anti-Semitism. So, while Schlomo and Esther stayed behind, five of their seven children left Schaki and Lithuania.

Most of the Jews left in those years. By September, 1923, a census counted 153,743 Jews in all of Lithuania, a mere 7.5% of the population -- yet they were the largest national minority! Only 0.5% of the Jews lived in small towns. And only 1,267 Jews were still in Schaki, making up 62% of the town's population!

Between 1928 and 1939, 13,898 of the remaining Jews emigrated from Lithuania, 25.5% went to Palestine and only 10.8% to the United States.

Aron, the Friedmanns' first child and my paternal grandfather, was born on August 22, 1855. He became the famous cantor and composer and the first of the family to leave Lithuania, in 1878, for Berlin.

One after another, five of the children left the country. After Aron went to Berlin and stayed, the second son, Samuel, also went to Berlin, then to England, and finally to the United States to become "our Uncle Sam." (See Chapter 7.)

Schlomo and Esther's third son, Jacob Friedmann, went to London and changed his name to John Planter. My father always said that he renamed himself after Planter's peanuts. "John" visited the family in Berlin often, so my father knew him very well. In London, "Uncle Planter" bought and fixed up old houses and had a cigar store. In 1914, he married Louise Gluckstein, who was born around 1893 and was nicknamed "Luxie." They had two daughters, Esther and Eva, who, my father wrote, "married to Johannesburg (South Africa) and we lost track of them."

Reuben, the youngest son, also came to America. His family's story is Chapter 46.

Two of the three Friedmann daughters, Frade and Jochbed, stayed in Schaki and were still there when Lithuania became part of Russia. Only the oldest girl, Rochel, later known as Rachel, went to the U.S.A. and married Schlomo Fisher here.

Unfortunately, I know nothing more about Frade Friedmann. All I know of Jochbed is that she married Solomon Gittlemann and that they had four children, the youngest of whom was named Martha. In 1869 or 1870, an "M. Gitelman" came to the U.S.A. Was that Martha who dropped a "t" and an "n"? Possibly.

4. Fifty Years in Berlin

Aron Friedmann wrote his autobiography, his *erinnerungen* or remembrances, of his fifty years in Berlin (1878-1928) entitled *50 Jahre in Berlin*. Published in 1929, the profits went to help German cantors, their widows and children.

His opening paragraph is: "My father, Schlomo Friedmann, from Schaki, Lithuania, who often led the German congregation in prayers on the High Holy Days, already instilled a love of Germany into my earliest youth. His deepest wish was to see me as a cantor in Germany. His wish was fulfilled through God's Providence: he saw me officiate as a cantor in Germany's leading congregation, in Berlin."

That is all he wrote about his father and his own earliest upbringing.

Although born in Schaki on August 22, 1855, Aron's first German congregation was in Czersk, West Prussia. "Often a piece of wood was my pillow, my smock was my blanket, and a hard, wooden bench my bed."

Then he went to Buetow in Pommerania where the idea hit him, "as it first hit Moses Mendelssohn, to go to Berlin in order to learn." He simultaneously applied as a student and a teacher. It was April, 1878. Aron was 22.

He first rented a room with friends and then he took the entrance exam. He did not do well and was only accepted as an auditor of the classes. The reason he gave was that many subjects were "new and strange" to him.

His room was quite a distance from the school and, since he had no extra money for carfare, he walked both ways. As an orthodox Jew he would not light a fire or lamp on Friday nights and so he sat in the dark, reciting from memory the previous week's lessons. "But God always helped."

He recognized the "holes," as he put it, "in my education and in my wallet." So he took on students, officiated on the High Holy Days, and even borrowed money. A year later, Aron took the examination again, passed, and was proud to be a seminary student.

Louis Lewandowski, the famed composer and Master Teacher of music, theory, and song, asked his students to compose music for synagogue liturgy. Lewandowski's first remark to Aron Friedmann about his first creation was, "you will ruin your taste with your composition. You're better off singing my composition to those words."

On the first evening of Chanukah Aron went to the New Synagogue, Berlin's largest, which had opened 12 years earlier on *Oranienberger Strasse 29/30*. It was designed by Eduard Knoblauch with a dramatic 50-meter high gilded dome. It was (and has been reconstructed in 1995) in an awesome neo-Byzantine style with Moorish influences. Rector Horwitz asked him what he'd thought of the service. Aron answered, "It was like in a small village."

The rector was amused. Aron explained that in a large town like Vilnius, the service begins with an orchestral selection, then the cantor sings with a choir, then cantor and orchestra perform, until it reaches a climax with cantor, choir and orchestra. It builds up and up and up. I think he was proud of his somewhat nervy response to the rector.

The rector recommended congregations to Aron and Aron to them, which led to Aron's singing at various cities while he continued his studies and gave private lessons.

Rector Horwitz suffered a stroke and died. At the funeral a colleague went up to Louis Lewandowski and, pointing to Aron, said, "The deceased wanted this young man to perform in the New Synagogue on the High Holy Days."

Lewandowski answered, "Whatever Horwitz wanted will be done!"

So, Aron was immediately hired, but only for the High Holy Days.

In January 1882, Aron was given a job as an assistant cantor although he was still in his first year of Seminary School. Aron Friedmann introduced many Lewandowski compositions to various services. After one, the organist came up to Aron and said, "I am a Christian and do not understand Hebrew, but I was so moved by your singing that I almost fell off the organ's bench!"

In April 1883, Aron passed the oral exam to become an "elementary teacher." And he took the final examinations at the Jewish "high school" as well as at an academy. He officiated at the Old Synagogue in addition to his regular job at the New Synagogue. He performed at the *Kaiserstrasse* Synagogue and in other German cities.

At this time, social changes were happening in Germany. And in Judaism, too. Changes in the prayer book as well as the music. Aron Friedmann, it seems to me, was a new force on the scene, one that even Lewandowski listened to … sometimes.

Occasionally Lewandowski held musical evenings at his home and invited Aron. Sometimes Aron sang, other times he played the violin, and at times the piano.

Once, while Aron was singing one of his own compositions during a service, the choirmaster and a member of the chorus started to laugh. The head of the congregation upbraided them: "Why did you laugh during the service?"

"Because it sounded like an opera melody," was the response.

Interestingly, someone else had a similar reaction: A retired Duke University professor, Albrecht Strauss, told me recently that he remembers hearing Aron sing in Berlin's *Lewitzonstrasse* Synagogue on *Rosh Hashanah* and *Yom Kippur*. He told me, "it was like an operatic performance! His voice was beautiful and he chanted with such skill -- it was almost too effective -- like an opera singer performing!"

Aron's operatic-like singing could have come from the cantorial grace notes which he added. Or that he strutted on the *bimah* like on a stage. It might have been a tendency to dramatize the music, especially his own music.

Albrecht Strauss described the black *kittel* or robe and the round, black hat that my grandfather wore with his *tallis* or prayer shawl. He also said that sometimes Cantor Friedmann wore his black top hat or *cyllinderhut* -- which I later owned and eventually donated to the Chappaqua Drama Group.

When the post of chief cantor opened up in Cologne, Aron asked the head of the congregation for a leave of absence. He answered, "Don't go! We'll raise your salary!"

To which Aron said, "I am of the age where I want to establish a home. A raise is not enough." The head replied that Lewandowski had just recently set Aron's wage and suggested that Aron think it over for 14 days.

Aron wrote: "What did I do? When the time was up, I went to the head of the congregation and kept the Berlin job for various reasons. I wrote off the Cologne job."

After his position was secure, Aron continued, "I got married in 1885 to the piano teacher Hulda Saul. Since I now had a family, I was forced to discuss my pay very often, as the increases were minimal. I didn't have the same income as my colleagues, not by a long shot!" (That is one of only two short mentions of his family in his autobiography covering fifty years of remembrances!)

Lewandowski said that he knew no cantor in all Germany who could sing his, Lewandowski's, compositions as well as Friedmann. And in 1882 my grandfather was appointed *Oberkantor der Juedische Gemeinde Berlin* or Head Cantor of the Jewish Congregation of Berlin, yet he continued to officiate with Lewandowski usually selecting the music to be sung.

From 1886 to 1892, Cantor Friedmann also took music theory classes and always sat shoulder to shoulder with Bruno Schlesinger, who, Aron thought, was extraordinarily gifted. That man later dropped his last name and used his middle name instead, gaining fame as the conductor Bruno Walter.

The death of Kaiser Friedrich III caused Aron to compose two mourning songs, one of which Aron sang at the funeral to the thanks of the Kaiser's widow.

In December, 1890, when Lewandowski celebrated his 50-year jubilee, one of the committee members was Professor Wilhelm Wolf, the same man who welcomed my parents and me to America at our arrival in New York harbor.

The directors constructed a women's choir in addition to the men's at the *Oranienburgerstrasse* Temple. They debated about whether the cantor/soloist should be a tenor or a baritone. Was the show overwhelming the religious service? The discussion raged until it was decided that the cantor is the leader of the prayers -- the primary reason why people go to the synagogue.

Aron continued to attend the Master Musician's School and began to compose his own masterpiece, *Schir li Schlomo,* or Song of Solomon, named for his father as well as Salomon Sulzer and the biblical Solomon. It took him almost ten years to complete. At the same time he continued to compose other religious music for various psalms, holidays and services as well as a few, very few, secular songs, mostly for family affairs.

In 1898, a third synagogue was included in the Berlin congregation. They then rotated the assignments with three cantors effectively performing the services in all three. The city's chief cantor did not necessarily spend most of his time at his "home synagogue," the one closest to his home. Since orthodox Jews would not travel on the Sabbath, a guest cantor would spend the weekend at his host temple or synagogue. Aron divided his time among the three in Berlin, with occasional voyages to other German and even other European places of worship.

Aron's *Shir li Schlomo* was printed in 1901. In 1904, he published *Der Synagogale Gesang,* which included biographies of Salomon Sulzer and Louis Lewandowski. The first printing was an immediate sellout and a second one was published in 1908 and also sold out. (It was later re-issued; see the following chapter.) Aron also published several newspaper articles over the years.

In 1904, Aron tells us, he sang at the Odd Fellows Hall in Berlin at a celebration of Dr. Theodor Herzl, the founder of Zionism.

A critic said that Aron's strong conservatism belies the fact that he performs in a synagogue with an organ. He answered that the organ gave him inner peace whereas when he sings with no musical accompaniment, "it gives me a certain unease."

On January 1, 1907, Aron celebrated 25 years as a Berlin cantor and wrote, "Sadly my dear wife was not able to witness my 25th jubilee since, already on the 30th of April, 1906, my dear Hulda, the mother of my four minor children, died after a short illness at age 46." (She had died eight months earlier but he never mentioned it except in the context of her missing his jubilee! My father said that his father only cared about music and religion, not his family. I think this oblique reference proves him right.)

Shortly after his jubilee Aron was transferred to the *Heidereutergasse* Synagogue. A congregant asked, "How did we sin so that you no longer serve the New Synagogue?"

Now to fill the emptiness in his house, as he put it, he started to collect the melodies for a "Liturgical Songbook," which he published in 1910. He went to libraries and archives to find documents and correspondences, including non-German sources such as Cardinals and Popes. He continued this work into 1914. Thereafter he collected the works of Louis Lewandowski.

Aron wrote, "In the summer of 1914, I went into my second marriage with the science teacher Johanna Bermann from Frankfurt am Main. In my second wife I found likewise a true, loving life-partner, who took part in all my endeavors."

In 1915, the hard times started with "my three sons standing at the front." They were in the German army in World War I; he wrote no more about the war or about them except to say: "My children pleased me with the publishing of the second edition."

Aron also worked with Isidor Caro who was a rabbi. Many years later their widows, my grandmother Johanna Friedmann and Klara Caro, were together in the Theresienstadt concentration camp and again thereafter in New York City.

Aron's book, *Lebensbilder beruehmter Kantoren,* "Life Pictures of Famous Cantors" was published in 1918 in three volumes. He was kept busy singing and now also lecturing. Another book of his came out in 1922, Aron's collection of *"kantoral-wissenschaftlicher Aufsaetze* or cantoral scientific compositions."

He retired the next year, 1923, but continued to publish. His 70th birthday was in 1925. The third edition of his "Lives" came out without his active participation. His remembrances end with the conviction that the Almighty guided him with "a loving hand" and, quoting Jehuda Halevi, he says "my heart belongs in God's House."

In July, 1935, *Der Juedische Kantor,* a bimonthly publication of the "united German cantors," devoted its entire issue to Aron Friedmann, telling his life story.

My grandfather died June 9, 1936 -- when I was only two. I remember his white beard most of all. In fact, I called him *Opa-bart* (Grandpa-beard) but I added another word, *sauer,* which literally means sour, but which I used to mean anything unpleasant. At that tender age, I must have meant that his beard was unpleasant, not his personality.

More than fifty years after his death, Aron's great-granddaughter Evelyn Lipson held a concert of his music at her home in California. It featured piano, violin, guitar, and singers. My son David videotaped it and I have a VHS copy.

5. In Excellent Company

I remember my grandfather, Aron Friedmann, as a cold, stern, didactic and dictatorial man. According to my father, his father only cared about religion and music.

In 1904, Aron Friedmann wrote the book he entitled, *Der Synagogale Gesang,* or The Synagological Song. A greatly expanded version was published a mere two years later. And it was reissued again more than seventy years after that!

That latest 1978 version was put out by the so-called atheistic, communistic, anti-Semitic East German regime. Yet it was the only religiously oriented book published in the group they called Peters Reprints. It was one of the series on "The Science of Music Library Studies," which featured the work of such composers as

Johann Sebastian Bach,
Wolfgang Amadeus Mozart,
Ludwig von Beethoven,
Franz Schubert,
Carl Maria von Weber,
Arnold Schoenberg,
Aron Friedmann,
and 13 others.

My grandfather, the chief cantor of Berlin, was certainly in excellent company!

Aron Friedmann's opening sentence in *Der Synagogale Gesang* was "Every person brings with him, through his entry into the world, the urge to sing."

He claimed that singing is more natural than speaking; it expresses the individual better. He suggests that Adam and Eve discovered singing, that singing frees our heart and is effective for every emotion. Every emotion? An interesting notion.

Aron noted that when King Saul was so aggravated that doctors could not help him, he was calmed by young David playing his harp and singing to him. My grandfather may have been among the first to use biblical references for modern medical, psychological, and physical truths, not just religious dogma.

While he called the bible the oldest and truest book ever written, Aron Friedmann called music the truest accompanist anyone ever has. He thought it almost impossible to consider any celebratory occasion without music. The cantor said we raise our voices in music to sing praises to the Almighty and could offer no higher devotion. Quoting Jellinek, Aron wrote "a prayer without song is like a body without a soul."

His book is difficult for me to read because it is in three languages: German, Hebrew, and Music. *Der Synagogale Gesang* was subtitled "A Study" and dedicated in honor of the one-hundredth birthday of Salomon Sulzer and the tenth anniversary of the death of Louis Lewandowski. Aron ended with biographies of these two men.

Salomon Sulzer (1804-1890) was from Austria. As a small boy he fell into a torrential Alpine river and was miraculously saved from drowning by a farmer whom he later rewarded with a lifelong pension. The boy told his parents that he had seen a light and had felt no fear.

Thereafter his mother dressed him only in white and dedicated him to the Almighty. She made him swear he would always devote himself to God. As a result of his dedication, Sulzer was named a cantor in his small hometown at the age of thirteen! There was a protest over the appointment, and the Kaiser himself decided that Sulzer could become the local cantor if he first devoted three years to liturgical study. He did this and led a string quartet at the Kaiser's birthday.

At 21, Sulzer became the cantor in a Vienna synagogue, bringing superb music to the congregation. Schubert and Liszt came to hear him sing and became his friends. Schubert wrote, "only now do I understand my own music, having heard him!"

Sulzer's masterpiece, *The Song of Zion*, was published in 1839 and is still used around the world. My grandfather followed Sulzer with his own *Song of Solomon*.

Salomon Sulzer remained the cantor of that synagogue for 45 years. Kaiser Ferdinand came to hear him and rewarded him with a diamond ring! What did Ferdinand's wife, Kaiserin Caroline Auguste, think of that? She demanded that he appear in a famous Vienna theater and she offered him 100 ducats in pure gold!

Aron wrote that Sulzer's singing "was at its mightiest at an open grave."

Aron's other biography is of Louis Lewandowski (1821-1894.) Born in Poland to parents from rabbinical families, Louis left home for Berlin when he was twelve. He became the first Jew to attend the Berlin Academy of the Arts. He exhibited talent at composing and directing as well as playing music. But a devastating illness forced him to concentrate on religious music which he considered the highest form of expression.

For 24 years he was the choirmaster at the *Heiderlutergasse* Temple in Berlin. But in 1864 the construction of the *Oranienburgerstrasse* Temple, which had an organ, let him create an entirely new Jewish service harmonizing the entire liturgical cycle for organ, cantor, and choir. He also composed music for psalms which he dedicated to King Ludwig II of Bavaria. He was honored by the Kaiser and named Royal Music Director. And he taught cantoral students, among them my grandfather.

Aron Friedmann introduced many of Louis Lewandowski's compositions to various services. Once Aron sang a Lewandowski composition that Louis himself did not recognize. So he asked Aron if he had composed it. "No," he replied, "it was your own composition which you wrote for your own birthday!"

In the 1950's, my father attended a lecture at the Herzl Institute in New York by Irene N. Heskes, an American music historian. Irene N. Heskes published *The Golden Age of Cantors* in 1991 which included a section on Aron Friedmann and she was planning to write a book on the life and influences of Cantor Aron Friedmann for the Cantors Institute of the Jewish Theological Seminary in December 1963, but was unable to complete it before her death.

Hans wrote that she often mentioned Lewandowski in her lecture and said of Aron Friedmann, "He was one of the greatest; a very well-known musicologist with a great knowledge of the history of music and Jewish music."

A man at that lecture said, "I was a choir boy under Lewandowski in Berlin."

My Dad answered, "That's impossible; Lewandowski died before I was born!"

To which he replied, "Yes, you are right; I was a choir boy under, under …" At first he could not think of the name, finally, enthusiastically, he said, "Aron Friedmann! Aron Friedmann was the greatest!" Then my father revealed that he was Aron's son.

More than a hundred years after Lewandowski's death, Aron's granddaughter-in-law, Herbert's widow Inge, happened to meet Lewandowski's granddaughter on Catalina Island. They became friendly, got together thereafter, and it came to light that Aron had not just been his pupil but had also written Louis Lewandowski's biography.

Aron Friedmann was given the same honorific title by the Kaiser that had been held by both of his heroes, Sulzer and Lewandowski; that is, *Koeniglicher Musikdirektor* or Royal Music Director. Once again, my grandfather was in excellent company.

6. Piano Teacher and Poet

My grandfather Aron didn't write much about his children or his two wives. His first wife, Hulda Saul, was five years younger than he, very intelligent, obviously educated, even intellectual, and she had a

16

wonderful sense of humor. I know that primarily through her poetry, some of which she wrote in slang.

On March 8, 1885, the day Hulda Saul got engaged to my grandfather, she wrote a poem to him. I first translated it on March 31, 1989, more than a century later:

Lonely sat I, all alone,
And thought of your love;
Thought of those dear words
That you, at the house's door,
Softly whispered in my ear,
Full of love, burning hot.
Oh, I felt myself uplifted
As I gave you my word.
I felt a hot kiss --
Which I must think of -- instead of myself.
It sealed a promise to you
That I can never break.
So you may firmly rely upon,
Build solidly upon, my love.
Be it in joy, be it in pain,
Though I carry for you in my heart
True love, which I carry
Dear man, for you, forever.

She wrote the following two months before their wedding. "To my dear bridegroom -- dedicated in deepest love -- from Hulda -- Berlin, March 12, 1885." I translated it in its rhyme scheme of first letters.

All my luck, all my joy
Ripened by you in me to the fore.
O! How nice that God made both of us
Now into a pair!
For this luck to praise Him,
Raise I His name on high,
I always, forever want Him to know
Ever and ever on the right track,
Dat we two, truly tied together,
May happily pull our way through life,
All the luck that we have found,

Now may blossom freely, in luck,
Name, oh God, my banner upward,
Sanction our lifetimes.

Early on the morning after the wedding, May 17, 1885, "your truly loving Hulda," wrote a poem to her sleeping husband. She wrote another for his birthday that year and then, a love poem in slang, "In Memory of our Engagement-day, March 8th." On their first anniversary, Hulda dedicated a poem "to my dear husband." Its first verse is:

Wake up you golden-red morning,
O beautiful day, begin!
So I can do as my heart bids:
Greet my husband today.

Aron Friedmann never mentioned her poetry; he only wrote that his wife was a piano teacher. But Hulda wrote the words for some of Aron's musical compositions. She wrote three bridal songs to melodies composed by Aron in 1885 and sung at the wedding of their son Paul and Dorothea ("Thea") Kohn in Berlin in 1928.

My father's mother, Hulda Saul, was born on March 31, 1860, in Breslau, the same city where my mother's father was born!

Hulda bore Aron seven children. First was Selma, the only girl; two boys, Ludwig and Walter, died in infancy before the last two were born.

On November 27, 1900, Hulda wrote a "Prolog to the Bar-Mitzvahs of Sigmund, Paul and Hans," her three sons, which was recited by Selma, her daughter. Hulda lived to see Sigmund's and Paul's *bar mitzvahs* but she died when her last child, my father, was only 11 years old.

So he hardly remembered her and could not tell me much about her. Yet it is clear that he loved his mother and missed her terribly. Hulda passed away on April 30, 1906, at age 46. She is buried in Berlin's Jewish Cemetery, Wannsee, next to Aron, in graves marked with very large black marble headstones, still standing today.

After his wife's death, Aron concentrated all the more on his music, practically ignoring his children, as my father said, "My father's life was his music and his religion. It left him no time at all for his family."

7. Our Uncle Sam

The name, "Uncle Sam" conjures up the image of America itself as a thin man with a goatee beard, wearing red, white and blue. My father's uncle Sam, Aron's younger brother and Schlomo and Esther's second son, was a thin but clean-shaven man, whom I remember wearing only black suits, white shirts, and conservative ties. He was the one who truly symbolized America to us. He was our Uncle Sam.

Samuel Friedmann helped us get to America because he was the first one of our families who got here. He gave us the affidavit that we needed to come. By that time he was really Americanized, married with three children, a rabbi in Philadelphia.

Sam went from Schaki, Lithuania, to the U.S.A. by way of Germany and England. It couldn't have been easy. The boy who began his Jewish education in Eastern Europe studied at a seminary in Germany. Sam's grandson Bud Rubin says that Sam studied in Hanover with his older brother Aron and became a rabbi because his brother was a cantor. Yet Sam was a musician and a composer as well! He wrote *Sheerai Mikdosh*, music for the sanctuary, among other scores. And I believe that my grandfather Aron only studied at the seminary in Berlin.

Sam continued his training at the Rabbinical Seminary called Jews' College in London. Thereafter, Sam became the rabbi of the North West London Synagogue.

Then Sam emigrated to America and, one source says, became a real estate salesperson in Pennsylvania. Soon thereafter he took up his real calling as the rabbi of Temple Israel in Amsterdam, New York. Next Samuel Friedman became the rabbi of Temple Ohev Shalom in Harrisburg. The founding rabbi of the Yeshiva school remembered Sam Friedman as "a well-regarded reform rabbi with a very orthodox bent."

Uncle Sam married Jenny Myers and they had three children, Sidney, Ivy, and Annette Friedman.

8. Selma and Siegmund

All of Aron and Hulda Friedmann's six children were born in Berlin. The oldest child, Selma, the only girl, was born on July 20, 1886. She lived in Dresden and was later described as matronly.

Selma Friedmann married Kurt Tirshtigel, a rabbi, who was something of a mystery man. Both my father and Hilde Levy believed that he was a homosexual. He was effeminate. He may have been impotent. They had no children.

Selma divorced him and married another mystery man, Dr. Bernhard Isaak, who was seven years older. His doctorate was a PhD. One pupil who took Hebrew lessons from him was Walter Heinemann, a cousin on my mother's side. Although the Isaaks lived in Dresden, Walter's lessons took place in Meissen.

Before World War II, Selma's younger brother Paul helped her and her husband get to England. Although they lived in Leeds, Dr. Isaak taught school in London.

He and Selma also never had any children. But the man's mystery increased after his wife's death in London in 1952.

Soon thereafter, Bernhard Isaak got in touch with a friend's widow who lived in Washington, D.C. She came to England, they got married, and, according to Hilde Levy, they went on separate honeymoons. Was this another man of questionable sexuality? The newlyweds traveled back to England together and on that return trip Bernhard dropped dead on the platform at Victoria Station in the London Underground!

Selma's brother Siegmund, Aron and Hulda's second child, never married. He was taken to a concentration camp but was released. Then he, too, got to London. For a while Siegmund lived with his brother Paul's children, Walter and Hilde Levy. But their mother Thea thought that Siegmund became "too difficult." So he went to a retirement home in Kew Gardens, England, where he passed the time until he passed away.

The next two boys born to Aron and Hulda were named Walter and Ludwig but they both died young, about ages 4, 5, or 6, sometime before 1892. Neither was alive when the next two sons were born.

9. Paul and Hans

Aron and Hulda Friedmann's last two boys were Paul and Hans.

Paul Friedmann was born on June 13, 1892 and always considered 13 his lucky number. My Uncle Paul died on November 25, 1950.

Little Hans, my future father, the youngest child, was born at 7 AM on June 26, 1894, at home, *Elsasserstrasse 56*, in Berlin. Hans was eight years younger than Selma and six years younger than Siegmund. But only two years younger than Paul.

Their mother, Hulda, died when my father was eleven years old and Paul was 13. They grew up with a succession of *kindermaedchen* taking care of them. They do not seem to have been trained as nannies. Not one of them lasted any length of time. My father believed they were all young, perhaps only teenagers.

One of those *kindermaedchen,* my father told me, taught him the facts of life at a very tender age. I am sure this does not mean that they had sexual relations. She most probably only told him what he wanted to know.

Aron Friedmann must have been a strict disciplinarian in the Teutonic style of that time. But in many other respects he virtually ignored his children. Motherless, they grew up, my father felt, loveless. Hans Friedmann once wrote that "as a small child" he "doubted to believe in God" although his father had no such doubt whatsoever.

I am certain that Hans very often felt like the little boy in the song:

"Hanschen klein,
Geht allein,
In die Grosse Welt hinein"
That is:
"Little Hans
Goes all alone
Into the huge world"

As my father remembers it, he and Paul were always linked together, *Paul und Hans,* but never *Hans und Paul.* Hans often tagged along after his bigger brother and usually felt inferior to him. Hans wrote that he and his brother were bathed together in a bathtub, sharing the hot water, at least up until he was ten and Paul twelve.

Hans had not inherited his father's gift for music -- but Paul did. Hans was not as quick with a quip or a joke as Paul was. Nor was he as popular as Paul. But Hans was virtually always with Paul, feeling somewhat in his shadow. It may have been hero-worship because Hans had no one else to look up to. While only two years separated them, my father felt like a much younger hanger-on, although Paul was always sure that his little brother was there with him, was all right, was taken care of, or tended to.

Hans learned four foreign languages in school: Latin, Greek, French, and Hebrew. That's in addition to German, of course, a language with complicated grammar. He wrote that he began his interest in politics at age ten. His education ended with a degree from the *Gymnasium,* equivalent to more than a high school.

I think it is not surprising that my father rebelled against his father at an early age. Hans had studied his Hebrew lessons, Bible lessons, Jewish history, Sayings of the Fathers, etc. He learned his lessons well but then he did not practice his religion. Paul remained religious all his life. Hans resented his father and became an atheist.

, Paul was interested in the nature of individual people. My father once wrote, "I am not interested in nature, but interested in [the] achievements of people."

The Friedman boys grew up in Berlin, the capital and cultural center of Germany, one of the truly great cities of the world. At the time they were young, the Roaring 1920's, Berlin was <u>the</u> place to be. It was in the forefront of the arts, theater, literature, music, and politics -- all of which fascinated my father and his brother.

The citizens of Berlin were then and are now Germany's New Yorkers, with an accent and a big-city attitude all their own. Even non-Jews in each of those cities often use Yiddish words. The natives of Berlin have "the gift of gab," a unique brashness, a cynical attitude, a fast-paced lifestyle, and a sense of humor that is often blunt and biting, deflating and democratic. Their characteristic style of speech is anti-authoritarian, delivered in harsh and terse accents, vibrant, and vital. Their way of speaking is known as a *Berliner schnautze* -- a Berlin snout! Paul had it, Hans didn't.

The personalities of the two Friedmann brothers, so close in age, were totally different. Paul was the extrovert, Hans the introvert. Paul was the life of the party everywhere he went, he was "always on." My father was the quiet one. Yet for all his exhibitionist ways, Paul was not the one who actually began a career as a stage actor for the world-famous Max Reinhardt; that was my father.

My uncle was really a fun guy, the traveling salesman type. My father was not at all like that. But he, like Paul, became a traveling salesman!

On February 4, 1918, in Berlin, Paul married Dorothea Kohn (my *Tante Thea*) who was a member of the Cohen family, no matter how they spelled it. That particular family is charged in the bible with being the caretakers of the Temple and as such have certain dos and don'ts. For example, Cohens are forbidden to go to any cemetery before their own parents' funerals. Like her husband, Thea was also born on the 13th of the month, in her case it was July 13, 1893. So she, like her husband, considered 13 her lucky number.

Paul and Thea were more orthodox, more religious, than my parents ever were. Their children, my first cousins, were Herbert and Hilde Friedman; their descendants are our California cousins. While they were all born in Germany, Paul, Thea, Herbie and Hilde had emigrated to England before we left *Deutschland*.

Paul Friedman was a charmer who entertained every group he was in. He told many jokes and came up with quick quips, perfect puns and word plays. *Onkel Paul* was particularly fast with a telling remark or humorous tale. Whenever he went somewhere he met interesting people and made friends easily. I remember my Uncle Paul best as a world traveler who would tell fabulous stories, usually of his own travels and adventures; he was a raconteur. As a boy, I always asked for more stories ... and there always were more!

My father wrote that he was interested in the German Social Democratic movement ever since he was 15 years old, "and at the same time in the Zionist movement." Later, he even went to Palestine to try to create a new country. His brother Paul was also interested in Zionism and he actually did help create Israel! But that's a later chapter.

Uncle Paul and *Tante Thea* came from London to visit us in Boston, New York, and even at Camp Edgewood. In his fifties and sixties, when I remember him, Paul was somewhat overweight, balding, with a fringe of dark hair, and an enchanting, humorous, and delightful person. "Fat, jolly and balding" applies perfectly.

My Uncle Paul died in London on November 25, 1950. A copy of his death certificate, certified by his wife's brother, Dr. Rudy Kohn, lists three causes of death: apoplexy, cerebral hemorrhage (left side) and hypertension.

However both Paul's granddaughter Evelyn Friedman-Levy-Garson-Lipson and I heard the same two stories about his death. One was that he dropped dead while talking on the telephone; the other, that he died while sitting on the toilet. We both believe that the telephone tale is a cover story for the somewhat embarrassing truth. And we also agreed that having a cerebral hemorrhage anywhere is a quick, easy, and therefore most desirable death. But there is much more to tell about my Uncle Paul's life. Read on.

10. Careers

Moses Mendelssohn wrote about his own son in 1785 that "as a Jew he must become a physician, a merchant, or a beggar."

In Berlin in 1807, Jews owned 30 of the 52 banking houses and as late as 1862, 550 of the 642 banks in Prussia.

But Aron Friedmann had other ideas in the early 1900's. He certainly knew the prominent members of his Berlin congregations. So he singled out three of them to ask each for a favor, which they were happy to grant him.

Then Aron assembled his three sons and announced to them that they were each to be apprenticed to a good Jewish company, to learn a basic trade, a steady trade, one that would always stand them in good stead, no matter what. They were each to have a different career with an assured future. He was taking good care of his sons. It almost didn't matter which one he pointed to for which trade. But he told them in age order:

"Siegmund, you are going into the paper business!

"Paul, you are going into the metal business!

"Hans, you are going into the leather business!"

That was it, there was no choice. That was each boy's prescheduled apprenticeship. That was the job each had, the trade he learned. And so, that is what they all did for the rest of their lives. Their careers were set.

All I know about Siegmund's career is that he was indeed in the paper business.

Paul spent his life working with one metal or another. Although he was an apprentice with *Hirsch Kupfer*, a copper company, he learned all about all kinds of metals and later dealt with scrap metals of every kind and shape and condition.

Paul's metal business know-how was transferred, years later, to his son Herbert and even to his son-in-law, Walter Levy. These two brothers-in-law went into the aluminum extrusion business together. They each had their own metal company at some point. Their stories cover a few interesting chapters.

My father's leather apprenticeship began when he was only 15 years old. He spent a year with the largest Jewish tannery, that is, a leather factory and wholesale leather firm, named *Isaac Josef.*

Like his brothers, Hans learned his trade well. He could touch any kind of leather, feel it just a little, perhaps twist or bend it a bit -- be it goatskin or cowhide or horse -- tanned or raw, with or without hair, a narrow strip or an entire hide, a shoe or a wallet or a belt -- and he could tell its quality. He would often know its originating country, or where it was tanned, what city, or even the factory where it had been manufactured. He developed an incredible, unerring feel for leather. He could determine its value and what its proper pricing should be.

But after his apprenticeship in leather, my father's mind drifted elsewhere. For he was living in Berlin, Germany's thriving capital, an international center, and young Hans was delighting in the nightclubs, cabarets, and theaters.

11. The Great Magician

My father decided to go to acting auditions and soon won a job as an extra in a show. Although my father was seven years older than his first cousin, Curt Bois, they both became actors and were truly close. Hans Friedmann had a very short interlude on stage, Curt a very extended career. Both appeared in Max Reinhardt productions in Berlin but never in the same show. And only Curt made movie history.

Let me tell you something about Max Reinhardt first. Born in 1873, he became Germany's most influential figure in the Expressionist movement of the early twentieth century. As a famed director and the owner-director of the *Deutsche Theater* in Berlin, he was responsible for training numerous actors who began their careers in the theater, many of whom eventually went on to work in the movies. Curt Bois was one.

No other director discovered or nurtured as many great actors as did Reinhardt. The names sound like a roll call of the outstanding actors of the 20th Century. Many went on to fame as directors. From 1905 to 1930, Reinhardt staged an incredible 452 plays (totaling 23,374 performances) of ancient and modern playwrights including 2,527 of Shakespeare's and 1,207 of George Bernard Shaw's works. Just to exemplify his extraordinary casting consider Mickey Rooney and James Cagney in Shakespearian roles!

In a German television program about Max entitled *The Great Magician*, Curt Bois starred as himself. In celebration of Max Reinhardt's 100th anniversary with the *Deutsche Theater*, the December, 2005 issue of *Aktuell* began, "He was the greatest magician of the theater."

When Hitler came to power the Nazis expropriated Reinhardt's theaters and he emigrated to America in 1934. He was very active on Broadway and ran an acting school in New York until his death there in 1943.

Jumping ahead thirty years to 1974, my parents attended an exhibition of the work of Max Reinhardt in Manhattan. Among many photographs of different Reinhardt productions, my mother saw one of *Oedipus Rex* dated 1910 and ran to my father saying, "I found you in a picture!"

Looking at the photo he agreed, "Here I am!"

Just his face was visible behind other people in a crowd scene of toga-clad actors and actresses. My mother said, "He was sixteen then! I never knew him that young!"

They bought the exhibition catalog with that picture in it. I have it now.

Some time later, Max Reinhardt's son Gottfried was in New York for a symposium which my parents also attended. I quote my father, speaking about Gottfried: "The son began to tell stories about his father. When [that] was over, I went to the son and I said, 'My name is Friedman. My father, *Musikdirektor* Aron Friedmann, was in a correspondence with Max Reinhardt [who] wrote to him first, and I still remember that in the last year, the older he [Reinhardt] got, the more he was interested in Jewish affairs.' Gottfried Reinhardt knew of it and agreed wholeheartedly."

My father often imitated the German star Albert Bassermann in a deep bass, demonstrating different roles in different voices to me. Yes, Hans Friedman truly was an actor!

His career did not last long. His first cousin's did. But that's the next chapter.

12. The Actor and the Singer

My father's first cousins, Curt and Ilse Bois, were the children of his mother's sister. Curt became an international stage and screen star; his older sister Ilse became a comedienne and nightclub singer.

Curt Bois acted in Berlin theater and on Broadway. He appeared in more than 40 Hollywood movies, 111 in total. In addition to film and stage acting, he directed three shows, wrote at least one screenplay, appeared as himself in four films and was on many television shows. He is in the *Guinness Book of World Records* as the actor with the longest career in show business! My father spoke of him quite often and I believe that it was with family pride rather than a failed actor's envy or jealousy.

Ilse Bois was one of three featured performers in a 1913 movie, *Der Geheimnisvolle Klub* or The Super-Secret Club, directed by Joseph Delmont, produced by Franz Vogel, and done by Eiko Films, Berlin. An Italian book, *Prima di Caligari,* and a Danish review in 1995 point out that this detective story predated Fritz Lang's films. Acting longevity must run in the Bois family.

In the 1950's, my parents and I saw Ilse perform -- she had top billing in a night club in Manhattan! I remember her as a torch singer who sang risqué specialties sort of a German Sophie Tucker, as well as straight love songs and comedic ones. Sometimes she teased her audience coquettishly and they loved her for it. With curtain call after curtain call, the audience kept calling for more. Her show went on long past midnight, possibly even after one o'clock, the latest I had stayed up until then. I was just a teenager, but it was New Year's Eve.

Curt was born in Berlin on April 5, 1901. His father left the family when Curt was young. His stepfather, who married his mother in 1907, was the playwright Albert Bernstein-Sawersky, a great influence on his adopted children.

Although my father was seven years older than his cousin, the two Berlin boys must have bonded over their love of Max Reinhardt and acting. Curt was the first to appear on stage. In 1908, he started his lifelong career at the age of seven! My father started at sixteen. Curt's first role was as Heinerle in Leo Falls' operetta *The Loyal Farmer* in Berlin's Theater of the West. His biography says that acting "never let its hold on him go." That's certainly true. It all started with Heinerle and didn't end for 83 years! One of the first child stars, Curt played various children's parts on stage and on film. From 1920 to 1924, he was a "salon humorist" and cabaret player throughout Germany, Austria, Hungary, and Switzerland. He also appeared in the famous Berlin *Kaberett der Komikker*, (Cabaret of Comedians) and certain songs were identified with him as his hits. Bois was deemed by critics, "extraordinarily popular."

From 1923 to 1925, he was at the Berlin Theater on the famed *Kurfeurstendam*, mostly in comic parts because he had the talent and because of his big nose.

Then Max Reinhardt won him over for even bigger roles. In 1925, Curt Bois had his first great success as a character actor in *The Excess*. This was followed by many major roles. A critic praised the tall, thin Bois as "a featherweight master in all the arts of pure theater."

In the 27 silent films that he appeared in until 1933, his biography says, "many people hoped he would ripen into a tragic-comic in the style of Charlie Chaplin." His first talkie was in 1931, *Der Schlemiel*.

Because of the Nazis, Bois made his way to America -- via Czechoslovakia, Austria, and England. He arrived in New York City and had some success on Broadway but went to Hollywood in 1937. He was often cast in comic roles, sometimes as a lead or supporting actor, but mostly in bit parts. Among the films Curt Bois was in from 1938 to 1988 were *The Great Waltz, The Amazing Dr. Clitterhouse, The Hunchback of Notre Dame, Bitter Sweet, The Lady in Question, Boom Town, The Tuttles of Tahiti, Casablanca, Caught, Wings of Desire, Das Boot ist Voll,* as well as *The Boat is Full.*

I remember going to the movies with my parents and them easily pointing out which actor he was. It was as obvious as the nose on his face.

A black-and-white film that was released in 1940 but made entirely in German was entitled *Der ewige Jude,* or The Eternal Jew. Its subtitle was "A film contribution on the problem of World Jewry." I am sure it is Nazi propaganda. Its complete credits show that it starred, "in alphabetical order, each played by himself, Curt Bois, Charles Chaplin, Albert Einstein, Adolf Hitler, Fritz Kortner, Peter Lorre, Ernst Lubitsch, Rosa Luxemburg, and Anna Stern."

According to his biographer, "In 1950, Curt Bois surprised the film industry by returning to Germany."

He went back to his beginnings, to the Soviet sector of East Berlin in the German Democratic Republic. And he became a big star once again. He celebrated an impressive "comeback" (as they called it in German) in the title role in Gogol's *Revisor.* Bois was in plays by Berthold Brecht, Shakespeare, George Bernard Shaw, Schiller, and Moliere. He worked in the *Deutsche Theater* in East Berlin and the *Berliner Theater* in West Berlin as well as the German Opera. His last stage part was in 1978 in Shakespeare's *The Tempest.* One of his directors called him "a completely unteachable big child," but added that what Bois did was "a virtuoso performance which was absolutely unlearnable."

Hans Friedman often visited Curt Bois in East Berlin, in the Russian sector of the city. My father last met with his first cousin in Berlin in 1977. After my father's death, my mother wrote to Curt Bois and he replied, "We wanted to meet again and he [my father] said he would be back the next year, but, sadly, he has gone the way we all must."

My mother praised Curt's performance in *Das Boot ist voll* which she took Paul Robert Friedman to see, writing that acting blood is in the family. In his reply Curt said: "I wish [Paul] success and much luck, because that is very important in an acting career."

In addition to the theater, Curt Bois made German movies and TV shows including *Bert Brecht in Front of the McCarthy Board* and *The Magic Mountain.* He directed *Splinters Bring Luck* and wrote and directed *A Prenuptial Evening.* This versatile talent has also written a small book, *So schlecht war mir noch nie,* or I've Never Had It So Bad, which includes his own diary as well as his drawings or cartoons. And he made two records, recorded in front of live audiences.

Curt Bois was given a German National Award and a Golden Film award in 1972 and the European film award for Best Supporting Actor in 1988 for *Der Himmel ueber Berlin,* The Heavens Over Berlin. He appeared in the German television documentary entitled, "Curt Bois, or It All Started With Heinerle." And it ended where it started, in Berlin. Curt Bois died there on December 25, 1991. He was 90 years old; he had an 83-year-long acting career! An amazing record.

His biography, *Humor kommt aus der Trauer,* Humor Comes From Sadness, by Gerold Ducke, was published January 1, 2001. All I know about his personal life is that he was married twice, first to Hedy Ury, then to a woman named Dagmar. I do not know if he, or Ilse Bois, ever had any children.

13. My Oma

Both of my grandmothers were named Johanna Friedmann. While I did live with my mother's parents in Bielefeld for two years, I was really too young then, from age two to four, to remember much.

But my father's stepmother was the grandmother, the Oma, that I knew well and truly loved. This Johanna was the daughter of Simon Bermann and Jettchen Raunheim. Oma was born on June 3, 1870 in Frankfurt-on-the-Main -- before Germany became a country, united by Otto von Bismark. That explains why there is another Frankfurt in Germany, on the Odor River.

Klara Caro, her good friend for almost all of my Oma's life, said that "already as a young girl, Johanna was unusual for her cleverness, her sharp sense, who had a wide view and a good heart and for her unusual character. Add thereto her charm and natural understanding, so that it was no wonder that in her profession as a science teacher she had a special feeling for the young."

I have a copy of Klara Caro's typewritten autobiography which she willed to my parents. Speaking of herself, Mrs. Caro added, "We have witnessed the nicest evidence for that since her favorite student, who was closer to her than a daughter, was true to her throughout her life."

Records show that Johanna Bermann married my grandfather, Berlin's chief cantor and music director Aron Friedmann, her only marriage, on September 3, 1913, when she was 44 and he was already

69 years old (although she once wrote that they were married in August, 1914). As his wife she was usually addressed with the honorific *Frau Musik Direktor.*

Oma's good friend Klara married a Berlin rabbi, Dr. Isidor Caro. Mrs. Caro said that my Oma "was especially helpful to her [own] husband at the evening of his life and improved his life's work by taking part."

Johanna Bermann was a science teacher; Aron's first wife, Hulda Saul, had been a music teacher. They were both very religious, of course. They were both poets. And I can describe Aron's second wife in much the same words as his first. Johanna Bermann was very intelligent, obviously educated, even intellectual, with a wonderful sense of humor. She, my father's step-mother, the grandmother I called Oma, is the only survivor of a concentration camp in our family. She was the grandparent I knew best.

My Oma defended me without my being aware of it. Only recently, in 2006, did I find and translate a letter that she and Aron had written to my parents in 1936. It shows his annoyance at me, a three-year-old, for calling him *"Opa bart sauer,"* a sourpuss, as he took it. But my Oma, even then, excused my brashness and vocabulary limits. She wrote that I'd said "Opa scratchy-beard" and was sure that I, in my childish way, had not meant that <u>he</u> was *sauer* or unpleasant, it was just his beard that had bothered me. She went on to praise "Little Walter" and adored his photographs. So my Oma and I had established a wonderful relationship early in my life which we happily resumed much later.

She never had any children of her own; the only one she ever helped grow up was me. She lived with us through my formative years, from my 13th birthday, when the Jews considered me a man, until I was 19, when I thought I was one. My Oma always treated me as an adult. She and I loved each other very much.

14. The First Zionists

Theodor Herzl originated Zionism. He was born in Budapest in 1860 and educated in Vienna. Ironically it was not German Nazis but French anti-Semites who gave Herzl the idea. During the Dreyfus Affair, the trial in France of a Jewish captain unjustly accused of treason, Herzl heard mobs shout, "Death to the Jews!" He realized that Jews were not safe anywhere and so needed a homeland of their own. A journalist, he wrote that Jewish statehood was an international political question and proposed a stock company, later called the Zionist Organization, to create a modern, neutral, peace-seeking, secular nation.

Herzl published a novel depicting a model Jewish state as a socialist utopia in the Land of Israel; a cooperative society using scientific methods to develop the land.

His writing made a tremendous impact on my future father. He had finished his internship in the leather business, at least for that time, and the theater was finished with him, at least as an actor. But he took to the new idea of Zionism with all his heart.

Herzl worked tirelessly and wrote eloquently but unsuccessfully about this ideal Jewish state. He died, disappointed, in 1904. But my father had been inspired.

At the same time, another Jewish writer gave my father -- only a teenager -- yet another idea: Karl Marx had defined his ideal state, a Socialist country. One which would bring to life the slogan, "from each according to his ability, to each according to his need." To Hans, it really looked good. He resolved to help turn it into a reality!

Also about that time, on November 2, 1917, Arthur James Balfour issued the *Balfour Declaration* at the instigation of Chaim Weizmann, later Israel's first president. It said, "His Majesty's Government view with favour the establishment in Palestine of a national home for the Jewish people." It seemed to my father to be an inevitability. Yet it took his brother Paul to make it a reality!

Strictly a city boy, my father went to Halbe, near Berlin, or as he put it, "the countryside," to learn how to farm the land in preparation for going to Palestine to literally create the land of Israel. My mother's cousin Friedrich Buchholz wrote to me on May 17, 1985 that he had met "your father in July, 1922 [in Halbe] ... a much older man, to become after 30 years my good, unforgettable Hans."

It took my father two years to feel that he was ready. Hans Friedmann, the young intellectual city boy, paid his own fare to Palestine and there began the hard, physical labor involved in tilling the soil.

He thought himself a visionary, one of the few making Hertzl's dream and Marx's theory into a reality ... a shining example for the whole world: A new Jewish country! Reclaiming Jewish history! Establishing an ideal nation! Revitalizing an ancient heritage! It would be a magnificent achievement. A marvel for the whole world. A bright new future. A truly perfect nation -- a socialist state. The Hertzl idea and the Marxian ideal.

Young Hans went into the future with his eyes wide open. But those who were there did not see things his way. Amos Oz saw those pioneers, these intellectuals turned workers, as German Jews who had not managed to recover from their Germanic ways, like Russian Jews who lived Chekhovian lives.

My father saw things very differently. To his surprise the reality he saw in Palestine was nothing like his idealized picture. In his just-opened eyes, the immigrant Jews were actually taking the land away from the native Arabs! Cheating them by buying it too cheaply or even stealing their property. The country these Jews were trying to build was not what Herzl had envisioned nor what Marx had theorized.

Instead it was more like the early settlers in the United States who got rid of the Native Americans by forcing them off their land. Palestine was not a peaceful, agricultural land; rather, it was akin to the old wild American West, with lawlessness and a lack of respect for the inhabitants. My father had sought a law-abiding, progressive new state. He did not find it in Palestine and so Hans became an anti-Zionist for the rest of his life. But he did not lose his Socialist ideas or Communist ideals.

My father, now a disillusioned young idealist, returned to Germany a disappointed man, uncertain of his future. Leather would be all right as a career, he supposed, especially since acting hadn't worked out for him and Zionism definitely didn't.

Meanwhile, Jews in Russia flocked to a movie in 1913 called *The Life of the Jews in Palestine.* A documentary, it was a silent, 35mm, 78 minute, black-and-white film. It showed European and Eastern-European Jews working alongside Middle-Eastern Jews. It did not show any local Arabs. It was effective propaganda. A one-sided picture. Millions believed the image; my father had seen the reality.

He was unusual in that he wanted to see things for himself. Much later in life, Hans Friedman was one of the first Americans to visit the Eastern Zone of occupied Berlin and also the Soviet Union itself.

But the question of what to do next was answered for him: He was drafted into the German army. He had to fight for his country in the world war.

15. The Great War

When the Great War began, all three of Aron and Hulda Friedmann's sons went into the German army and had their basic military training. But they did not stay together.

I know nothing about the oldest, Siegmund, as far as his military service. But there is a picture that I had (and Evelyn Levy Lipson has) which shows my father's brother Paul in German Army uniform at, I was told, the front lines. A group of soldiers are singing, with one of them at the piano -- *a piano at the front?* -- as Paul holds up the sheet music to the camera. Clearly visible is the composer's name: Aron Friedmann.

Incidentally, Paul's daughter-in-law Inge has and plays his piano now.

Hans, the youngest son, then 24, was in the infantry and said he was "the oldest in the front lines." He also wrote that he "spoke freely against the Kaiser ... and in spite of my political opinion [was] highly regarded as a solider."

My father faced French or possibly American forces in what the U.S. calls the Meuse-Argonne Offensive of World War I. The Germans called it the Battle of the Maas -- that being the Dutch and Belgian name for the river we called the Meuse.

They did not know it, but it was less than two months before the end of the war.

As my father described it to me, it was literally trench warfare, the kind depicted in World War One movies like *All Quiet on the Western Front*, *Paths of Glory*, and the French film, *A Very Long Engagement*. When called upon to attack, soldiers leapt from their bunkers or tunnels and ran forward, a frontal attack against the enemy. He believed, but could not be sure, that he was facing the French who were dug in, fighting for their homeland. And they had machine guns trained at the German line.

But it may have been Americans that he faced. Official American reports called it the biggest operation and victory of the American Expeditionary Force (AEF) in that war. The offensive took place in the Verdun area, between September 26 and November 11, 1918. U.S. Forces consisted of ten divisions of the First Army under General John J. Pershing until October 16th and thereafter under Lt. Gen. Hunter Liggett. The logistics were planned and directed by then Colonel George C. Marshall (later the top 4-star General of World War II and still later, Secretary of State under President Harry Truman).

German forces comprised about 40 divisions. The American attack began at 5:30 AM on September 26. On the 29th, six new German divisions were deployed to oppose the Americans. The attack began on October 4 against 20 German line and reserve divisions. American casualties required 90,000 replacements, but they only got 45,000 until November 1st. The Allied commander-in-chief, French Marshall Foch, urged that the attacks continue, aimed at the chief German line. By October 14, U.S. units reached and crossed the Hindenburg line.

My father did not know what day it was when his unit, in the German trenches, heard the shouted order to attack. He ran forward with the others. But he was almost immediately struck by machine-gun fire! He didn't even know where he was hit. Or what hit him. He just fell to the ground and lost consciousness.

Some time later, he woke up. He realized that he was lying in wet, cold mud. But it hadn't rained; the mud was made by his own blood. He became aware of his pain. Then he lost consciousness. He wakened to pain and lost consciousness again. Hans slipped into and out of awareness. He didn't know how long he lay there. Or how much blood he had lost. Time passed slowly. Pain came and went and came back again.

Sometimes, when he came to, he heard what seemed like far-off shooting; other times, there was complete silence. Daytime or night, he couldn't tell, for he lay quietly, not daring to raise his head up to look around for fear he would be discovered by the enemy. He was hungry, tired, in pain, not sure of what had happened or what might happen next. All Hans knew was that he was all alone out there, somewhere. What had happened to the attack? Had the war moved away? Was there anyone near him?

Gefreiter (that was his rank, equivalent to private) Hans Friedmann lay there for three days -- three whole days! And three long nights! But he didn't know how long it was at that time. It seemed as if it was forever. At last, during the third night, someone came to drag him away.

Was it a Frenchman who took him away or a German? Where was he? Hans wondered if he was behind the German line. He did not know and worried about it.

Eventually Hans realized that he had been dragged behind the German line. And he discovered that he had been wounded in three places at once, obviously by machine-gun fire. He often quoted the official form describing him as "wounded in the left leg, the left arm, and the left head."

Was it his head wound that had him confused? He didn't know. What was sure, the Battle of the Maas was over for him. Actually, the American offensive stopped when the armistice that ended all the hostilities was signed at 11 AM on the 11th day of the 11th month, November, 1918. For years thereafter people wore red poppies on that day, commemorating the fields of poppies that grew in the nearby Flanders Fields, under which so many men were buried.

Eventually, my father was taken further back, away from the front, away from the battlefield. He was operated on and the bullets removed from his left leg and left arm. But they did not dare operate on his head. That bullet was lodged in the bone right at his brain. It was never removed. It showed clearly on his X-rays all the rest of his life.

And for all the years thereafter, whenever he forgot anything, his standard excuse was, *kopfschuss,* or headshot. The operations on his arm and his leg left small scars. And I could always feel the small bump on the left side of his head.

He had permanent war wounds from what was then called the War to End All Wars, or the Great War, Later, when there was a second, this one was called the First World War. I do not know how many German soldiers were killed or wounded in that battle, but 26,277 Allied Expeditionary Forces (AEF) troops were killed and 95,786 were wounded in that war.

Hans Friedmann was awarded the Iron Cross medal for being wounded. He never wore it because he became a pacifist, a relatively inactive pacifist, opposing war in general but not officially joining any anti-war organization.

But, about twenty years later, he was all in favor of World War Two against the Germans, now the Nazis!

16. Adler & Oppenheimer

As a young man, my father, Hans Friedmann, wrote, "With the end of the war (in) 1918, as every young person in Berlin, I began to read Freud. A few years later, went into analysis, as [did] all my other friends."

But what could he do to earn a living? He had been an apprentice with a leather company, a stage actor, a Zionist, an anti-Zionist, and a wounded veteran of what was then the Great War. Now what?

His father had insisted that each of his sons learn a trade, something to stand them in good stead, no matter what. Hans had learned leather. So he worked for a year for a leather company in Halbe. Then he joined the largest Jewish-owned leather company in all of Europe, with 6,000 employees, named *Adler und Oppenheimer*, and known as *A&O*. It was a listed on the stock exchange, with many offices in a few German cities and headquarters in Berlin, located on *Neue Friedrichstrasse 2* but with its entrance at *Schicklerstrasse 2.*

It was there that the well-trained ex-apprentice applied for a job. He got it, starting on September 1, 1922. He was hired by A&O, first working in the warehouse, then as a buyer of leather goods. Then his assignment was to go to tanneries all over Europe. He next worked at their Berlin central office, at their so-called bottom-leather store and quickly rose to become the supervisor of sales and service.

This was the Berlin of the Roaring 20's and my father definitely enjoyed all of the theater, cabarets, and bachelor lifestyle that Berlin was famous for. I believe it was at this time that he met three sisters and dated them -- one at a time. They were named Ilka, Olga, and Lena, but he gave them the nicknames of Ilksha, Olgsha, and Lensha. About thirty years later, when we lived in New York City, Ilka, now the widow of Paul Fleischmann, was once again a good friend of our family.

Next, A&O promoted *Herr Friedmann* to the same responsibility and duties at their second branch office, in Frankfurt-am-Main. His stepmother Johanna, my Oma, came from Frankfurt. Many years later, when I was in the American Army, I was stationed in Frankfurt. And many more years after that my family, that is, Betty and our three sons and I, lived in suburban Frankfurt while I worked in the city.

So my father became a traveling salesman, which is what he did for the rest of his life. According to a deposition by A&O's big boss, Julius Oppenheimer, "We can testify that Mr. Friedmann is a capable, intelligent, and knowledgeable co-worker, who, in all positions which he held in our company, demonstrated his great business sense and special abilities which we valued highly."

He wrote that my father "quickly achieved great success through his knowledge and understanding and intelligent presentations so that our directors decided to promote Mr. Friedmann to traveling salesman for our second branch in Cologne-on-the-Rhine."

The date of my father's promotion to Cologne (*Koln,* in German) was May 1, 1931. In one year he earned another promotion. On May 13, 1932, he became the head buyer for the Cologne office which meant that he was responsible for the branch.

My father referred to himself at that time as "getting to the top as branch manager." His assistant manager, a leather buyer, the second in command, was named Kurt Bachmann. More about him later.

Up until August 6, 1936 -- a significant date -- my father was A&O's best salesman, probably earning a commission on top of his salary. I know he did well because we lived well. At the time I was a baby, our family had three live-in maids, one to clean the house, another to cook (my mother never did learn how to cook), and the third, the *kindermaedchen* or babynurse took care of me. Of course my mother didn't work; she supervised that staff. In addition to those servants, one man came to our house every day to shave my father because a gentleman did not shave himself. Another man arrived daily to drive my father to work or to his customers -- a gentleman didn't drive himself, either. We lived the life of good, successful, well-to-do German citizens. Which we were.

Later, when we arrived in America unable to speak English, my father went to work in a leather factory again and my mother started cleaning other people's houses! It's evidence of their industriousness that they were successful in starting over again, and we ended up well off once again. It reminds me of the old Jewish joke which is so true: "I've been rich. And I've been poor. And, take it from me: rich is better."

It's not just the opportunity offered to every immigrant by the United State. And it's not just "the American way." I think it is also the Jewish way ... a never-give-up spirit, a determination to overcome obstacles, the lesson learned perhaps from the Book of Job. Or, perhaps, something assimilated by a people who have never lost their spirit no matter how great the oppressor. If we didn't get it from Haman in the Book of Esther, or the Babylonian Exile, or the Spanish Inquisition, or the Pogroms of the Cossacks, or Russian or Polish anti-Semitism, we definitely got the point from Adolf Hitler.

II. MY MOTHER'S FAMILY
(1800's - 1930's)

17. The Stollers of Silesia

My mother's mother's family and my mother's father's family both originally came from Silesia in east central Europe, the part of Germany that is now Poland.

The land was already inhabited in the Stone, Bronze and Iron Ages and then it was taken by the Vandals, Romans and Mongols. It became Moravian, Bohemian, Polish, Czech, Polish again, Austrian, Hungarian, Prussian, German, and Polish a third time.

I have a typewritten copy in German of a bill of sale for a house purchased by my two great-great-great-grandfathers, Manuel Simon Stoller and Lobel Baruch Oelsner, my mother's mother's progenitors. Both are described in the paper as "believers in the Old Testament." They purchased the house from Carl Bayer, on September 20, 1816. The two became *mechutten,* a Yiddish word for which there is no English translation. It means that their children married each other and they shared grandkids.

The contract is for house number 53 on the Ring in the city of Militsch for a price of 3,250 "Rthlr," the abbreviation of *Reichs thaler.* By the way, *thaler* is the German word that led to our English word, "dollar."

It is interesting that only 250 Rthlr were paid, with 3,000 Rthlr being the mortgage held by the Hyptheg bank at a rate of 5%. The contract also stipulated that the buyer's father guaranteed the loan. But the seller could call in the loan by giving a quarter of a year's notice. And the seller reserved the life-long right to have a room on the back street, Polish St., as well as use of the woodpile, the cellar, and a basement room. Included in the sale were the fire extinguishers and everything that was already nailed down, but the new owners could nail down whatever they wish. Beds for soldiers were not included and the buyer had to furnish any. Since the upper floor was rented out, that contract remained as it was. But the buyers had to furnish the seller a place to set up his bed in case the need arose.

The note says, "Since Baruch previously rented from the seller, the buyers must arrange any details between themselves although they both will own the house equally."

A picture of the Stoller family home in Militsch, probably the one in the contract, reveals a large house, immediately attached on its left side to another similar house. It is on the T end of a street, a corner house. The building has two chimneys, a long, sloping roof which could house two stories above the two that are visible under the roof. There is a central front door with two windows on either side and five windows on the floor above it. It is certainly in a prosperous, well-to-do residential area with many somewhat similar houses on the facing street and a wide road leading directly to it. Militsch was a mid-sized city near the Niese River, then on the border of Poland.

Silesia was still a part of Prussia when, on July 12, 1811, Salomon Stoller was born there. He was my mother's grandmother's father. His father was Manuel Simon Stoller, one of my great-great-great-grandfathers.

Salomon Stoller, who was described as intelligent, married Ida Oelsner, who was called efficient. She, ten years younger than he, was born in Militsch February 22, 1821. Her father was Lobel Baruch Oelsner, my other great-great-great-grandfather.

Salomon and Ida Stoller, the children of the two partners in the contract, had seven children, all born in Militsch: three boys -- Louis, Emil, and Paul -- and four girls -- Anna, Jenni, Klara, and Mathilde. Salomon Stoller died in Silesia in 1870, a year before Count Otto von Bismark merged Prussia into a new country, Germany.

Louis, the oldest child of Salomon and Ida Stoller, was born in 1841 and he had two wives. The first, Malwine Zueler bore him a boy named Fritz. The second, Marianne Wigadszynski (no, that's no misprint), gave him a daughter, Helene.

I have professionally made photographs of four family members, who are well dressed but unidentified. I guess the photos are from the late 1800's. It looks like two generations are pictured, possibly the grandparents are Salomon and Ida Stoller and the middle-age couple are Gustav and Anna Friedmann. If so, Salomon wore a round, black hat atop his white hair, a bandana-like tie, white shirt, vest, and suit jacket or coat. Ida has full, white hair and wore a silk dress. The young husband, probably Gustav, is hatless, with a somewhat receding hairline. He has a bow tie, white shirt, vest with a gold watch chain, and jacket. His wife, Anna, has dark hair parted down the middle and a white blouse with a long-sleeved dress, pinched above the waist.

Anna was the second child, the oldest daughter, born on October 12, 1844. She had an "intelligent father and efficient mama," according to a 20-verse poem written in her memory. She was my mother's Oma, the grandmother she knew well, loved deeply and respected. My mother often referred to her as Anna Stoller, her maiden name. Anna married Gustav Friedmann, who was originally from Hamburg, but who lived in Breslau when they got married.

18. The Breslau Friedmanns

The name Friedmann does not mean a freed man, although it is pronounced that way. Many Southerners say "fried man," and it certainly does not mean that, either. No, the correct translation of our name is "man of peace." Peace, in German, is *frieden*.

Two Friedmann brothers, Ludwig and Gustav, married two sisters, Clara and Anna Stoller. Ludwig and Clara celebrated their Golden Wedding Anniversary in Breslau in 1921; they had two sons, Karl and Erich Friedrich Friedmann.

Gustav Friedmann was born on the 4th of July, 1865. Gustav and Anna had three boys, Ernst, Paul, and Franz -- all born in Breslau. The youngest, Franz Friedmann, was born on June 20, 1871, the year Germany was created. He was my mother's father.

41

Then as now, Breslau was the capital of Lower Silesia, at the foot of the Sudety Mountains, on the Oder River. In the 10th century it was ruled by Polish kings, then the Germans, Bohemians, and Prussians. In 1741, Frederick II, known as Frederick the Great, named it Breslau. It has 12 islands, 112 bridges, and city walls which go back to medieval times.

Anna and Gustav named their son Paul because the child's uncle named Paul had passed away. In the best Jewish tradition, one names a child to honor a deceased person, but not necessarily with the identical name.

A poem about Anna says that she loved to eat and was a cooking magician; she started making "chocolate fish" for children's birthdays; she taught her daughters-in-law, and the tradition has continued for four generations now. My mother always made it for a kid's party! It is for children, although it is a mixture of chocolate, nuts, and some alcohol! John had the recipe and the vital fish-form and now David has it all.

Anna Friedmann loved peace and quiet, the poem tells us, but "her way was sometimes loud."

Above all, she valued cleanliness. She made toys by hand and loved to give them; she told fairy tales that "always had a meaning for daily life."

She wrote letters often, disbursing good news "that very hour" throughout the family whenever she could.

Another verse translates:
No birthday was ever forgotten!
Not only within the Family Circle,
Also acquaintances far and wide
She remembered them all.
The same could be said of her granddaughter, my mother.

After her husband Gustav passed away, Anna took her three sons and moved to Hamburg. There was a celebration of her 80th birthday at which another poem to her mentions how thin she remained and how she enjoyed listening to records and going for a drive in a car. Of course such a woman was especially fond of her grandchildren "and her last year even brought her the first great-grandchild who was pure joy in her heart."

That was me! She died almost 90 years old, on June 10, 1934, just 2½ months after I was born.

Anna Stoller Friedmann's sister, Jenni, became the grandmother of the Krebs and Buchholz families. Friedrich Buchholz visited the U.S.A. and was a favorite of my Betty's. In November, 2004, my son David and I visited him when he was 98 years old and in amazingly good health. It took a little while for him to understand who we were.

We two also visited with some of the surviving members of that Krebs family branch in Holland and Germany. The fact is that, thanks to my son David's Internet work, we can now trace exactly 109 direct descendants and their spouses from Jenni!

The third daughter of Salomon and Ida Stoller, Klara, also married a Friedmann, Ludwig. The name Friedmann is pretty common among Jews; we know many who are not related to us. But Ludwig and Klara's two sons, Karl and Erich Friedrich Friedmann, surely were. Yet that line died out with Erich in Berlin in 1941 during World War II.

It is so ironic that one sister had so many descendants for so many generations while another had so few, and eventually, none.

The fourth daughter, Mathilde, was born in Militsch in 1854 and died only 24 years later in Berlin. There is a picture of Mathilde Stoller in which my son David sees a resemblance to his brother John. She is his great-great-grandaunt. She became Ursula and Fritz Wolff's maternal grandmother. Fritz, an international businessman, was a charming gentleman who I met a few times. He passed away just recently in Israel at 93. His almost-last words were, "Don't be sad because I am happy to go."

There is a picture of a man in my mother's ancestral family to whom John also bears a great resemblance. It is probably my mother's Uncle Ernest. The only reason I know it is not John is that my son never dressed up in such old-fashioned clothing!

In the 1905 census, 75% of Silesia's population was German and only 25% Polish. The Stollers and Friedmanns all considered themselves good German Jews.

In 1919, Silesia was divided into Upper and Lower Silesia. In 1938 it was also split into three districts. All of my mother's mother's ancestors came from Upper Silesia, in the Breslau district, but not from Breslau. The Friedmanns, my mother's father's family, came from Breslau, the largest city in Silesia, now in Poland and called *Wroclaw*.

19. The Co-Co-Co

My mother's mother's family were the Altmanns from Silesia. We can only trace back seven generations from my grandchildren, as far as my great-grandparents, Koppel and Rosalie. But we count 219 relatives on that branch of the family tree! And counting!

Koppel Altmann was born on July 10, 1839. Rosalie Feuerstein was born on January 18, 1840. They got married and had ten children. That's the reason I have so many cousins on my mother's side of the family. That, and the fact that those cousins became a tightly knit group simply by organizing themselves in a kind of a club called The Co-Co-Co or *Congress von Cousins und Cousinen* (Congress of male Cousins and female Cousins). They got together often, usually at the wedding of one of them, and created a unique flag for each such important occasion.

Both Koppel and Rosalie Altmann died in 1902. Here are their ten children: four girls in a row (Selma, Sophie, Marie, and Lina) then two boys (Siegfried and Samuel) then three girls (Dorothea, Else, and Johanna) and finally David Altmann. The girls were known as "the seven sisters." The three younger ones were particularly close, probably because of the age gap between the oldest and youngest groups of girls. The youngest girl became my grandmother, my mother's mother, Johanna.

The seven Altmann sisters were all said to be very good looking. Their descendants are certainly a handsome group. There is a photograph of a small meeting of the Co-Co-Co, probably taken in August, 1916, when sisters Johanna and Else (Friedmann and Burin, nee Altmann) rented a house at Travemuende on the Baltic Sea *(Ostsee)*. It shows thirteen of the next-generation cousins sprawled out on the beach.

The oldest of the seven sisters, Selma (1865-1931), married a Dutchman, Morris Van Praagh, and moved to London. There they had three children, Sam, Harry, and Lina. Sam married Ethel Jones and they had three children, David, Anthony, and Zelma. I met Ethel and David Van Praagh in London in 1955 at the unveiling of Sam's tombstone. At that time David was a grossly overweight man who insisted on eating the fat that I cut off my meat. He and Doris had two sons, John -- who married a Karen, as my son John did, and Michael --

who married a Kathryn, unlike my son Michael, who married a Mary. David's sister Zelma married David Kremer starting that line in London and California.The second sister, Sophie, also went to London, married a Ruby and had a daughter who married a Silver. That's how we got some jewelry in the family! But I'm afraid we're are not related to the Friedman Jewelry Store chain.

The third sister, Marie (1869-1949), married Maximillian Goerlich. He was quite a character, a tall man who wore tall and distinctive hats, dramatic coats and capes, horn-rimmed glasses, and sported a glorious white beard. He didn't walk or stroll or amble but marched down the street, carrying a stick or cane which he flourished like a baton.

The cousins joked that Maximillian's name wasn't long enough; so they called him *Maximillianaum*, after a museum of that name. It was Max (if I may shorten his name instead) who lived in a large house by a lake in Caputh, a suburb of Berlin.

Maximillian had had four daughters with his first wife who died. When he married Marie, she was twenty years older than his oldest daughter but just a few years older than his youngest, who I believe was named Martha. They had no children together but Marie moved into his house where Martha also lived. Many of the Co-Co-Co cousins spent a lot of time with them in that big house.

There, too, Max and Marie had a very successful in-home business. He was the editor of a trade newspaper (foreshadowing a job I had) and its publisher (which I am doing now). He and his wife also made herbal, medicinal teas of their own secret formulations which they mixed up in a large zinc bathtub which stood in the center of their Great Room. They bagged the teas there. My mother said their whole house always smelled of one herb or another. They sold the teas through mail order (foreshadowing another job I had). Successfully combining the two businesses, he wrote the ads (the last foreshadowing of my career) and ran them at no cost -- only in his trade paper, a union publication.

Max and Marie's home remained in the Goerlich family, even after the war, or so it seems from the correspondence to Walter and Rosi Heinemann from Marie and Martha Goerlich. *Tante Marie* was a favorite of my mother and my cousin Ellen-Ruth Fass who also spent a great deal of time with her "Oma Caputh."

Back to the Altmann sisters. Lina was born in Cologne or Schrimm; she married Max Kochmann who was born in Cologne or Schokken. I have two differing sources for this. I will quote from one, a woman who knew them well, but whose name I don't know. She is the granddaughter of Michael and Beatrix Schoenen.

"Max and Lina's children were Leo, Karl, and Marga. Between 1910 and 1935, they lived in a third-floor apartment on *Ehrenstrasse 19*, Cologne, a building owned by the family who lived below them, the Schoenens." Their granddaughter wrote that the Kochmanns also rented the ground-floor storefront from them.

I believe it was the shoe store established by Ernst Simon (see Chapter 23). If so, the family business was run by Karl Kochmann, Ernst's wife's nephew, and later taken over by him.

The owner's granddaughter continues, "Max Kochmann was a thin man and his wife, Lina, a heavy-set woman. Both had dark hair. Lina Kochmann was a kind matron and Marga a very nice child with a round face like her mother's, with somewhat curly, dark hair and freckles.

"For New Year's and special holidays, Mr. and Mrs. Kochmann came downstairs about 11 o'clock in the morning; he in evening clothes and top hat, she in a fine, black dress, to wish their landlords a good new year. They were rewarded with a glass of 'morning wine.' Also for the engagement of my grandfather, they came dressed that way to congratulate. My grandmother, Hilde Schoenen, who lived as the daughter-in-law in the house from 1925 to 1930, liked both of them and wrote of them as formal and pleasant. Especially Marga and Karl were congenial to her."

The Schoenens' granddaughter describes Marga's girlfriend Beate Zimmermann as spending a lot of time with her, especially inside the store. "There [were] balls of wool on shelves on the walls and a small two-step ladder. The two girls sat on the steps of this ladder and used the top surface as a playtable."

She describes Beate as enjoying visits to the Kochmanns, "particularly when the family celebrated the Sabbath. There Hebrew songs were sung, candles were burning, and there *Mazzen* [sic] were eaten, which is unleavened bread."

She said that Marga went to the Jewish school on *St. Aprenstrasse*. "After 1933, the Nazis came to power, the Kochmanns gave up the business." She wrote that, but I don't think so. Or, if they did, they got it back after the war.

She continued, "They also moved to a different apartment. From there, Max and Lina Kochmann were collected, on June 15, 1942, and deported to Theresienstadt. There she was murdered.

"Their daughter, Marga, had married Alfred Mosbach, who was born in *Leudenscheid* and who was also a Jew. With him she moved to *Rheinaustrasse 18* in Cologne. They had a daughter, Johanna. This family emigrated to Amsterdam where they were also later arrested by the Nazis and deported to the Sorbibor concentration camp. All three of them were killed there on July 23, 1943.

"The son, Leo, emigrated at the right time to Shanghai. From there he went to California, where he died in 1969."

Leo Kochmann married Elsbeth on the 4th of July, 1948, in Cologne. But long before that, his younger sister Marga married Alfred Mosbach in Cologne in 1932. Then Max and Lina Kochmann's middle child, Karl, married Hedy Zeus in Cologne on February, 2, 1933. There was a Co-Co-Co celebration, complete with a new flag.

1933 was the start of the Nazi era in Germany and Hedy was not Jewish; Zeus is certainly not a Jewish name. Karl converted to Christianity and they joined a neighborhood church.

The previously quoted woman continues her story: "Karl stayed unmolested, since he married a non-Jewish wife. However, she was regularly hauled to the Gestapo [Headquarters] in EL-DE Haus in Cologne at *Appellhofplatz* and put under pressure to divorce her husband. She withstood that and had her first child with him, Klaus. In 1946 she had her second son [Manfred]. Karl carried on the shoe store and later turned it over to her second son, who still continues in Cologne even today, a wholesale shoe business."

She continues, "My grandfather, Joseph Schoenen, met Karl Kochmann after the war (about 1948) and learned from him that his parents and his sister's family, were dead. My grandmother told me that her husband was completely beside himself and actually sick when he came home and told her that. She was also very taken with it. She had especially known Marga Kochmann since 1925, more than ten years, and liked her. After she herself had moved from *Ehrenstrasse 19* to a neighboring street, she practically daily had met her on the street while shopping. They both had little children and every time spoke with each other."

It was ten years after their marriage that Karl Kochmann's and Hedy's also euphonious son, Klaus Kochmann, was born in Cologne in 1943, during World War II. As he told David and me in November, 2004, Klaus felt that his father had seemed to him to be a very private man who often left the house for periods of time and did not talk about where he had been. Only once, long after the war, did his father take young Klaus to a place they boy had never been before. He recalled it as a somewhat mysterious small stone structure in a strange kind of courtyard.

Long after his brother Manfred was born in 1946, and long after the end of the Second World War, Klaus came to understand where his father had disappeared to and what that special courtyard had been. It was a church's cemetery and the burial crypt of a priest. That was where his father had hidden himself whenever he thought the Nazis might be after him for being Jewish.

I believe it was Klaus Kochmann who wrote that there never was a Nazi or swastika flag flown in that house on *Ehrenstrasse*. "On a Nazi holiday in the year 1937, the eldest son of my great-grandparents, Jean, already almost 60 years old, and his son, Hans-Joseph, witnessed the following scene:

"It was directed that [every] house be decorated with a Swastika flag. [The Nazi emblem.] Jean hung the yellow-and-white church flag out of his window. [I believe it to be the papal flag.] While on the narrow *Ehrenstrasse* now all the [other] houses were decorated with the red flags with black swastikas, the house at number 19 was noticed. The [Nazi] party members came to the house and confronted Jean mightily; didn't he have a swastika flag? He answered, 'On the contrary, yes, of course, we have a flag, come into the living room.'

"He led them to a closet and pulled a flag from the lowest drawer. 'But my mother does not allow me to hang this out.'

"Then call your mother!"

At that time she was 85 years old, but the official spoke to her sharply: "What is this? You must hang this swastika flag outside!"

She answered energetically, "As long as I have been living in this house, there has always been a yellow-and-white flag flying. And as long as I live in this house, there will always be a yellow-white flag. There is the door. Get out!"

And the party officials left.

Klaus Kochmann is today an extremely fascinating man. His English is so good that he translates important books professionally from English into German. Among them are Bill Clinton's *My Life* and Daniel Jonah Goldhagen's *Hitler's Willing Executions* which tells of the thousands of ordinary Germans who killed Jews.

Klaus Kochmann married Brigitte Speith who is a superb cook. He and his wife have long lived in a very large, very well located, downtown Berlin apartment house at *Momsenstrasse 50.* They have a lease and cannot be evicted from their third-floor flat. At the time David and I visited them in October 2004, the owners were converting the building into a co-op and every other resident had moved out, except Klaus and Brigitte. They continued to stay, quite legally, while the construction was going on all around them. Not only was the exterior of the building open to the elements and only partly covered with planks but the three flights of stairs leading up to their apartment were only partially there! Later the couple went to China and returned when their home was finished.

Brigitte had had a son, Wolfgang, born in Berlin. Klaus adopted him long ago and he is now named Kochmann, too. He is in his 20's and runs a local motorcycle shop, participates in cycle races, goes camping, and often helps his parents.

When I met the Kochmann family for the first time in October 2004, Klaus misunderstood something I said about my father and he had an anxiety attack. I didn't understand why at the time. Evidently, Klaus felt that he was spiritually and emotionally closer to my father than I was! Perhaps Klaus was politically closer, yet Klaus is a blood relative of my mother, not my father!

It was thereafter that Klaus wrote me a "Remembrance of Hans Friedman," which helped me understand my father better. But I'll save that for a later chapter.

Klaus' brother Manfred Kochmann continued the euphonious tradition when he married Marion and they named their three sons Michael, Martin, and Markus. David and I spoke with Manfred on our 2004 visit and had a delightful dinner with his three sons: Martin and Markus are twins, born on June 1, 1979; Michael is two years older.

The boys took us to a typical Cologne bar where they serve very fresh local beer and traditional foods. But, as a long-standing local joke, the specialty dishes are not named what they are, much as a hot dog is not literally that. So a so-called liver-and-cheese sandwich contains none of those ingredients; it is not even a sandwich! Things like that amuse the locals at the expense of the tourists. The M&M&M boys, along with Michael's girlfriend, interpreted the local lingo for us.

Back to the Altmanns. Siegfried Altmann married Johanna Salomon and their daughter Gertie started the Sichel line, also in Cologne.

Brother Samuel's progeny took the Altmann family to South Africa, the Nahums went to Israel and the Steins to New York, California, and Korea.

Tante Dora was another favorite of my mother's. She's the one who married Eduard Simon and they owned a shoe store or two. They also had the three daughters: Nannette, Rosalie, and Else (most often called Nanni, Rosi, and Else, and also known as the Shoe Store Simon Sisters). They led to all my New York and Boston cousins -- the Fass, Zilka, Freeman, and Roth families, the Heinemans and Marshalls, as well as the Silversmiths and so on.

Else Altmann married Paul Burin, leading to the Buffalo, NY, families of Klees, Poseners, Landress, and McCabes.

Johanna married Franz Salomon Friedmann, who begat Paul, Lotte and Karl, and the next generation, me and my first cousins in England, Australia, and South Africa -- Frank, Ruth, Vivian, Etan, and Kalene Friedman, etc.

Finally, the youngest of the ten Altmann children, David (1883-1961), married Johanna Lesem and they had only one child, my uncle Alfred. The youngest of that generation of cousins, Alfred was born in 1921 in Dusseldorf, Germany. He married Denise Aaronson on March 23, 1952. Theirs was the last of the true Co-Co-Co wedding celebrations, complete with its own flag. Those are my Canadian cousins.

The only time my parents and I ever went to Niagara Falls, Canada, I was a young teenager. As we crossed the border, I mentioned that we knew only one Canadian, my Uncle Alfred. I looked up and said, "There he is!" It was indeed Alfred Altman on one of his very few visits to the Falls! I think that the only time I had seen him before that was at my *bar mitzvah*.

Alfred and Denise's daughter Jacquelyn (Jaqui) was born on July 6, 1961, four days after our son David. Their son David was born in 1964, a year before our Michael.

All in all there were 15 Co-Co-Co flags made, each celebrating a wedding in the Altmann family, from Georg and Nanni Fass in Cologne on July 3, 1927, through Alfred and Denise Altman. But we continue to celebrate, even without flags.

My mother's 80th birthday party in New York was one Co-Co-Co convention. The most recent meeting of the Co-Co-Co had about 40 family members in London at Heddy Friedman's (nee Wagener) 95th birthday on New Year's, 2004. My son David and his wife Debbie and daughters Sarah and Rachel were there with me.

20. From Breslau to Bielefeld

My mother's father, Franz Friedmann, was born in Breslau on June 20, 1871.

Franz Friedmann's father had been in textiles and so Franz, naturally, started off in that business. It was the era when you did what your father had done. Franz married the youngest of those seven pretty Altmann sisters, Johanna, on June 7, 1903, and they started their family in *Essen-an-der-Ruhr*. There they had their three children. Paul was born March 4, 1904, Lotte came along two years later, March 11, 1906, and Karl on December 13, 1907. We did not learn it until much later, but Lotte's real first name was Rosalie. Lotte was her middle name. But she was always called Lotte and grew up believing that her initials were LRF. They were on our best linen napkins.

My future grandparents attended a gala dinner on January 28, 1906 -- while Johanna was pregnant with my mother -- at the *Hotel Berliner Hof* in *Essen-an-der-Ruhr*. They saved the full-color printed script for a celebratory "melodrama" and the embossed folder and menu from that party. Caviar on ice was the appetizer, then turtle soup, filet of veal with mushrooms next, then lobster from Helgoland with Kaiser's-length asparagus and English celery; finally, assorted fruits, dessert, and "exploding candy." Franz and Johanna surely knew what the good life, the high life, was and they enjoyed it. They resolved to "make it" in their own business.

As a young family man, Franz saw that the Industrial Revolution had changed the world. In particular he noted that Jewish manufacturers were producing various goods, paper, metal, leather, but above all, textiles. Jewish entrepreneurs were active in that new phenomenon, the department store. With it came a whole new style of shopping, One particular pioneer in Silesia converted his dry-goods business to include clothing, linens and even bridal trousseaus.

Franz realized that this department store concept was an opportunity for him. His idea was to establish a department store that featured textiles, ideally in a place where they knew something about fabrics and quality. He wanted to put his idea into practice somewhere other than Silesia, in an area that didn't have a department store yet. He literally went around Germany in search of the ideal location.

He got to a city in Westphalia called Bielefeld. It was actually an ancient town, historically. And Franz Friedmann became fascinated by the town's history. Originally spelled *Bilivelde* in the year 1015, meaning "field at the foot of the hill," it was located at the *Sparenberg* or Sparen Mountain in the Teutoburge Forest, at the confluence of the Rhein and Weser rivers. Organized on the left bank in feudal times and ruled by the Earl of Ravensberg, it became a free city in Saxon times. In 1256, they began a new town called *Neustadt* on the right bank and each built its own wall around itself. Jews were massacred there during the Black Death (1348-1349), but many returned in 1370. In 1511, Johan von Cleve united the twin territories. By 1559, a linen factory had started there.

The city of Kleve is in Germany near the border with Holland. In October, 2004, my son David and I visited relatives on my mother's side, Wolfgang and Christa Krebs, in Kleve. They had put on an exhibition about the Jews of Kleve and now house the only collection of historical materials on that subject in the area.

It wasn't until 1574 that the two parts, *Bilivelde* and *Neustadt,* officially became the city of Bielefeld. The Hanseatic League took over in 1580 until 1614, when the 30 Years' War began. (The fortress atop the *Sparenberg* dates from that era.) When the last Count of Cleve died in 1609, the town of Bielefeld stayed neutral in the 30 Year's War.

Spanish and French forces fought there until 1647 when the Dutch took over! They invigorated the spinning and weaving trade. In 1782 the first damask factory was established in the city. Soon Bielefeld's linens became famous all over the globe.

Otto von Bismark united Germany in 1871, including the state of Westphalia and its Bielefeld. In 1905, a synagogue that seated 800 was consecrated in town. The Jewish population was 65 in 1783 and 800 by 1933.

My father, who came from the capital city, Berlin, Germany's largest city, joked that Bielefeld was a small town. Detractors called it *Bieledorf,* or Biele-village. But it was and still is a medium-sized city, not at all like any small, provincial burg. Today it is the 18th largest city in Germany with 320,000 inhabitants while Berlin has more than ten times that many, 3,275,000.

When Franz Friedmann arrived in Bielefeld about 1910, he recognized that it was a factory town with textile mills that employed mostly young women. There was then and still is a statue in Bielefeld, the town symbol, called the Linen Weaver, who is depicted as an old man smoking a long pipe. This city was exactly what my grandfather had been searching for.

Franz realized that the female linen workers in Bielefeld earned good salaries and would want to have all the latest fashions. They made linens and they knew good fabrics. He also figured that when they got married they'd want to stay around their home town and keep up with the ever-changing styles. The city had gained a reputation for quality products. This was an ideal place for a fashionable, modern department store. One that would feature linens and fabrics in its street-front windows. He found the perfect site, just off the city's main crossroads, Jahnplatz, right at a street-car stop. That was where Franz opened his *Kaufhaus,* (department store). His name was dramatically displayed over the entrance: *Franz Friedmann.*

It was a 4-storey structure that had an impressive steeple and big front windows facing the corners, the intersections of two main streets. The enticing displays were changed to reflect the appropriate times of year. They always showed the very latest, up-to-the-minute things -- just like Berlin or even Paris. The local newspaper had a drawing of the store and a short story which sounded a lot like an ad.

Under a headline of *Die Firma Franz Friedmann in Bielefeld,* it said: "In the main business quarter of the city, on the corner of *Niedern* and *Hagenbruch* streets, (elsewhere described as *Niedernstrasse 15 und Guesenstrasse* 2) in place of the old *Reichsbank,* stands the business building of Franz Friedmann's company. Women's and children's clothing, dress fabrics and silks, fashion ware, wools, linens, and washables, mostly unique in Bielefeld, are sold here. Also rugs, drapes, curtains, and leather goods are the main articles of the house. Manners, the best taste, and large selections will satisfy the many needs of our women's world. We expect the reputation of the Franz Friedmann Company to flow far past the borders of the city."

I have the opening advertisement which shows a sophisticated and elegant lady in a large hat with a feather plume, a fur-lined coat and huge fur muff, wearing a long silk or satin gown with a low-hanging necklace and pointy shoes. The ad's headline says, "MODERN SPECIALTY HOUSE."

A later ad in the city news section of the local paper headlined, "Bielefeld's White Sensation Is Friedmann's White Week." A white sale means a bargain in fabrics.

Another day, the news section carried an article about the store with pictures of a Japanese tea table, an evening table with wine, and a breakfast table in a game room.

Most of all, the window displays showed the very latest fashionable fabrics. Franz felt it was important to show off the finest of finery and to keep changing the scene frequently enough to lure new business into the store. It is no wonder that many years later, Franz's youngest son, Karl, went into the window display business.

Franz had been absolutely right, the store was a big success. He was a big success. He and his family soon settled very comfortably in Bielefeld at *Falkstrasse* 12, in a large, comfortable apartment not far from the store. It is a short street in the Jewish section, quite near the synagogue.

Naturally, the Friedmann family home had all the latest fashions and furnishings with luxurious linens and the finest silverware. It was the epitome of elegance. My grandparents were every bit as up to the minute as their store's latest fashions.

There is a German saying: *Sehn wir uns nicht in dieser Welt*

So sehn wir uns in Bielefeld!

I translated that to mean: If we don't see each other in this world,
Then we'll see each other in Bielefeld!

It was a paradise. And Franz Friedmann's business was an immediate and tremendous success. A fantastic success. It made Franz and Johanna wealthier than they had thought possible. They truly prospered. I believe they were the equivalent of millionaires -- the first (but not the last) in our Friedmann families!

At first Franz saw to every detail of the business but as things continued to prosper, he realized they could act as wealthy as they had become. They had servants, one to cook, another to clean. My grandparents always dressed themselves in the finest, most elegant, tasteful, and up-to-date clothing that the business could feature. They were truly walking advertisements for their store.

Franz had come to love his adopted city of Bielefeld and he decided to become active in local, especially religious, affairs. He spent more and more time on the nearby synagogue's activities. He became a civic leader, a prominent citizen, recognized by the local politicians, religious leaders, and other businessmen. His family enjoyed the pleasures of the department store's success. They had earned it all.

And *Herr und Frau Friedmann* also realized that they could now do what they had always wanted to: travel. They went to Paris to see the great city. They took a steamship to North Africa to see the pyramids of Egypt. Franz and Johanna traveled far and wide, first class all the way. They truly lived well.

Until World War One. And its aftermath.

21. Paul, Lotte and Karl

Franz and Johanna Friedmann's children, Paul, Lotte and Karl, were close, not only in age. Paul was born March 24, 1904; Lotte March 11, 1906; Karl December 13, 1907, all in Essen on the Ruhr River. Franz moved his young family to Bielefeld when the children were still small. In the fashion of the times, little Karl was dressed in girl's clothes for a special occasion such as a formal photograph. (See the boy on the horse in the upper right cover photo).

Throughout their childhood, the Friedmann children lived a prosperous life. The department store could easily furnish them all the clothes, all the toys, all the luxuries.

In those happy, even idyllic pre-World War I times, the three often visited their relatives. They especially enjoyed going to their mother's sister, their *Tante Marie* and her husband Maximillian Goerlich, in a suburb of Berlin, Caputh. Their large house on a lake became a convenient, central, hospitable meeting place for all the cousins, the largest home available to house all the children of all the Altmanns, the Co-Co-Co.

During the Great War, in the summer of 1917, Lotte and Marga Burin (later Klee) spent four weeks in the country together. They stayed on a farm with a flour mill near Soest in Westphalia. They helped with the harvesting of hay and grain and watched cows being milked. The milking was, according to Marga, "sometimes directly into our mouths."

It was there that, as Marga put it, "we learned about the birds and the bees."

Marga continued, "The food and the home-baked bread and the cakes were terrific, especially considering the food shortage in Germany during World War I."

The family gatherings, in Caputh or other vacation spots such as the seashore, became enjoyable meetings of the Co-Co-Co. In today's terms one would say that the cousins bonded. The closeness of those cousins was to become beneficial for those who left Germany before, during, and after World War II.

My mother enjoyed her stays in Caputh so much that she decided, after her graduation from school, to attend the teacher-training program in Caputh. I do not know if that decision was because of the location or the career, but she went there to learn to become a kindergarten teacher.

That was where she met Hilde Wagener who was nicknamed Heddy. The schoolmates became roommates. One day during school vacation, Lotte brought Heddy home to Bielefeld to meet her family. She liked them all, especially Lotte's brother Paul. In fact, as my Aunt Heddy told me in 2004, she was determined to marry Paul the day she set eyes on him. But of course she didn't let Paul in on her decision until much later. So the two roommates who became best friends eventually became sisters-in-law.

Both Paul and Karl often went to their father's department store and, as naturally as their father before them, learned the family business. It was to stand them both in good stead, in ways and places they never imagined at the time.

World War I did not really affect the Franz Friedmann family as much as its aftermath did. No bombs fell on Bielefeld; the town saw no invasion, no action. That would have to wait for World War II. But the victorious allies insisted that Germany pay for its sins and bear the cost of rebuilding the countries it had invaded. The price they demanded was steep. It was enough to give Adolf Hitler an excuse to start another war.

22. After World War I

Germany had lost the war and the reparations demanded by the victorious allies, especially the French, helped to create the most horrendous post-war inflation that became the worst depression. The entire population was made to pay for the devastation that Germany had caused.

It may be hard for you to understand this inflation-depression. I think of it this way: When I was young, gasoline for a car cost 25 cents a gallon. Inflation of 100% is only 50 cents a gallon. I recently paid $2.50 a gallon and that's 1,000% inflation. Gas has gone to more than $3.25. Yet we are not living in inflationary times!

Germany's inflation was not just many thousands per cent! It was literally in the millions per cent, if you can imagine that. The aftermath of The Great War saw the *Deutschmark* fall into freefall, virtual worthlessness. Very few people had any money and those that had some, found it was not worth the paper it was printed on, much less the cost of printing it!

A daily newspaper that had cost pennies now literally cost millions! There were pictures in the newspaper showing people taking a wheelbarrow full of money to buy bread. In the 1920's a streetcar ride was 10 million marks! A sausage cost 12 million per pound and it actually went up to 240 million per pound! It was written at that time that "one can only go shopping with billion-mark notes."

Unemployment was rising; the collapse of the German economy was complete. The post-war inflation was what Hitler used to denounce foreign countries and to blame on the Jews.

I do not mean to compare that economy with our present American economy. David has said that I have correctly predicted eleven of the last four downturns. I am not a "doom and gloom" forecaster. Yet economies, all economies, go in cycles. And the post-World War One German economy was the worst that ever hit any country.

It was hard for my mother's father, Franz Friedmann, to maintain his department store business and almost impossible for him to buy for the store much less to sell from the store. Times were tough. But Germans are even tougher. And Jews tougher yet. Of course the Friedmanns survived.

My mother remembered that after World War I her family had to use cut up newspaper for toilet paper! They, who had become so wealthy, now had to scrimp and save. No more servants; now my grandmother had to cook and clean and take care of the children. My grandfather had to do so much more than supervise his staff, he became the floor manager of all four sales floors. I think that the comedown had to be so much harder for people who had been all the way up. But they did what they had to do; what else could they do?

Yet people simply had to buy the necessities of life. And what had been a luxurious store started to sell relative necessities. However as soon as it was possible, Franz built up the quality of the merchandise and it became a department store that sold not just necessities but also the luxuries that made life worth living. Thus the business continued. Slowly he rebuilt the store's reputation for quality merchandise. It took time and a great deal of effort, but Franz Friedmann built it all up again, practically from scratch. It wasn't easy, but with dogged determination, the department store began to prosper again. It kept its customers. It even regained its former status and reputation.

The war was over and the quality of life was improving. The Friedmann family was able to enjoy the good life, the rich life, once again. Life actually returned to its pre-World War I splendor and luxury and happiness. Bielefeld and the Friedmanns endured!

Until the Nazi time. To think of what my grandparents lived through twice seems absolutely incredible to me. They had recovered from what they thought was the worst that could possibly happen to them, and then something so much more horrible happened!

23. The Shoe Store Simon Sisters

The three youngest of the seven Altmann sisters were close in age and their descendents, among the many cousins who formed the Co-Co-Co, were also very close.

The youngest Altmann girl was my mother's mother, Johanna.

The middle sister was Else who married Paul Burin, which led to the Klees.

The eldest of the three was Dorothea, my mother's *Tante Dora*, who married Eduard Simon. It was he who owned and operated a shoe store in Cologne. I do not know its name nor its address. But I cannot overemphasize its lasting importance to my mother's side of the family. Because it seems that Eduard created a real family business. Dora and Eduard had no sons but they did have three daughters, the so-called Shoe Store Simon Sisters: Nanette, Rosalie, and Else. His three girls definitely were not the reason Eduard hired only men as shoe salesmen. Rather, it was the custom at the time; all shoe salesmen were men. But Eduard did hire relatives or those who would become relatives by "marrying into" the family.

The Simons' oldest daughter, who was called Nanni, married a traveling wholesale shoe salesman, Georg Fass, who sold shoes <u>to</u> the store. Their children were Ellen-Ruth and Gerd, who "became letters" and changed their names. (See Chapter 31.)

The youngest daughter, Else, married an in-their-store shoe salesman named Fritz Silberschmidt. Their children, Donald and Peter, became the Silversmith Doctors.

Only Eduard and Dora's middle daughter, who was known as Rosi, married "outside the shoe store." Her husband was Walter Heinemann and their only child was Vera, who was always known as Putzi, although I don't know why.

There's much more about the three Shoe Store Simon Sisters and their progeny who came to Boston, Massachusetts, in later chapters.

The family business did so well that Eduard Simon opened a second shop, a wholesale shoe store, and he hired his wife's nephew, Karl

Kochmann, to run it. This store was also in Cologne, and I believe its address to be *Ehrenstrasse 19*.

Karl's son Manfred still runs that store today!

But Eduard Simon's request during the Nazi time to the German Red Cross for a travel permit to Cuba was either denied or unanswered. He did not survive.

III. OUR FAMILY
(1932 - 1939)

24. How My Parents Met and Married

My mother, Lotte Rosalie Friedmann, having finished her education at Caputh in northeast Germany, was now a licensed kindergarten teacher. But there weren't many jobs available as Germany was coming out of its post-World War I depression, especially for a young teacher with no experience. So she decided to begin instead as a *kindermaedchen*, someone who takes care of children, sort of a governess, nanny, or glorified baby-sitter. My mother would take care of a child or children by living in someone's home, usually but not only when the parents went away for a period of time.

My father had had *kindermaedchen*. Many years later, when our family lived in Cologne, I had a live-in *kindermaedchen* to take care of me. But at this point in her young life, my mother took a job in Cologne taking care of Herbert and Hilde, the children of my father's brother Paul and Dorothea Friedmann.

The children called their live-in, semi-permanent caregiver "Aunt Lotte." But the coincidence of their *kindermaedchen* having the same last name as the family she was working for was not lost on any of them; the children especially enjoyed the idea.

So when Herbert and Hilde's father's brother, their *Onkel Hans,* came to their house in Cologne for a visit, Herbert and Hilde laughed at the idea, and said, "You're both Friedmanns. If you two get married, *Tante Lotte* doesn't have to change her name!"

"Nor change the initials on my fine white linens," my mother added, jokingly. They all laughed -- prophetically. For her parents had given young Lotte a full set of the best table linens from their department store, with her own, artistically designed, L.R.F. initials embroidered on each piece, as a kind of early trousseau.

And, to the children, the idea of their *Onkel Hans* and their *Tante Lotte* getting married to each other meant that they, Herbert and Hilde, could legitimately keep calling them Uncle Hans and Aunt Lotte!

Thus, my father got a full dose of thinking about marrying this woman the very moment they met. Right away he thought that she, who was eleven years younger than he, had very attractive legs, a delightful smile, sparkling *schlitzaugen,* as well as a winning personality. (Klaus Kochmann recalled that his father, Karl, considered his cousin Lotte Friedmann the only Jewish girl he thought was very attractive.) Indeed, Hans and Lotte hit it off the first time they saw each other. The attraction was mutual.

My parents dated a while and really enjoyed each other's company. She was impressed with this successful businessman with his handsome moustache (which would later be called a Hitler moustache). Hans was enchanted by this vivacious young lady with her charming smile and manner. They enjoyed the same things when they went out. He took Lotte to the theater and impressed her with his knowledge of acting, staging, presentation -- things he had learned from the greatest master theatrical director and showman -- Max Reinhardt. And he was taken by her inquisitive mind and eager, sympathetic understanding. Yes, they hit it off immediately.

The thought of marriage never far from his mind, Hans asked her -- and her father -- who both said yes.

My parents were married in my mother's hometown of Bielefeld on September 7, 1932 at the *Rathaus* or City Hall. I must say that in addition to Herbert and Hilde, I'm also very glad they did! The celebration included a meeting of the Co-Co-Co with a flag made for the occasion.

My father had been a bachelor living alone for many years. He got married in a black suit. Or so he thought. It was only after the ceremony when they got his suit back from the dry-cleaner that his new wife saw stripes in the material. He had forgotten his suit's original design and evidently hadn't had it dry-cleaned before the wedding! Any woman would say that he was a man who needed to get married.

Nevertheless the marriage was a good one, a lasting one, a happy one. I frankly believe that my mother was not my father's intellectual equal, nor was he as concerned as she was with appearances. She did not care about politics, economics and world issues; he did not concern himself with details and technicalities. They each filled voids in the other's personality and thus made a happy marital arrangement.

It was still the era when the man was the boss of the house and the woman did what she was told. They had both grown up that way. She had a lot of respect for him and gladly did whatever he asked her to. And while my father beat me whenever he thought I deserved it, he never hit my mother.

They lived through awful times. Two world wars, the Cold War, Korean War, and Vietnam. Like her parents, both my parents grew up in wealth and then had to work their way up from the bottom to achieve riches once again. They had it hard.

Yet they shared many wonderful things: their love of music and theater and a recognition of quality. And I have no doubt whatsoever that my parents truly loved and were devoted to each other and to their only child.

25. Walter Erich Friedmann

My father had read Adolf Hilter's *Mein Kampf* (My Fight.) He made his intentions perfectly clear in the book he wrote in 1924 in prison, ten years before he gained power!

At that time, Hitler's threats were absolutely unbelievable and so completely implausible that very few people paid attention to them! His views were so extremist, they would never become popular. What he proposed was incredible, even impossible! Germany was one of the most civilized countries; it was a modern society. What Hitler had written, most people thought, was just political rhetoric; in the improbable event that Hitler achieved power, he couldn't carry out such a program.

Then, when he was appointed Chancellor in 1933, most Germans could not believe that Hitler would be able to radically change German public opinion so quickly and so horrendously. Yet my father was among the very few German Jews who realized that the threat was real, the attitude was catchy, and the horror was possible.

That is why my father had sent my mother to London so that the baby would be born with dual nationalities, a British subject and a German citizen. His idea was that I might be able to go from Germany to England if and when, years from then, things got worse for Jews in Nazi Germany than they were in 1934.

My father was working in Germany for Adler & Oppenheimer; he was in charge of their Cologne office and the head buyer of leather goods. As such he often had to travel to various leather tanneries and to key customers. He simply could not leave the country for the time it would take, at least a month, before the baby was due. But he had made arrangements to come to London well before the baby would be born.

They miscalculated. I, Walter Erich Friedmann, was born early. As I mentioned in Chapter 1, my father got there while my mother and I were still in the hospital. And he immediately started making arrangements for our return to Germany. After all, that was where my parents lived. We left England when I was 28 days old.

We flew to Cologne and my parents brought me to their apartment on the *Zuelpiltscherstrasse*. From the many photos I have seen, I was a happy, somewhat chubby baby. Those pictures help me realize that I was potty trained at about three years of age. They show my mother to have quickly returned to her slim figure and my father to glow with unmitigated pride in his young offspring.

Of course I was too young to understand it, but things were getting worse and worse for the Jews in Germany.

26. The Gestapo Arrest My Parents

My father never told me this. My mother did not tell me until he had passed away and I was 51 years old! Most of this account I base on what I wrote down at the time I was told. But I did not find out the whole story until October 2004, when my son David and I, then age 70, went to Germany!

I was an infant when it happened and did not know what was going on. Later, when I was a child, my parents felt that I was still too young to understand. Still later, in the 1950's, during the McCarthy anti-Communist era, I was in the U.S. Army, in Military Intelligence, and personally under investigation for a top secret security clearance, so they dared not mention it. And later, when I had married Betty Klein, my parents felt they could not trust my father-in-law. Alex Klein had been a leftist but had gone all the way over to an ultra-rightist political stance. My father was also concerned because Alex's best friend was a policeman, possibly an undercover cop. My mother, when she told me, thought that our three sons were still too young to understand it. And they were 20, 22, and 24 years old then!

The truth came out on November 14, 1985, at the insistence of our good friend Herta Lowenthal who was visiting my mother, Betty, and me in New York City. Herta felt it simply had to be told to the family; my mother was persuaded to agree.

It started when Adolf Hitler became Germany's Chancellor. Hans Friedmann, a young, intelligent, educated, politically active Jew, did all he could to oppose the legitimate government. He joined the only political party that was actively working against the Nazis: the Communists.

Herta gave me permission to quote from her autobiography, *Herta*. She clearly describes their attitude at that time: "As young Communists we looked at it all from such an idealistic international viewpoint and identified ourselves with such slogans as 'Workers of the World Unite' and 'No Nationalism, No Wars,' etc. At that time we felt -- and indeed it was a fact -- that nobody, but nobody [else] was fighting Nazism. The Social Democrats said, 'Let them try, they won't last.'

"Nobody actually seemed to realize the terrible danger that was threatening the world, and it really was only the Communists who took up the fight ... We were all too naïve. Nobody then could even begin to envisage the consequences or could possibly imagine the atrocities of the Nazi regime."

Herta Lowenthal's maiden name was Friedemann -- with that extra "e" in there. She and Karl Rosenberg, her boyfriend at that time, were my parents' friends and neighbors on *Zuelpilcherstrasse* in Cologne. (My mother's cousins, the Karl Kochmanns, also lived on that street.)

The four friends shared leftist sentiments. My father never changed his opinion and was, in fact, a Communist for life. But he never again joined any political organization. (Today at age 95, while Herta Friedemann, later Rosenberg, and finally Lowenthal, has changed her name, she has not altered her leftist political leanings!)

When Herta and Karl Rosenberg got married on March 10, 1934, my parents were the only witnesses to the civil ceremony, the only wedding they had. It was conducted in an officiously legal way by a clerk, a civil servant who cared more about documents than romance. The four waited on hard benches for the deliberate and slow paperwork. Impatient, my mother yelled at the official, "Hurry up the wedding before the baby comes!"

She was the one who was pregnant, however, not Herta. And I was the baby who was born very soon thereafter. But that's another story (see Chapter 1).

The two young couples did many things as a foursome and shared many activities. They went out together often, to cabarets, movies, theater, and discussed politics much of the time. Although the Rosenbergs moved to a larger apartment in Cologne, the four of them continued to be the best of friends. Together they plotted opposition to the German government in their Communist Party cell or group.

In Cologne in 1935, according to official records I have seen, a group around Otto Kropp and Ulrich Osche began to organize a resistance to the legal government. I believe that meant creating small, secret cells. The Friedmanns and Rosenbergs were in one of that group's cells.

My father was the buyer and head of the local Cologne office of the biggest leather company, Adler & Oppenheimer, for which he had been working since September 1, 1922. On August 6, 1936 the Gestapo -- officially the *Geheime Staatspolizei* or Secret State Police -- came to the A&O leather company's offices between *Blaubach* and *Griechenmarkt* in Cologne where my father worked. The assistant buyer and thus second-in-command, Kurt Bachmann, saw them first. Thinking that they might be after him, he hid behind some furniture, avoiding the possibility of their seeing him or his spreading any warning. Without a moment's notice, therefore, it was my father whom the Gestapo took into custody.

After World War II, the Gestapo was found by the Nuremberg Charges to be "the executive agency of the police system established by the Nazis for the purpose of combating the political and ideological enemies of the Nazi regime ... [with] authority to make police investigations in cases of criminal attacks upon Party as well as upon State."

The day they arrested my father, the Gestapo also went to my parents' home on *Zuelpilcherstrasse.* Heddy Wagener, who had been my mother's college roommate in Caputh, was visiting my mother and me at that time. They arrested my mother and took her away.

A half century later, Heddy still vividly remembered me at that moment, crying and screaming *Mutti!* or "Mommie!" at the top of the stairs as the Gestapo arrested her. Just two and a half years old, I was impressed by the fact that the police wore clean, pure white gloves, as cops usually only did when they directed traffic.

A pregnant Herta and her husband Karl Rosenberg were also arrested.

I found out from Heddy at her 95th birthday party in London in December, 2003, that it was she who was there then and she who took me to my mother's parents' home in Bielefeld. But she didn't become my aunt, she didn't marry my mother's brother Paul, until April 3, 1938 -- more than two years after she took me from Cologne to my grandparents' home in Bielefeld!

I stayed with my maternal grandparents until my mother was released. Then *Mutti* and I remained there for two years.

But I digress. My parents were both held in Cologne's Gestapo Headquarters and interrogated separately, each not knowing of the other's arrest. They were cross-questioned by teams of Gestapo questioners and torturers. My mother knew nothing about any plots or political plans or subversive goals; she had usually stayed home with her baby when my father went to meetings.

My parents were kept totally separated. My father was imprisoned in one of the very narrow prison cells which already had many previous prisoners' graffiti on its close, white walls. The Gestapo believed that my parents were members of the Kropp-Osche Group. But they wanted to know which particular communist cell, who else was in it, and especially, under whose local leadership the cell was.

One day in prison my mother was going down the only staircase in Cologne's Gestapo Headquarters, keeping to the right. A full flight below her, my father was going up the same stairwell, under armed guard. As they passed each other in silence, she whisper-shouted one word -- not too loud -- *Lieber!* -- darling. That was when he realized she had been arrested, too. It was the only time they saw each other for years.

Lieber -- that one word sustained my father's mind if not his body. He later told her that the word convinced him that she still loved him. It helped give him the courage to go on, the strength to resist torture. He was reassured, comforted, secure in the knowledge that his wife was standing by him.

It was in Cologne that Nazi terror hit the German Communist Party (KPD) first and hard. As early as February and March, 1933, its leaders were arrested and part of its organization destroyed with great brutality. Since 1933, the KPD went underground, keeping their illegal plots and plans secret. But the Gestapo constantly was able to discover some cells and destroy them. There were frequent mass arrests and show trials. One hundred thirteen of the 142 known trials which were held in the years between 1934 and 1938 against Cologne's resistance fighters were against communists because the German Communist Party gave the Nazis the greatest resistance.

My parents were both held for a period of time in the Gestapo Headquarters in Cologne. Then they were separately transferred to the prison on *Klingelputzstrasse*. The Gestapo was suspicious of this group of young Jewish intellectuals meeting secretly in Cologne -- these communists, these enemies of the state. What were they plotting? Were they actually planning to overthrow the legitimate German government of Adolf Hitler? The torturers were determined to find out. Were Hans and Lotte Friedmann and Karl and Herta Rosenberg indeed part of the Kropp-Osche Group? And who was the leader of their particular cell?

Hans underwent one extraordinarily tough inquisition more than a month after his arrest, in September 1936, being interrogated by a group of questioners. It took a great deal of courage; because this unathletic successful businessman was truly cross-questioned by experts and tortured -- brutally, unmercifully. "Gestapo tactics" became infamous. They suspected my father of being a member of the Communist group plotting the overthrow of the legal German government, now completely in Hitler's hands. Hadn't my father discussed with his close friends and associates what the fate of Jews might be under a notoriously anti-Semitic regime? Didn't they have meetings? Weren't they plotting against the German government? Isn't that treason?

I do not know what form his torture took. Yet my father resisted as best he could and kept to himself the big secret that his torturers were after. They wanted to know the other cell members and, in particular, the name of the cell's leader. But my father steadfastly would not reveal this information.

The particular session that September was the roughest he had yet faced. He felt himself slipping, becoming unsure of past realities, feeling almost hopeless, alone, afraid. He was at his lowest point, perhaps about to give away some vital information, possibly even the name of the man he was protecting, the person they were really looking for. Just then his questioners abruptly stopped their probing. They walked out on him because the radio started broadcasting the 1936 Olympic Games at that moment being held in Berlin with Adolf Hitler himself conspicuously in attendance.

I just found out recently from Maury Lerman that the German announcer who broadcast that event was Horst Slesina. Ironically, forty years later, when I was the Creative Director of Ted Bates' German office, that same Horst Slesina was my boss! In fact, the company was named Slesina-Bates. You might say that my boss had saved my father's life. But I didn't know that at the time I worked for the tough old man.

My mother, after five months in prison, without any evidence or charge or indictment and truly innocent of any crime, was released. It was just before Christmas, 1936. Her mother had been preparing to visit her in prison and that had embarrassed my mother. For, even though it was strictly a "political crime" of which she was almost accused, she was by then in the Cologne prison, on *Klingelputzstrasse*, where real criminals were held. In Cologne, when anyone said he was going to Klingelputz Street it meant going to prison. My mother was truly innocent, having spent most of her time taking care of her little baby. When she was finally released for lack of evidence against her, she left my father still imprisoned there. He was indicted to be tried in court! His trial was to take place in the city of Hamm in Westphalia.

My mother rejoined me at her parental home on *Falkstrasse* in Bielefeld. Her parents had hired a baby nurse, a *kindermardchen,* to take care of me up to that time.

My father's father, the Head Cantor Aron Friedmann, had died just before all of this. But my mother's father, Franz Friedmann, took care of things. For one thing, they took care of me. For another, he went to my father's longtime employer, Adler & Oppenheimer, and asked what they were going to do about my father's impending trial. They immediately handed him 20,000 *Reichmark*, a substantial sum, to hire a defense attorney for my father. (My father had a contract with A&O that called for a payment of 20,000 German Marks whenever he left their employ, which he effectively did then.)

In 1936, the German government indicted 152 "co-conspirators" in the Kropp-Osche gang and put Hans Friedmann and Karl and Herta Rosenberg on individual trials. As I said, my mother had already been released from prison.

Herta was temporarily removed to a hospital so that she could have her baby, a girl named Ruth Rosenberg. (She is today Mrs. Barry Fluss, living in Haifa, Israel.) But Herta was sent back to prison to nurse her infant. She later had a separate trial, herself alone in the docket, and was found not guilty. (She lives in London and Haifa today and I have visited her in both.)

One leader of their group, Ulrich Osche, was sentenced to 15 years of hard labor. Otto Kropp was sentenced to death by the court. On May 25, 1937, he was executed.

I learned in October 2003, that my father was found guilty by the court in Hamm, Westphalia, and sentenced to two years of hard labor which he served. He was visited in prison by Dr. Isidor Karo, previously a Berlin rabbi and friend who knew my father's father, and who was then the rabbi of the local Cologne synagogue. He visited the sick and imprisoned as part of his rabbinical duties. He was a source of great consolation -- and information. For, although he was personally apolitical, he passed messages knowing their content and kept vital secrets.

His wife, Klara Caro, always known as "Klaerchen" (Little Klara, for she was short), visited my mother in prison as a social worker. My mother recalled that Klaerchen brought her a toothbrush. Klara had been a lifelong friend of my father's stepmother, my Oma, as well as my mother's parents in Bielefeld and my father's brother Paul who was living with his wife Thea in Cologne at that time. Isidor and Klara's daughter was married in the London home of Paul and Thea Friedman. The Caros were later in the same concentration camp, Theresienstadt, as my Oma. It truly is a small world.

I have translated an "affirmation in lieu of an oath" given by a Mrs. Johanna Dreyer, nee Marx, the widow of Dr. Felix Dreyer, formerly of Bielefeld. She stated that "I remember perfectly that ... about July, 1938, Mr. Hans Friedmann returned to Bielefeld from the concentration camp. Immediately after his arrival, he consulted my husband, since he had returned sick. However, I do not recall which sickness he had or about what he complained."

I know nothing further about that, but through the efforts of my mother's father, we were allowed to leave Germany in August of 1939. My father said that he arranged for our departure, aided by Julius Oppenheimer, part of whose declaration I quoted in Chapter 16. He wrote it to help us secure an exit visa in order to leave Germany. He wrote his deposition and mailed it to my mother, addressed: "at this time at 12 Falkstrasse, Bielefeld." Mr. Oppenheimer wrote that "Mr. Friedmann, who wishes to establish an existence and emigrate overseas, goes with our best wishes for good fortune."

Herta's husband Karl Rosenberg also had been tortured, tried, and was given a two-year prison sentence. He was sent elsewhere to serve his term and remained in custody through 1938. He was released but soon re-arrested. This time it was not on political charges, now he was just one of the six million Jews who were sent to concentration camps. He died at Auschwitz.

It was only in 1974 that my father revealed to my mother for the first time -- what he had never told anyone, even those who had tortured him to find out -- that the one who was the Communist cell leader was actually Kurt Bachmann, the assistant buyer who was second in command under my father at Adler & Oppenheimer in Cologne. He was the one who had hid when the Gestapo came and did not alert his comrades. His name never came up in the proceedings. Bachmann got away because my father did not reveal his identity. My father had not even told my mother that truth for more than 30 years! But in 2004 I learned that my father had visited Bachmann after the war; so did Herta with her second husband, Julius Lowenthal.

Kurt Bachmann had avoided arrest and led an interesting life. He was one of the 16 anti-Nazis profiled in the book, *Gegen den braunen Strom*, (Against the Brown Stream). He was born in 1909 and his father was a tanner and trade unionist who had opposed World War I. Kurt learned how to grade leather and worked in a tannery in Luxembourg. He joined the tanners' trade union and was fired when he opposed his employer at the union's request. He joined the Communist Party of Germany (KPD) in 1932 and headed the cell code-named "opera house." It was part of what the book called "the Kropp conspiracy," which the Gestapo called "Kropp-Osche."

Bachmann described his regular job with an unnamed leather company as "one step below the buyer ... until Spring of 1938." My father was the buyer, his boss at *A&O*.

Gegen den braunen Strom says that Kurt Bachmann's job gave him the use of a company car which he utilized, with Otto Kropp, to transport illegal materials.

Bachmann said that he started off a democratic anti-fascist, not a communist anti-fascist but he realized that capitalism took advantage of workers while communism helped the helpless. In 1933, Kurt Bachmann ran for election on the Communist Party ticket but emigrated to southern France with his wife Alice when the party became illegal in Germany. Arrested by the French police in 1939 and put into a camp, he escaped in 1940. Arrested again in 1942, he and his wife were handed over to the Gestapo and deported. She was killed in Auschwitz; he was sent to four other concentration camps, finally to Buchenwald.

Freed after the war, he went back to Cologne and became the Secretary and later the Head of the West German Communist Party from 1969 to 1973. In 1978 he wrote the book, "*The Truth About Hitler*," and in 1983 the book, "*The Year 1933*." Bachmann remained politically active until his death in 1998.

I recently learned from my mother's cousin Klaus Kochmann, that my father's annual visits to Germany in the 1950's, 60's and 70's, included not only visits to Berlin but also sometimes to Russia. I know he met his first cousin Curt Bois and Kurt Bachmann and possibly Communist party officials in East Germany.

In October, 2004, David and I went to Cologne's former Gestapo Headquarters -- now a museum called the *EL-DE Haus* -- where we obtained much information and bought the books mentioned in this chapter.

We saw the 4-story staircase on which my parents glimpsed each other, where my mother had whispered *Lieber*. I had imagined it as a spiral staircase but it was not. It actually was square, with a central opening going up all four flights. I was also surprised to see that it was white. David and I saw the narrow, white, close-walled cells in which prisoners were held and saw the graffiti on practically every inch of every cell.

On the uppermost floor of this museum there is now a series of rooms depicting what the Gestapo had done in that building. You pass through rooms with evidence of their treatment of gypsies, homosexuals, dissidents, until finally you reach the last room, showing their torture of Jews and Communists.

One permanent exhibition is on the Kropp-Osche Group, with Page 1 of the list of 153 suspects. That initial page includes the names of my father, mother, Karl and Herta Rosenberg. Part of the display includes Karl Rosenberg's prison photos -- front and side views. The Gestapo had arrested everyone -- except Kurt Bachmann, the cell leader.

Post-World War II West Germany might have been very different if the cell leader they sought at Adler & Oppenheimer had not hidden behind furniture but had been arrested by the Gestapo instead of my father. Or if my father had revealed his name.

The museum director, Dr. Werner Jung, said that he would try to get me a copy of the indictment or court records of my father's trial. I sent him a copy of this chapter but I have no response and assume that nothing can be found.

27. Leaving Germany

When both my parents were arrested in Cologne by the Gestapo, my aunt Heddy, later my mother's brother Paul's wife, took me to live with my mother's parents at their apartment, *Falkstrasse 12, Bielefeld*. I stayed there two years, until I was 4½ years old.

I really do remember my grandparental home. It was near the end of a long street in the Jewish section of downtown Bielefeld. It was from that home that my grandfather and I took long walks every evening after supper. He smoked his cigar, which he wouldn't do in the house in order to not stink up the fine curtains. We went on what he called a *Falkstrassen Bummel,* which really only meant a walk on Falk Street but, with his aromatic cigar which his wife would not let him smoke indoors, he equated it to bumming around!

The synagogue my grandparents attended, and were prominent in, was virtually around the corner from their home. We sometimes walked to it but didn't go in.

In 1955, as an American soldier in Germany, I visited that house on *Falkstrasse.* And I met, once again, the upstairs neighbors, the Baumanns. They remembered me as *Bueber,* my nickname at the time. They had a son about my age, Jochen, with whom I had played. He had an older sister whom I hadn't remembered from my childhood but did meet in 1955. She was a stewardess for Lufthansa then.

The Baumanns lived directly above my grandparents so I got to see the same kind of living room as they had had. Only my grandparents' living room was decorated with much nicer furniture and furnishing, curtains and drapes, lace tablecloths, all the best linens, keepsakes from their foreign travel, fine artwork and the finest silverware.

My son David and I saw *Falkstrasse* again in 2004. By that time the front of the house had been renovated but we don't know about the inside. To my great surprise, Falk Street was now quite short, only a few blocks long! When I was two, three, and four it certainly seemed much longer.

I remember my grandfather as a successful and debonair man, a bit overweight, balding, with a small moustache. Franz Friedmann had a wonderful sense of humor. As one example, in a display of trick photography, he was pictured playing cards with two men who were both himself!

While my father was in prison, my mother's father arranged for our emigration from Germany as soon as my father was released. I know that my grandfather did it with Julius Oppenheimer, the big boss of A&O, a man my father always mentioned with the utmost respect and admiration.

Yet it was my father's own foresight that made my parents pack up their good furniture and ship the lot to England. They had ultra-modern taste and their furnishings were the very latest fashion, the style that started in the 1930's in Germany and became very popular in the U.S.A. much later. It was called post-modern or art deco.

It was on September 14, 1938, just a few weeks before *Kristallnacht* (Nov. 9th) that Hans Friedmann, who had served his two years of hard labor, was allowed to take his family out of Germany. A police certificate of that date gives our last address in Cologne as *Julygurtel 36*.

Julius Oppenheimer had sent a written deposition addressed to my mother "at this time at *Falkstrasse 12, Bielefeld*," from which I quoted earlier. It said: "On May 13, 1932, Mr. Friedmann became the buyer for our Cologne office from which time on Mr. Friedmann was the responsible leader of this branch which he did until August 6, 1936."

That was the date of his arrest by the Gestapo.

Mr. Oppenheimer's statement ended: "Mr. Friedmann, who wishes to establish an existence and emigrate overseas, goes with our best wishes for good fortune."

On the very day we were to leave the country, my *Onkel Fritz Silberschmidt*, later to become my Uncle Fred Silversmith, took me to the *Heintzelmaenchenbrunnen*, a Cologne fountain of fairy-tale characters. He filmed me reading a book. He titled that scene *Absheid von Bueber*, which uses my nickname at the time. It would be almost fair to translate it as "Farewell to Bubba!"

He took me out to film me while my parents finished packing. They completed their job before we returned and were very worried about my uncle and me. Where were we? Had we gotten lost? Had we been picked up by the Gestapo? Their last-minute fears were justified. But we made it back just in the nick of time.

I have since transferred that film to videotape (VHS) and have it on a reel with my bar-mitzvah and scenes from Camp Edgewood.

In anticipation of leaving Germany, my parents had bought me new clothes, and a nice new pair of shoes. My father made sure that they were made of the best quality leather. That one pair might have to last me a long time. So they bought the shoes a size too large, "to grow into." And my mother stuffed some cotton inside the shoes, in front of my toes, so the shoes would fit and wouldn't be uncomfortably large for me.

At the airport we had to pass the rigorous inspection by the German border guards who were very carefully searching all Jews leaving

Germany in the expectation of finding money or gold or diamonds. Their attitude was, we know you are smuggling something valuable out of Germany, our job is to find it. Perhaps some guards were looking to find something they could take for themselves or to find something that would make them a hero or simply doing their duty. Whatever the rationale, they searched all departing Jews, and certainly the three of us, completely and thoroughly.

They looked especially carefully at me, my clothes and the toys I had brought along for the trip. They sensed that this was a rich kid so they paid particularly careful attention to me. They suspected that my parents had somehow used innocent-looking little me, only 4½ years old, to hide something, probably unbeknownst to me at that. And two expert searchers looked and looked until one of the guards finally found something -- aha! That was it! Something had been stuffed into these too-large shoes, of course that was the hiding place! He carefully pulled out whatever it was.

At first, all he got was cotton. So he reached in again, carefully. Then he looked at the cotton itself more thoroughly. There were probably diamonds or jewels or some such hidden in there. As the guard pulled at the cotton, I said to him, *Das ist mollich* -- that's comfy!

He was amazed that it was just plain cotton, nothing more. And so, reluctantly, the border guards had to let us leave Germany. We got on the plane to England.

28. The Vollendam

My parents and I were in London for quite a few months. England was to be only our initial stopover. At that time, there was a possibility of our going to a South American country, I do not remember which one, possibly Cuba. So my parents made preparations by studying Spanish. But the exact date of our trip to South America was not yet set, giving us an opportunity to visit with my father's brother Paul, his wife Thea, and their children, Herbert and Hilde, who had introduced my parents to each other.

Something went wrong with the South American connection but my parents continued to learn Spanish. It was 1939, and rumors of impending war were everywhere. We were stuck in England with no place to go. For some reason we couldn't stay there. Finally we got a chance to leave. The opportunity to go to America! It was only a matter of time before the war would start and the U.S. might not be in it. There were plenty of isolationists in America who thought that Hitler was a strictly European problem.

It was my father's uncle, Aron's brother Samuel, who sponsored us and made it possible for us to come to America. We booked passage on the Holland-America line's *Vollendam*. (Another ship with the same name now sails up to Alaska.) It was a twin screw, turbine steamer, 575 feet long and 67 feet wide with six passenger decks, one a sun deck for sports, a smoke room, social hall, library, dining salon, a cocktail bar, lounge, and a glass-enclosed promenade. I still have the brochure which pictures those rooms and promises that the *Vollendam* "is the choice of a distinguished group of travelers whose congenial company adds immensely to the pleasure of the voyage."

I was not yet five years old at that time and don't remember much about our voyage but my parents often related a story to me about the trip: It seems that there were some English boys onboard ship who had tricycles which they rode around the deck. I watched for hours, longingly, as they kept riding the bikes. I don't know how many boys there were or how many tricycles, but it seemed like every time I went up on deck some of them were there, riding around and around, very happily. They yelled and shouted to each other but I didn't understand anything they said since it was in English.

And then, one day at sea, there was an unattended tricycle out on deck and none of the boys were there. I took the golden opportunity, got on it and started riding around and around. I had a grand old time.

Even after one of the boys came up and started yelling something at me in English, I continued to circle the entire deck. I didn't know what he was saying; I was having such good fun. Not the least little bit seasick! I didn't want to stop. This was great! More of the English boys had come on deck and started running after me, but nothing could make me stop. I didn't know what it was they were all shouting -- and I didn't care!

British children are more polite than American kids. Those boys were all yelling at me but they wouldn't physically try to stop me. They just kept on shouting things like, "get off, boy, that's our bike! It's not yours! Right now! Straight away! Get off, boy!"

Some German-and-English speaking passenger told my parents what was being said and they told me -- in German, of course -- to get off. Which I did, immediately. But I don't remember having any other fun on that ship.

We arrived on February 7, 1939, and were met at the dock in Hoboken, New Jersey, not Ellis Island, and taken immediately to Manhattan by William Wolff, who became Lewandowski's successor. My father always spoke of him as *Herr Doktor Wilhelm Wolff.* He arranged for us to pass through customs and immigration without a hitch and probably for our first few nights' stay in New York City.

Like any refugees arriving in America we certainly gawked at what we called the *wolkenkratzern,* which translates literally to cloud scrapers.

It was William Wolff, probably the only person we knew in New York City, who suggested that we go to Boston because he knew of a leather firm there where my father, who spoke no English, could find employment. I have often wondered why we didn't go to Philadelphia, where my father's real Uncle Sam was a rabbi.

World War II broke out on September 1, 1939, when Germany invaded Poland.

I heard that on one of its next trips from England to the U.S., the *Vollendam* was torpedoed by a German U-boat, or submarine. No one survived.

IV. World War II
(1939 - 1945)

29. Kristallnacht

Adolf Hitler had published his racist ideas in 1928. One statement he wrote says a lot: "In standing against the Jew I am defending the handiwork of the Lord."

When Hitler was legally appointed Chancellor of Germany on January 31, 1933, he and his National Socialist (Nazi) Party immediately began to pass anti-Semitic laws, restricting Jews in many specific ways.

He blamed the Jews for the economic problems Germany faced; they were the easy scapegoat. Hitler had his Minister of Information, the infamous Josef Goebbels, spew out hatred of the Jews and repeat The Big Lie, that it was their fault. His theory was: "If you repeat a lie often enough, people will believe it."

A little history is necessary: The Nazis passed one humiliating anti-Jewish law after another: Jews were not allowed to own cars, radios, telephones, and typewriters; use public libraries, parks, cinemas, and swimming pools; buy cigarettes, tobacco, and flowers; food rations were reduced and they could not even own pets; you had to get rid of the ones you had. Every Jew had to wear a yellow Star of David with the word Jew. Then things got worse.

On November 7th, just two days before *Kristallnacht*, a German diplomat was assassinated in Paris by a Jewish teenager whose parents, along with 17,000 other Polish Jews, had been expelled from the German Reich. That was the pretext for the Nazis to unleash a wave of terror against Germany's Jews. Although they claimed that it was a spontaneous outburst of outrage by ordinary people, *Kristallnacht* was in fact a carefully calculated and prepared plan carried out by Hitler's stormtroopers and Nazi party members and organizations.

On *Kristallnacht*, or night of broken glass, November 9, 1938, which historians count as the start of the Nazis' violent campaign against the Jewish people, gangs smashed the glass windows of synagogues and storefronts owned by Jews. Along with the torahs and other Judaica destroyed that night were tablets commemorating Jews who died for their fatherland in World War I.

In the space of a few hours in one night the gangsters damaged or destroyed thousands of Jewish places of business and homes, dozens of temples and cemeteries, and killed at least 91 Jews. A local fire department prevented a synagogue fire from spreading to nearby homes but made no attempt to put out the fire in the building. It was obvious that the night of terror had been carefully planned.

It was the first time that Jews were arrested on a massive scale and transported to concentration camps. That first awfully horrible night about 30,000 Jews were sent to Buchenwald, Dachau, and Sachsenhausen where hundreds died within weeks of their arrival. *Kristallnacht* was the beginning of the mass murder of Jews by the Germans, when what could still be harassment of a minority turned into the measures that led to the "Final Solution." It is the point at which most Jews realized that there was no one to protect them and nothing they could do.

But we were already in England <u>before</u> then. My father had seen it coming in March, 1934, even <u>before</u> I was born! His foresight had sent my mother to England for the baby to have dual nationality. And my mother's father had helped us escape in time.

30. The Holocaust

How can I, how can anyone, explain the inexplicable? Many members of our extended families did not survive the Holocaust. The few who did, however, managed not merely to escape or survive but to actually do very well in many different parts of the world. The international success of our family is, to me, absolutely astounding.

After *Kristallnacht,* life became terrible for Jews in Germany, many thought it couldn't get worse! They were wrong.

On January 20, 1942, fifteen high-ranking Nazi and government leaders met in a villa by a Berlin lake, the Wannsee. There they developed the so-called "Final Solution to The Jewish Problem" -- the deliberate, carefully planned genocide of all European Jewry. They called it the Final Solution in public but privately spoke about methods of killing, of liquidation, of extermination.

The Wannsee Conference was where non-Nazi officials were informed of the genocidal plan; their help was needed to arrange for the transportation of Jews from all over German-occupied Europe to their slaughter. No one present objected although no modern state, no cultured and civilized society, had ever committed itself to murder an entire people. Genocide became official government policy.

It all led to mass arrests, deportation to concentration camps, and extermination. That is what the world now calls The Holocaust.

The Indian Ocean Tsunami of December 26, 2004, called the worst natural disaster in recorded history, killed about 200,000 people. The Holocaust exterminated about eleven million human beings! That's 11,000,000! About six million of them were Jews, two-thirds of Europe's 9.7 million Jewish population! About five million were gypsies, homosexuals, communists, and other political opponents. Add to that all the millions of deaths on both sides of World War II that the Nazis' policy caused. What people have done to other people is so much worse than what "nature" has done. What civilized, educated human beings have consciously and carefully planned to do -- and literally executed -- far exceeds any "natural" disaster.

Many members of our family were killed in the Holocaust, some committed suicide, others escaped, still others converted to Christianity. Only two members of our family got out of Germany to England in the *kindertransport*. Just one family member survived a concentration camp.

Betty and I visited Auschwitz, the huge death camp where millions were gassed. We also went to Theresienstadt, the camp in which my Oma, Cantor Aron Friedmann's second wife, Johanna Friedmann, somehow managed to survive.

In the Holocaust Jews were Jews, there was no choice. Observant Jews, liberal Jews, Communist Jews and Jews who were sure they weren't Jews were crammed into the ghettos and camps. Their one and only offense: being Jewish.

The Holocaust stretched over six difficult years. Six long, hard, torturous years. The worst years in Jewish history which had previously included pogroms, inquisitions, internments, exiles, and exterminations. The *New York Times* wrote, "Those were years when every minute, every second, every split-second held more than it could bear. Pain and fear reigned in the midst of hunger and humiliation."

Daniel Jonah Goldhagen's 1996 book *Hitler's Willing Executioners,* which my cousin Klaus Kochmann translated into German, points out that ordinary Germans did most of the killing of their fellow citizens, Jews.

Another more recent book, from 2004, by Goetz Aly, *Hitler's People's State,* points out that average Germans heartily supported the Nazis because Hitler made them feel good and important and well cared-for.

Aly wonders if it was a deplorable weakness of human nature or insatiable German avarice. He advances the claim that about 95% of the German population benefited financially from the Nazi's killing machine. That the Germans maintained the war by robbing from others, not just valuable paintings and homes and businesses, but everything down to the gold in Jewish mouths.

Aly's analysis proves that 70% of the war was financed by plunder. He wrote that it is easier to blame a small group of others than to admit to your own greed. The book will be published in English in 2006.

An article in *Der Spiegel* explains that Hitler gave Germans huge tax breaks, social benefits, and raised military salaries by robbing and murdering others, slave labor, and plundering other countries. Hitler couldn't stop, Aly says, because peace would have meant certain bankruptcy for the Reich.

Some members of our extended families survived the war and have remained in Germany. But many in the family managed to get out and find a future in Israel, England, Australia, Africa, China, Canada, and the United States of America. Some fought against Nazi Germany in World War II. But many of our family members died in the Holocaust. Yet enough survived to create better lives for themselves and their -- our -- families.

31. They Became Letters

Nanette was the oldest of the three "Shoe Store Simon Sisters" in my mother's family. She was known as Nanni, and married Georg Fass, a traveling salesman who sold to shoe retailers. They met at the shoe store in Cologne. But they made their home in Berlin.

They had two children. Ellen-Ruth Thea Fass was born on October 6, 1928, in Berlin, the first grandchild on her mother's (and my mother's) side of the family. Her kid brother, Gerd, was born five years later. Neither of them retained their birth names. Instead, it was said, "they became letters!"

Nanni and her children often visited their uncles and aunts, particularly those on our mothers' side of the family, the Co-Co-Co. When Ellen-Ruth Fass and her first cousin, Vera "Putzi" Heinemann, wore identical homemade dresses they called each other sisters. That was only the first time they did so. Years later, "they became sisters."

In 1938, the Nazis forced the Fass family to relocate to a smaller apartment in Berlin at *Johannisstrasse 8*. Ellen-Ruth remembers going to school and being chased down the street by her supposed school chums who shouted hateful anti-Jewish names at her.

The family moved just two blocks from the *Oranienbergerstrasse* Synagogue which they attended long after my father's father had officiated there. It was from that apartment that they saw the flames on *Kristallnacht,* November 9, 1938, leaping from that synagogue.

It was also from there that their parents put them on a train, the famous *kinder transport,* which took them to England where "children became letters."

"It was a common expression among Jews in Nazi Germany," according to a brochure from an exhibition entitled *Aus Kindern wurden Briefe,* i.e., children became letters. The exhibition was held in Berlin's *Oranienbergerstrasse* Synagogue from September, 2004 to January, 2005. It recalled that Jewish parents put their children on the *kindertransport,* destination unknown. Thereafter, most parents only got letters back, instead of their children.

Ellen-Ruth and Gerd wrote many letters to their parents. After a while they were limited to writing only 20 words via the Red Cross. Their parents wrote daily, but then the letters stopped. "I wondered why," Ellen said years later, "but I don't think I was able to figure it out."

I have translated one letter, dated December 21, 1939, from Nanni to her sister Rosi, Walter and Putzi. She wrote that "For some days I have been [in Cologne] with the dear parents. We have it nice and comfortable here, the apartment is very friendly, nice and warm ... We hope that we will soon receive our boat tickets and in time all will work out." It did not; they did not survive.

The two Fass children got out of Germany, just in time. My cousin Ellen-Ruth always acknowledges my mother's vital role in their story. We were in London then, so their *Tante Lotte* got their names put on the evacuation list for the *kindertransport* in the organization's headquarters.

Gerd left first, in June, 1939, when he was almost five. Ellen-Ruth left a few weeks later, in July. Her parents put her on the *kindertransport* train and then they took the Underground Subway, the *U-bahn,* to the train's next stop to be able to wave to her. Nanni had sewn name tags onto all her children's clothes and possessions, not so much to identify them as to prove to the Nazis that those things were not for sale.

Ellen-Ruth's train went to Holland. That night the children were put on a boat which crossed the English Channel, almost always a rough trip. Then the children were all put on trains to their individual destinations.

Transporting Jewish children out of Nazi Germany took place in the nine months just before the outbreak of World War II. The story is well told in two documentary films which I have on videotape. The famous one, *Into the Arms of Strangers,* won the Academy Award (Oscar) for best documentary in 1999. The other is *The Children Who Cheated the Nazis* which is narrated by Richard Attenborough.

There were fewer than 8,000 children between the ages of 3 and 17, according to one source. Another says that Great Britain took in more than 10,000 children, 90% of them Jewish, from Germany, Austria and Czechoslovakia. A third says that children from infants to 17 year olds were sent away from their homes, most of them all alone, first by train and then by boat, over to England. Most were met at Liverpool Street Station. Some were put into private homes, others into schools and orphanages.

Ellen-Ruth Fass arrived in England on July 25, 1939, and was put into a convalescent home for women called Hillside The Edge, in the countryside near Stroud in Gloustershire. It had connected cottages and was run by Kate Eleanor Richmond, a retired headmistress, whom Ellen always called Miss Richmond. It became a kind of nursing home, rest home, and children's home, as well as a country home for evacuees from London during the blitz.

In England, Ellen-Ruth dropped the hyphen and used Ruth as a middle name. In one of the few letters my teenaged cousin got from her parents, they expressed their surprise that Miss Richmond was not Jewish. In fact, it was, as Ellen put it, "a good Christian home." Yet Miss Richmond saw to it that this Jewish girl got religious instruction, by mail, from a reform synagogue in London.

Miss Richmond knew that her young charge should not or would not eat ham or bacon which the English usually had with their eggs for breakfast. So Miss Richmond came up with a substitute: Spam. It was years later, when Ellen got to America, that she found out what Spam really was. (Perhaps you think it is unwanted e-mail but the word was coined for a brand of cheap, fatty pork parts which were certainly not kosher.)

The daughter of German-Jewish refugees who lived nearby was placed in the same home just to be a companion to Ellen and to go to school with her, a long walk or bicycle ride. It literally was downhill all the way to school but uphill back. Only in winter did they take a double-decker bus to school. There were Christian religious ceremonies every morning in Junior High and High School as well as religious instruction but the ten or so Jewish refugees were excused from them.

Ellen worked in the kitchen at the home, often using herbs and spices grown in their garden, making mustard, chopping parsley. She lived in a basement room which was part of the air-raid shelter, although she had a window to the garden.

Some of her parents' letters have survived, as did some of her letters to relatives in America. Young Ellen wrote in German to her parents in Berlin and her aunt and uncle, Rosi and Walter Heinemann, who were originally from Erfurt, Germany. They then were living in Boston, yet she addressed them as "my dear Erfurters." At that time her Aunt Else and Uncle Fritz Silberschmidt were still in Germany. I have translated four of her letters. One of them, from Stroud, England, dated June 10, 1940, said that she was missing *"Mutti und Pappi."*

Her letters reveal a normal young teenager concerned with going out to a birthday party, but having to run for a half hour each way to get there ... forgetting the exact date of her cousin Putzi's birthday (the 16th of March or the 16th of May) ... and buying her first pair of high heeled shoes, "but they are not very high. I wanted to buy real sports-shoes but they did not have any, so I bought these."

Early on, Ellen called her aunts grandmothers. She referred to "Oma Caputh" (her aunt Marie Goerlich) just as she later referred to "Oma Boston" (her aunt Rosi Heineman) and "Oma New York" (her aunt, my mother, Lotte Friedman).

Ellen visited her brother for two weeks in Derby (pronounced "darby") every spring vacation at Passover. She wrote that "Gerd has grown a lot and only speaks English. If someone speaks German to him he says, 'I don't know what you're saying.'"

I find that interesting because, while she went to school in Germany and wrote those letters in German, nowadays Ellen says she can't speak or understand German at all! I was too young for school in Germany and consider myself fluent.

Her brother Gerd Fass was taken in by an English-Jewish family named Freeman -- not related, of course -- and not adopted by them but anyway changed his name to Gerald Freeman. His sister was visiting him in Derby at V-J Day in 1945. (V-E Day was the allied victory in Europe, V-J Day was victory over Japan.)

Ellen left England just before Gerald's *bar-mitzvah*. Since then, he has gotten married, had a son named Martin, got divorced, and moved to Manchester. I have seen Gerald a few times at family functions for which he has come to the U.S.A.; one was my mother's 80th birthday, another was Sam and Ellen's son Jeff's wedding to Ivy Stern.

On September 23, 1997, Ellen Zilka, nee Ellen-Ruth Fass, participated in Steven Spielberg's "Survivors of the Shoah," or Holocaust project, from her home in Bayside, Queens, N.Y. She commended her parents for having had, "the strength and courage to send their children away. It must have been very hard for them."

Ellen's daughter Diane was kind enough to lend me the videotapes, feeling that, as she put it, "they capture the extraordinary strength and dignity of my Mom." Diane also thought the tape shows "Ellen's tenderness, kindness, loving, respectful, and optimistic way." She asked me to "please give her <u>very</u> personal reminiscences all due respect," which I hope and believe I have done.

Steven Spielberg, in his letter to Ellen Zilka, wrote, "you have granted future generations the opportunity to experience a personal connection with history.

"Your interview will be carefully preserved … far into the future, people may listen and learn, and always remember."

32. Dunkirk

My first cousin, the daughter of my father's brother Paul and his wife Thea, was named Hildegard Gretel Hannah Esther Friedmann. She was born in Cologne, Germany, in 1923. She hated her first name, especially when I, an awful child, 11 years younger, teased her by calling her *Hildebobbe die hexe,* after a witch in a children's story. Not because of me, but for whatever reason, she was always called just Hilde. I am forever grateful to her and her brother Herbert for helping my parents meet and marry.

Hilde and her family immigrated to London as German-Jewish refugees before World War II. It was there that Hilde met a handsome young soldier with an attractive moustache who was also a German-Jewish refugee named Walter Max Theodore Levy.

These two people, with so many more names than most people, fell in love but Hilde often said that while Walter was a very handsome fellow, especially in his uniform, it was his moustache she really adored.

They got engaged; it was the kind of long-term engagement so many servicemen and their girlfriends had: planning to get married after the war ... if, of course, he survived the battles he'd be in and she survived the London Blitz -- the almost daily or nightly bombings by the German *Luftwaffe*.

Walter M. T. Levy became an engineer in the army and was sent into the thick of the battle in France as a member of the British Expeditionary Force against the Nazi army. I learned recently that Walter was wounded in battle when an explosion caused him to suffer hearing loss and shrapnel in his eyes! Whenever he later went to an eye doctor there was always amazement at the still visible fragments *in his eye!* But as far as I know, it never bothered him.

On the European mainland the Brits, French and Belgian forces were fighting overwhelming odds. They were completely outnumbered and totally outgunned -- stopped by superior equipment and firepower. With their far greater fighting force, the Germans forced them back, cutting off all escape routes. The allies retreated ever backward toward the harbor and beaches, until they could go no further. They had reached the coast, the relentless German Army in front of them. Now they had their backs to the sea, the English Channel behind them.

The allied troops were low on arms as well as ammunition. To make matters worse, Walter had somehow lost his rifle and all that he could get as a replacement was a wooden stick! He was virtually defenseless.

Those troops who were armed were not much better off. The entire British Expeditionary Force was facing a tremendous battle. It truly seemed hopeless. They were prepared to die at the small French town called Dunkirk. It was June, 1940.

The British navy sent what they could: enough destroyers and transport ships to evacuate about 30,000 troops. But there were 300,000 troops!

And very quickly German planes and guns sank many of those ships, partially blocking Dunkirk harbor, making it impossible for the rescue ships to reach the troops on shore. The water was simply too shallow for the few remaining British vessels to attempt to approach them. There was no way out -- German troops in front of them, they had their backs to the sea. With escape impossible, it was going to be a major disaster!

But little ships, sailboats, motorboats, fishing smacks, trawlers, rowboats, even paddleboats came to help, manned by ordinary local sailors. Most of them were elderly because all the able-bodied young men were in the military. Some small boats came from the nearby French areas but even more came from England, all the way across the ever-rough waters of the Channel.

For the most part they ferried the troops from the beaches to the destroyers and transport ships laying offshore -- about 30,000 men took those big ships back to England. But so many thousands more troops came all the way back across the rough waters to England in those tiny boats. They were truly rescued in the nick of time! Every last one of them! All three hundred thousand of them! Including Walter Levy.

Dunkirk energized the hearts of the British people at a time when it looked probable that they would soon be invaded. It seemed like a victory in just getting the troops back -- a third of a million of them -- to fight another day.

British Prime Minister Winston Churchill said it was "a miracle of deliverance."

Hilde's Walter was safe and sound. But he had shaved off his moustache to win a bet with an army buddy! She married him anyway ... and he never grew it back!

33. Theresienstadt

My father's stepmother, my Oma, Johanna Friedmann, did not take advantage of the opportunity that her children offered her to emigrate from Berlin after the Nazis took power, according to Mrs. Klara Caro, in order to save her late husband's work. Instead, she was evacuated from Berlin on September 14, 1942, and delivered to the Theresienstadt concentration camp the next day.

No one in our entire family knew it at the time.

Rabbi and "Klaerchen" Caro were also sent to Theresienstadt. He did not survive; she and my Oma did. Walter Heineman's mother, Wilhelmine, nee Cohn, was transported to Theresienstadt, too, and died there October 15, 1943. At least six members of our family perished there: Lina Altmann, Martin Buchholz, Max Kochmann, Agnes Krebs, Marie Thilo, and Gertrude Tockuss.

Ironically, a lady named Rosenberg had been sent by the Nazis from her home in Lubeck to Bielefeld where she lived with my mother's father, the widower of Johanna Friedmann, my maternal grandmother. She was later sent to Theresienstadt where she lived with Johanna Friedmann, my paternal grandmother. Mrs. Rosenberg also survived the camp and ended up in New York City.

Theresienstadt is the German name for the Polish city they called Terezin. Long after my Oma's death, Betty and I visited the camp. There was an ironic sign over the entrance to the Theresienstadt camp: *Arbeit macht frei* or Work Sets You Free.

Terezin is about 90 miles north of Prague, just south of Litomerice, in what is now the Czech Republic. The big fortress there was originally built in 1780 by Emperor Joseph II of Austria and named after his mother, Empress Maria Theresa. This big fortress was surrounded by ramparts and used until 1882. There was a small fortress nearby which was used to house dangerous criminals. And a farming town of peasants.

The small walled fortress became the concentration camp.

In a meeting in Prague on October 10, 1940, Rudolf Heydrich, the Nazi boss of the "Czech Protectorate," decided to make Terezin into a "collection camp," a "transit camp," or a "holding camp," different words in German as they are in English. They later called it, falsely and deliberately misleadingly, a "ghetto". It was administered by the SS, guarded by Czech gendarmes, and run internally by a Jewish Council of Elders.

The Nazis sent the first Jewish prisoners there on November 24 and December 4, 1941, four days before Hitler declared war on the United States. These first transports consisted entirely of men who became the construction detail which rebuilt the old town. They transformed the town which had about 7,000 residents into a concentration camp for

60,000. But, incredibly, they did not enlarge the place. So there was never enough housing; bathrooms were scarce, water was limited and contaminated; the place lacked enough toilet or sewage facilities and had insufficient electricity right from the start.

I heard Julia Bos, a survivor of the camp, present her memoir on May 5, 2005, *Yom Hashoah*, literally The Day of the Holocaust, or annual Holocaust Remembrance Day. She described her transport to the camp: "We were put in freight cars packed together, too many to move. We had two buckets, one for water and one for toilet purposes. And no food. It took three days to get to Theresienstadt."

I attended a University of North Carolina seminar on the Theresienstadt concentration camp, entitled *Confronting Darkness*. I also went to another UNC seminar called *Escaping the Holocaust and Starting Life Anew*. The first obviously applied to my Oma, but the second applied to my parents and me.

Theresienstadt was very different from all the other camps in many significant respects. For one thing, here the Nazis ingeniously, devilishly, had Jews make many important decisions. Here, too, there was a cultural life that seemed unbelievable. The Nazis appointed Jakob Edelstein as the *Judenaelteste* or Jewish Elder and set up a *Judenrat* or Jewish Council. Oma's great friend Klara Caro said that "he hurled courageous words at the Nazis before they shot him, together with his wife and child."

The 7-man Council was assigned the tasks of creating a Jewish police force and fire department, and of deciding the food distribution in the camp. They determined that the children should get the most food since they were the future of the Jewish people, that those who worked for the German war effort should receive adequate rations to sustain life, and that the eldest would get the least. The Jewish Council protected those who were their friends and family and those working in the ghetto's administration. Nearly half to two-thirds of the camp's population was "protected."

Klara Caro wrote, "It was one of the meanest tricks of the Nazis that the Jews themselves had to provide the lists for deportation. By cooperating, the Jewish leaders hoped to buy their own freedom. But it did not do them any good, they all ended in Auschwitz."

Theresienstadt was also different from other concentration camps because the Jewish Council saw to it that the children received some education, that there was some music, art, and entertainment to keep the populace pacified. They saw in the children the only hope for a Jewish future in Europe.

Women and children were placed in barracks separate from the men's barracks.

The Nazis realized that some information about concentration camps had been leaked to the outside world, most of whose populace simply would not believe the horror stories they heard. The Nazis needed to keep up appearances and also recognized that elderly and prominent Jews could not all simply disappear suddenly. The regime decided to continue their "final solution to the Jewish question" but they resolved to make this one camp the "model ghetto," the one that would "temporarily" house those Jews famed enough to possibly have international authorities question their whereabouts. The Nazis wanted to show off to any potential Red Cross and the few possible international visitors that the Jews were not being mistreated.

The Germans put mostly well-known Czech and Austrian Jews or leading German-Jewish citizens into this so-called model camp. My Oma was probably considered one of those since she was the widow of a famous Berlin cantor.

A famed Berlin rabbi, Leo Baeck, was arrested by the Nazis at 6 AM on January 27, 1943 and sent to Theresienstadt. He said, "Only the Gestapo would come at that hour."

Prominent Jews, especially those the Nazis thought might be sought by international authorities, were sent to this place they called a ghetto. It wasn't. That was a cover story which even allowed the Nazis to make some Jews pay to get into the so-called ghetto. Jews were "rewarded" by being sent to Theresienstadt instead of a concentration camp. But the latter is exactly what it really was.

Later many Austrian and Dutch Jews arrived. Like the others, they were crammed into cattle cars with little or no water, food, or sanitation. They were unloaded at the nearest train station about two kilometers away, then forced to disembark and march into the camp's checkpoint, called the floodgate.

Some few important Jews were given small, overcrowded rooms in apartment buildings but about 60,000 people were crammed into triple-tiered bunk beds stacked in rows inside many buildings. All those beds were covered with vermin, rats, fleas, flies, and lice. Norbert Troller wrote that their calves were bitten by fleas that could only be removed with kerosene.

Pavel Friedmann, no relation, was sent to Theresienstadt in April, 1942. He wrote a poem there, *The Butterfly*, which, along with other poems and children's drawings from that camp, has been made into a book I have, *I Never Saw Another Butterfly*, and a play, *The Last Butterfly*, which I saw in Durham, NC. Pavel perished in Auschwitz.

Adolf Eichmann, who attended the Wannsee Conference which decided on the "final solution to the Jewish problem" and who was executed in Israel many years after the war, was one of those who personally supervised Theresienstadt.

Food was a dire concern in Theresienstadt. In the beginning one problem was that there weren't enough cauldrons to cook for all the people housed in the camp. So in May, 1942, rationing with special treatment for certain segments of the society was established. Lack of nourishment, of medicines, and a general susceptibility to illness made the fatality rate extremely high.

Norbert Troller wrote, "It took three or four months until one reached a plateau where the pangs of hunger -- real pains that reduced one's thinking and working abilities -- were less apparent; it seems that the human organism can get used to hunger."

Klara Caro organized meetings and lectures in the camp. In 1946, she wrote of what she called *An Unforgettable Seder Eve*. Three thousand prisoners declared before the Passover holidays in 1943 that they would not eat leavened bread. They got 3 matzos each day and that meant being even more hungry than usual. The Seder ceremony, led by her husband, Rabbi Isidor Caro, was attended by 25 people crowded into a small room. On the Seder plate there was only a single carrot, some inedible greens and salt water. Suddenly the lights went out (that happened in the camp quite often), but the ceremony was not interrupted. Rabbi Caro knew the *Haggada* text by heart, a cantor from Prague sang Hebrew and Yiddish hymns, and so they sat till morning.

Mrs. Caro later wrote her memoirs, *Staerker als das Schwert,* (Stronger than the Sword), and dedicated it to the victims of Theresienstadt. She wrote about my Oma, "Even in the Camp through her 3-year imprisonment, she gave others a bright example in the way to behave … through her humility and selflessness, modesty and through her faith in God, she gave her fellow Jews comfort, hope, and courage."

Norbert Troller wrote, "I do not believe there are many people who have the dignity, the courage, the fearlessness to face death bravely without any weapon, without any means of resistance. Most of us were young."

I do not know much detail about my Oma's own life in the concentration camp. About the only thing that she told me of her three years there was that she had a job in the kitchen, peeling potatoes. That is what she did all day, day after day after day. At least she had something to eat. From Norbert Troller's book *Theresienstadt, Hitler's Gift to the Jews,* I learned the Czech word for potato peels, *slupky.* They were an important part of the diet.

Betty and I visited the tiny kitchen which was indeed too small to feed the population. We had no idea, we could not imagine, what it was like to work in that kitchen. But now we know. In *The Jewish Voice* of June, 2005, a former inmate of Theresienstadt, Julia Bos, wrote, "I was lucky. My extra job was in the kitchen … The kitchen was built in 1780 and everything in it, I guess from the same period. Huge rats squirming on the floor and walls and, once in a while, one falling in the soup pot. I was scared to death of them, but what can one do, eat the barley soup or not. At least the rats were boiled."

She wrote that some days they were marched outside of the camp to pick up potatoes and could easily see pushcarts going to the crematorium with bodies, mostly the elderly who were not able to exist on the meager rations.

In her memoir Julia Bos stated, "We had two meals a day: at noon, watery barley soup, at night, potato soup or potatoes. Every ten days, a piece of bread and if you were careful, it would last four to five days."

I know that my Oma always kept up her deep faith in God; she was certain that He would protect her from the very worst fate. She prayed every day. Alone. A Jew does not need a synagogue or temple. Like Tevye in *Fiddler On The Roof* anyone can speak directly to God in prayer. My Oma always did.

But I must admit that I have lost my faith! I cannot believe that God answers prayers -- if He never answered the prayers of 6,000,000 innocent Jews and others who were killed by the Nazis! I am, like my father, an atheist. But a Jewish atheist! Judaism is my heritage, my background, my family's place in the world. But that does not mean that I believe in God, or prayer, or any afterlife.

The Nazis devised a solution to Theresienstadt's overcrowding. On January 5, 1942, less than two months after the arrival of the first transport into the concentration camp, the first train left, bound eastward for the extermination camp, Auschwitz.

Betty and I visited that camp, too. One memory remains etched into my mind: The crematoriums with fingernail scratches on their walls. Betty and I also saw European schoolchildren there, quiet, respectful, reverent. I wonder if American kids would be.

In September, 1942, a crematorium was built in Theresienstadt to get rid of the corpses that had piled up for lack of burial space. It disposed of 190 bodies per day, every day of the week. The ashes were searched for gold (from the teeth) and the remaining ashes were shoveled into cardboard boxes -- 25,000 boxes! Inmates had to pass each box from one to another to put them in a pushcart. Then the cart was wheeled to the Ohre River, according to one source, and the boxes were opened and the ashes thrown into the water. Another eye-witness, Norbert Troller, wrote that the ashes were dumped into the Eger River which flowed into the Elbe, a source of drinking water.

There were many children in Theresienstadt. Seventeen thousand young inmates died in that camp just from summer to winter in 1942.

The Nazis in charge of Theresienstadt decided how many Jews, from 1,000 to 5,000, were to go on each eastward train. But they devilishly left it up to their appointed *Judenrat* to fulfill the quota. We do not know how many prisoners in Theresienstadt knew the truth about the trains headed east to Auschwitz or how many believed the incredible rumors they heard. The truth was indeed almost impossible to believe, even in a concentration camp. The head of the *Judenrat*, Edelstein, simply could not believe it and asked that the rumor not be spread. Also in the camp Rabbi Leo Baeck heard stories of gas chambers but did not repeat them. He believed it was better that the inmates in

Theresienstadt did not hear horror stories. In fact, 140,000 Jews died either there or in a camp thereafter.

UNC Professor Christopher Browning reported at a seminar that this "model showcase camp was a clear and conscious act of political theater." He told us that 85% of its inmates did not survive -- while some death camps actually had higher survival rates!

Paul Weiner, a Czech survivor of the camp, called it "a model of deception." He told us, "It was not a ghetto; it was a gateway to death." And he told us at the UNC seminar: "It is a testimonial to the Jewish Administration that children were educated."

He explained that diseases were rampant: "Impetigo from malnutrition, fever, and jaundice; typhoid was endemic, and depression constant."

He added, "it is hard to write about life when all you see are graves."

On October 5, 1943, the first Danish Jews arrived and soon thereafter, the Danish Red Cross and the Swedish Red Cross declared that they were coming to inspect the conditions at the camp. The Nazi guards decided on a scheme to fool them: they planned an exact route for these special visitors, one that they had the prisoners enhance with green turf, flowers, and benches. A playground, sports fields, and even a monument were added along their route. One billet even got furniture, drapes, and flower boxes. They put up a sign that said "Boys School," another read "Closed for the Holidays."

Joel Shatzky reported that on November 11, 1943, a "census count" of the 40,000 inmates was held. They all had to stand in a field through the long, cold night. Between 200 and 300 died then and there.

On May 12, 1944, SS Colonel Karl Rahm, the commander of the camp, ordered 7,500 prisoners deported, including all the orphans and the sick. The transports continued until only 400 able-bodied men, plus women, children and elderly were left in camp.

Everything was ready for the day, June 23rd, 1944, when the Red Cross representative -- there was only one, Mr. Dunant, -- arrived. He stayed exactly five and a half hours. He saw that bakers were baking bread. A load of vegetables was delivered. And workers sang. Some signs, such as "To the Beach", are still there from that time.

The artificial façade made a great impression -- on the Nazis! They decided to make a film of it to show the world that the camps weren't so bad. And they even made a film of the film being made.

Did the great deception fool the sole visitor? (Not until 1990 was his report to the Danish Red Cross found by scholars.) He had immediately recognized that the place was horrendously overcrowded. Yet he phrased things diplomatically. He described the activities he saw. But was it sardonic? Was it believed? It is still impossible to tell.

Yet Dr. Franz Hvass, the head of a Danish delegation, expressed his "admiration for the Jewish people … for creating such relatively good living conditions for their fellow Jews."

Then, in April 1945, new transports and death marchers arrived at Theresienstadt. Some of them were prisoners who had left the camp just months before. They had come from Auschwitz and Ravensbrueck and other camps further East, retreating from the Russian Army. Some had typhus and infected the camp with it. They also brought word of the extermination camps in the East. So the awful rumors were indeed true.

Klara Caro reported that, "the last transport in those days before liberation, in which Rabbi Baeck was to go, was a trick, and was to be gassed. The lucky, timely arrival of the leader of the Red Cross, Mr. Dunant, prevented the gruesome deed."

The officials who were left in charge of the camp debated among themselves as to what to do with the remaining prisoners. Some wanted to deport them all; others wanted to free them in the hope of clemency from the oncoming allied troops. Still others wanted to negotiate with the neutral Swiss. They even sent a transport of Jews to Switzerland. Rabbi Caro's widow got the last train which took her via Constance to Switzerland.

Just before the Russians got to Terezin, as they called it, many of the Nazi guards deserted their posts. A few others, however, threw away their guns and remained there. No Jew raised a hand against any one of them, according to one source. However Julia Bos remembers it differently: She saw three gallows where some of the prisoners had hanged German officers of the camp.

On May 8, 1945, Theresienstadt was liberated by the Soviet Army and placed under the protection of the International Red Cross. Of the 87,000 human beings who had gone eastward from Terezin, 83,000 were murdered or perished on forced marches. My Oma was among those few who were still there when Theresienstadt was liberated. So was Rabbi Leo Baeck.

I tell you the story of this camp and this survivor because the truth about the concentration camps is hard to believe, almost impossible to comprehend, even difficult to understand. One young college student, upon meeting concentration camp survivors, asked incredulously, "Were you never given any dessert?"

It was June 10, 1945, after the Russians got there, that the inmates received their first pat of butter in almost three years and Oma wrote *The First Butter* in rhyming slang:

I'm glad 'bout this evenin'
'cause we're gettin' butter,
Even cheese n' cabbage,
Kids, we've got it good!

After a 3-year-long fast,
The bread'll fill our box.
Sugar, eggs, margarine,
All rich in vitamine.

Meat, lettuce, all good things
Should make us strong again.
The Russians ordered it thusly,
So we'll recover thoroughly.

They tossed out our enemies
We stayed alive luckily.
God did a wonder for us
One can't thank Him enough.

The face was drawn and haggard
The bodies were frightfully thin.
Enteritis and Vitaminosis
Were the doctors' diagnosis.

Bones so weak you'd hardly stand
Just walkin' felt so difficult
Bloodless brain, head so empty,
Ya reeled as if ya were drunk.

All that, the false diet brought
Infamed 'n devilish doctors thought
Tis true, believe, friends, my word
A giant, bloodless, mass murder.

Thank G'd, our sufferin's over,
Finished are the hard times,
The trial and soul's need
G'd saved us from certain death.

We're rousin' ourselves, goin' forth
'Most ev'ryone to a diff'rent town
Takin' with us, to our constant reminder,
Our dear dead's holy legacy.

Let's reach out our hands to each other,
The word *Theresienstadt* is our sign
That we Jews are always ready
To practice <u>love,</u> <u>truth,</u> and <u>justice.</u>

On July 11, 1945, her last day there, my Oma wrote a poem,
"Farewell to Theresienstadt" to the melody of *So leb' denn wohl*, which
I translate as, "So liv' well then":
    So liv' well then, Theresienstadt,
    That for 3 years put us up "as a guest."
    Freedom was for us Room and Board and a Lie
    We lived splendidly as never before.

    Even the clothes and the shoes
    Were free for us there
    A small piece of soap and some toilet paper
      Lasted many weeks for every four "people"

From hunger also not a trace,
We were in the spa town
We were fat, I hardly understand it
In fact, unfortunately, it was only in my dream

In the bed, a true paradise,
One lays so rich, one sleeps so sweet
In truth, one found oneself
On hard earth, next to a cold wall

The war was outside. We were free
All around, arrives the month of May
Where everything blooms and is bustling
For us, though, the pain stays in our hearts.

These poems show my Oma's biting cynicism, clever wit, ironic bent -- in spite of all that had happened to her!

Oma was in that horrible concentration camp until her liberation day. She was the only relative of ours to survive any concentration camp. Of the 140,000 people sent to Theresienstadt, almost 90,000 were sent to death camps, 33,000 died in Theresienstadt, only 16,832 survived!

The last remaining Jews left Theresienstadt on August 17, 1945. In a *New York Times* article, Aharon Appelfield described the few survivors as being in "the shock of liberation." My Oma must have been.

He wrote that God did not reveal himself in Auschwitz or in other camps. Yet my grandmother continued her faith. Appelfield said, "some entered hell as pious people and came out of it just as pious. That position deserves respect." My Oma was one of those.

We did not know where she was, that she was alive, or who had survived -- until a chance encounter on the streets of Washington Heights in New York City. My parents had read in the *Aufbau,* an American newspaper in German for Jewish refugees, that Klara Caro was in New York, but they did not know where. My father or mother or both, I don't remember exactly, just happened to run into her in our neighborhood one day. And it was she who told them that Johanna Friedmann had been in Theresienstadt and had survived. But Klaerchen did not know where she was now.

From her liberation until the end of September, 1946 -- more than a year! -- my Oma was in a Displaced Persons or D.P. camp in Deggendorf, Bavaria. She did not know where her family was, who was alive, or where else to go.

It took time for us to locate my Oma in the DP camp. Then her son Paul came from London to get her and brought her to England. Paul and his brother, my father, decided that their stepmother should live with us in America. She was delighted.

34. Wartime in Bielefeld

While my father was in jail, my mother's father arranged for our departure from Germany almost as soon as he would be released. My parents and I left for England and America.

Meanwhile, in Germany, the Nazi times were tough, especially in a relatively small town like Bielefeld where my mother's parents decided to remain even though their children had gone. Bielefeld had been so good to them for so many years. Their department store was well known. They were respected members of their community.

Franz had been particularly active in the congregation, and, soon after the synagogue was burned on *Kristallnacht,* Franz started serving as the chairman of the Jewish congregation. (Now there is a plaque showing where the temple had been.)

Bielefeld was a small enough town so that a prominent merchant was revered. They were pillars of the local society. The town was indeed their paradise. Besides, they were getting too old to leave Germany.

But the Nazi anti-Semitism was growing, gaining members everywhere. And Bielefeld was the kind of place where almost everyone knows everyone else's business. Often a busybody or tattletale tried to learn information. Someone could curry favor by telling the authorities what they wanted to know. It was a time for Jews not to trust strangers.

One day my mother's mother went shopping in a butcher shop. She said something to a friend of hers whom she happened to see there, some anti-Nazi remark. Another woman overheard what she had said and stared at Johanna Friedmann, a look of sheer hatred! She may even have said something to my grandmother, and if so, it certainly frightened her.

My grandmother went home, told her husband about it, and then promptly went into the bedroom, swallowed pills she had gotten from their friendly pharmacist, and committed suicide. It was November 1, 1939, a year after *Kristallnacht,* and she was only 58.

Franz was overwhelmed. Devastated. Horrified. His grief was total. His despair was palpable. He could not get over the sudden death of his beloved wife. He never recovered from the shock.

On December 14, 1939, in a letter sent by Transatlantic Airways Clipper via Lisbon, Portugal, addressed to his beloved children and grandchild (he had only one, me, at that time), Franz Friedmann wrote, "the house is empty -- empty -- and I have to go to the cemetery to visit the beloved mother. How have we lived together happily for these 36½ years, how have we always understood each other; we have completed each other, I could discuss everything, everything with the beloved mother, and the beloved mother had a complete understanding of everything."

His wife had the foresight he may have lacked. She had written that he should "go to the children," meaning to join us. He did, however, sell his department store and it became a *Sporthaus,* or sports-oriented store, which I visited in 1956. By 2004 it had been completely modernized into a much taller glass building, still labeled *Sporthaus.*

In July, 1942, Franz Friedmann got the notice from the Gestapo to appear at the Bielefeld *Hauptbahnhof,* or Main Railroad Station, for transport to *Theresienstadt* (where the other Johanna Friedmann was). It was truly too much for him to bear. He settled his affairs and wrote to his three children, "Your dear mother lies under the earth, in peace … I belong with your beloved mother; I belong by her side."

On July 26th, Franz joined his wife by swallowing pills. He was 72. My age.

When David and I visited Bielefeld's Jewish cemetery in 2004, Franz and Johanna Friedmann's graves next to each other were undisturbed (although other parts of the cemetery had been changed). At our visit their names were being regilded in gold.

35. World War II

Hitler plunged the world into World War II when he invaded Poland on September 1, 1939. But it was not until the Japanese bombed

Pearl Harbor on December 7, 1941, that the United States of America entered the war.

President Roosevelt called it "a date which will live in infamy" when he asked the U.S. Congress to declare war on Japan on December 8th. Then Hitler declared war on us on December 9th! The U.S. and "the allies" fought "the axis" of Germany, Japan and Italy. It was a long war, fought hard by all sides, with tremendous casualties.

Germany invaded her European neighbors, one after the other, conquering the continent. England was bombed regularly, by planes and then by rockets. And Japan invaded its neighboring islands, one by one, holding much of the Pacific.

Our allies were England, France, and Russia. Europe, Asia, and Africa were battle sites. Allied bombers flew missions from England, blasting the German homeland. While the Russians fought the German army in the East, the other allies invaded German-occupied France on D-Day, June 6, 1944. So, toward the end, Germany was attacked from the East and the West. They did not surrender until Berlin itself was conquered. Hitler and Goebbels committed suicide.

The second World War did not end with VE Day, Victory in Europe, May 8, 1945. It wasn't over until VJ Day, the victory over Japan, August 14, 1945, just eight days after the first atomic bomb hit Japan.

Early into the war, Gerhardt Riegner, a lawyer and member of the World Jewish Congress in Geneva, Switzerland, was told by a German industrialist about the concentration camps that housed tens of thousands of Jews. Riegner sent telegrams to Winston Churchill and Franklin Delano Roosevelt and wrote about it in his memoirs. But the allies deliberately took no action and did not publicize the camps. The horrors were not revealed until the camps were liberated and the war was over.

The Germans had a saying at that time, *Berlin bleibt doch Berlin*, meaning that whatever happens, Berlin will remain Berlin anyway

In the early 1890's, Germany's last emperor, Wilhelm II, built a neo-Gothic Protestant church at the east end of the *Kurfuerstendamm*, Berlin's main shopping street. He called it the *Kaiser Wilhelm-Gedaechniskirche* as a remembrance of his grandfather, Kaiser Wilhelm I. It was bombed into a ruin during World War II and left that way as a reminder. Today, students gather there and have scrawled graffiti on it. It is a wonderful symbol of the freedom that Berlin now enjoys.

36. International Cousins

Most of our Friedman families' members managed to escape from Germany, although some remained. Many emigrated to England, some to the U.S.A. Still others went to Poland, Hungary, Italy, Holland, Switzerland, Israel, Canada, Russia, China, Korea, and Australia as well as Nigeria, Rhodesia, and South Africa -- seventeen countries!

My mother's brother Paul and his wife Heddy went from Germany to England. He got a job with Lever Brothers as a traveling salesman -- but his assigned territory was Africa! Paul and Heddy's daughter, Ruth Joan, was born on February 2, 1946, in Port Harcourt, Nigeria. I was twelve years old when my parents told me I had a first cousin born in Africa; I was delighted, absolutely thrilled to have a Negro cousin. I knew that people born in Africa were black and was disappointed to learn that she was white.

My mother's younger brother Karl also went to London. In 1947, he married Miriam Mehl and they also went to Africa for Lever Bros. When their daughter, Vivian Ann, was born in Livingston, Rhodesia, in 1953, I was 19 and knew she was white.

Paul and Heddy returned to England and their son, Frank David Friedman, was born in London in September, 1948. I visited them when I was in Europe in 1955 and my family and I visited them when we were in Europe in May, 1976. To our surprise and pleasure, we arrived a day or two after Frank's marriage to Chris Anders, an Australian girl. Frank had become a skilled carpenter and the couple went to Australia.

He loved Australia but he and Chris got divorced. Frank came to New York at the time of my mother's 80th birthday party in March, 1976. So did his sister Ruth and her husband, Robert Bruckner, from London.

Frank later married another Aussie, Particia Hall on March 28th (my birthday) 1987. They have two children, Joshua and Maia Friedman.

My Uncle Karl remained in Africa and turned to a career he enjoyed more than direct selling. Based on his experience in his father's store in Bielefeld, he became a window dresser for African department stores. Store openings were a big business for him and he established a reputation for doing it up right, helping a new store or branch have a gala opening.

Karl visited us once, in Rye Hills. I remember his red hair. He was very happy in Africa but Miriam wasn't. When former British colonies became independent, she decided to return to England with her daughter. Karl and Miriam divorced.

He stayed in Africa and married Renee Rosen. They had two children, Etan in 1971 and Kalene in 1977 -- when Karl was 70! Both these first cousins of mine were born in Natal, South Africa. Kalene married Quentin Jacobs in 2001 and to be timely, as I write this on February 13, 2006, Oriana Eilidh Hannah Jacobs was born today! (South Africa is 6 hours ahead of our time zone.)

V. THE BOSTONIANS
(1939 - 1947)

37. Brookline and Brighton

Soon after our arrival in the U.S.A. in September, 1939, we moved to the section just outside of Boston, Massachusetts, known as Brookline (not to be confused with the section of New York City known as Brooklyn). We rented two rooms from a Jewish family named Balicer in their home on Addington Road, I think it was number 72. My parents had one bedroom, I the other. I believe we shared the Balicers' kitchen, bathroom and dining room with them, but I'm not sure.

My parents thought of themselves as refugees from Hitler and immigrants in the United States. Professor Lillian Furst prefers to call such people escapees. We were all three, and even more. But not yet Americans. Legally, we were stateless. We were delighted to be in America but we did not yet feel comfortable here. Dr. Alan J. Stern, a psychiatrist, said, "All the escapees were traumatized."

In his book, *The German Refugee,* Bernard Malamud wrote that although many of these people were articulate, their greatest loss was their loss of language. They could no longer say what they wanted to say. One such escapee from Germany said he felt like a child, or sometimes even worse, like a moron, as if his tongue were useless.

Imagine how my father felt, forty-five years old, a traveling salesman who could not speak English so he could not sell and could not travel. He could not do any business at all! Since he had no other useful training, my father started to work in the only trade he knew, in a leather factory or tannery in downtown Boston named Agoos.

My mother, who had had servants in her parental home as well as her own, now had no means of communication at all. She went to work cleaning other people's houses. She never did become a kindergarten teacher although she had a diploma which qualified her. I, however, was actually oblivious to all that. I was too young to understand.

Alice Kaplan compared the loss of language, or being between languages, to be as miserable in its way as to be without bread. But my parents were not miserable. They were grateful that they got out of Germany in time.

It took my parents quite a while to learn English. Learning a language is harder the older one is. My parents went to language lessons. They read the newspaper. But, most of all, my parents listened to the radio. They mostly listened to the news and to political speeches during election years. And to President Franklin Delano Roosevelt's "fireside chats."

My parents never lost their German accents but they became fluent in English. One word always bothered my father. He needed it to sell. It was the word *genuine* as in "genuine leather." He and I went over and over it but he never did get it quite right.

Someone, probably Mr. or Mrs. Balicer, told my parents that their boy, at five not yet old enough for regular public school, had to go to Hebrew School. So I dutifully went to Temple Ohabei Shalom twice a week and on Sundays. I learned Hebrew just in order to read the bible; it was not then a living language. And I studied Jewish history, culture, and religion. My diploma from that school is dated 5706 or 1946.

When both of my parents had learned enough English to feel some confidence, we moved from Brookline to our own apartment, Suite 2, on the ground floor of 24 Colborne Road, in the section of Boston called Brighton. It was May of 1940. My father also bought a car, a used or second-hand or previously-owned Chevrolet. The fact that he had a car and his own apartment impressed his father-in-law. Franz Friedmann wrote that my father "was already a real American, going at super-speed."

Our apartment was a railroad flat: it had a central corridor with two rooms off each side and one room, the bathroom, straight ahead down the hall -- the one room you looked at upon entering the apartment. The first room to the right was the eat-in kitchen. The second on the right was my parents' bedroom. The first room to the left was, at first, my room. The second to the left was originally the dining room.

Things either could not have gone quite as well as planned, or else -- and hopefully more likely -- we were doing new immigrants a favor. My parents started taking in male boarders. This gave the renter, always a German refugee, what had been the dining room. So my bedroom also became a part-time dining room.

Boston is a proud old New England town, a proud college town, a proud baseball town, and a proud historical town. Bostonians also take pride in their "proper English," the pronunciation closest to British English, as in "Bahston" or "pahk the cah in Hahvahd Yahd." Later, when we moved to New York, or as Bostonians would say, "Noo Yahk," I changed my accent to the New Yorker's: "Noo Yawk."

My parents told me that I had to go to school to learn to read and write. So I went to the Harriet Alice Baldwin School in Brighton, the local public school. I came home from my first day of school and told them, "can't read yet, can't write yet!"

My teachers were all female, all old maids, all Catholic, with names like Mary or Mary-Catherine or Mary-Alice. There were not many Jews in school but there were various white ethnic groups. I remember Greek, Italian, and Irish kids.

I looked up the school on the Internet in 2006. Baldwin had only 81 students in 2003-2004, of which 32.1% were Asian, 22.2% black, 28.4% Hispanic, 17.3% white -- and 98.8% graduated. Wow, how my old neighborhood has changed!

I also became a Boy Scout, advancing only as far as the lowest rank, Tenderfoot. But I did take part as a Boy Scout in a major Bostonian tradition: the annual march from Concord to Lexington. Those two sections of Greater Boston were the sites of the first battles of the American Revolution. And Boston is very proud of its position as the starting point of America's War of Independence. It's celebrated in the city as Patriot's Day, the day the Boston Red Sox play a double-header.

I felt truly honored to be chosen to carry our Scout Troop's American flag in that day's parade. I wore a leather belt that held the flagstaff at my crotch level. And I was told that the flag could not be dropped, or even as much as lowered; that it must be held with two hands at all times. I started the parade with my head up and the flag high. But I had a cold and a runny nose. I could not reach for the handkerchief in my back pocket. So, unfortunately, my nose dripped as we marched for what felt like hours. It was. I dared not move my hands as my nasal drips reached the pole, my left hand, and the leather. I was simultaneously proud and embarrassed!

My parents and I often listened to the radio, partly to learn English and partly to keep up with what was going on in the world. My father maintained his interest in politics and got me interested, too. During World War II the news became a truly personal, vitally important information source. We sat quietly by the radio and listened intently. When the news was over, we talked about it at length.

The radio was a part of our family. We lived with it. In those days, believe it or not, people sat and looked at the radio while they listened. My mother and I would listen to soap operas like "Our Gal Sunday." We three really loved Jack Benny and Fred Allen who had weekly half-hour evening programs. Hans Friedman's involvement with Berlin's cabaret life and his love of good comedians were reflected with his radio days. Years later, his enjoyment of Sid Caesar's pseudo-German on the "Show of Shows" was the only reason he bought us a TV set.

One Sunday morning we turned on the radio and heard names, a long list of names, mostly men, many with military titles. What was going on? The date was December 7, 1941; it was Pearl Harbor, as Franklin Delano Roosevelt said, "a day which will live in infamy."

It was the start of the U.S. involvement in World War II. And we followed the action of the war daily. After the invasion of Europe, we followed the action on the radio with maps spread out on the table.

Another Sunday morning we turned on the radio and heard another long list of names, but this time males and females. What was this? The infamous Coconut Grove fire in Boston on November 28, 1942, when 492 people died.

After the invasion of Europe on D-Day, June 6, 1944, we kept careful track of the allied progress through Europe by monitoring on maps where "we" (allies) and "they" (Germans) were. We considered ourselves Americans although we were not yet citizens. I recall that we were called "enemy aliens" and therefore an F.B.I. agent came to our home and removed the wire, or whatever, that made our radio a short-wave set. That's nothing compared to what happened to Japanese who were, in fact, U.S. citizens as we were not. These Nisei, American-born Japanese, were put into concentration camps.

My parents had already earned and saved enough to sponsor family members and others, to help them come to America. My father's brother Paul and his family were in England; my mother's brothers Paul and Karl and their families were in Africa. We did help the Silversmiths and Heinemanns, my mother's relatives. My mother's father, Franz Friedmann, wrote to us that he appreciated that my parents had "arranged for jobs for Else & Fritz [Silversmith] even before they arrived and also you have helped them immigrate. For hard-working people one can do that, but for lazy ones -- not."

We did not know about anyone on my father's side who was in Germany.

38. The Broken Stick

My father had theories of child-rearing that would be called into question today. But they were not at all unusual for the times and "where he was coming from." Yet for someone who was interested in Freudian psychology, he acted as if he'd never heard of it!

My father became a frequently absent and abusive father, just as his father had been. He also became a strict disciplinarian, like his own father. My father valued one trait: being *tapfer,* brave or stoic. One had to "take it," to "tough it out."

Psychologists say that sons who are beaten often beat their sons. If he learned it from his father, he certainly tried to teach it to me. Sometimes I thought my father beat me just to teach me to "take it like a man." I tried very hard to be *tapfer,* not to cry. And often succeeded.

Hans Friedman truly had no patience, a fierce temper, and a very short fuse, often beating me with a stick. I remember that he once broke a bamboo stick on my rear end. I remembered that for a long time (as you can see) and resolved that I would not beat any children I had.

He also kicked me, especially under the table, whenever I said or did something he thought was wrong at any time, even during a meal, not only privately but also in front of company. When he did so, I felt embarrassed even more than hurt. Often, of course, he was justified (in my own mind) because I had indeed said or done something that was wrong. But I honestly believe he did not think that I was a bad boy.

And I respected him. He was, in his way, teaching me to be good and do right. And to be *tapfer*. I think the lesson took.

But he did not beat his wife and I did not beat my wife or my sons or anyone, not even when I had boxing in Physical Training, in high school.

Another child-rearing theory of my father's backfired. When I was 12 years old he offered me a cigarette, hoping I would cough, choke, or otherwise be sickened by it and never want another. When I smoked it all the way down (although I did not inhale as Bill Clinton said he didn't when he smoked marihuana) without any ill effects, my father made his second mistake. He said he would buy me all my cigarettes if I promised not to buy any myself, on the theory of limiting my use of the "noxious weed." He paid for pack after pack of Philip Morris.

I continued to smoke for thirty years, eventually more than a pack a day, but I quit -- cold turkey -- more than thirty years ago.

39. My Childhood Friends

I had three friends in particular in those pre-teen Boston years, boys my age: Daniel Glatzer, Claude Oulman, and Uri Mayer.

Danny was the son of Nahum Glatzer, a Brandeis University professor, editor at the Shocken publishing house, and a noted Jewish author. Danny and I wrote (and drew) comic books -- which could have been a forerunner of my career as an advertising copywriter that included not only writing but drawing some storyboards. A storyboard is like a blueprint of a TV commercial in a kind of comic book fashion, with frame by frame drawings of what the video would be above a typed audio script.

Another friend, Claudio Marcus Oulmann, was the Italian-born son of German- Jewish refugees who moved into our apartment house. He became Claude Mark Oulman when he became a citizen, just as I went from Walter Erich Friedmann to Walter Eric Friedman. I did not realize it then, but Claude's parents paid my mother to watch him after school while his folks both worked. We always played together and were the best of friends until he and his family moved to Portland, Oregon in 1946. I lost touch with him.

But that was before the Internet. Betty managed to locate him in 1999! Claude and his wife, Callie, had moved to Butte, Montana but had sold their house in Portland to one of their five daughters who forwarded the Email. They also had one son. We got together in Portland in 2000 to renew old, old memories.

I had remembered that Claude was allergic to peanut butter and that is why I never ate it. Never. Yet when we finally got reacquainted, he admitted that it was not really an allergy; he just didn't like peanut butter and had said he was allergic. Now he sometimes eats peanut butter but I still don't!

Claude recalled that we two were such close buddies -- and so disruptive of the first grade -- that the teachers in the Harriet Alice Baldwin School kept us in separate classes for all the next five grades. Claude had moved from Boston, however, before I was graduated and so I went on, alone, to Thomas Alva Edison Junior High School, where, incidentally, I had two years of French. That was my only formal education in that language. But it stood me in good stead in all the years we lived on St. Barthelemy in the French West Indies.

I do not remember anyone in that school being anything other than white. I looked up the Edison School on the Internet. It had 616 students in 2003-2004. They were 13% Asian, 29.4% Black, 44.5% Hispanic, and only 13% White.

My good friend Uri Mayer and I "hung out together," as a more modern phrase would put it. One place we often went was a construction site. They were preparing the place for what would become an apartment house. But they first had to dig down deep and then pour in concrete to create footings or foundations for the building. They put wooden boards at ground level with gaps between them for the footings. After school, when the construction crew had gone, Uri and I would jump from one board to another, and, incongruously, make believe we were on the war's front line.

One day Uri went there by himself. I had to go straight home, I don't remember why, but I didn't go there with him. When he didn't come home, his mother called us to find out if I was with him or knew where he was. Then she called the police.

All alone at the construction site, Uri had jumped from board to board, just as we always did. On his last jump, he didn't make it! They found Uri Mayer's body on the bottom of a deep excavation. His death changed my life.

I was devastated. Such a close friend dying doing what I had done with him, was horribly upsetting. I gave up my daredevil ways and became a "chicken."

Uri's parents, of course, were shocked, too. So was his big brother Paul. They were Jewish but, with the senseless death of his little brother, Paul became a Benedictine Monk for 18 years, then a Catholic priest, went to Panama, then became executive director of an interfaith coalition for justice and peace. Paul Mayer opposed the Vietnam War, led demonstrations for peace and for the environment. Co-founder of "Children of War," an international teenage organization, he became a dedicated practitioner of yoga.

Uri's death completely changed his big brother's life.

40. The Heinemanns

My mother's cousin Rosi was the middle daughter of the Shoe Store Simon Sisters. She and her husband, Walter Heinemann, with their daughter Vera (known as *Putzi,)* left Germany after we did.

Their son-in-law Sal Marshall told me that Walter Heinemann had actually been in the Buchenwald concentration camp and that he and his wife and daughter got out of Germany on the last ship to leave in 1939.

A family that owned a furniture shop on Boston's Boylston Street provided the three Heinemanns with visas and financial assurance to help them come to America.

Also in 1939, my parents helped start an organization to help German Jews (and later others) come to America. It was called the Immigrants' Mutual Aid Society, the IMAS. I think that my parents and the IMAS helped the Heinemanns in some way. They did help my mother's other cousins, Fritz and Else Silberschmidt.

It was then necessary under American law for every individual immigrating to the U.S.A. to prove that he or she or a sponsor had at least a thousand dollars in the bank. The idea was that every immigrant would not be indigent and would be able to live until he got a job. As soon as they could, my parents put up many such bonds through the IMAS. They helped relatives of friends, strangers, and refugees from other countries. I know that, many years later, they also aided Hungarians after the anti-communist revolution there -- even though my father remained a communist himself!

The first of our relatives who came were the Heinemanns. (The record shows that the family name had been Heynemann in 1923). My Uncle Walter had been a horticulturalist in Germany. But not being able to speak English, not having another trade nor advanced education, he figured he could only find some kind of outdoor work. His first job was at a farm in New Jersey, but he didn't know how to milk cows. Next he and his wife were employed by A. A. Shapiro in Ridgefield, Connecticut. Walter was the superintendent for $100 a month and Rosi the cook for $15 a month plus food and lodging in a cottage on the property.

Finally he got the perfect job for him -- at least until he got severe arthritis. The job even came with a wonderful home for his family. Walter Heineman -- now without the last 'n' -- became the head gardener at a Jewish cemetery outside of Boston. Sometimes he was the only gardener, and thus had to dig graves, too. But, for the most part, he supervised a staff that dug the holes and filled them up again, tended the graves and the flowers and the greenery. He kept the place looking perfectly inviting and peaceful for many, many years.

Putzi was a bit ashamed of living on a cemetery and seldom invited friends over. But the problem was solved when the Heinemans had the greatest Halloween parties!

They also had terrific picnics. Someone wrote a poem in German entitled, "Picnic," dated April 26, 1953. Here's my translation of the beginning:

The Spring has hit,
We've all got it.
April seems so wet
We're looking for grub yet.

The buds have sprung.
The birds have sung.

In the garden it's so cold
The HOBOS call us scold.

The poem has eight stanzas and trying to make it rhyme in English doesn't really work out well. But my point is that it refers to the gardener twice and the last verse says:
The gardener was still Walter,
The poetry was by an oldster.
The list was done by Ro
With Jo.

I think that Ro is Rosi and Jo is Jorlande Gottschalk, a friend from IMAS.

On July 24, 1947, Walter Heineman received word from the United Nations Relief and Rehabilitation Administration that his mother, Wilhelmine Heinemann, nee Cohn, "was transported to Theresienstadt and died there October 15, 1943."

My Uncle Walter seemed to me, when I was a child, to have a head that was small for his body. Later I realized that he actually had a well-developed muscular body, so he was really in excellent condition, an ideal physical specimen until he was crippled by arthritis and could hardly walk, much less do physical labor. He supervised a staff yet he continued to garden, uncomplainingly, even on crutches. I don't know how he did it.

I considered my Aunt Rosi to be the most attractive and the nicest one in the family. With snow white hair and an excellent taste in clothes, she always looked her best. Besides, she was an superb cook and had a most pleasing, welcoming, friendly personality. And she laughed a lot.

The Heinemans' daughter Vera, whom we always called *Putzi,* was just a few years older than me -- but she was a girl! In those preteen years, I was absolutely shy, especially with my very pretty big cousin.

41. Silberschmidts and the Red Sox

The next of my mother's family members to come to the Boston area were the Silberschmidts, Fritz and Else and their baby son, Donald.

Fritz was the uncle who took movies of me in Cologne the day we left Germany. Else was Rosi's (and Nanni's) sister, the youngest of the Shoe Store Simon Sisters.

Else soon became pregnant and had the first family member on my mother's side born in the U.S.A., their second son, Peter. I saw his mother breast-feed him, the first time I ever saw that!

Onkel Fritz certainly assimilated fast, becoming very "American" very quickly. For example, he learned and understood baseball and was a real fan. Luckily for me, his two sons were much too young to go to a game so Uncle Fred (by this time he had become Fred Silversmith) took me to my first major league baseball games.

It was 1945. He took me to Boston Red Sox games in Fenway Park and I became a Red Sox fan for life. Uncle Fred also took me to Boston Braves games at Braves Field. The Braves had only two good pitchers, Warren Spahn and Johnny Sain. Their pitching rotation was "Spahn and Sain and pray for rain!" I saw Spahn pitch and it was exciting: he kicked his right leg up higher than anyone else and gained more momentum on his fastball. He's in the Hall of Fame and Sain became a famed pitching coach.

In 1948, just after we left Boston, the Braves won the National League pennant and the Red Sox tied for first place in the American League on the last day of the season. Both Boston teams lost to the Cleveland Indians. The Braves moved to Milwaukee and then to Atlanta.

However my favorite team, then as now, was the Red Sox. Their big star was Ted Williams. I remember one game that Uncle Fred took me to. Ted bobbled an easy catch in left field. He didn't get an official error on the play, but he didn't look good out there. The rabid Bosox fans booed him. As luck would have it, he came up first the next inning and hit a towering home run. I was cheering along with all the fickle Boston fans as "The Splendid Splinter" ran the bases. Ted circled the bases while making a gesture with his right arm and left elbow. And the fans' cheers turned right back to boos. I didn't understand that. Nor the gesture. And I didn't understand Uncle Fred's explanation.

The Sox won the American League pennant the next year, 1946, as my uncle and I watched a few games. I followed many others on the radio. It was an exciting World Series, too, against the St. Louis

Cardinals. The Bosox lost when Johnny Pesky didn't relay the ball quickly enough to the catcher as Enos Slaughter ran all the way from first base to home on a single that ended the seventh game and thus won the World Series.

"My Sox" lost another World Series to the New York Mets. The fact is, the Boston Red Sox did not win a World Series from 1918 until 2004; starting the year they sold their best young pitcher -- George Herman (nicknamed Babe) Ruth -- to the rival New York Yankees. That was the "curse of the Bambino" which, theoretically, kept the Sox from beating out the Yanks year after year. The Sox always were in the running, always close, in "the greatest rivalry in professional sports."

For many years a part of the rivalry was between fans of Boston's Ted Williams and the Yankees' Joe DiMaggio. Then, one year, Joe signed a contract for $100,000. At the time, Ted was making $60,000 -- and insisted that he get $100,000 as well. He got it. I never dreamed that I would ever earn that much -- and more!

As I said, the Boston Red Sox did not win another World Series … until 2004. They beat the hated Yankees in the playoffs (after losing three games in a row) and then beat the Cardinals in the World Series (again after losing three in a row)! I had lost a lot of bets over all those years, mostly bets with Betty of 25 cents. But this year I bet -- and won -- $20! I'm sorry that neither Betty nor Uncle Fred lived to see it.

Fred Silversmith was a very talented, multifaceted man. I do not think that he had a college education. But he was amazingly self-educated. For one thing, he became a ham radio operator, learning it from books he had sent away for, and "broadcasting" from his home, contacting people in far-flung countries. He also carved wood into works of art and created unique designs.

Most of all, he became a master electrician, but self-taught, possibly even learning it all from books. He became an electrician -- later the Head Electrician -- at famed Massachusetts General Hospital. He was the one who helped develop some of the fantastic machinery they created for miraculous operations. Fred ran such major medical devices as heart-lung machines when they were just coming out. He worked there for years and years as the one electrician to "go to" when there was a crisis.

114

Fred and Else's two sons, Donald and Peter, were also very successful; they both became doctors, but that's another chapter.

When Fred finally retired from Mass General, he and his wife moved to Florida. I would like to think that he went to see the spring training of some major league teams. The Red Sox train in Fort Myers. Did he see them there? Or watch the Florida Marlins win the pennant? Or see the Tampa Bay Devil Rays? My dear Uncle Fred lived there only a short while and passed away. Else died, too, a few years later.

42. Edgewood's Aunts

My mother was a trained kindergarten teacher but was not licensed to teach in America. What could she do here? She was wonderful with children, especially the little ones, but she really didn't know what to do about it, until she met Erna Beihoff, a woman who had been a nurse in Germany but had no U.S. nursing license.

Miss Beihoff lived in New York's Washington Heights, which would later become our neighborhood. The woman we came to know as Aunt Erna was not related to us at all. She owned a small summer camp in the tiny town of Edgewood in New York's Catskill Mountains. It was perfect. The camp started off very small and eventually progressed to be just small. It probably never had more than thirty children, boys and girls, in any one year at its peak capacity. It started off with less than twenty, only taking children up to age ten.

It was very Jewish, very orthodox, and strictly kosher, keeping all meat and milk dishes separate and saying the prayers every *Shabbos*. I had learned Hebrew and now I was really reading it; we said the proper prayers before and after meals.

Aunt Erna was the oldest of three sisters who worked at the camp. The middle one, Aunt Grete, was also a spinster-lady. But the youngest, Aunt Alma, was not. She was a single mom with a young son, Kurt Mohr, although he was sometimes called Kurt Beihoff. He was just about my age, give or take a month or two. My mother and the three sisters, four middle-aged women, were the only counselors.

My mother was the Head Counselor and she became Aunt Lotte to a hundred or more children over the years. Instead of paying her, Aunt Erna let me come to camp for free. Edgewood, the town, was far off the beaten path. Edgewood, the camp, was next to an apple orchard and -- its real drawing card -- it had a pool.

It was in that pool that Aunt Erna taught me how to swim. At first I had a rubber inner tube around my waist. That kept me afloat so I "swam" no matter what my arms and legs were doing. Aunt Erna insisted upon teaching me proper breaststroke by walking alongside the pool, holding onto my tube. When I swam away from her and she fell into the pool, she confiscated the tube and made me swim without any aids. I did.

With my mother as Head Counselor, or for whatever reason, the camp grew and grew, most probably as campers grew up and had brothers, sisters, cousins, friends, plus a growing reputation among refugees. The number of children outgrew the facilities at Edgewood. And Aunt Erna bought another building, this one in Tannersville, a bigger, better-known Catskill community. But Camp Edgewood retained its name.

Next door to the big, new house was an old, almost-falling-down building with a sign on it, *Antiques*. Its caretaker was an old man, possibly in his 80's, named Montana Hublitt. Montana was probably a nickname, but it was what everyone called him. He enthralled me with tales, possibly even true, of his former adventures as a cowboy. So my initial ambition was to become a cowboy. Aunt Erna called me, "The Yiddisher Cowboy."

But the bigger house didn't have a pool. We walked, perhaps a mile or more, to Rip Van Winkle Lake in Tannersville. That's where I really learned how to swim! I did mostly breast stroke and swam across the lake -- and back!

One year there was a major polio scare in the cities and Camp Edgewood had to extend its season a week or two longer than originally planned. Harry Knopf, the son of the camp's cook, had polio and recovered with only a limp that he still has.

Then there was the year when some of the bigger kids were eleven and twelve years old and had outgrown Camp Edgewood's 10-year age limit. I went to other camps those summers while my mother stayed on at Camp Edgewood.

Finally, in 1947, the year I was thirteen, my Oma came to America . She was able to rent a room directly across the street from the camp and she ate and prayed with us all. My mother and Aunt Erna had decided that Camp Edgewood would take 13-year-olds, after all, including me, Kurt Mohr, a boy named Charlie Matusovitz and his sister, and others. Charlie later legally changed his name to Charles Matson.

My mother had found the perfect job, one she truly loved: creating activities for and playing with little children. We had parties, sang songs, performed plays, dressed in costumes, bobbed for apples, learned dances, celebrated birthdays and Jewish holidays. We went on hikes, the big one was up Hunter Mountain. I once did it dressed as a cowboy, pretending to be on horseback. (Hey, my imagination came in handy later in life!)

One thing my mother did at camp every year was to dress up in a costume as a magician. She had learned some magic tricks as part of her training as a kindergarten teacher. She put on a pointed hat, a cape, smeared black (which was burnt cork) on her face to simulate a beard, and somehow made her voice much deeper. One trick I remember she did was to eat a burning candle. Actually, the candle was an apple, the wick was its stem, and she blew out the flame by exhaling as she put it in her mouth.

Many years later she managed to fool our son John completely when she did her magic show at our children's birthday parties. Her costume and blackened beard really made her look totally different. He never recognized her! He didn't even detect the one thing she could not change: her German accent.

43. A Fish Tale

I got my first goldfish and fish tank when I was about eight or nine years old. My parents would not let me have a dog or a cat in our apartment; perhaps the landlord forbade it. So I bought the only pet I was allowed and could afford.

He, its gender being a presumption on my part, was kept in a round glass bowl with some marbles on the bottom. The fish just swam around. It could not have been a good life for the animal, but that was all I could give it. The fish kept gulping water with his mouth wide open, so I named him "Bigmouth."

After a while it died; that's what fish do. I was sad and quickly bought myself another goldfish. He was named "Bigmouth, Junior."

One day my teacher at the Baldwin School had a kind of show-and-tell, without the show. When it was my turn, I told my class about my pet named Bigmouth, Jr. The teacher quickly interjected, "Well, we all know for whom he's named!"

I had never been so embarrassed; I must have been because I remember it to this day. And I have never been so embarrassed since. But the reason I am telling you this is because it started me on my lifelong hobby.

When Bigmouth, Jr. went the way of all fish, my replacement was a real fish tank with tropical fish. That, of course, meant a heater and lights and aerator bubbling away. My parents used to send me to bed at night and soon thereafter called, "lights out." My room's and the fish tank's lights, as well as my radio, were all to be put out. Not wanting to get up out of bed after having enjoyed its warmth for a while, I rigged up a wiring system that was, now that I think about it, totally illegal and dangerous.

I ran electrical wires under the rug and under the bed to a small switchboard I made which turned off the lamp, the fish tank light, and the radio -- only I didn't turn off the radio. The tank bubbler's noise made it impossible for anyone outside my door to hear the radio. So I kept it on all night. I fell asleep with it on and whenever I woke up at night I listened and promptly fell asleep again. I have always listened to the radio every night ever since.

I rarely admitted that to anyone. But it came up twice: our great friend Marvelle Gilbert and my first cousin Hilde Friedman Levy had the same all-night radio habit.

The other habit that I developed from that time, however, was having a fish tank of one kind or another. The tropical tanks I got when we moved to New York were bigger and better and had a greater variety of fish.

When I left home to go into the army, my girlfriend Betty Klein promised to take care of the two tanks I had with perhaps 20 to 25 tropical fish of various kinds. It was, among other things, an excuse for her to come over to my parents' home regularly and read excerpts from my letters to her as they read her all of those addressed to them.

I was gone a year and a half and in that time all but one of the fish had to be flushed away. The day I came home from Europe was the day the last gourami died!

When we got married and moved to New Rochelle, we had no fish tank. Nor did we have one in Rye Hills. But I really missed having them, so when we had our house built in Chappaqua, I carefully planned for a special kind of tropical fish tank. Since our downstairs playroom would share one wall with the laundry room, I had the builder frame out a space in that common wall to build in a fish tank. Toward the playroom it would be like a living picture on the wall, framed and flush with the wall. Toward the laundry room, into which it jutted, it could have direct access to water, electricity, and lights.

The space became a convenient pass-through because a fish tank never happened. Instead, we started snorkeling and got to swim with tropical fish! For me, that turned out to be better than any fish tank.

But that doesn't quite end this fishy story.

One of our sons, David, a superb swimmer, was nicknamed "Fish" in college. When Michael went to the same school, they gave him the same appellation.

David, in his home in Roseville, California, has a large swimming pool in his backyard and a small artificial waterfall in his front yard. They also have a little pond of goldfish who reproduced in captivity. It has a wire net over it to keep the egrets away. Mike, in his former home in Reston, Virginia, had a flowing self-made small brook in his backyard with fish, frogs and turtles in it. Of course he has built another, bigger "pond" in the backyard of his new home in Ashburn, Virginia. So he has goldfish and koi and their progeny living the outdoor life.

Of course John has a tropical fish tank, too. Every time we visited any of our sons, Betty continued her tradition of feeding the fish, whether they needed it or not.

And our family's attraction to fish continued through the years. In fact, we became sailors, Mike and I owned sailboats, and we all got so close to tropical fish that Betty, the three boys and I went from fish tanks to scuba tanks.

44. Eastern Supply & Belting Co.

After working in the downtown Boston leather factory long enough to learn sufficient English to pass his driving test and buy a car, my father decided he had to go into business -- not quite for himself, but with a partner. That was Mr. Hans Sachs, and later a Mr. Christman, who,

119

incidentally, was a Christian. In the proper old German fashion, my father would not be on a first-name basis with *Herr Sachs* and would always call Mister Christman that when talking about them and to their faces.

Mr. Christman -- I never knew his first name -- lived in Worcester, Mass., about an hour-and-a-half's drive north of Boston. By the way, that's pronounced "Wooster." I don't know how they first met or got to know each other, but the arrangement they made was 50/50. My father was a middle man, positioned between the manufacturers and the end users who in this case were textile, fabric, clothing, and apparel makers. The company's only product was leather machine belting. So it was called the Worcester Belting Co.

At that time leather was the material best suited for the belts used on sewing machinery. Leather was better than rubber or any artificial material. Much like an automobile's fan belt, belting had some give but not too much, yet was not brittle or easily broken. The quality of the leather used for belting varied widely.

Some of the leather for belting was imported. My father, who truly knew the quality of the leather he handled, felt that the imported goods were generally better than domestic leathers. But the imported raw material cost more: there were always import duties, taxes and shipping charges so that the American-made belting was invariably less expensive. That is why he carefully graded each spool, domestic and imported.

My father was also the "outside" man, the traveling salesman, who now drove himself, staying in cheap hotels. He left home every Monday and came home every weekend when his customers' businesses were closed. What Mr. Christman did as the inside man, other than store all the merchandise and ship it, I really don't know.

My father arranged that when he died my mother would continue the business with Mr. Christman. But Mr. Christman died suddenly, unexpectedly. So my father went into business for himself.

He called that company Eastern Supply & Belting Co. since by then he was also selling auxiliary materials for sewing machines, such as thread, needles, and blades. We rented space above some stores, near the post office, where we kept the merchandise.

Hans Friedman knew leather so well that his belting lasted longer than any competitors' and that saved his customers time, trouble, and money. The opening scene of the Broadway musical, *The Pajama Game*, which I saw with my parents, features a crisis in the apparel factory when the belting breaks.

My father had perfected his leather know-how. He hardly did more than touch the belting in a potential customer's machines to determine its quality. Then my father carefully selected each roll of belting to give his customers a better quality product than whatever they were using. He graded each spool to assign it his own quality designation.

The absolutely worst grade, he marked Grade A. He would tell a customer who he thought didn't know "the goods" that he was getting Grade A leather.

The next-best, but still not very good, was Grade AA. Then Grade AAA. Then A+, A++, A+++, AA+, AA++, and so on, up to AAA+++, a total of 12 grades. He credited his expertise on his having learned all about leather long before he joined Adler & Oppenheimer, during the apprenticeship his father had arranged for him.

With Mr. Christman gone, we, my parents and I, shipped everything by mail. Every Saturday morning we would go to the shop. My father selected the merchandise while I packed it into cardboard cartons. I had to judge the size of the box that an order would fit into and then package the belting spools, the thread cones, the needle and blade boxes into it, stuffing it with newspaper -- just enough but not too much to add expensive weight. Then we hand-carried the boxes to the post office. The highest compliment my father ever gave me, which he said quite often, was that I was a good packer.

My mother then typed the bills. Checks came in the mail. Rarely my father had to collect an overdue payment. If that happened often, my father dropped the customer.

We lived in Brighton, but my father drove to Western Massachusetts, lower Vermont and New Hampshire, upstate New York, Connecticut, and Pennsylvania to visit his customers. Textile businesses were then generally in the Northeast.

New York City was the center of the garment business, "the rag trade." My father had to buy all the merchandise he sold. So my father rented a room in an apartment in Manhattan from a family named

Marx. Hans H. Friedman did hardly any selling in New York -- there were many competitors there -- but it was a necessary stopover. His rented room, instead of an expensive hotel room, was on the road to elsewhere.

Eastern Supply & Belting Co. supplied shoe and garment factories. My father's unique expertise in leather helped him determine for the manufacturers exactly what belting they needed for their various sewing machines, what size, thickness, and quality. He did not talk much because, he wrote, "my English remains very poor; because I talk only German with my wife; I hardly understand anybody, including customers, and nobody understands me, but I do not complain a bit about my sales and my customers have always appreciated my correctness and honesty."

In the mid 1940's many textile manufacturers moved out of the Northeast to the Southern states like North Carolina because labor there was not unionized and therefore cheaper. In 2004, Southern states lost fabric and fashion factories to China and India because their laborers are much less expensive.

Our lives changed dramatically shortly after my *bar-mitzvah*. So it was that in September, 1947, after the summer at Camp Edgewood in Tannersville, N.Y., our family plus my newly arrived grandmother, my Oma, -- as well as the Eastern Supply & Belting Co. -- moved from Boston. His customers had moved south, so we moved south, but not all that far south! We moved to New York City, home of the hated Yankees.

45. U.S. Citizens

When my family became American citizens, on August 8, 1944, we dropped the final "n" from our last name. My mother became Lotte Rosalie Friedman, which is the way she was always known, although we found that her birth certificate gave her name as Rosalie Lotte Friedmann! My father added a middle name, Henry, because I was embarrassed by his all-too-German name, Hans. Thereafter he called himself H. H. Friedman. And I dropped the "h" off Eric. So I lost one and he gained one.

I legally became a citizen of the United States the same day that my parents did, when I was ten years old. But to obtain my own citizenship certificate, I had to appear before a magistrate when I was thirteen. I asked, "Daddy, what's a magistrate?" He didn't know.

I had to personally swear allegiance to my new country, repeating certain phrases after the magistrate. I denounced any allegiance to "any foreign king, queen, or potentate." I asked, "Daddy, what's a potentate?" He didn't know that either.

According to the official description of me at 13 years of age, I had a medium complexion, whatever that means, blue eyes, brown hair, and was 5 feet 1½ inches tall, weighed 103 pounds, and had no visible distinctive marks.

My photo, affixed to my citizenship certificate, shows a chubby-cheeked boy with close-cropped hair combed slightly down my forehead, wearing a white shirt, tie, and dark suit. I signed with my full new name, Walter Eric Friedman. My own citizenship certificate was issued July 24th, 1947, the 172nd year of my new country's independence.

Now my parents could vote in the 1944 presidential election. Indeed, my father took me to Fenway Park, the home of "my" Boston Red Sox, to see the president, Franklin Delano Roosevelt. He was running for a record-breaking fourth term. To check out the public address system, they normally say "testing 1, 2, 3," but this announcer said, "One, two, three, testing four." I understood my first political joke.

I remember F.D.R. being driven around the field, waving his hat and, I believe, he had his trademark cigarette holder clenched in his teeth. One did not see him get out of the car, nor view him lifted up to the large lectern that covered his crippled legs, but I did notice how he gripped both of the lectern's sides for support as he stood there, otherwise unaided, throughout his speech. Few people knew how crippled by polio he was. The president was fighting the Nazis in World War II, as I felt it, for our sake. Roosevelt was on "our" side so "we" were voting for him.

Living in Boston during that war, we participated in air raids. It was nothing like the real thing that was happening in England. Yet every block had an "air raid warden," who wore a helmet emblazoned with those words. He made sure every window was "blacked out" with dark shades. There never was an air raid on the U.S., but lots of practice alerts, with siren wails signaling "air raid" and siren beeps for "all clear."

We saved the tin foil from gum and cigarette packets, rolled it up into balls, and turned them in for the war effort. Red and blue "points" allowed one to buy meat and dairy products. Gasoline was rationed; each car had a sticker on it. My father's car was Class A, he could buy unlimited amounts as a traveling salesman. Class B or C cars were rationed as to how much they could buy.

My parents and I were truly thrilled to have become Americans. I remember wishing I were old enough to vote. Since I have been to so many different countries and fully recognize the different mind-sets and ways of thinking and beliefs of other people, I truly prize my U.S. citizenship and appreciate its unique value. Even though I disagree vehemently with our current president, George W. Bush, I am still proud and glad to be an American. It is vitally important to me.

46. Native-Born Americans

I was delighted to join all our relatives who are native-born American citizens. There are many. Let me start with my father's side of the family. My father's "Uncle Sam" (see Chapter 7) and his wife Jenny had three children, Ivy, Sidney and Annette. They're older than I am but my generation.

Ivy Friedman was born in 1897 in Amsterdam, NY. I remember visiting her and her husband Irv Rubin with my father on a business trip to Pennsylvania. Their children are Bernard, born in 1922 and known as Bud; Harry Theodore, known as Ted; and Annette Rubin.

Bud and his wife Helen lived in Newark, New Jersey. I met Bud and Helen at a memorable Thanksgiving dinner at their home in 1948 (see Chapter 52) before the birth of their first child. Jerryl was born in 1949, Kenneth in 1951, Sandy in 1952, and Mitchell on the last day of 1954. So he counted as a tax deduction for that entire year.

I last saw Bud in Palo Alto, California, in 2004. He's a dozen years older than I am and at 83 recently celebrated his "second bar mitzvah." His wife, Helen, was from Chicago. She retired as school psychologist for the San Jose system and passed away in 2000.

Irv and Ivy Rubin's other son, Harry Theodore Rubin has had a fascinating career. He was born in 1926 in Harrisburg, PA, and married Bunny Rosenthal. They were both ardent liberals who were very active politically. H. Ted Rubin, as he is known, became a Colorado State Representative, Denver Juvenile Court Judge, recognized expert on juvenile delinquency, and the author of significant books on teenage crime and its punishment. One of his titles is *Behind the Black Robes*, which sounds intriguing. Its subtitle reveals more: *Juvenile Court Justices and the Court*.

My father especially enjoyed political conversations with Ted. Later Betty and I did, too. He was always soft-spoken yet firm in his views; a good, kind, thoughtful man. Bunny, whom I knew less well, was also a particular delight to talk to.

Bunny and Ted had three children: Marjorie Joan Rubin, in January, 1955; Steven Douglas Rubin, in January, 1957; and Jefferson Darrow Rubin, in January, 1959. Notice the pattern here as well as the honorific names.

Steve is a photojournalist who was born in Denver but lives in Baltimore now.

Betty and I met young Jefferson when he was working for New York City's famed Metropolitan Museum of Art. He was a sculptor in his own right, but had trained in a highly specialized field and was working as the expert classical sculpture restorer, repairing valuable ancient Greek and Roman statues for the museum. He was obviously tremendously talented and skilled in a very esoteric and difficult profession. Unfortunately, he was killed in a truck accident in Colorado when he was only 36.

"Uncle Sam" and Jenny Friedman's son Sidney was born in 1896. He became a lawyer in Philadelphia and married Mary Clough. He died in January, 1966, in Harrisburg, PA.

Sam and Jenny's third child, Annette, was born in 1903. She married Lewis Isenberg, known as Lew, an automobile dealer who died in 1976. Annette died in Philadelphia in 2001. They had no children.

Uncle Sam was just the first of three siblings to come to America. So did his sister Rochel, who changed her name to Rachel in the U.S.A. She married Schlomo Fisher and they had four children: Bessy, Joseph,

Louis, and Albert. Of these my parents and I only met Joe and Lou, who lived on Long Island until Joe moved away. We also met Joe's daughter, Jewel. The Fishers were the orthodox branch of our family.

The youngest of Schlomo and Esther's children, Reuben, was born on September 9, 1877, in Schaki. Reuben also came to the U.S.A. via England. He was very athletic and ate meat three meals every day. He used to wash cocoa bags for the Hershey Chocolate Company, driving to Hershey from his home in Lancaster, PA, every day.

Reuben married "Eva" Solsky in 1920 in Middletown, PA. She was born in Lancaster, but when she started school she could not speak English. When the teacher asked her name, she answered "Rifka," which was the Hebrew version of Rebecca, her real name. The teacher thought she had said "Eva," so she became known as Eva.

She worked in her brother Benjamin's grocery store and had a heart attack and died when she was only 48. Eva and her husband, Reuben, who died in November, 1929, just before the stock market crash, are both buried in Lancaster. Their children, Esther and Stanley, started the Migdon and Wachtel lines.

A grandson of Rabbi Sam Friedman and son of Reuben and Eva Solsky Friedman, Stanley Friedman was very active in his beloved Temple Beth El in his birthplace, Lancaster, Pennsylvania. He was the president of the synagogue. And he had a dream: Stanley wanted to move Beth El from North Lime St. Because he was a real estate developer, he made his dream come true. He sold the building and relocated the temple to Rohrerstown Road. At the groundbreaking ceremony, Stanley was honored with digging the first shovelful of dirt. The lobby was named in his and his family's honor.

Born in 1923, Stanley was graduated from high school in 1941, the start of World War II. He enlisted in the army immediately and served as a bombardier/navigator. His plane was shot down and Stanley was listed as missing in action. Actually, he was forced to land in Sweden.

After the war, he started Keystone Aluminum Window Corporation, which he ran for many years. He was the first of three members of this family in that business. When fire destroyed the plant, he rebuilt at as a public storage warehouse.

Stanley was retired for all of two months when he earned his real estate license, first selling homes and later commercial properties as the co-owner of Crown Properties. He brought the first outlet development to Lancaster County. Today it's known as Tanger Outlet Center, one of a large multi-state chain. He also developed Regency Square and several other commercial venues. He and Faye were married for more than 57 years when he passed away at age 80.

The native-born Americans on my mother's side are the children of the Heinemans, Silversmiths, Klees, Zilkas, Marshalls and, of course, their grandchildren. I must also add the Altmans who are Canadians.

47. Herbie Comes to America

The son of my father's brother Paul, my first cousin Herbert Friedman, lived in London at the start of World War II. But when he heard that anyone coming to America and joining the U.S. Army would earn U.S. citizenship after his tour of duty, Herbie came to America. He visited us in Boston and then did a cross-country tour before volunteering for active duty. He got as far as California -- which he fell in love with instantly. He was inducted, and about four years later, discharged in California.

But he had to serve his time first. Having been born and lived in Germany, he spoke German perfectly, but as is the army's S.O.P. -- Standard Operating Procedure -- his language ability was not put to use. Instead, they gave him basic training and then signal training; he was put into the Signal Corps and sent to Alaska.

It is true that the closest U.S. territory to Japan was Alaska. (Both Alaska and Hawaii were not yet states at that time.) My "big cousin" -- Herbie was about 6'3" -- spent much of his time at the largest, furthest-away island in the Aleutian chain, Kodiak.

Afterward, he told me great stories of hunting the world's largest bear, the big brown Kodiak bear. (No, they are not Polar Bears.) Herbie's father Paul was a famed storyteller. I'm not sure how true some of Herbie's fantastic stories were that he told his awed little cousin; I recall that they scared me. There was something about a frozen rifle as a giant bear stalked him, but I don't remember any details any more. Herbie told me tales of what he had thought might be Japanese ships or planes on the horizon. But I know that there never was any real action on Kodiak..

When Herbie visited us in Boston in his army uniform I was very impressed. After the war he had lots of "hash marks" -- I think there was one for every six months he'd served and he was in for about four years -- plus "three up and three down" stripes that signified his rank of Master Sergeant. I was as proud of my big first cousin as I would have been of a big brother.

Herbie had set up a business office in New York City which I once visited by myself. I don't recall what Herbie did; all I know is that he was in the metal business as his father was. The office was in one of the taller skyscrapers and consisted of one room which Herbie and his secretary shared. A young teenager, I thought she was very pretty. I also remember that Herbie asked her to buy me an ice cream soda.

His office was in Manhattan but it was California that Herbie loved. He wrote to his family in England and spoke to them by phone about the wonders that the Golden State offered … and the golden business possibilities. It was the Land of Opportunity! Herbert convinced his sister and brother-in-law to come … not just across the pond but across the whole country. And to start a new life.

48. My Bar-Mitzvah

My father knew that cigarettes were really no good for you and he no longer smoked. In those days, however, the only admonition against smoking was that it would stunt your growth. Well, everyone knew that was a lie. My father proposed that if I not smoke at all on the day of my bar mitzvah, then I could have a giant party that weekend. I agreed. I deserved a great party after all the Hebrew I'd studied.

Always the stern taskmaster, my father had me rehearsing by repeating the passages endlessly, mostly with him saying, "again," every time I finished. "And again!"

Then, in March, 1947, my first cousins Walter and Hilde Levy with their 2-year-old daughter Evelyn, my father's brother Paul and my *Tante Thea*, as well as my Oma, all six of them, came to America from England. They sailed on the Queen Mary, the vessel that's now docked at Long Beach, California and we toured.

My cousin Herbert met his family in New York when they arrived. Then they all came to Boston -- as planned -- in perfect timing for my *bar-mitzvah*. Almost all the relatives on my mother's side of the family lived in the Boston area. Alfred and Denise Altman came from Canada. And we had lots of family friends, almost all refugees from Nazi Germany, at my bar mitzvah.

The big event was at Brookline's Temple Ohabei Shalom on March 29, 1947. I guess I did all right; I certainly had studied hard and long, more with my father than with the temple's new rabbi, Douglas Weinberg. (I never heard that rabbi's name again until, more than 50 years later when I attended Aviva Marshall's *bat-mitzvah* in Omaha! He and Rabbi Stern from Chappaqua were on the committee that wrote the prayer book.)

Both of my little cousins, Donald and Peter Silversmith, about four and two years old at my *bar-mitzvah*, were sent outside for making noise. They sat on the temple steps.

Everyone says I did a good job, never stumbling. But my granddaughter Sarah did an even better job. She actually chanted the Hebrew; I merely recited it, reading from the Torah the words I had rehearsed, but without any vowels. That's the way it is written.

It was the culmination of three or four years of studying Hebrew twice a week after school and at Sunday School. Now, my father said, "the Jews think you are a man, make your first grown-up decision: do you want to quit Hebrew School or continue?"

What an easy decision that was! As my father knew I would, I quit cold. He had wanted me to learn my heritage, my background, what my religion was all about. But he really did not want me to practice it any more than he, the confirmed atheist, did. Indeed, like my father, I am a Jewish atheist! Judaism is my cultural heritage but atheism is my firm conviction; I am sure that there is no god, no heaven, no afterlife.

The party that evening was truly a grand affair. My uncle Fred Silversmith, who had filmed me the day we left Germany (see Chapter 27) took movies, black-and-white of course, of all the people there which I have since transferred to VHS videotape for your viewing pleasure. They were all our relatives and friends, a very big group. Every time Walter and Hilde saw the camera (with its lights) coming, they kissed. So we have lots of pictures of them, always kissing. My father's brother Paul made up a short poem.

This was surely the biggest family party outside of Germany up to that time, until recent history. Because of those movies I can recall all the people who were there. In addition to the family there were members of the Immigrants' Mutual Aid Society (IMAS,) friends, neighbors, and Camp Edgewood campers and counselors. Together with the non-family people, it was a huge throng.

There was a band, of course, and at the appropriate moment, the band leader stopped the music to announce that the *bar-mitzvah* boy had not yet delivered his traditional speech. He said that we had waited until absolutely everyone the family had ever met was there. He gave a "settle back in your seats" kind of introduction. As planned, I then made my speech. Here it is, my entire oration:

"I want to thank you all for coming and hope you have a nice time."

I remember my little cousin Evelyn crawling around on the floor, her dress hiked up and her diapers showing. Perhaps she was talking, but she wasn't walking. At least, not on her own. Not in any of the movies.

A few days later we took movies of me, age 13 now, in my *tallis,* with all my *bar- mitzvah* presents around me. Boy, what a haul! I still have some of the books. I look very confident and self-satisfied in my first film appearance (now on VHS) as a man.

VI. THE NEW YORKERS
(1947 - 1953)

49. From Boston to New York

My father and his brother Paul decided that their stepmother, my Oma, Johanna Friedmann, would come to America and live with us. But our Brighton apartment was too small for four and, besides, my father's business trips took him further and further away from New England. He decided we would all move to New York City. Not that he had any customers there, but it was a much closer point from which to go to upstate New York, New Jersey and Pennsylvania, where his customers were.

After the big family event in Boston, the three Levys went on to California with Herbert. Paul and Thea went back to England. And we four, now including my Oma, moved to the home city of the "damn Yankees."

Her great friend Klara Caro said that my Oma, "had the great good fortune to be rescued and found in time for her grandson's bar-mitzvah. In the home of her children, whose crown she was, she found a home, a new life, and despite her years of horror, she found a life's work, taking part in her children's lives and she had the luck in her old age to help the growth and future of her grandson."

Because I came to know Klaerchen Caro, I believe that she felt she achieved something very important. She survived. She came out of the camp alive. That alone was her success story. Perhaps my Oma felt the same way.

I remember my Oma vividly from the time she was 77 and older: her dark-rimmed circular eyeglasses, her snow white hair up in a bun, her sweet, tender, caring smile. Always dressed in black, stressing her widowhood, she wore her black dresses with a white lace, doily-like collar. She was hunched over, even humpbacked, which made her seem even shorter than she was. She was truly short; I towered over her as a 13-year-old. I still remember her smile, her enduring and loving smile. She was such a warm-hearted person who really cared about me and truly loved me. And I loved her in return.

Every morning she got up, washed, got dressed, and prayed. Standing in her room, which was also our dining room, Oma recited her morning prayers to herself. I do not remember evening or any other prayer time for her; perhaps it was after my bedtime.

This deeply religious woman, now living with her stepson, the avowed atheist, kept her religion to herself, never discussing it with my father or me. She was proud of me, however, at my *bar-mitzvah*, and often praised me for it, even months after the fact. Perhaps she was subtly questioning my nonreligious lifestyle, but she never directly mentioned it. A very wise woman.

She lived with us in New York City's Washington Heights, in the area my father called superorthodox, at 44 Bennett Avenue, Apartment 4B. Right outside our windows the street was filled with religious Jews walking every *Shabbos* and Jewish holiday. But we never attended the local temple which was on the next block.

I learned a great deal from Oma, even if I didn't directly apply the life lessons I should have. Yet she took lessons from me! She learned baseball! I explained the rules and tried to convey my devotion to the Boston Red Sox, although what we watched together on television were the New York Yankee games. And she actually rooted for my beloved Bosox! Now, that's a loving grandmother.

I spent much more time in Yankee Stadium than I ever had in Fenway Park, but to this day I am still a Boston Red Sox fan; I simply could never transfer my allegiance to "the enemy." I used to sit with a few die-hard Red Sox fans in the center field bleachers in Yankee Stadium, yelling: "He's better than his brother Joe ... Dominic DiMaggio!"

I still have fond memories of Boston and I really loved all my years in St. Barths. I spent more time there than in Boston or New York. And those years in Westchester County during which I commuted to New York City add up to my spending more time in Manhattan than anywhere else. And I married a native-born New Yorker. So now I think of myself as a New Yorker. But when I first arrived from Boston, I felt out of place in New York City.

50. George Washington High

When my parents, my Oma, and I arrived in New York City we naturally moved to the German-Jewish section in uptown Manhattan called Washington Heights. The house was off 184th St., near an entrance to the A train's 181st St. subway station.

It was 44 Bennett Avenue, called Bennett Court on its front door, although we never called it that. Our Apartment 4B had two bedrooms and one bath off the entry, then a long hall that led to separate living and dining rooms and the kitchen. My bedroom was also the office from which all my father's business was conducted, with my mother acting as his secretary-typist. We also rented storage space on 168th Street for all the belting, thread and needles that Eastern Supply & Belting Company shipped to its customers.

Shortly after we moved in, directly from Camp Edgewood, Bernie Simon came to our door early one morning. He was the son of Eugene Simon, therefore not a blood relative, but a distant cousin of the "Shoe Store Simons" in my mother's family.

Bernie came to show me the way to my new high school. It turned out to be a long walk to 190th St. and Broadway, where we entered a

3-block-long tunnel built in 1913 that led to elevators going up an 18-story hill to 190th St. and St. Nicholas Ave. It was really a subway stop's elevator that we took without taking the subway. Then we walked a few more blocks to 193rd and Audubon Ave., the site of the George Washington High School.

GWHS put its students on one of three tiers: academic, commercial, or general. I was in the headed-for-college category before I ever thought about it.

School was where I made most of my friends. We played baseball on the field where the New York Giants' shortstop Buddy Kerr had played, where the future Pittsburgh Pirate Arnie Portocarero was then pitching, and where the Red Sox's Manny Ramirez later set the all-time record for high school batting average -- over .600! More important to me at the time was the story that the movie star Paulette Goddard had gone to GW and had been raped by a teacher in the tower. Who knows how true that was?

Betty Klein actually was three years behind me in the same high school but we never met in the one year when I was a senior and she was a freshman.

Early on I met Mark Jaffe, whose real name is Mordechai Jacob Jaffe. We became best friends and often spent time at each others' homes, though we were most often at his apartment. His mother was a single mother and his grandmother lived with them as my Oma lived with us.

Mark was in the group of us guys -- Roger S. Jones, Tony Blandi, Bill "Bones" Bernstein, Warren Weinstein, the twins Armand ("the smart one") and Leon ("the cute one") Diaz, a few others. Most often we met after school to play baseball and again in the evening, after supper at home, on the street corner of 181st and Broadway, outside the subway entrance, where, downstairs, Falcaro's Bowling Alley had a bar attached. We bowled rarely; but often sat in the bar and talked for hours. I am sure the legal drinking age in New York at that time was 18 and we were 16 at first. There was no Army draft then, so no-one had any official card as proof of his or her age. We didn't have enough money to go to a bar very often. At times we drank in other bars; the Audubon was one. We usually just had a beer or two but when we ordered "hard liquor" it was "7 and 7" -- Seven Crown whiskey and 7-Up.

Often we went to the movies. A few times we went to a baseball game at Yankee Stadium, especially when the Boston Red Sox were in town. Rarely we'd go to the Polo Grounds where the New York Giants played before they moved to San Francisco. We usually only went there when they played the Brooklyn Dodgers.

Sometimes we'd take a bus and go to the burlesque show across the Hudson River in Union City, New Jersey. I recall the acts -- comedians and strippers and, best of all, the girls on the occasional "amateur nights." When they twirled their tassels -- wow!!

We occasionally played hooky from school and went to the Coliseum Movie Theater at 181st and Broadway. I wonder what a truant officer thought when so many of us were out on the day that a highly-heralded movie opened.

I also had my first after-school job at that time, delivering (and picking up) laundry for a Chinese laundry. I earned ten cents a bundle, that is, a dime for bringing the neatly wrapped, cleaned and pressed laundry package to someone and also schlepping back their bag of dirty laundry -- but nothing at all when nobody was home and I carried the package both ways. That job ended when I got chicken pox and couldn't work.

My next job was delivering much smaller packages for much more money: I worked for the corner drug store, Wadsworth Ethical Pharmacy, at 181st St. and Bennett Ave., delivering medicines and earning sixty cents an hour, plus tips. I was paid even when there was nothing to deliver and I just hung around, dusting off the shelves. I remember one time watching my watch as it ticked off a minute and I had earned a penny for doing nothing at all.

Then there was a summer job one year. Many of my friends and I went to work for Montgomery Ward's in downtown Manhattan, we called it "Monkey Ward's," in their mail-order shipping center. My boss was Jack Sharkey and every morning he clocked in and took his *New York Times* into the bathroom for at least an hour. I learned something that stood me in good stead later.

Everyone in the New York City school system had to take and pass P.T. -- physical training. One of the tests was that one had to swim the length of the pool. I had learned to swim in Camp Edgewood so I did that easily. But a friend of mine, Bernie Friedman, another unrelated

134

Friedman, just could not swim. So I took his test for him when they called out, "Friedman," and of course he passed, sort of.

There was a more significant test that I recall from high school. We had to pass the N.Y. State Regents Exam, the same test given on the same day, statewide. Everyone in every high school studied for it by going over previous years' tests.

Some time after the Regents, we had our chemistry final exam scheduled for the next day and someone managed to get a copy of the test the day before. Copies were secretly handed out to all the guys in our group, and others, and so that was what I studied. I doubted that it was the actual test but rather thought that it, like those pre-Regents tests, might be an excellent preparation for the real exam. So I got a copy.

Mark Jaffe was planning on becoming a scientist, which he did become. Scientific accuracy and honesty was very important to him. So he alone refused to even look at "tomorrow's" chemistry test. I was somewhat surprised when it did, indeed, turn out to be the real test. But, later, not surprised that most of the class got A's on it. Mark Jaffe did not do as well and so did not get, as I did, an A as his final chemistry grade.

All of the guys graduated from GW together and most of us went to City College uptown. And we all still met "at Falcaro's," that is, on the street corner above the bowling alley-bar-subway stop. A few girls who also graduated from GW "hung around" with us guys: Brenda Saunders, Louise Gross, and others. Brenda was then Mark Jaffe's girlfriend (although they both married other people). Louise, however, married Roger S. Jones, who later became an atomic physicist.

Roger was doing well -- until the end of the Cold War also ended his job at the famed Brookhaven Lab. I never thought I'd find a guy named Jones on the Internet, but I did! So I now know that he retired as a physics professor at the University of Minnesota.

51. How Israel Was Created

He would never have put it that way; in fact, he declined any publicity on the subject. But if it weren't for my *Onkel Paul,* my father's brother, the state of Israel would not exist!

135

It was toward the end of November, 1947, that the United Nations was debating the possible partition of Palestine into Jewish and Arab sectors. The U.N. General Assembly determined that it would take a two-thirds affirmative vote to achieve partition. After much debate, it was obvious that it would be a very close vote, and it looked like the pro-partition nations would be two or three votes short of a 2/3 majority!

Paul Friedman had been in the metal business all his life. He even taught his son Herbert the business. Herbie was now a veteran who had earned his stripes as a Master Sergeant in the U.S. Army. World War II had left many guns, tanks, planes, and equipment made of various metals starting to rot in far-flung corners of the globe. The American administration sought to sell this scrap metal to legitimate buyers. Paul and Herbert saw this as a business opportunity. They traveled together to sell the stuff.

One of the best customers they developed for this scrap metal was the government of the newly independent Philippine Islands, a staunch ally in the war. The Philippines' first president was Manuel Roxas who designated his secretary of state and vice-president, Elpidio Quirino, to negotiate for the metal they wanted. (Quirino later became the Philippines' second president.)

The following are translated excerpts from a letter that Paul wrote in German to his family in England, dated December 1, 1947, on Hotel Manila stationery:

"…This letter will contain such a unique and enjoyable message that surpasses in significance all business or personal affairs of our nearest family. A significance for the Jewish world and the entire world which cannot yet be fully measured even: the acceptance of the partition of Palestine and the establishment of a Jewish state…[which] stood on the razor's edge and grotesquely the decisive vote is the vote of the Philippines.

"And now listen and marvel how a Friedman helped to achieve this wonderful result."

Paul and Herbert were in Manila, negotiating with Vice President Quirino about the scrap metal. They had read in the newspaper about the back-and-forth, yes-and-no and possible postponement of the "Palestine Question" until next year, *"but when we read that the Philippines had spoken sharply against partition, we were very depressed.*

"While Herbert and I were having breakfast Friday morning, Rabbi Schwarz and Dr. Schalscha came, and said they could not sleep since the

136

previous night's radio broadcast, and they had been thinking if among the 18 million Filipinos or among the 600 Jews there was not one man who knew a high minister personally well enough to dare to go to him and beg for our people."

They all realized that personal influence is crucial in the Philippines. And they figured that if the Philippines would abstain the necessary 2/3 majority could happen!

Paul reported, *"I said yes without hesitance.*

"Yes! I shall go to Quirino!"

Paul knew that President Roxas was out of the country and the acting president, Quirino, was in town. He also knew that in the Philippines, unlike in the United States, whenever the president is out of the country, the vice-president is temporarily in complete control. And their country's representative in the United Nations at that time, General Carlos Romulo, who was personally opposed to the partition of Palestine, had previously been told by President Roxas to vote his conscience. Romulo was determined to vote against partition and another country had agreed to go along with his vote in exchange for the Philippines' vote on an issue they cared more about. But I do not know the exact trade-offs of votes that were bargained one way or the other, or which country it was.

Paul told Herbert and the two gentlemen that he would tell Quirino, *"if you cannot say yes that the Jews want to have a homeland after two thousand years, then at least don't vote against it!"*

In his letter Paul reported that he went to the Presidential Palace and had to wait for a long time but was finally received in audience. *"I really felt like Esther or Mordechai going to King Ahasverus to beg for a mitigating verdict!"*

Someone else was in the room so Paul started quietly telling Quirino that he wanted to speak to him personally, that he had not come for business affairs. Paul was so bold, so courageous, he reported, because Quirino had given him a picture of himself with the inscription, 'in friendship.'

"I told him that I had read that morning Romulo's report and in as much as his vote is decisive for the 2/3 majority, I had come to ask him if he found it impossible to say yes - at least to abstain.

"Then he said something about Romulo and took the newspaper and read every word as if he read it for the first time."

The Vice President then asked Paul if he was for partition. When Paul replied, "Yes, sir," Quirino immediately left the room.

When he returned Paul said to him, *"You, as a good Christian, and I as a Jew, particularly in the Philippines…know best what independence and liberty mean. I felt like the biblical Esther talking to the Persian King -- Trees will be planted in your name, sir! -- destiny has brought us together this time.*

"He rang a bell and had the text of a cable read to him which he had composed and then he read every word to me. After a short introduction, it read: If your voice is decisive, abstain from voting and discuss matters with American committee members to insure cooperation. The introduction said somewhat this: instructions are given here on how to vote on said question.

"When he read the words, 'to abstain form voting,' I stood up and kissed him on the forehead [a Philippine custom among friends] *and said, 'God bless you!'*

"Then he asked once more his private secretary to make sure this goes 'rush.' <u>Only on account of a difference of a day in time was all this possible.</u>"

The International Dateline made all the difference! The Philippine Islands were a day ahead of the U.N. in New York.

When Paul was about to leave the Palace and say goodbye,*"Quirino said to me: Is this your only mission today? And again I answered, 'Yes, sir. God bless you!'"*

Rabbi Schwarz, Dr. Schalscha and Herbert were waiting anxiously in the lobby of the hotel for Paul's return. *"I waved them with a newspaper and from my happy face they could read my immense success."*

I must explain that the then U.N. Representative Romulo was so anti-Jewish, so pro-Arab, that he refused to obey Quirino's orders and angrily stormed out, leaving his deputy to vote as he was instructed. Because Romulo had previously arranged for another country to follow the Philippines' lead and vote as they voted, Paul Friedman's action caused two anti-partition votes to vote for it instead! On November 29, 1947, the United Nations voted in favor of partitioning Palestine -- it passed by two votes!

Paul Friedman's letter to Thea and Hilde and Walter Levy concludes:

138

"The result will be a blessing for the whole world and the Philippines and for our Jewish people…I want no publicity for many reasons, at least not now. I don't want to be too modest: I only want to say that I believe, even if and how my audience influenced the position the P.I. Government took, it is to Rabbi Schwarz's and Dr. Schalscha's credit to have awakened me to take this step.

"And whatever the results of this journey may be, we Friedman-Levys are convinced it will remain unforgettable for us and for our children and children's children's destiny!"

On May 20, 1973, my father, Hans Friedman, wrote a confirmation of this story. "A month ago, IMAS [the Immigrants' Mutual Aid Society, which my parents had helped found in Boston] held their 35th anniversary party and we were among the 200 people invited to attend. Naturally, we were delighted to see so many of our old friends."

He explained that the festivities started with the introduction of the honored guests. "The first to be greeted was the chairman of the organization of Jews in Europe, the second was Mr. and Mrs. H. H. Friedman from New York, and third, the vice-consul of Israel, in that order.

"During the meal … the president of the *Chevrah* asked about me … so I went to [the head table] to speak with him. The man seated next to him mentioned something about 'Manila' and then rose to speak with me. It was the Israeli vice-consul.

"I immediately said to him, 'You mentioned Manila. Let me tell you a story which comes to mind.' My father then told the story detailed above.

"When I finished telling the Israeli vice-consul the story, he said, 'I know it; I have heard this story <u>so</u> often. Many, many times. One of the Jewish men who called upon your brother in Manila was my father-in-law!'"

We just do not know if he was Rabbi Schwarz or Dr. Schalscha!

It is ironic that my father, the disillusioned Zionist, was undoubtedly proud of his brother's role in the creation of Israel.

Another coda to this story comes from page 183 of the novel *Exodus*, in which Leon Uris wrote of the Philippines being called upon to vote in the United Nations on November 29, 1947: "For a breathless second the world stood still. Romulo had been called away from Flushing Meadow. The alternate stood up. 'The Philippines votes <u>for</u> partition!'

"A roar went up! The members of the Jewish delegation looked to each other with dazed expressions. 'Dear God,' said Barak, 'I think we have made it!'"

My Uncle Paul's daughter-in-law, Inge Friedman, gave me a signed, bound, first-edition copy of David Ben Gurion's memoir, *Israel: A Personal History*. The day after Ben Gurion read the Declaration of Independence establishing the state named Israel, U.S. President Harry S Truman gave the new country diplomatic recognition.

Finally, Paul's story was told in the Israeli historical records kept, I believe, in the Jewish Museum in Jerusalem. Originally it said that a British-Jewish businessman had called upon Vice-President Quirino to persuade him to change the Philippines' vote. When he read that, Paul Friedman persuaded the authorities to put his name into the official Israeli record. And so it is. He is duly credited with helping to create Israel.

52. Thanksgiving, 1948

It was Thanksgiving, 1948, and my parents and I were visiting my father's cousins, Bud and Helen Rubin, in their Newark, N.J., home. She was pregnant with Jerryl Lynn at the time. Helen had prepared a real old-fashioned, authentic Thanksgiving dinner as a mid-afternoon meal. We were eagerly awaiting the feast. The Rubins were real Americans, having been born here, unlike us.

I had learned about Pilgrims and Thanksgiving, a local event in Boston; my mother had even served turkey, a strange bird to Europeans, at past meals. However, she was never a cook and she certainly didn't know anything about "all the trimmings."

But Helen surely did! I vividly recall the sweet potatoes with melted marshmallows on top! Wow, what a treat for a 14-year-old boy! Marshmallows were like candy. I had only known them to be toasted (and usually burned) over a campfire. And the sweet potatoes were really sweet. They may have been yams -- whatever the difference was, I surely didn't know. And my parents didn't know, either.

At first we only ate the appetizers; the big, main meal was to come later. It was to be a late afternoon dinner. Anyway, we had to wait for one more guest to arrive, my big first cousin, my father's brother

Paul's son, Herbert Friedman. At this time his office was in midtown Manhattan and he lived elsewhere in New York City. But now we had to wait; he was late. Very late. He didn't come and didn't call. So we were all beginning to get worried.

Finally, the telephone rang and Helen answered it. It was Herbie. He had a bad cold, she reported, had drunk some Scotch as medicine, fallen asleep, and only now awakened. But, we shouldn't worry, he would be right there.

Naturally we waited for him. Helen reheated whatever needed reheating and refrigerated the rest. She served more appetizers. And we all talked about this fantastic idea of treating a cold with Scotch! Who had ever heard of such a thing? I certainly hadn't. My parents also hadn't. And "the real Americans," Bud and Helen, also had never heard of this treatment.

We waited. And waited. And waited some more. We theorized about traffic on Thanksgiving. Then we began to get really worried. Helen, ever understanding and cheerful, said that Thanksgiving dinner could be eaten anytime. It was, in fact, almost dinner time!

Finally, the front doorbell rang and there was my big, tall 6'3" cousin Herbie ... and a short woman! (Well, next to him, everyone was short. But she seemed *very* short to me.) She was introduced as Inge Fridberg, his fiancée.

Wow! The whole story of the cold and the Scotch was a "cover story" -- the truth was, her airplane from Los Angeles was late getting to what was then called Idlewild Airport, today's JFK. Herbert wanted to introduce his future bride to the family -- the New York family -- the only family he had in America that did not know her.

And she turned out to be a fascinating and charming woman even though she had not had an easy life. But that's another story -- starting with the next chapter.

Herbert and Inge were married soon after that memorable Thanksgiving.

53. From Fridberg to Friedman

Ingeborg Ursula Fridberg, who was always called Inge, was born April 4, 1919 in Berlin. Her father, Emil, was a dentist with his practice in their home. Her mother, Elly, whom she always called *Mutti,* supervised the live-in staff: a cook, maid, nurse, and children's nurse. Inge and her parents, as well as Inge's two older brothers, Horst and Klaus, lived on *Koepenickestrasse* in Berlin, in the area which later became East Berlin.

By coincidence, *Obercantor* Aron and Hulda Friedmann and their children -- including Inge's future father-in-law, my father's brother Paul -- also lived on *Koepenickestrasse* at that time! But they lived on opposite ends of that street.

Although her family was not religious, Inge remembers going to the temple on *Oranienbergerstrasse* for the High Holidays. She recalled that Leo Baeck was a rabbi there but doesn't remember any cantor. Cantor Aron Friedmann officiated there every third year, so she probably saw and heard him.

Her parents loved music; her mother sang in a choir (could it have been at that temple?) and played the piano and flute. Inge played the cello and always took it with her. Years later in the U.S., she won awards as a cellist.

Inge went to school in Berlin and remembers that the schoolteachers became more and more Nazified. Jewish children were first teased by the teachers as well as the children, then picked on mercilessly, and finally were made to feel unwanted. They were told to get out of regular school and attend Jewish school.

Her parents divorced and each remarried. The boys stayed with their father, Inge with her mother and stepfather, Hermann Militscher, whom Inge called *Oncle Hermann* and with whom she never got along.

In 1933, Inge's father, Emil, whom she dearly loved, decided to keep his sons at home but to send her to Catholic boarding schools, first to France, then to Switzerland, and finally, when she was 14, to Hastings, England. He sent her money regularly.

She would come home to Berlin on vacation. She was there in 1936 for the Berlin Olympics and her father took her to see the competition and Adolf Hitler. But, in 1939, when she went to Germany from school in England, she was arrested by the Gestapo and taken to the police station. She was 19.

She did not know it, but her father was also arrested that same day. One thing they wanted to know about was the money he had sent her. It was 55 pounds sterling.

The cruel Gestapo man questioning her father told him that they had arrested Inge. Emil was tortured as only the Gestapo know how to do. Because of that, as well as the heat, he started sweating profusely. So he asked that a window be opened. And he jumped out to his death!

Inge discovered the horrendous news as soon as she was released. Now she felt truly deprived as well as horrified. She had loved her father very much. Emil Fridberg was buried in Berlin's Weissensee Jewish Cemetery.

Inge and her mother were both devastated. They left Germany together and went to London. There Inge finished her training as a baby nurse and took that up, staying with each family. Because she was given room and board, she was paid only one pound sterling per week. Yet even with such little income and not much time off, Inge Fridberg managed to attend a sewing class. It was at that class that she met another student, Hilde Friedmann, her future sister-in-law.

When the *blitzkreig,* the bombing raids of World War II, rained devastation onto London, Inge decided it was time to move on. She took a job taking care of two old ladies and escorted them to Quito, Ecuador. They took a small steamer to Rio de Janeiro, Brazil. Inge had only ten pounds sterling, which she thought was a lot of money.

It was a rough crossing that took four weeks from Southampton to Buenos Aires, Brazil, and was especially difficult for the elderly ladies in her care. When they got there, they found that the train to Quito was not leaving for a week.

Inge could not afford food or shelter. But she found them places to eat and to stay by looking up Jewish names in the phone book and asking for help. She learned a life lesson: that whenever you are in trouble, find a Jew. One Jew will always help another.

They borrowed the trainfare and the train took a long time to get from the seacoast up the Andes Mountains. They arrived with no money left.

Inge immediately took on a job as a baby nurse in the home of the owner of Ecuador's biggest, most popular, fashionable nightclub. The owner, Mischa Saslovski, became fabulously wealthy.

Young and attractive, Inge Fridberg ended up marrying her boss and became Mrs. Mischa Saslovski. They were rich, celebrated, in high society. Inge arranged for her mother and her stepfather, *Onkel Hermann,* to come to Quito. She felt herself a million miles away from the Gestapo. Her life was starting over.

But her happiness was cut short when she realized that Mischa had become a drug addict. After surviving and escaping the horrors of Nazi Germany, Inge's husband's addiction was her latest shock.

And then an overdose killed him! She had lost her father and her husband! The death of both men who meant so much to her was almost too much to bear.

Now she was a young widow. She felt alone, even when she was with her loving mother. Like the biblical Job, she told me, she thought "why me?"

Meanwhile, her two brothers had moved to California and changed their names from Horst and Klaus to Harry and Charley. So Inge decided to leave Ecuador and also begin a new life in the U.S.A.

Harry filled out an affidavit, declaring that he had one thousand dollars to support his sister, if necessary. Inge thought that he must be very rich -- a thousand dollars seemed a great fortune! But when she arrived at Los Angeles airport and her brothers took her to their car, the rundown jalopy showed her that they were not rich. That is when she learned they had borrowed the money for the affidavit.

Inge resumed her maiden name and her career as a baby nurse. As soon as she could, she brought her *Mutti* and *Onkel Hermann* to the U.S. One day she went to an affair at a local temple to meet some Jewish people. To her surprise, a woman there walked up to her and said, "I know you!"

It was Hilde Friedman, now Levy, from the old London sewing class! She invited Inge to her home. There she met Hilde's husband, Walter, and their daughters, Evelyn and DeeDee, who spoke reverentially of their Uncle Herbie in New York City.

Inge and Hilde got together a few times, and there was often talk of Uncle Herbie, who had always given his little nieces presents. Inge still remembers how glowingly they always spoke of their uncle.

One day she met the living legend. And "Uncle Herbie" asked her out on a date! Then he flew back to New York. The next time he came to L.A., another date. And back to N.Y.C. On their third date -- Inge swears it was the third date -- he asked her to marry him! Then he flew back to New York. It was 1948, shortly before Thanksgiving.

That holiday is when my parents and I met Inge. My first cousin Herbie and Inge got married soon thereafter, changing her name from Fridberg to Friedman.

But there is much more to Inge's story. Her future, like her past, seems too unbelievable to be true. It's almost a soap opera.

So this is a cliff-hanger, to be continued.

54. Other Summer Camps

When I was 15 and no longer eligible for Camp Edgewood but ready to spend the summer away from my mother, I went to a work camp. We had construction projects. Among other things, we built a cement sidewalk. I did it but didn't enjoy it. In fact, I had a minor accident with the teeth or gear of a cement mixer which left a small scar on the first finger of my left hand. Little did I know that I would, in the distant future, build another cement sidewalk, terrace a landscape, and create rock walls.

The next year, at 16, I had grown up enough to become a waiter in an all-girls' camp! At the interview I assured the owners that I would indeed dance with the girls. That part was easy and I enjoyed that summer though my boss, the cook, was Chinese and he worked us, as we put it, like coolie laborers. We had to clean up the mess hall after each meal and scrub the floor once a week.

The summer of 1951, when I was 17, I was a C.I.T., a counselor-in-training, at a children's camp called Farm Camp Loewy. It was a real, working farm, owned by German-Jewish immigrants. Mr. Loewy had virtually nothing to do with the camp but welcomed anyone who would do farm work. Mrs. Loewy, like my mother, had been educated as a kindergarten teacher and spent her summers running a camp. My mother knew her and got me the job.

Farm Camp Loewy was "upstate" in Windsor, NY. It was bigger than Camp Edgewood and was divided into a boy's camp and a girl's camp. And it had two C.I.T.'s; I was the one for the boys and Susie Fels was the girl's C.I.T. I was seventeen, she was probably sixteen. A well-developed 16-year-old.

Whatever my duties with the boys were, and I had many, what interested this city boy was farming. I learned to saddle and ride a horse, do "cow chasing," that is, getting more than 40 cows into the barn at milking times. I put on the milking machines, one metal thingamajig onto each of the four teats a cow has on her udder. And I "stripped" the cows, hand-milking the last of the milk that the machine couldn't quite get from each cow. I squatted on a stool, studiously avoiding not just her swishing tail but also the cow's excrement. I guess I learned about bullshit then and perhaps it prepared me for the advertising business. Of course I also had to clean out the barn, pitchforking hay and straw as well as shoveling and sweeping the whole barn. Farming also involved feeding chickens and slopping pigs. The camp was kosher but the farm wasn't.

I detail all this to say that after a day of swimming in the nearby lake and various sports activities with the boys, I usually did some farm chores and ended up pretty tired, beat, exhausted every evening.

Nevertheless, on one of those evenings, I managed to entice Susie into the barn and even up onto the hayloft. We started to "make out," as one said then. But I fell asleep on top of Susie! Poor girl, she didn't know what to do. I think she fell asleep, too!

I always think of the song, "Wake up, Little Susie," when I tell this story:

"Wake up Little Susie, wake up;
"Wake up Little Susie, wake up.
"We've both been sound asleep;
"Wake up Little Susie, and weep.
"The movie's over, it's four o'clock,
"And we're in trouble deep."

We both could have been in deep trouble. I acted confident and told her not to worry and not to tell anyone anything.

She was worried but we didn't tell anyone and nobody ever found out about it.

Not long afterward, Farm Camp Lowey ended because summer was over. Like any normal 17-year-old boy, I asked for Susie's address and phone number in Manhattan and promised to call her when I got home.

But I never did.

So I was truly surprised when I did see her again!

55. California, Here I Come!

Now I was 18 and a high school graduate. I had passed the test and gotten my New York State driver's license. And my big cousins, Herbie and Inge Friedman, the former Master Sergeant and his wife whose father had jumped out of the window and whose first husband had died in Ecuador, invited me to come to Los Angeles for the summer. Alone! Wow, I was all grown up. A real adult. I was going to fly cross-country by myself. And be far from home. I would be staying at my cousins' house, of course, but ... California, here I come!

They had two children at that time. Michael was two years old and Paul Robert Friedman, named for his late grandfather, my father's brother Paul, was really a baby, just learning his first words. There was a TV show with a character named Beanie at that time. When he saw him, Paul said, "Beanie," one of his first words, proudly. One day soon thereafter, baby Paul was watching that program and his mother, Inge, put a beanie on his head, a cap with a propeller on top. When his father saw him there, he said, "that's my little Beanie!" The nickname stuck and Paul was called Beanie for a long time thereafter. I still call him that at times and he's in his mid-forties now!

At that time, my first visit to California, I slept on a bed in Paul's room. He was in a crib. On the night of July 21st, 1952, at exactly 3:52 AM, I was rudely awakened by the banging noise of the window shutter outside our room. The room, the whole house, was shaking. The baby did not wake up; he was probably used to being rocked. But I was shocked, rocked and mentally blocked, because I didn't immediately realize it was an earthquake. I didn't get up, nor did anyone else in the house. They slept right through it.

The next morning we found out that it was indeed a very strong earthquake. (The Richter Scale was not yet in use.) It was called the Tehachapi Quake, after the town southeast of Bakersfield, California, that was at its epicenter. Fourteen people were killed, at least 53 seriously injured, and the damage in the area exceeded $70 million! It was one of the worst quakes up to that time.

I had my driver's license and eagerly wanted to drive Herbie's car; wise man, he never let me. I went to a few tourist sites all by myself or with rides from friends and family and I even used some public transportation in L.A.. I visited the La Brea Tar Pits and Grauman's Chinese Theater with its famed Walk of Fame where movie stars' hand- and footprints are in the sidewalk. I gawked at them, opened a side door with curiosity, and walked inside the architecturally interesting pseudo-Oriental building. It was only when I got inside that I realized that Grauman's Chinese Theater was actually a movie theater. I sat down and watched the show, never having noticed a box office or ticket-taker.

Herbie went to work and Inge and I stayed home with the children. I remember taking a shower one day while she made breakfast. She got annoyed because I took so long and the eggs were getting cold. Inge was never reluctant to speak her mind.

One day, my loving cousin Inge suggested I get a job. So I applied for, and took a test for, a local civil-service job. In the meantime, my helpful cousins got a job for me.

It was for a friend of theirs, another German-Jewish refugee, named Rudy Bruch; he was a gardener. Actually, he was the boss of a company that hired Mexicans as gardeners and he was willing to put me on one of their crews. So I helped mow lawns in L.A. and plant flowers and trim bushes and water gardens. Rudy had a long list of customers and we would go from one to the next, in a sequence he set up, spending an hour at each one. I was picked up early every morning by a truck full of Mexicans and I worked alongside them. I had had three years of Spanish in high school and we managed to communicate very nicely.

My cousin Inge arranged that I would house-sit for a friend of theirs while they went on vacation. So I did that. My only instruction was to turn on the automatic sprinkler system early every morning, when I got up, and turn it off before I left for work.

One day I got up late, turned on the sprinklers, and then the Mexican truck came for me and I had to hurry, momentarily forgetting about the sprinklers. I worried all day. I had a watch and I think none of the Mexicans did. So they asked me to keep the time; they were to spend one hour at each job. I was worried about the sprinklers flooding the garden I was responsible for, so I short-timed every hour by five minutes. I was trying to get back to that house as quickly as I could. When I got there, I saw that a neighbor had turned off the sprinklers. I was saved!

After my house-sitting, instead of my moving back to Herbert and Inge's, they suggested that, since I was now working and earning money, perhaps I could rent a room somewhere. They were even kind enough to find a newspaper ad for me to answer. A nice little old Italian lady had a back room with its own entrance and bathroom that she rented to me. But she warned me clearly, "No bring-a de girl-a!" I didn't.

Of course I also spent a great deal of time with my other cousins, Walter and Hilde Levy. They lived in the San Fernando Valley, at 2222 South Bentley Avenue. A memorable address -- I remember it to this day.

By this time their daughter Evelyn, who had been in diapers and crawling at the time of my *bar-mitzvah* four years earlier, was already six years old. Her baby sister, Diane, known as Dee-Dee because that was how Evelyn first pronounced her name, was less than a year old.

One day we were riding in Hilde's car; she was driving. I think her mother, my *Tante Thea,* was next to her and we children were in the back seat, left to right, Evelyn, me, and Dee-Dee. We were on the extreme right lane (thank goodness!) of a freeway when, suddenly, the right rear door opened and Dee-Dee fell out of the car!

It was the biggest shock of my life! And hers. I did manage to grab onto a part of her clothing which probably softened her fall.

I also shouted something so that Hilde immediately stopped the car on the freeway shoulder, got out, and picked up her crying baby. Thankfully, little Dee-Dee's tears were due to shock. There wasn't a scratch on her!

Hilde got back into the driver's seat but we did not move for quite a while. Her heart had to resume normal beating. There were no safety locks on car doors then and accidents like this one were the reason they were created. That was the biggest adventure, the greatest excitement, of my first trip to L.A!

Of course it is something we, Dee-Dee, Evelyn, and I, still talk about whenever we get together. However, now that "little Dee-Dee" is married and has children and grandchildren of her own, Diane Levy Dorney has shortened her nickname to Dee.

Here's another interesting tid-bit: many, many years later, my kid cousin (on my father's side) Paul Robert Friedman, dated my kid cousin (on my mother's side) Annette Zilka! He remembers that he liked her a lot. I informed him that she is married and has twins!

56. CCNY, Uptown

I had been in the academic program in high school. All of my friends were planning on going to college. But my parents and I knew nothing of the prestige of particular universities. Nobody told us that which college one went to mattered for the rest of one's career. That it would be in college that one made future business connections and friends for life.

No one we knew had gone to college. Everyone in our circle was either a refugee from Germany or my own age. Although my folks didn't understand the true importance of a college education, they certainly wanted me to go "to further my education."

There was no thought given to my going out of town; if I went to college, I would live at home. There were good colleges in commuting distance. College is expensive, we reasoned, why pay room and board, too?

Which college? That decision was easy. Columbia was very expensive. If I went to any college, it would be New York University or the City College of New York. I applied to both NYU and CCNY.

NYU accepted me on my high school record but City said I had to pass a test first. NYU cost $40 a credit but CCNY was free -- if I passed their test. I did. (Betty's grades got her into City without having to take the test. But we hadn't met yet.)

The year was 1952. I was 18 and registered for the draft. The Korean War was on and every male had to register. I would get a deferment if I was a college student.

So I started college that September in "Uptown City" which was downtown from our home. CCNY was known academically as one of the best colleges in the country at that time. The uptown campus was around 135th St. and I took the Broadway bus, getting on at 181st St.

I gave Colin Powell, who became a 4-star General, Chairman of the Joint Chiefs of Staff, and Secretary of State, his first marching orders! In our first semester at City College, he and I joined the ROTC, the Reserve Officers Training Corps, at the same time. Someone in charge asked the milling group of freshman if anyone had had any military training. Those who had all knew enough not to volunteer.

Then we were asked if any of us had been Boy Scouts. Not knowing better, I raised my hand. I was given temporary Corporal stripes on an arm band and told to march this half of the group from here to there. In my group were the only three black men there. I yelled, "Group, Attention! Right Face! Forward March! Group Halt!"

Those were his first marching orders. Colin Powell later described his ROTC days at City College as one of the happiest experiences of his life: finding something he loved and could do well, he had "found himself.".

While I was at Uptown City, I also worked late afternoons, evenings, and weekends behind the candy and popcorn counter at the Loews' Theater on 175th St. and Broadway, working for the Peoples Candy Co. I ate about as much candy as I sold. And saw lots of movies.

As a freshman I did not have to declare a major and I wasn't sure what to major in. Perhaps history, I thought, simply because I liked history -- and still do.

That first semester one had to take a lot of required courses, one I took eagerly was American History. The final exam had an essay question which I misunderstood or misinterpreted and guessed at, incorrectly. My final grade in American History was a D, the worst grade I ever got.

That D made me rethink my potential major. I had done well in philosophy and enjoyed Philosophical Logic. But what does a philosopher do? I had no idea. I simply went on to my sophomore and junior years.

I enjoyed Modern American Literature and Current American Authors with Professor Leffert, plus Novel Writing and Short Story Writing with Professor Irwin Stark. I considered becoming a writer. Not factual writing, not journalism, no. Fiction. But not novels, either. I preferred short stories. Magazines published short fiction. Authors wrote books of short stories. I could write short fiction! My major would be English, with a minor in Philosophy.

Prof. Leffert presented readings in our Current American Authors class by Saul Bellow, Dylan Thomas, and others. I sat in the front row, both enthralled and spit-spattered by Dylan Thomas' reading from his *Under Milk Wood*. I'll never forget his mellifluous words as he read them in his rolling, musical Welsh accent. Our class paid him for his appearance, of course, and I heard that he put that check on a bar and he and his entourage of new-found friends drank it all up.

Dylan Thomas was found unconscious in his hotel bed a few days later and died in the hospital. It was November 9, 1953, just a few days after his 39th birthday. His reading to our class was his last public appearance. I felt terribly sad because the world lost a true and rare talent and I felt some slight responsibility for that great loss.

Professor Stark's class had me writing. Hey, I could do that! He collected our work and had some students read their stories to the class while he and we critiqued them. But I was never called upon to read my work.

57. My Oma's Last Days

My father's stepmother, Johanna Friedmann, never had any children of her own; when she married Aron his children were already grown and out of the house. Now we were Oma's closest family. I was the only child she ever helped grow up. We loved each other very much. She spent her last six very happy years with us. And we all truly enjoyed her company tremendously.

When she was liberated in 1945, she still had most of her teeth. Now all were removed and the gold was made into a ring with my WEF initials on it. I wore it proudly and then, after getting engaged to Betty with the diamond ring I had purchased in the Frankfurt P.X., I gave my new gold ring to Betty. Unfortunately, she lost it.

Oma had one other close relative in America, her nephew, Max Rosenthal, who lived near us in Washington Heights. (Her other Rosenthal relatives lived in South Africa.) I visited Max and his first wife, Inge, and their son Robert, every Tuesday night. They had a TV set in those early days and I watched Milton ("Uncle Miltie") Berle religiously. As a young child our son David did not understand Bobby Rosenthal's name correctly; to our delight, David called him, "Bobby Rosyballs."

Johanna Friedmann and her long-time good friend, Klara Caro, were reunited. "Klaerchen," Little Klara, as she was known by her close friends, was very active in the U.S.A. as she had been in Germany, on behalf of Israel and women's rights. She was feisty, strong-willed, determined. She wrote pamphlets and made speeches. I have a 13-page speech by her on "The Beauty of the Bible."

My Oma agreed with her generally on Jewish matters but was no activist. Oma was the shy, retiring type. Now she did all our cooking, for which we were very grateful. She was an excellent cook and my parents and I really appreciated it. And her.

In early 1953, Johanna Friedmann suffered a stroke that affected her left side, her arm and leg, but not her speech. On March 4, 1953, my parents decided that she would be better off in the University Nursing Home in the Bronx, under the medical care of our doctor, Dr. Joseph "Jup" Lazarus, a distant relative of hers.

On one of my last visits to that home, she talked about the beauty of the statues and artwork that surrounded her. Unfortunately, there were none; she was hallucinating. At that time it was a relief that she had beautiful and peaceful thoughts. The horrors of Theresienstadt were no longer with her.

That summer, the nursing home authorities decided that she had to be moved to another facility. We found Halcyon Rest, in Rye, N.Y., which served her kosher meals. I suppose it was a kind of hospice, although I believe that word did not exist at that time.

Oma's friend Klara Caro said that "despite her years of horror, she had the luck in her old age to help the growth and future of her grandson. And it was typical that in the pain and difficulty of her last weeks, only he was able to unlock some laughter from her."

On December 7th, "a date that will live in infamy," as President Roosevelt put it, my Oma suffered another "arteriosclerotic attack" which affected her speech and touch. She was, however, clearly able to say "I love you very much," her last words to me.

At that time my father was in the hospital undergoing surgery to sever the vagus nerve in his stomach, an experimental procedure intended to cure his persistent acid indigestion. His physician, a Dr. Jacoby, told us after the operation that my father reacted poorly, "as only one in two hundred do." On the third day after the operation my father had what the doctor called "the expected relapse," and was clearly not well, spiking a high temperature.

That morning I drove my father's car with Max Rosenthal, Oma's nephew, to Halcyon Rest. Oma was, as I wrote just three days later, "completely unconscious, from which she, thank God, never awoke. She had no knowledge of anything any more and had no pain. She felt nothing. Max and I tried to wake her up and we spoke to her. All she did was to hold our hands very tightly."

Max and I went to see Dr. Carlen who said that she had only about 24 hours. It had been raining that morning but just then it started to really pour. I drove Max home in very stormy rain and we decided that I should go to the hospital and tell my mother.

Afterward I wrote, "When I got there I had her called out of Dad's room and I told her how Oma was. We decided that we couldn't tell my father."

That Saturday afternoon, at my mother's suggestion, I drove out to Halcyon Rest with my best friend, Mark Jaffe. He decided to stay in the car while I went to see my Oma to say goodbye and to recite the *Shema Yisroel.* Shortly thereafter I wrote, "I have not yet described the way my grandmother looked (3½ hours before she passed away) to my parents and I will not describe her to you. Let me just say that I could see that she didn't have much time and that death, for <u>her</u> sake, would be welcome."

Her son was still hospitalized when she died on Sunday, December 13, 1953, age 83½ years. The cause was coronary thrombosis due to arteriosclerotic heart disease.

Hans Grunewald, the man who five years later married Betty and me, arranged for Oma's funeral and burial at the Cedar Park Cemetery in Westwood, New Jersey, just over the George Washington Bridge from Washington Heights. Perpetual care for her grave was fully funded.

The funeral was that Tuesday. Klara Caro gave the graveside speech. It is her oration as well as her other writings that I have quoted in these chapters.

I have a 14-page handwritten letter that I wrote, dated December 15, 1953, addressed to "My very dear ones." It begins, "Now you all have the awful news about the death of our dear Oma. My mother and I have just come back from the funeral and we will most probably soon leave to tell my father as much as he is capable of bearing.

"The weather on Tuesday was beautiful, bright, clear, crisp, sunny, in contrast with the rainy Saturday, Sunday, and Monday. The funeral began at 10:30 AM so that my mother would not miss her regular afternoon visit to the hospital. The funeral was small, simple, and orthodox, combining what Oma and my father wanted."

Oma's lifelong friend, Klara Caro, is buried near her and my parents have both joined them there.

58. Julius and Martin Oppenheimer

One Julius Oppenheimer in my father's life ran *Adler & Oppenheimer* and was his boss. He helped us get out of Germany. My father admired him.

Another Julius Oppenheimer had a chicken farm on Good Intent Road in Deptford, New Jersey. My father envied him.

That Julius Oppenheimer was related on my father's mother's side of the family, through Herman Minkowski, Albert Einstein's physics and math teacher. Julius had been a lawyer in Soest in Westphalia, with a doctorate of jurisprudence. He was married to Jenny and they had one son, Martin, who was three or four years older than me.

They had come to America in 1937 two years before we did. Julius had retired by the late 1940's and his chicken farm seemed, to my father at least, the ideal kind of retirement. Hans Friedman often talked of some day retiring to New Jersey to raise chickens. But I know he was not serious. He could never possibly have become a chicken farmer nor endured any retirement other than just reading the *New York Times* and watching his three grandsons at play. So that is what he did.

When we moved to New York City, we visited the nearby Oppenheimers on their chicken farm a few times; I don't recall them ever visiting us. Their place was on flat land and most of the chicks, chickens and roosters were out in the open, unlike today's huge chicken farms where the animals are all indoors or under cover.

A growing teenager, I inherited a pair or two of shoes that Martin had outgrown. They fit me perfectly, but I had to scrape chicken droppings off them before I wore them.

Martin had frequent and fierce sneezing attacks. There were times he just couldn't stop sneezing. I seem to have inherited that from him, too. My sons used to count mine; my best score was 17 in a row. I may have beaten Martin's record.

Speaking of sneezing, I sometimes have a "sneezing fit" after sex. Having researched the Internet, I find that sneezing is listed there as one of nine "physiological reactions to sex" and it adds, "idiosyncratic reactions are myriad."

155

Martin went to college and got his Masters from Columbia and a Doctorate in Sociology from the University of Pennsylvania, continuing the Minkowski intellectual tradition. He became a professor at Bryn Mawr and Vassar. He joined the staff at Rutgers in 1970 and became head of the department of Sociology at Livingston College.

He also became a Quaker, a pacifist, and an anti-Vietnam War activist. Martin married Sally in July of 1961. They had two children, Miriam and Joel.

In May of 1976, Dr. Martin Oppenheimer went to the *Freie Universitaet* in West Berlin, through the John F. Kennedy Institute, as a guest lecturer from Princeton. He spoke in German about workers' movements and problems of the last decade in America

Martin wrote a book, *The Urban Guerilla*, which has been translated into several languages. It deals with the problem of terrorism in many countries, for he was far ahead of his time. Martin's book is quoted in the *Columbia World of Quotations,* 1996: "Today's city is the most vulnerable social structure ever conceived by man."

Martin and Sally divorced. He met Hannah Fink, a painter, in 1980 and they began living with his children in Rocky Hill, NJ. They bought a second house nearby and converted the barn into a studio.

Prof. Dr. Martin Oppenheimer of Rutgers University is listed by the *Westfaelische Wilhelms-Universitat* in Muenster as lecturing in 1995-1996 and 1997-1998 and he got a Fulbright lectureship for the Spring of 1982. His daughter Miriam went there with him.

59. Seeing Susie Again

In December of 1953 my father was still hospitalized when his stepmother passed away. We did not tell him until after her funeral. It was a very difficult time for us all.

My mother was terribly worried. Doctors were cutting my father's vagus nerve in what was an experimental procedure, not a routine operation. He was her husband, her lover and provider. You could truly say that he was everything to her.

And she adored her mother-in-law, who did so much for us all. My Oma was such a kind and gentle woman, very soft spoken and quiet. But when she spoke, she said something friendly and nice or helpful.

I loved her very much and mourned her passing. And I, too, worried terribly about my father. It was tough.

Yet something wonderful happened at about that time!

I had passed my sophomore year and was now a junior at Uptown City and a regular rider on the Broadway bus which went from 193rd St., going downtown. Whenever I got on with a bunch of pals, at 181st Street and Broadway, it was already quite full.

I noticed a girl in the rearmost seat most days. It was Susie, the girl from Farm Camp Lowey, the one I'd fallen asleep on top of, up in the hayloft. I had promised to call her three years ago and never did. She avoided my glance and I looked away from her. But I did peek to see if she was there every time I boarded that bus. And I saw that when Susie was in the rear seat, she was always with another girl, always the same one. But I carefully avoided eye contact with them.

Then one day in the City College lunchroom, I was sitting with my friends at "our table," when the bell rang and they all went away to their next classes. I sat there, alone. And I recognized the girl who approached me as Susie's friend from the bus.

She said, "I'm Betty, what are you?" and sat down on the table next to me!

We talked. I don't know if she or I had a class that hour but we sat and talked. I don't remember any details of the conversation. Or how many classes we missed.

But that evening Betty Klein went home and told her mother, "I met the man I'm going to marry!"

Many years later John reminded us that her mother had asked Betty at that time, "Poor Devil, does he know it yet?"

Of course, I wasn't in on that plan for a long time.

I also did not know it then, but Betty was only 16 years old.

60. Christmas, 1953

Her real name was Babette Klein but she was always known as Betty.

Meeting Betty Klein was the bright spot in that terrible time. I had just met her and started to get to know her, and to like her very much. She was sympathetic and understanding. And she invited me to a day-after-Christmas party at her friend Laura's house in the Bronx. She also asked me to bring along some of my male friends, as there would be lots of girls.

Well, "the guys" had been talking about "new blood" -- girls other than those we'd all gone to high school and now college with. So four or five of us went to Laura's.

I did not realize it at the time but the entire party was designed for Betty to "get" me! The party had not been planned until I had agreed to come. She had set her sights on me and started to make her wish come true.

Betty and Laura had a hard time buying a Christmas tree the day after Christmas! After all, they were both Jewish and hadn't had one. Laura's parents were out of town and the two of them quickly got a few other girls just as easily as I had gotten "the guys." It was, in fact, Betty and my first date.

Laura didn't know Ernie Weber at that time but they got married and had three sons, just as we did. And we have remained friends over the years, although they live in California and have a home in England as well. Now Laura continues to send contributions to the American Lung Association in remembrance of Betty.

That Christmas party certainly changed my mood that day-after-Christmas.

Betty and I "went out together," as dating was called then. Sometimes to the movies, but most of the time we went on long walks, talking all the way from CCNY to her home in Washington Heights, or 138th St. to 193rd. (In Manhattan, 20 blocks equals one mile.) You do the math; I'm not good at it.

At other times we sat together in one of my classes or talked with each other in the back of the lecture hall while a speaker was teaching something. Sometimes she sat through my geology class (which I took because it was interesting) and even my German class (which was mostly Goethe and Schiller, printed in the old German Gothic typeface).

My ex-girlfriend Shelly told Betty that I was a football hero and, poor Betty, she believed it. Shelly had seen me score two touchdowns in Lewissohn Stadium for a required Physical Training course. I really couldn't convince Betty that I was no football star until many years later when I tried to play a little backyard football with our sons.

There was no doubt whatsoever that she was better than I in math. When I had to take calculus and I didn't understand it, she explained it to me. Immediately after the final exam, I forgot all I learned. But Betty had done so well that I got an A in calculus!

VII. BETTY KLEIN'S FAMILIES

61. The 18th Child

Jozsef, the son of Simon Klein, was born in Budapest in 1843 and died in 1927. Jozsef's wife Babette (nee Geldzahler) was born in 1856 and died in 1932. They had 18 children!

Sandor (pronounced "Shan-door") was born in Budapest on February 9, 1897, when his mother was 41 years old. He was the youngest and became Betty's father.

The eighteen were, in order, Janka, Simon, Lajos, Gyula (pronounced "Jewla" and later called Julius,) Fanny, Dezso, Olga, Irma, Vilma, Jeno (later Eugene,) Geza, Bela, Oscar, Imre, Erno (Ernest,) Rozsi, and Sandor. Their mother, Babette, who was always called Betty, wanted to earn the medal which the Kaiser gave to anyone who had twenty children. She was disappointed that she had had "only eighteen."

Surprisingly, the family name, Klein, died out in just one generation! Most of the children were girls who either married and thus their name changed, or never had any children and the boys either never married or had only girl babies. And, many died in the World Wars.

Also unusual is that Vilma married a man named Mor Katona. Katona is Hungarian for small while Klein is German for small. And the town of Katonah happens to be near Chappaqua, where we lived.

At a young age, Sandor had an accident that somewhat crippled his left arm. It never healed properly and was "frozen" at the elbow. When he said that he left Hungary in order to escape the military draft, I was somewhat skeptical because his "bad arm" would have kept him out of any army. He immigrated to the United States sometime during World War I, I think it was 1917. But his name is not listed on the rolls of those who landed at Ellis Island at any year.

Once in the U.S., he never left New York. Sandor -- which is the Hungarian equivalent of Alexander -- legally changed his name to

159

Alexander when he became an American citizen. So he was known as Alex Klein.

Of all the 18 children, none of the girls and only four boys came to America. I met only one Geza, ("Gay-za") a few times. I thought him something of a dandy -- a snappy dresser who wore brown-and-white shoes and even spats, carried a cane and always wore a hat. His were obviously expensive, colorful clothes, possibly even tailored for him. I believe that he lived in Philadelphia. I know he had had no children.

Brother Gyula, called Julius, lived in Manhattan but died in 1952. His wife had been Irma Patrovitch.

Bela had a wife named Tessie, but I never met them and don't know where they lived; it might have been Baltimore.

The only other brother who came to America was Dezso (pronounced "Desh-oo") who was also known as David. For whatever reason -- which Alex did not want to disclose -- Alex and Dezso never spoke to each other in all the many years they were both in America! It was a feud from the Hungarian days. I do not know where Dezso lived, although I suspect it was New York City.

It was not only with his family that Alex was basically antisocial. Alex did not like to go out, or go anywhere at all. But at least he didn't object when his wife's sisters came to visit, which they often did. Nor when I came around, which I very often did. He had only one friend that I knew of. I met him once and I recall that he was a policeman and he told me he did not wear a uniform. Perhaps he was an undercover narcotics cop.

Alex Klein worked all his life in "the rag trade," that is, the clothing business in the garment district in midtown Manhattan and he always lived uptown, in Washington Heights, going to work by subway. He became very skilled as an embroiderer, working on a specific kind of sewing machine. At first he had to work long, hard hours. Then the trade was unionized and he became an active member of the ILGWU -- the International Ladies' Garment Workers Union. It favored the Democratic Party and was considered a leftist organization. And Alex originally went along with that wholeheartedly.

Alexander Klein married Frieda Zwickler on September 11, 1930. They moved to a small one-room apartment in Washington Heights on Wadsworth Avenue. Alex was very adept at delicate embroidery so, after

160

a while, he decided to go into business for himself. Unfortunately, that was right at the time of the Great Depression, the 1930's, when literally millions of people were out of work. Alex's business went bankrupt.

There was unemployment insurance and Union relief, vitally necessary because Alex was out of work when, on December 1st, 1936, they had a little daughter. She was named Babette after Alex's mother and, just like her, was always called Betty.

Shortly after my future wife was born, the Kleins moved to 193rd St., just off Wadsworth Avenue. They literally had two rooms, one was a kitchen-dinette-living room and the other was the bedroom with a tiny bathroom. The apartment was small, but they had a large black-and-white dog, a mixed breed, named Chubby.

They doted on Betty, their one and only child, doing everything they could for her. She was the apple of her father's eye, as the saying goes. When the baby crawled on the floor and poked the dog in his rear end, they quickly got rid of the dog.

They scrimped and saved for her. Alex and Frieda ate <u>pea soup,</u> and <u>only</u> pea soup, <u>every day</u> so that they could afford to give their baby a varied diet of real, healthy, good baby food. They cut every corner to give little Betty nothing but the best of everything. Frieda went to work at Worthheimer's Department Store on 181st St., as a saleslady in the notions department.

Alex slept on the couch in the multi-purpose room and Betty and her mother shared the bedroom. It stayed like that until Betty got married to me and moved out. It is fair to say that she grew up in poverty and certainly lived frugally all her life, yet when she passed away we were worth millions!

Alex tried opening another embroidery business -- it was the only trade he knew. But it, too, went bankrupt. And despite the fact that Franklin Delano Roosevelt's Democratic Party's New Deal and the ILGWU Liberals provided what little money they had, Alex became not just a conservative but a right-wing Republican, which my father and I never understood! Alex Klein remained a reactionary the rest of his life, even after his embroidery earned him a decent salary when times got better. He was also always something of an isolationist. And he resented the Puerto Ricans, born American citizens, when they started to move into "our" Washington Heights.

He spoke of Budapest as a beautiful city. Betty and I both wondered how he could know, since as far as we knew, he never saw any places other than Budapest and New York City. But when we got there we found out he was right. It is beautiful.

I once said that Alex was vain with no reason for vanity. He always thought of himself as handsome, or acted that way, and he was a handsome young man. But I met him as an older man, when, brushing back the little hair on his bald head, he asked, "Have you ever seen a better-looking man?"

He was an expert poker player, which I was not. I don't think he cheated, but he'd often ask me to play cards with him, Betty, and her mother. He insisted that I put up my money, usually about $5 or less. He would proceed to <u>almost</u> wipe me out and then, when it was <u>almost</u> time for me to go home -- somehow -- I'd win back just about all my outlay or a tiny bit more. To this day I still believe he was just incredibly good at cards, or at understanding my betting better than I understood it myself.

I only met one friend of Alex's, a policeman, who told me that he didn't wear a uniform. I think he was a detective or, perhaps, an undercover cop.

Alex Klein seldom went out, probably because he couldn't afford to. Most often Frieda's two sisters would come to visit her, but there were times Frieda went, alone or with Betty, to their homes. And when I couldn't afford to take Betty out, I usually went to the Klein home. With its one room (plus one bedroom) we often talked for hours, her parents, Betty and I. Or we played some board game, Monopoly, Scrabble, Clue, or such. I didn't play Pinochle, Canasta, Mah-Jongg, or any of the games the Zwickler sisters played. And I do believe they usually played for pennies.

Alex knew that I was his daughter's serious boyfriend. He knew that we had talked of marriage. When I officially asked him if I could marry his daughter, his only answer was, "You're a sucker if you do!" I think he was joking.

Alex complained about the cost of his only child's wedding. It was in the home of the rabbi who performed both the New York State and Jewish ceremonies, and his wife baked the cake. He had kept the price down to $20. But Alex finally agreed that it was worth it, "to get rid of Betty." Again, I think he was joking.

Betty had never spoken to her father on the phone until after we were married. For it was only then that she realized he had a marked Hungarian accent. She also had not known that he knew Hebrew and German until the Kleins came to a Passover seder at my parents' home. So it was 1956 or 1957 when she discovered that he remembered both languages after at least 40 years!

A doting grandfather, Alex was especially proud of his only grandchildren. But he played very gingerly with them, seemingly afraid he'd break them, undoubtedly because of his own bent arm. He never roughhoused with his grandchildren, shuddered when they played roughly with each other, and was truly frightened whenever the boys went on our backyard swings, climbing bars, or geodesic dome. Alex would turn away and not watch them play "dangerously."

He never, after the first time, went to Chappaqua Pool to watch them swim, dive, race, or just enjoy themselves. Alex was afraid for them because he loved them so much.

Alexander Klein, a heavy smoker, died of lung cancer on July 19, 1978 in Mt. Sinai Hospital in New York City, age 81. He was in the hospital only about a week. His body was cremated and his ashes spread around rose bushes.

Our son John and Karen named their son Alexander Henry Friedman after both of John's grandfathers.

62. Zwicklers, Kemplers and Preisers

Jacob Zwickler married Lena Stil and we can trace six generations from them to my grandchildren. They had seven children, only four of whose names I know: Pesachyo, Chaim, Arje, and Leibish. Aren't you glad you weren't named after one of them?

My grandchildren are eight generations removed from Abraham Kempler, but that line is a little fuzzy at the beginning. We don't know who he married, nor the names of any of his children. Yet we do know of three of Old Abe's grandchildren: they are Elias Neuhof, Irving Kempler, and Anna Preiser.

Anna Preiser was born on December 15, 1879, in Zakopane, Poland. She married Chaim Zwickler and she died on March 17, 1954, in New York City. She was Betty Klein's maternal grandmother and, as a little girl, Betty actually hated her. That was due to the simple fact that Anna Zwickler never spoke English but often yelled at her in what might have been Polish or German or, most likely, Yiddish. Betty never knew what she had done to antagonize the old lady. In fact, about the only thing Betty did know was that the old biddy always seemed angry at her.

Chaim Zwickler was born April 17, 1878 in Timberk, Poland and died in New York City on September 3, 1943, when his granddaughter Betty Klein was only six and she did not remember him at all.

Chaim and Anna Zwickler, nee Preiser, had seven children in this sequence: Henry was born in Krakow, Poland; Lena was born in Austria; Max was born in Mannheim, Germany; Frieda, Rose, and William in Darmstadt, Germany; and Jack and Samuel in New York City. The Zwicklers arrived in America before World War I, since Jack was born here in June of 1915.

I knew all of those Zwicklers, some better than others. Henry was born in 1899 and had an Army-Navy Store in the Bronx. Those stores started soon after World War II selling "surplus," unused, or leftover Army and Navy equipment. Then they sold anything and everything, not just actual military stuff.

Henry was a widower when I met him; his wife Anna had died in 1952 and they had one son, Danny, who was eleven years older than I was, and one daughter whose real name was Leila but was called Libby. She was in a home for the retarded or mentally disturbed. Wherever she was, Betty and I never met or visited her.

Henry was short, a little overweight, and was generally a genial fellow who loved to smoke cigars. He entertained the few customers he had in his Army-Navy store, which was not in the best part of town, but in a section of the Bronx which was a mostly black and Puerto Rican neighborhood. I think he told his friends and customers war stories, although I believe that he was never actually in any war. They might, however, have been true stories nevertheless. Henry lived in the Bronx, not far from his store.

In my first real advertising-related job, while I was still in college, I was the assistant editor of, among other publications, *Army-Navy Store Magazine*. So I interviewed Betty's Uncle Henry and photographed him and his place and he was delighted when I did, and even more thrilled that it was actually published. He displayed the article proudly in his storefront window. Frankly, I didn't think it was flattering; it showed the reality. An ordinary, or I should say typical, Army-Navy store.

We got along very well. Henry had an old jalopy, I think it was a Ford, which he very generously lent me a few times while I was dating Betty. We gave the car a name, Herman, but I don't remember why.

Henry Zwickler had Dupuytren's contracture, which I now have in its early stage. It's a thickening of the tissue in the palm that can cause a finger or fingers to curl inward. It progresses slowly, is unstoppable and incurable as yet. But there is an operation that can be performed.

Two of Henry's fingers curled inward and he developed diabetes. The diabetes finally got to the point where they had to amputate one of his legs. That's when Henry gave "Herman The Car" to his son Danny. Henry died in 1967.

Max Zwickler and his wife Ida lived in the Bronx. He, too, was a nice guy, but as I recall he either worked late hours or worked nights and was usually tired. I don't remember what he did but when we visited he always had to go to bed early and we were hushed and didn't stay long.

Willi Zwickler and his wife Jean lived in Los Angeles and I think we met only once. They had no children.

Jack, whom Alex Klein always called Jakey, was a kosher butcher in the Bronx. He often brought delicious cuts of meat to the Kleins which I gladly helped eat. His wife was named Bea and their children, Phyllis, Howard, and Ellen, were all younger than Betty. We did get together with them a few times but not very often.

The youngest of Chaim and Anna Zwickler's children was Samuel. Sam and his wife Gloria had three children, Steven, Susan, and Adele. Sam was a mailman who delivered mail on foot, carrying his bag over his shoulder. It was a tiring, thankless job, although he earned tips at Christmas time.

They lived in the nearby Bronx and we got together more with them than with any of the other brothers. Sam's wife Gloria had a mental condition and was among the first (at least the first I had ever heard about) who took a daily pill that actually made her quite normal. I believe it was a tranquilizer. The story was that she had threatened her children with a knife, but on medication she was most pleasant and nicer than many other people.

Sam and Gloria's three kids were often Betty's playmates although they were all younger than she was: Susan got married and they lived in North Tarrytown when we did, but we never got together. Betty just didn't want to and Susan didn't contact us either.

All I can think of is that Betty did not have any real "family feeling," no desire to see relatives more often than she had to. She was always very social with comparative strangers, made many friends very easily, and definitely enjoyed people; she was always a real "people person," with almost anyone except her family. Perhaps she got some of that from her father who was deliberately antisocial and found fault with almost everyone except himself.

But the three Zwickler sisters, Lena, Frieda, and Rose, were very close. They often played cards or board games, usually at the Kleins' apartment, sometimes needing a fourth player, most often Alex but, when the game was poker, also Betty and me.

I believe that all three of them had diabetes. I remember that Betty and I bought the then-new sugarless candies for her mother and she shared them with her sisters. It is important that you, my grandchildren, know of the possibly genetic diseases.

But if you inherited anything from the three Zwickler sisters I hope it was a sense of humor and a "take it" attitude, no matter what happens to you in life. I would consider the three of them realists, just as I think of myself as such. Alex Klein, however, was anything but a realist.

Betty's mother Frieda was undoubtedly the nicest, friendliest, most outgoing of the three. She was very kind, caring and loving, seemingly always in a good and cheerful mood. Someone had told me when I was a teenager that I should study a girl's mother to see what the girl would become. If she was all the things Frieda was, her daughter would make a wonderful wife. That turned out to be excellent advice.

Frieda Klein went into the Jewish Home for the Aged in the Bronx in December of 1979, a year and a half after her husband died. Her good mood never changed; she enjoyed playing cards with the other old folks, usually with a cigarette in her mouth.

I was working at the Thompson Agency on June 3, 1983, when Betty telephoned me that her mother had dropped dead. A heart attack. It was totally unexpected. We were in a most hectic pre-presentation time at the office and the Thompsons did not understand that I had to leave immediately, but of course I did.

166

Frieda's body was cremated and her ashes spread at rose bushes.

A warm, wonderful, kind, generous woman, my mother-in-law and I truly loved each other. But Betty and I agreed we would never name a daughter Frieda Friedman.

63. In Love!

I was in love with Babette (Betty) Klein, there was no doubt about that in my mind. And I truly believed what she told me: that she loved me. That was the amazing part, that she was in love with me, too!

After all, I thought she was the one who was wonderful. She was cute, adorable, cuddly, sugar and spice and everything nice. Sweet, kind, gentle, thoughtful, considerate, truly loving. In addition, she was intelligent, insightful, a thinking human being with a mind of her own. We could talk, discuss, even argue rationally and reasonably. We usually agreed on most things, nevertheless and importantly, we had a respect for each other's opinion. I loved her, her mind, and everything about her.

Betty was clever, witty, fast with a quip, a spur-of-the-moment joke. I loved that!

Who wouldn't fall in love with her? She was so very warm and affectionate and just plain lovable! She was just right: Betty's name was Klein, which means little in German, but she was exactly the perfect height for me to kiss.

She and I had similar backgrounds, children of European immigrants, but she was born in the U.S.A., Manhattan, in fact. "My gal's a corker, she's a New Yorker," was a timely song.

My father, ever the German, always admired her efficiency. Betty knew what she wanted and pretty much got what she wanted. An only child -- as I was -- she was her father's darling: He wanted to give her everything, but they had so little!

It was the '50's, the Eisenhower era (although we both favored Adlai Stevenson). We really didn't have much money so we spent a lot of time walking and talking. We did more talking than "necking." We talked to each other a lot, got to know each other well, enjoyed being with each other.

Betty Klein knew her own mind yet listened to my ideas, thought them through, and agreed with me much more often than she disagreed. We were very comfortable with each other. She was an active, vital, alive, and wonderful person with a delightful personality, someone who did things, went places, had many friends. Betty had three very close girlfriends, Audrey Hutt, now Mrs. Jerry Bricker, who lived near her; Laura, now Mrs. Ernie Weber; and Arlene, known as Cookie, who became (for a while) Mrs. Tony Musto.

Betty didn't really like shopping but loved bargains. She cut coupons, bought the store brand rather than the national brand -- even in later years when I advertised the name brand! My parents, by contrast, bought Rolaids when I worked on that product, even though my father was on a prescription antacid! Yes, Betty was an independent thinker. She loved to read and to discuss ideas, plans, the future. She was interested in science and scientific things, but we talked politics, economics, social issues. We were both liberals, like-minded on the major questions of the day. We liked the same things. Yet her strengths were my weaknesses: she did arithmetic, I didn't. She undid knots, I did zippers.

We went to a few places together, to local bars even though we were under age. Legal drinking age in New York was eighteen but she started at 16. There was no way of proving one's age at that time. We started drinking "7 and 7," Seven Crown Whiskey with 7-Up. But we didn't go "out" much, instead we spent a lot of time at her house or mine. When we got some privacy, we were very loving, kind, gentle, passionate with each other.

We attended a Harry Belafonte concert in City College's Lewissohn Stadium and loved it. (Forty-five years later we attended another Belafonte concert at the University of North Carolina's Memorial Hall in Chapel Hill. We still both loved the same songs.) We got along wonderfully with each other! We were a pair, a couple.

She obviously brightened my life and so I began to think seriously about marrying her. I could easily declare my love for her, and I did. But she was a freshman and I was a junior. I had to declare a major now.

I liked to read and to write and I enjoyed my English courses. Could I, should I, major in English? What would that lead to? I didn't really know. I did not think I'd like being an English teacher! All I wanted to do was write short fiction stories.

One day in study hall, I read *The Ears of Johnny Bear*, a short story by John Steinbeck, to Betty. She didn't get it, so I explained it to her. Later she told me that my intelligence and comprehension of that story impressed her; that I was her intellectual superior and she was delighted about that.

It is only now, upon reflection while writing this book, recognizing that she had set her sights on me from the start, that I realize that Betty was certainly smart enough to make believe that she hadn't understood the story and wise enough to praise my "superior intellect."

Nicole Friedman, while she was editing this book, discussed that thought with me. She then bought me Steinbeck's *The Long Valley*, his book of short stories which included *Johnny Bear*. This was the first time I reread the story. So now -- and only now -- do I realize that Betty most surely had understood the story and understood me!

But at the time I was in college, I actually believed that I might have something others did not. I did not think of it as talent, but ability. I felt I could write short stories. Fiction. I had a good imagination. I could make up plots, characters, situations, dramatic scenes. But I did not want to write novels. And so I decided that my major would be English, and my career, short-story writer

I told my father my decision. He thought I was crazy, that I'd never be able to support a family on the meager income that, even then, short-story writers earned. But I was firm in my decision ... for a while.

And so I declared my major as English -- Short Story Writing -- in the second half of my junior year. I would go for a B.A., a Bachelor of Arts degree, in English.

Then, finally, I came around to the clear realization that I not only loved Betty, I definitely wanted to marry her! I was also struck with a new thought: Maybe my father was right about a short-story writer not having a real job, or paycheck, or regular income, or being able to support a wife, much less children!

Betty and I started talking seriously about getting married. We carefully considered how many children we wanted, what their names would be. We began talking about her working to support us, about her quitting work when we had children. What may seem like simple and obvious questions and answers were very complicated at the time and took a lot of discussion.

I was full of confidence in my ability to write short stories well enough to support a family. I took classes that had me writing. I submitted my work to City College's English teachers. One story that I recall was about my best friend Mark Jaffe; I showed it to him and he didn't like it although I thought what I'd written was good.

Mark and I both worked on City College's "literary magazine." He and I wrote most of one particular issue. I imagined my career as a short-story writer.

But I never imagined writing a non-fiction book of as many short stories as this!

VIII. ON MY OWN
(1953 - 1958)

64. The Cold War

As soon as World War II was over, the Allies divided Germany into four zones: Russian, American, English, and French; Berlin, entirely in the Russian Zone, was also split into the same 4 sectors. But it didn't take long for there to be just two zones and two sectors, Russian and Allied. The reason for this was the postwar division of the world into the Communist Soviet Union and its satellites versus the Westernized anti-Communist ideologies, with each side an armed camp, having atomic weaponry. That competition, mistrust, and threat of mutual nuclear annihilation was called the Cold War.

Because of the nuclear threat, children in American schools practiced diving under their desks when an air-raid siren sounded. People dug fall-out shelters in their back yards. The times were tense.

Cold Warriors gave rise to Senator Joseph McCarthy's anti-communist "crusade" that sought to identify the internal threat he perceived as undermining "the American way." The House Un-American Activities Committee searched for citizens they termed disloyal. It all became a witch hunt, seeking out "subversives" hidden in our own country. Vivian Gorman wrote in *Wild at Heart* about "the complicated aftermath of the Second World War, characterized by anxiety about the atomic bomb [and] a manipulated terror of godless Communism."

The Cold War's battle line was in Europe. There, American forces were on one side and Russians on the other side of the border that divided East and West Germany. It was where the danger was most obvious.

But, incredible as it may seem, there was also a hot war, a shooting war, with American forces in actual combat against Communists, going on at the same time as the Cold War -- although it was legally termed merely a "police action." The Korean War.

65. In the Army

During the Korean War there was a draft. Young men were conscripted into military service. One was deferred as long as one was in college. But I knew that sooner or later I would have to serve.

My best friend Mark Jaffe "moved his number up" and was drafted into the Army at a time of his choosing. He suggested that I do the same. So I did. I had my two-year military obligation start in the summer of 1954. Mark also suggested that I tell them I spoke German, hoping the army would send me far from Korea. So I did. The day I entered the Army, they tested my German language skills.

Every draftee's first eight weeks was Basic Training and I was sent to Fort Dix, New Jersey, for that. I endured the humiliation and exhaustion and dehumanization of the army. We were wakened early and driven hard. I learned to march, shoot, assemble a rifle, and obey orders.

Our barracks had double-decker bunks lined on both sides with absolutely no privacy whatsoever. I found it difficult to go to the toilet because they were all lined up in a row and fully occupied whenever I felt the need. I held out until Friday when the sergeant said, "Any of youse guys wants to go to Jewish Church, go ahead." I took that opportunity to use the bathrooms at the all-denominational "church."

It was a hot, dry, dusty summer at Dix. When we marched in the sand, which was often, usually with a heavy full-field pack, we were engulfed in clouds of dust. We were almost always hot, sweaty, exhausted, tired, and completely drained.

The only relief was the fact that visitors could come to the camp and my father drove to Fort Dix every Sunday with his *New York Times* and my Betty Klein. He said hello to me and then left us alone while he read the paper.

Betty and I did what we always did, we walked, we talked, we "necked." Our love for each other grew and grew; she was so tender, so caring, so very good for me and to me. She was definitely my true love.

Traveling together, my father and Betty really got to know each other and they got along very well indeed. They grew to love each other, starting then. My mother never went along and never had as close a relationship with Betty. Possibly no girl could ever be good enough for her only son.

The second eight weeks of military training were devoted to whatever specialized field the army wanted or needed at the time. Mark, the future scientist, was sent to Cook School. My orders were for Clerk-Type School in Ft. Dix. I was delighted to stay so close to home.

So I learned to touch-type and learned it well. I realized that for a writer, typing is an essential skill. (I was always a better typist than any secretary I ever had.) I also learned "the army way," the forms, the paperwork, the systems that a clerk had to know. It came in handy.

I learned enough of the army's methods to be able to -- totally illegally -- go AWOL, Away Without Official Leave, almost every weekend. My father lent me his car and I drove into Manhattan early Saturday mornings and back late on Sundays. It was when I had a legal pass that I had to wait to leave the post after lunch Saturday and return before lunch on Sunday. In the army, I had learned, it often did not make sense to do things logically or legally.

But I never realized that my training was a prelude to Military Intelligence, which is truly an oxymoron. Yet, of course, a German-speaking typist who knew the ropes was exactly what they needed in Germany during the Cold War. I was glad to be going to Germany since "the army way" is not often the sensible, reasonable way. And there was a shooting war in Korea.

I was first ordered to Camp Kilmer, New Jersey, before being shipped out. It was the day before Thanksgiving, 1954. Early that morning I was put on K.P. -- Kitchen Police -- a duty that is often a dirty job, like cleaning up grease pits or scrubbing floors, whatever. The job I was assigned was peeling shrimp for all of Camp Kilmer's Thanksgiving dinners. There was a huge pot of cooked shrimp on one side of me and two other huge pots on the other side, one for the peeled shrimp, the other for the shells.

Shrimp is not kosher. And while I did not care about that, I had never peeled a shrimp before. In fact, the only shrimp I'd ever eaten was in Chinese foods, mixed in with sauce and vegetables and stuff. I wasn't worried that God would strike me dead if I ate shrimp, so I tried one.

I loved it! I also realized that peeling shrimp was a very good job when you're on K.P. So I spent the day at it, not wanting to lose the job. I played one for you, one for me, and ate much of what I peeled. I ate shrimp for breakfast, lunch and dinner.

I had a pass for the next day, Thanksgiving Day. And I was to ship out to Germany the day after. But first I came home to say goodbye to my parents and to Betty and her parents. I no longer had my father's car but took a bus and the subway.

However overdosing on shrimp made me sick to my stomach. The trip home did not help. I was throwing up and feeling awful when I got to New York City and all the time I was with my loved ones. My last day with Betty Klein was horrible!

I took off the next day on the troop transport liberty ship still feeling sick to my stomach. I did not leave for Germany under ideal conditions. I really felt miserable, emotionally as well as physically. It was bad. Awful. Horrible.

Sure enough, things got worse.

66. Back to Germany

My boat trip from Germany to America on the Vollendam in September, 1939, had been fun for a 4½-year-old boy. But my voyage back to Germany on a liberty ship converted to a troop transport was hell on the 20-year-old I was then. We left from Hoboken, New Jersey, in New York harbor the day after Thanksgiving, 1954.

I was still sick from overeating shrimp and I was assigned to the lowest deck, way below the water line. It was one huge room, holding about 400 guys in canvas-and-rope bunks, in tiers four high, one on top of the other. I was in a third bunk, that is, one from the top. The overcrowding was horrible, but I did not realize how bad it was until the ship started to move.

On any boat there is yaw and pitch and roll, the three different motions while sailing. They are the up-and-down movement in the waves, the side-to-side sway, and the back-and-forth swing. You feel each in the pit of your stomach. At least I did. That alone usually causes what is called seasickness but more accurately is motion sickness.

With no windows or ventilation of any kind, 400 sweating, stinking men in close quarters really smelled awful. To get to the uppermost bunk one had to climb up the ones below. Each bunk did not offer enough room for anyone to sit up, just enough to lie still. Please pardon this graphic description: but when someone in an upper bunk throws up, he splashes the person in the lowest bunk. Pretty soon the vomit was sloshing around the floor and it was truly impossible to walk. I began to retch as the boat swayed. At least I wasn't throwing up. The "head," or bathroom facility, was even worse, so I won't describe it.

I went upstairs to the mess hall. The tables sat about eight men on each side. As the boat swayed, the trays of food slid down the long tables. If you didn't hold on to your tray, it would go back and forth. My tray slid away from me; someone else's appeared before me. I just couldn't eat. I left the mess hall. Then the loudspeaker began a long list of names, Private Walter Friedman among them: "All youse mens is on K.P. Report to the mess hall on the double."

I was not alone in not reporting. I simply couldn't. The truth is, I hardly ever went to the mess hall again. And I couldn't stomach the sleeping arrangements either. Because I was sick to my stomach before I got on board, Betty had given me a good supply of Dramamine pills (for seasickness or nausea). I ate little else.

I went out on deck to see the Statue of Liberty disappearing. The cold September air was somewhat refreshing. But I couldn't stay on deck all day and all night.

There was no choice but to go back inside. Instead of going below, however, I found a front stairwell and went down as far as it would go. Soon I was at the bow, the front-most point of the ship. There I found myself alone in a cozy little nook and went to sleep. The ship's movements didn't seem as bad there. While it did go up and down, there was less side-to-side movement, and hardly any sway at all.

The next morning I discovered the ship's library and took out a bunch of what were then called pocket books; small paperbacks, mostly mysteries. I took them to my little nook and read. And got completely engrossed in their plots. That's what I did all day, every day. I read book after book and didn't eat much besides Dramamine.

Every once in a while I went back out on deck for a breath of fresh air. I saw the Queen Mary pass us, as if we were standing still, heading in the same direction we were.

As the days wore on, the list of names on the loudspeaker grew shorter and shorter. My name was still being called. That felt strangely reassuring.

When I went back out on deck a few days later, the Queen Mary passed us again, going back to America. But it really got to me when she passed us a <u>third</u> time, heading in the same European direction we were, before we had made our one-way trip!

It took us twelve days to cross the Atlantic.

By the time we arrived in Germany, Private Walter Friedman was one of only three names unaccounted for. But, the voice said to the three of us: "We know you're on this ship somewhere!"

I resolved to fly back to America when my "tour of duty" was over. And I did.

We arrived in Bremerhaven at night and were immediately put on a German train bound for *Frankfurt-am-Main*. There were sleeping berths and the train's motion let me sleep and sleep well for the first time in twelve days! I don't know how many hours I slept -- we were in a different time zone and I hadn't set my watch properly. But I slept all the way to Frankfurt and woke up feeling well rested.

When the trainman and conductor started talking to each other, I realized that I did indeed speak and understand German very well.

67. Military Intelligence

From Frankfurt's railroad station, I was taken by car to the suburban town of Oberursel to an army base called Camp King. Twenty years later, in 1974, when I moved to Frankfurt with my family, the boys went to the Frankfurt International School, located in Oberursel. About forty years after that, Willi Geisel, a friend in St. Barths, also lived in Oberursel. And fifty years later, in 2004, when I moved to Carol Woods, I discovered that one of my neighbors, Byron Parry, had been in Camp King just before me!

Camp King was originally a German prisoner of war camp which was used after World War II by the Americans to interrogate German soldiers. But in December, 1954, it was a military intelligence base where civilians who had come from East Germany, the Russian zone, over to West Germany, were interrogated. I didn't ask why, but I learned.

I spent a few weeks there and went into Frankfurt by streetcar a few times. With my new army buddies I discovered Frankfurt's seedier section, near the *hauptbahnhof.*

Then I was shipped to Military Intelligence School outside of Oberammergau in Bavaria for another eight-week course of training. One of the instructors there, Art was his name, became a friend. And a girl in town became another friend. She was a film actress, a stand-in for EvaMarie Saint, and was in *Night People* with Gregory Peck.

This was 1954, during the Cold War, when Russian and East German troops were just across the West German border. The objective of military intelligence was to learn as much as possible about the potential enemy's troops and intentions. We wanted to know their "Order of Battle." What units, their strength, training, arms, and equipment. Who were their leaders, how was their morale, what were their conditions; we wanted to learn everything about them. What was our army facing?

To that end we had German spies. One could question the use of spies, the ethics of spying. But this Cold War could turn "hot" at any time. If it did, it would most probably happen in Germany. We were afraid the Russians would attack us there.

Some of our spies were Germans living in East Germany. But many were those who had come from there and could be persuaded to return for short periods of time to find out what we wanted to know. The spies were called sources or agents. Our guys were the "agent handlers," the ones who debriefed the spies and helped them do their spying, supplying them with what they needed, whether it be tiny Minox cameras and secret codes or money, liquor, drugs, women -- whatever it took. Most of our agent handlers were stationed in West Berlin.

That was truly dangerous activity. I did not want to go there and do that. So, when I was given another German language test in Oberammergau, I failed it. And when I was sent on a training mission to "spy" on an American Army base outside Munich, I was immediately caught. Again, one can question the ethics of what I did. But I truly felt that I was avoiding potential personal danger.

Not surprisingly, when I finished the training course, I was not assigned to Berlin but to Frankfurt, my Oma's home town. I got an office job in the former I. G. Farben building, then completely taken over by the American army. It was located on top of a hill and was six stories tall. The Germans called it the *I. G. Hochhaus* or high building, not quite a skyscraper. Our unit occupied the top two floors on one wing. There was a *Fahrkorb* instead of an elevator. It was a constantly moving dumbwaiter-like device that held 4 or 5 people at a time, going up one way and down next to it.

I was in a Military Intelligence Battalion, but we never, ever used that designation. We would never say M.I. No, we said we were in -- our cover name -- the "7982 USAREUR Liaison Group." (U.S. ARmy in EURope.) And we wore "Ike jackets" with the flaming sword patch also made famous by General Dwight D. Eisenhower.

I had to have a security clearance to work in military intel, a series of clearances actually -- Classified, Secret, Top Secret, and I eventually got even higher than that, Q Clearance. It took time for those "full field clearances," so I started at a low level.

My M.O.S. or Military Occupational Specialty was as a Military Intelligence Analyst. I sat behind a typewriter and turned the reports written by agent handlers about what their sources had learned into standard military format to be forwarded upward as actual intelligence. No one knew if I was typing an army report or a letter to Betty.

I worked in uniform but we wore civilian clothes during almost all our off-duty time. And we all lived in a German apartment house on *64 Henry Budgestrasse* off any base. I doubt anyone thought we were ordinary civilians, a bunch of guys all in one apartment house with no women. It was like a college fraternity house. In our apartment, a second floor walk-up, Sgt. Willie Wilson lived in the kitchen, three guys were in the living room, and I shared the bedroom for about a year with Joe Taormina. Some of the other guys in the outfit and in the building were Bob Inman, Bob Luoma, and Jack Blanshei. Because they all had somewhat unusual names, Betty was able to contact them via the Internet many years later, and we have recently been reunited.

During all my army time with him, I thought my good buddy Joe T. was kind of lazy since he usually stayed in his bed as much as possible, seldom joining me and the others in going out on the town. Later he discovered that he had multiple sclerosis and got a disability-pension from the army. Joe passed away recently with cancer.

My army buddies and I went out a lot, to German restaurants, nightclubs, jazz joints, and bars, but most often to one neighborhood bar just around the corner whose name I have forgotten. When I wanted to show that bar to my wife and children twenty years later it had become the Harry S. Truman Post of the American Legion!

In his autobiography, Bob Luoma wrote of "boozy scenes of me and my army buddies. Joe, Wally, and I once drank too much *Apfelwein* (apple wine) at a jazz club in Sachsenhausen, just across the Main River. Tipsy on a tram [*strassenbahn* or street car] on the way back, we fell down, tumbled out, and sprawled in the street, laughing boisterously. Although blotto, I was still conscious enough to garble apologies to the Germans gaping at us. Some were amused." I actually do remember that incident!

One day a source reported seeing a Russian rocket in an East German city. That was unusual and very surprising. So we sent spies to the area with tiny Minox cameras to check it out. Sure enough, a fuzzy and distant photo showed what looked like a rocket on a flatbed truck! If this were true it would be like the later Cuban Missile Crisis; we would have to alert Washington, maybe even President Eisenhower. More spies, more cameras, brought more photos. Most seemed to confirm the disastrous news. It looked like a rocket. But one close-up photo revealed that the "rocket" was on a *Fashing* or Carnival float -- and was made of *papier mache*!

Cigarettes were rationed to a carton a week and I sold mine every week to a German farmer. He and his wife fed me a farm-fresh breakfast and paid me well for the smokes. I started smoking a pipe because its tobacco was not rationed.

I went all over Europe, including visiting Vienna the week the Russians left and the Vienna Opera House reopened. I got a standing-room "seat" on the upper-rearmost steps. I traveled all over western Europe but had to avoid the East, although I did get to West Berlin on the diplomatic courier's airplane with orders I typed myself.

Joe Taormina and I went to Spain and the Riviera with a buddy we called "Freddie Darlink." I don't remember his real last name. We went to Spain in his car. Both Joe and I had studied Spanish and so we practiced our almost-forgotten skill.

When we got to downtown Madrid, Spanish soldiers suddenly appeared from trucks. They fixed bayonets and forced the crowd (including us) back. Then black cars whizzed by. The Sultan of Morocco was visiting Dictator Francisco Franco.

In Madrid, Joe and I had a suite in a fancy hotel -- I think it was the Ritz -- for all of $3 U.S. -- while Freddie Darlink slept in his car to save money.

When we got to Monaco, there were American flags all over the place and crowds of people with luxury yachts and fabulous cars. Freddy's license plate read "American Army in Europe" and we were welcomed with open arms, even at the famed casino. What was going on? Why were we treated so royally?

Simply because we were Americans and we had arrived, without knowing it, the week of American movie-star Grace Kelly's wedding to Ranier III, prince of Monaco.

Months later, my old friend from Oberammergau, Art, came to Frankfurt. He had almost completed writing a book, with his friends' help, which he called *The G.I.'s Guide to Europe*. (A soldier is called a "G.I." which stands for Government Issue, meaning that everything he has, is, or was, was given to him by the government.)

The book was all but finished when Art came to Frankfurt. It only lacked a chapter on Paris, an absolute essential for any European guidebook. So I went to Paris and wrote that chapter. Then I helped Art, who was a lawyer, negotiate with a German printer to create his book. When he headed back to the States, we agreed to meet with his girlfriend and mine at a French restaurant in Manhattan, the Champlain, when I returned. We did. By that time Art had rewritten the book and called it, *Europe on $5 a Day*. And that's how Betty met my old army buddy, Arthur Frommer.

Incidentally, Bob Luoma wrote of how helpful the *G.I.'s Guide* was for him.

Before I went back to America I bought a diamond engagement ring for Betty at the P.X. or Post Exchange as well as a complete dinnerware service for twelve, a Rosenthal brand, which are the dishes I use now.

I managed to get out before my two-year hitch was up -- legally -- and to fly back to the U.S. instead of suffering another excruciatingly long boat ride. I was discharged two months early, in June of 1956, to go back to college for summer session.

My military career ended with me wearing Specialist Third Class rank (equivalent to Corporal) and in the Inactive Reserve. I remain inactive.

68. CCNY, Downtown

Here's how I decided on my future career: It happened in the "dayroom" of our German apartment house on *Henrybudgestrasse* when I picked up a copy of *Time* magazine. I read an ad, I don't remember which, but I read it through completely. And then I realized that someone had written that ad. Someone writes all the ads in all the magazines. That might be something I could do!

When I mentioned it to Joe Taormina he said, "Sure. The people who write ad copy are called copywriters."

I don't think I had ever heard the word before.

"And," Joe added, "they're very well paid!"

That settled it. I would write ads.

Then Joe gave me another thought: "I'll bet you'd have to have a business degree to get that kind of job."

Everything clicked into place. I would switch from a B.A. (Bachelor of Arts) degree to a B.B.A. (Bachelor of Business Administration) and transfer from CCNY Uptown to CCNY Downtown, the Bernard M. Baruch School of Business Administration.

My military training had taught me how to do the army paperwork. So I used my know-how to get out of the Army early for a change of degree objective. I realized that some of the required courses for a business degree were different from those I had already taken. For example, I would have to take accounting, boring stuff like that. But

I could do boring stuff. After all, I'd been behind an army typewriter for a year and a half.

So I managed to fly home two months early and register at City College on 23rd Street; I'd take a subway instead of that Broadway bus. I had what I wanted from that bus, the girl I had written to so often on my army typewriter, the girl who had written to me even more often, the girl I wanted to marry.

Buying the ring for her and the dishes for us was easy. I knew what I liked. I was confident we both had the same taste. True, I hadn't actually asked Betty to marry me yet, but it was understood. I was sure. And I started CCNY Downtown, knowing I'd become a copywriter. And I was right.

I offered Betty Klein the engagement ring and it fit her finger perfectly. Betty accepted my proposal -- even though it would be a full year and a half before we got married! I also had a job as a copywriter even before I was graduated!

Starting in July, 1956, I became a full-time matriculating student, studying such courses as Marketing, Print Production, and, of course, Advertising. It didn't take long for me to join the National Professional Advertising Fraternity and become the chapter's president. I also became the Assistant Editor of five national trade magazines. In addition I got a government check every month. Plus I had a 12-hour-a-day job in the local Post Office at Christmas. And I went out with Betty! Here's how I did it all at the same time.

City College had a "work/study program," which enabled me to adjust my working and college schedules as long as I held a career-objective job. My friend Sy Reinhart got me a job as a "paste-up boy" (at first) for the Commercial Circular Co., a trade magazine publisher. It was run by Mr. Aronson, whom we called "Mr. A." He was a behind-the-scenes boss who directed his employees in every aspect of their jobs.

The five trade magazines were: *Pet Dealer, Beauty and Barber Supplier, Glove Review, Army-Navy Store Magazine*, and one other one which I don't remember. Some came out monthly, others bimonthly. In a year and a half, I did every job they had, from art director to typesetter (using a special typewriter which "justified" every column, left and right) to photographer to reporter and writer. There were issues in which I wrote practically every article, using various bylines. I also wrote a few ads. It was fun -- a great learning experience. I got paid a little for doing a lot. And, most important, I got samples of my writing in print.

I went out with Betty whenever I could. Most often, because we had so little money, we went for walks. And we talked and talked. About everything. We even planned our family: one boy and one girl, named David and Joan. David because we both liked the name. And Joan after my two grandmothers, both named Johanna Friedmann.

At Christmas time, the post office hired temporary workers on two 12-hour shifts. I was so busy, what with school and work and Betty, that on my first day at the P.O. I hadn't had time to go to the bathroom. So I started off by going to the toilet and promptly fell asleep there. I never got a real job assignment. I used my time at the P.O. to go to the bathroom and to sleep! So I got paid for doing nothing.

I also was paid by the U.S. Government on the G.I. Bill which sent me a check every month for $110.00 as a Korean War Veteran. Yet at CCNY my education was free. I took my classes, cutting just a few now and then to be with Betty.

I designed the cover of the Bernard M. Baruch School of Business and Public Administration folder, For Careers in Business, which even printed a credit for me on the inside.

At graduation, in January, 1958, I won the award given by the American Marketing Association's New York Chapter for "the advancement of science in marketing." I was elected to *Gamma Delta Sigma*, the business school equivalent of *Phi Beta Kappa*. And my grades were such that I was graduated *cum laude*. But I didn't attend the graduation ceremony because I was already working in my first advertising agency as a junior copy writer!

69. Alpha Delta Sigma

As soon as I heard that there was a chapter of "the national professional advertising fraternity" on campus, I decided to join it. Of course, one had to pledge for Alpha Delta Sigma first.

The "price of admission" was to complete a pledge project. Probably because I was a year or two older than most of the other six pledges, I was named the Account Executive on the project. We decided to do a television advertising campaign for a fictional product, All-Fast Glue. I wrote the copy and we created a photo-storyboard with pledge Sy Reinhardt's pictures of my girlfriend Betty posing as a housewife.

We six were all accepted and the next year I was elected president of the fraternity. As such, I inducted professional admen as well as undergrads as members. One of those pros was Sid Kallner, an account executive at Pace Advertising.

As the vice-president of ADS, my pal Sy Reinhart was in charge of vice. So he got us what we called dirty movies, all in black and white. Another ADS member and great friend was Jerry Deoul, who became our best man and lawyer when we bought our first house. He and his wife Louise were one of our renters in St. Barth's. And his later business partners also became our renters and friends.

I didn't know anyone in the advertising business and it was through ADS that I met some. One was Maurice Lerman, always known as Maury, just as Walter Friedman was always Wally. He went to Downtown CCNY two years before me. He was three years older than I but he had never been in the army.

Maury had come to address a class I was taking on advertising. As a recent graduate, he could talk intelligently about the job opportunities and what it really was like in the business -- as opposed to the glamorous picture being portrayed of admen in many popular movies and the Broadway show, *How To Succeed In Business Without Really Trying*. I believed it was a glamorous business but that's not what I cared about. I thought it paid well!

Maury was then a copywriter with the Maxwell Sackheim ad agency. And he set us all straight. Beginning salaries were not so great. If you were good enough, though, he told his eager young listeners, the pay was commensurate with your ability. That sure sounded fair to me. It was tough and really competitive but you had to develop a thick skin and not "fall on your sword when they kill your babies."

He told us that we'd probably change jobs more often than we wanted to. Maury said that when agencies lose an account, or merge, they fire people.

If he was telling it like it is, that's exactly what I needed to know. He made another point that hadn't really entered my mind before. He said that there were Jewish agencies and Gentile agencies, but most were definitely *goyish*. And some of them were prejudiced against Jews. I hadn't thought that anti-Semitism still existed in New York.

Doyle, Dane, Bernbach was a so-called Jewish ad agency. Both Maxwell Dane and Bill Bernbach were Jewish but Doyle, whose name came first of course, was not. Maury told us that Grey Advertising was owned and run by Jews; one of the few "shops" that didn't have a name or names on the door. That's why it was called Grey.

Maury mentioned at the time that Ted Bates & Co. was not known as Jewish since Ted himself was not, nor was their Creative Director, Rosser Reeves. But the Bates Creative Department was nicknamed, "Rosser Reeves and his 40 Hebes!"

And Maury told us that coming from CCNY was decidedly not an advantage: it would have been better, he told us City guys, to have gone to Harvard or Yale or Princeton. Well, that was something we couldn't change, any more than our religion. His main point: "It's a tough field to crack. But if you get in, it's worth it."

I introduced myself to him as the president of Alpha Delta Sigma, the same fraternity he had mentioned he'd been in when he was at City College. I knew enough about the need for "contacts," which is what it was called before "networking" became the word for it. Maury Lerman seemed like a straight shooter. But I didn't know if I'd ever see him again.

Yet our paths were to cross more often than I thought possible.

70. The Good Doctor

While I was in the army overseas Betty quit City College. Although she had done well and had been considering science as a career, she did not enjoy the required courses. I joked that she had what she wanted from college, her M.R.S. degree. Betty went, instead, to Manhattan Medical Assistant School. That school later became a client of mine!

Sylvan Theodore Sussman, M.D., known as Doctor S. Theodore Sussman or Ted, was the New Rochelle doctor who gave Betty her first job. She "reverse commuted," from her parents' home in Manhattan to New Rochelle.

Ted Sussman treated the other person in his office as his assistant. He taught her to give injections and prep patients, do paperwork, prepare treatments, take histories, bandage wounds, and do everything a physician's assistant would do. (Deborah Lynn Kach had much the same job when our son David met her. And our son John worked for the Physicians' Assistants Association.)

Betty and Ted got along so very well. To the silver-haired, mustachioed Ted, she was like another daughter. More than a teacher or mentor, he was also a true friend. And to teen-aged Betty, the man she called Ted to his face but Dr. Sussman to everyone else, he was like a beloved, kindly and helpful grandfather. All the years they worked together, she loved her job and looked forward to going to work every day. Ted, for his part, enjoyed the eagerness and youthfulness of the pupil he treated especially kindly.

When we became engaged, Ted gave us an 8mm movie camera that we used for years. Those movies and Fred Silversmith's earlier movies of me have been transferred into three videotapes (VHS) and cover our own family's history. Our films show Betty and me with Mark Jaffe going to Stamford, Connecticut; Betty and her family in her home and me and my parents in our home. Two VHS tapes cover the "Friedman Family 1960 - 1970" and "1970 - 1979." All shot on Ted Sussman's gift camera.

Dr. Sussman welcomed me home from Germany warmly, graciously and kindly, like a member of the family or a friend, not a boss. Betty's happiness in her job and wish to end her reverse commute made us move to New Rochelle when we got married.

Ted Sussman was cultured and cultivated, educated, informed, up-to-date and knowledgeable, yet also thoughtful, kind, sincere. He was a great friend and wonderful influence on both of our lives. One of those rare people who come into one's life and are a profound and helpful presence, a necessary asset to this world. He was terrific to me when I married Betty, happy for us. A real *mensch*.

So it was a tremendous surprise when Dr. Ted Sussman committed suicide! We had no idea of his mental instability. No one knew he had been going to a psychiatrist. And even he did not think Ted was suicidal.

Ted checked into a local motel and took pills he had prescribed, labeled for Walter Friedman. An ambulance rushed him to New Rochelle Hospital where they tried in vain to save him. He had thrown up and drowned in his own vomit. We can never know what makes someone take his own life.

We gave our son John the middle name of Todd in honor of Ted Sussman.

Betty took a job with another doctor. It was the same kind of work, but it simply wasn't the same; it couldn't have been. Her new boss' name was Dr. Bernard Friedman and he was not related to us (nor the Bernie Friedman I had known in high school.)

Betty quit that job almost as soon as she became pregnant.

71. Two Iraqi Jews

In a biblical sense, Judaism started in Iraq with Abraham at Ur, between the Tigris and the Euphrates Rivers, near what is now Baghdad. So it should not be a surprise that there are Jews living in that country.

Salman Mashaal was a Jew growing up in Basra, the second largest city, one of about 150,000 Jews then in Iraq. This was before the reign of Saddam Hussein, when there was a king. At that time they taught religion in the public school, the *madrass*, and when the Muslim religion was the subject, the Jews were excused. They went to Hebrew School, just as I did in Boston, to learn their religion. Young Salman took Arabic, English, and Hebrew in elementary and junior high school. But when he finished high school, Salman wanted to study civil engineering. So he applied to the very best engineering school in the world, doubting that he would get in.

MIT, the Massachusetts Institute of Technology, accepted him. So he left his family in a peaceful Basra and came to Boston. Now, as I write this, in December, 2004, there is warfare in Basra. It is occupied by British troops and the scene of frequent suicide bombings and insurgent or guerilla attacks that I call a civil war.

His studies were not easy, but they were worthwhile. And Sal, as Americans called him, did well. When the Jewish holidays came around, he was ready to relax. The local Hillel organization was setting up for a tea dance and he decided to attend.

My cousin Ellen-Ruth Fass, who escaped Germany on the *Kindertransport* and came to Boston, was a member of Hillel. She was supposed to help decorate the room. But she was ill, so her "sister" Vera substituted for her. When Salman entered the room he immediately spotted a quiet, demure, thin, almost delicate and very attractive young lady on a ladder, putting up balloons. Their eyes met. And then they met. It was love at first sight for him. Sal knew exactly what he wanted: he was determined to marry her!

Her name was Vera Heineman, nicknamed Putzi, the daughter of Ashkenazi Jewish immigrants to America who had become citizens recently. She was willing to go out with him, a Sephardic Jew, and when she did, she found him to be charming, delightful, entertaining, exciting, and very interesting. Sal was also gentle, kind, thoughtful, and considerate as he courted her as intensively as he studied his lessons.

The difference between Ashkenazi and Sephardic Jews is just where they come from: Northern Europe versus Spain and North Africa. I do not think those distinctions made any difference in our families.

Sal met Vera's family, which now included not only her parents, Walter and Rosi Heineman, but also her first cousin, introduced as her "sister," Ellen, formerly Ellen-Ruth Fass.

Salman Mashaal married Vera and he changed his name legally to Stanley Marshall. But our family still calls him, most affectionately, Sal.

It was not long thereafter when Ellen, having spent three years at Radcliffe and then two at Simmons to achieve a degree in Library Science, was in New York City's International House.

Someone else who went to the International House that day was another young Jew originally from Baghdad named Samuel H. Zilka. He thought it might be a good place to meet girls. When he noticed a young lady reading a *New York Times*, he tried a pickup line, asking her if she was finished with a section of the paper.

Ellen gladly gave him what he asked for and a conversation ensued. It soon came out that he was an engineer from Iraq and was Jewish.

"What a coincidence, my sister just married a Jewish engineer from Iraq," Ellen said to Sam Zilka. That certainly put the idea of marrying a Jewish girl in America into Sam's head, if it hadn't been there before. And Sam and Ellen started dating.

In stark contrast to the war zone of today, the Baghdad of 1957 was described in *Time* as booming, doubling in five years (to about a million). "Streets are jammed with American cars, creating a monumental traffic problem that the new bridges over the Tigris have not begun to solve. Bulldozers are flattening 300 slum houses and bazaar shops to open a new freeway through the city center ... the city is spreading beyond the dikes where handsome villas are rising for the new, well-to-do middle classes" to which the Zilkas belonged.

But the Zilkhas -- with an h, an important difference -- were among the uppermost class of Baghdad society! Khedoury Zilkha was known as "the Rothschild of the Middle East," having started in 1899 with a one-room bank in Baghdad. His four sons extended the family's reach to Lebanon, Egypt, France, England, and the U.S.A. They entered many businesses, including oil, with Zilkha Energy and Zilkha Renewable Energy. The richest members of the Zilkha family now live in Texas and California.

Khedoury Zilkha's cousin was also a banker in Baghdad; he was Sam Zilka's father. It's this less-than-wealthy branch to which our Zilkas (with no h) belong.

Sam introduced Ellen and my parents and me to his brother Ned, a Syosset, Long Island, eye surgeon, and to his sister Violet. Ellen had Sam meet her "sister and brother-in-law," the Marshalls; her "Oma and Opa Boston," the Heinemans; and her "Oma and Opa New York," my parents. As Ellen's only relatives in New York, my parents spent a good deal of time with Sam and Ellen.

My father and Sam Zilka got to know each other much better very quickly and really got to like each other a lot, although they must have had trouble with each other's accents. They got along so well partly because they shared a love of operatic and symphonic music, and both had subscriptions to the Metropolitan Opera and the City Center.

Ellen was forever grateful to my mother for having enabled her to escape Nazi Germany and take the *kindertransport* to England as well as my parents for helping her come to America.

When Sam and Ellen got married, I was the "bartender" at their party, thanks to a little book that told how to mix drinks. Whenever someone asked for something, I looked it up, mixed it up, gave it to them, and tested or tasted my concoction. No book had told me not to mix my drinks! Needless to say, I got very drunk very quickly.

My mother told me that the newlywed Ellen Zilka had asked her opinion about how many children would be ideal. And my mother said she told her: three. Ellen had 3, Vera had 3, and we had 3 -- but those nine kids were definitely not all born just on my mother's say-so.

Back to Sal and Vera "Putzi" Marshall as a young married couple. He got a job as a civil engineer on what was the biggest construction job in Boston. This was about 30 years before the "Big Dig" which became Boston's much, much bigger boondoggle. That was the underground highway tunnel which collapsed and killed a woman in her car. The job Sal worked on was an underground waterline which sprung a leak while it was being constructed. It wasn't Sal's fault, but he felt it wise to change jobs.

While looking in the newspaper for an apartment, he noticed one for a furnished penthouse apartment in Rio de Janeiro, Brazil! A 4- to 6-month job as the Project Engineer turned out to take eight months.

Their daughter Linda hated Rio and went home to Massachusetts, but their youngest son Gary got sick in Rio, staying in his room for three days. Then there was another job opportunity in Brazil. The so-called expatriate experience was a wonderful one for the young Marshall family; it lasted from 1971 to 1976.

They returned to Boston and Putzi developed breast cancer. She fought it for many years, valiantly, but passed away in October, 2001.

72. Pace Advertising

Walter A. Friedman is a historian at Harvard and no relation to me. He wrote *Birth of a Salesman*, subtitled *The Transformation of Selling in America.* It chronicles how our economy became driven by advertising, the chosen career of Walter E. Friedman.

In the *New Yorker* of March 28, 2005 (my 71st birthday), Ken Auletta contrasted the advertising business as it is now and as it was in my day. He wrote that "the ad game" was where failed poets became embittered copywriters and have too many martinis. Advertising was manipulative in books like *The Hidden Persuaders*, ruthless in movies like *The Hucksters,* and innocent fun in Augusten Burroughs' memoir, *Dry.*

I did not see it like that and I was in the business in its heyday. It has changed over the years but let me begin where I started.

My first advertising agency job began in January, 1958, while I was still in my senior year of college. It didn't hurt that Sid Kallner, an Account Exec, remembered me from ADS when I applied for a job as a Junior Copywriter at Pace Advertising. Perhaps Maury Lerman had been right: who you know may be as important as what you know.

There were two writers in the agency, that's all. The other one was called the Copy Chief. He was known as "Dolf" because his name was Adolf. We shared a room only slightly larger than our two desks, which faced each other.

Dolf never reviewed my copy. I worked directly with and for the Account Executives, two of whom were the partners who owned the agency.

I earned $60 a week. Betty was earning $65 working for Dr. Ted Sussman in New Rochelle That's what we earned when we got married. My college friends who were engineers all started at $100 a week!

Pace Advertising was owned by two partners, both Jewish. One of the Pace partners and most of the other Account Executives handled only real estate advertising. So I wrote ads for developments on Long Island, Westchester, New Jersey, and a few apartment houses in Riverdale and New York City. There were weekends when ads I wrote predominated in the real estate sections of the *New York Times, Post, Daily News,* and *Mirror.* In my first year, I wrote hundreds of ads for those newspapers!

The other partner, however, and some other Account Executives, had "real" clients, not real estate. There was Hudson Vitamins, Hotel Bar Foods, Hankey Bannister Whiskey, United Metal Cabinets, Warner Windows.

And there was Pez candy and dispensers. I often held in my hand the very expensive working models of the original Pez dispensers such as Santa Claus, Popeye, Superman, and many more. My commercials introduced those. Today, the manufactured versions of these are very valuable collectors' items. Imagine what those models are now worth!

I wrote many TV commercials for Pez and other products. In those days, I typed up a script with the video directions on the left column and the audio copy -- the words that the announcer or the "talent" was to say -- on the right. Once approved by client, we'd mimeograph copies and I'd go to the TV studio and rehearse the actors and actresses as well as the cameramen and director. For Pez, one talent was Shari Lewis who performed with hand-puppets that were socks. Another was Miss Frances of Romper Room. I'd rehearse the talent by going over the script, then having them read it to time it and I'd critique it, often telling them to "punch" the brand name. Usually one rehearsal was enough or all they had time for. We rarely made cue cards. The talent read the script and memorized it. And I told the cameramen when to show the product. Then the commercials were delivered and broadcast "live" in those early black-and-white days of TV advertising. They happened on the spot and were not recorded. This was just before kinescope or videotape recording. No copies exist and I kept no old scripts.

Pace also worked with a public relations affiliate owned by Tex McCrary and his wife Jinx Falkenberg. She had been a Miss America (the first one I met) and he was a radio "personality." In a meeting with them I met Bill (as he was introduced to me) Safire. Our common client was the Long Island builder whom we convinced to set up a model home in Moscow. It was the scene of then-Vice President Nixon's "kitchen debate" with Soviet Premier Khrushchev; it was where Safire met Nixon. He later became President Nixon's speechwriter and a *New York Times* columnist and author. When any of the Pace agency's real estate account executives went on vacation, I went to sell my copy to their clients. That's how I met Sid Farber, my first millionaire.

Betty and I got married while I was at Pace; that's the next Chapter.

I didn't attend my own college graduation because I was working as a copywriter. Then Pace lost some business -- certainly through no fault of mine -- but they no longer needed two writers. So I was let go. A newlywed and out of work!

Despite that initial rejection, I went on to have ads or campaigns I wrote or worked on elected to the Advertising Hall of Fame, win the top Clio for the best TV commercial under :60, The One Show, ANNY, ANDY, and an International Award of Merit. Three of the ads appeared in *Adverting Age's* "100 Best." I ended up in the then-rising field of international advertising and had my own recognized ad agency. I didn't do too badly.

And my entire career was indeed writing short, very short, stories.

IX. MY FAMILY
(1958 - 1989)

73. Our Wedding and New Rochelle

Betty and I rented an apartment at 175 Center Avenue in New Rochelle, within easy walking distance of Dr. Sussman's office and not too far from the train station. It was really just one room with a kitchen and bath. The "rule of thumb" in those days was to spend no more than a quarter of your income on housing. The rent was $110 per month; together we earned $125 a week. We bought a fold-away bed/couch and set our wedding date for the day after Macy's would deliver it.

Our wedding was Friday afternoon, March 8, 1958. Our "honeymoon" would be in our new apartment that weekend. On Monday morning we both had to go to work.

The wedding was at the Bennett Avenue home of friends of my parents, Hans and Else Gruenewald; he was a part-time rabbi and licensed by New York State to marry people. In addition to her parents and mine, we needed two witnesses to sign the *Katubah* or marriage certificate. We picked my best friend Mark Jaffe (I was later his best man, too) and her best friend Audrey Hutt Bricker (she and Jerry had recently been married). But Mr. Gruenewald said we had to have two male witnesses so we also invited my ADS pal, Jerry Deoul, who later became our lawyer. That was it. (Only Mike and Mary's wedding was smaller: one officiant, two witnesses and one friend was it.)

My father gave me his Chevrolet as a wedding present and we left the Gruenewald's apartment, drove up Bennett Avenue to 181st St., turned the corner and stopped for a red light behind other cars. I was so nervous *after* the wedding, that I took my foot off the brake and promptly rear-ended another car! What an inauspicious start to married life! But it was truly minor, a mere bumper-bump that caused no damage at all.

Every week we cashed both of our paychecks and put the money into envelopes labeled for their various purposes such as rent, food, furniture, and "savings for spending" and "savings for saving." We continued that system for years.

It was a few months before we each had a week off work and so could go on a "real" honeymoon. I drove the Chevy northward, first stopping at Saratoga Springs, then for a night in a motel at Lake George. Then I invited Betty for a horseback ride in the country; after all, I had ridden horses at Farm Camp Loewy, the place Betty knew I'd met her friend Susie so many years ago.

We galloped around a bend and I fell off my horse! Aside from the embarrassment, I scraped my elbow. Of course we drove on, reaching our final northward destination, Montreal, Canada. The first thing we did there, after registering in the *Auberge du Boulevard Laurier,* which we called our "Honeymoon Hotel," was to go to the hospital they suggested, up on the hill that is Mount Royal. They treated and bandaged my elbow.

While I was at Pace Advertising, one of the real estate guys got a hot tip on a Canadian uranium mining stock, Kerr Lake Mines, Ltd. I phoned Betty and convinced her to let me put $100 into it. Our very first investment. At $125 combined income per week, that was a lot of money. At her insistence, I agreed to sell if the stock doubled or halved.

So we sold our shares just a few weeks later when it hit $200 -- just before a scandal broke that deflated all those speculative Canadian Uranium Mining stocks down to virtually nothing. Kerr Lake, however, became a shopping center developer!

We took the $200 and invested it, through Merrill Lynch Pierce Fenner & Smith, as it was then known, in Boeing Aircraft stock and that started our real investing. We kept with the plan of selling at double or half. So we sold Boeing when it hit $100.

My old army buddy Joe Taormina visited us in our apartment after he got out of the army. We didn't have a room to put him up in, so he slept in the kitchen, or as he put it at the time, with his head in the dinette and his feet in the refrigerator.

Before our one-year lease was up we started looking for a house. We found what we wanted in what was then known as the Town of Rye in a development known as Rye Hills at 3 Jennifer Lane. It was a house built for returning servicemen after World War II and it had originally cost only $9,999 and available to ex-G.I.'s for no money down.

Those were magic numbers and words. I was writing ad copy like that for housing developments. I was, after all, an ex-G.I., but the now 7-year-old house was not available to me on those terms. Nor was the price as low as it had been. By 1959, it had doubled in value! They were asking $19,999 and it would require a cash down payment. But, at least, as a veteran myself, I could buy it from the vet who owned it and "pick up" his 4¼% G.I. mortgage -- if only I could put up $10,000!

Still living on a total of $125 a week, still saving our cash in envelopes, we had no money saved for that kind of expense! However my father came to the rescue. He wanted us to be the first in the Friedman family to own their house. He wanted us to have children. Actually, he wanted grandchildren. So he gave us the ten thousand dollars!

74. Biff and Rye

Our first house was in the unincorporated Town of Rye. Our taxes were lower than in the city of Rye. Taxes were included with the monthly mortgage payment. So we kept up our savings plan in envelopes.

One of the things we had to save up for was a floor lamp. When I found a lamp in Bloomingdale's that I liked which cost only $20, I asked Betty to drive to Manhattan to see the lamp and, if she liked it, we'd buy it and drive it home. It had taken us a while but we had saved up $20 in the furniture envelope. Walking from the parking space to Bloomie's, however, took us past a pet shop which had beagle-terrier puppies in the window. We stopped, looked and fell in love with the runt of the litter. The pet shop gave us this mixed breed in a cardboard box. We took him to the car and drove to my parents' home for dinner. The just-a-few-days-old puppy cost us our many-weeks-savings of $20.

My father got very upset, which he did easily and often. And it wasn't because the puppy peed on his apartment floor, which, of course, he did. Hans Friedman thought we'd bought a dog instead of having children.

It was a bit later, after we'd had the little mutt a while, that we noticed that the puppy often seemed to bat away or biff at things with his paws. A character in Arthur Miller's great play *Death of A Salesman* was named Biff. The pup became Biff.

We fenced in the backyard to keep the dog close to home. There are wonderful movies (VHS) which show Biff in summer and winter, in our blow-up pool and sled.

My old army buddy Joe Taormina visited us in our new home. Betty and I went with him to see his old girl friend, Mona, who had written him a "Dear John" letter while we were in the army. Joe had kept in touch with her. She was not only married but had four children already! At that time Joe said, "I always knew Mona was fertile!"

Betty became pregnant at the same time as Biff was enrolled in Dog Obedience Training School. Also at that time, I slipped a disc in my back. So it wasn't the dog's fault that he never was properly trained or obedient. He considered "come" a request. "Clean up" became the words he would come for.

Biff was part of our family for a long time. When Betty called the kids in for dinner, it was always, "David, John, Michael, Biff -- stop what you're doing and come home!" It was many years after Biff's death at age 14 that David started telling his daughters fanciful tales of "Biff, the Wonder Dog."

There was a homeowners' association for the Rye Hills and Rye Brook twin communities and I became the editor of their newsletter. Before our time there, it had been decided that the area needed sewers. I got involved and, using "the power of the press," we lobbied the powers that be, the local politicians, especially "Chappie" Posillipo, the Town Manager. We got our sewers at the whole town's taxpayers' expense.

Betty and I became angels when we lived in Rye! A friend in the area, I'll call him Don Sampler, worked for a theatrical production company in Manhattan. He often got the opportunity to buy shares in Broadway shows long before they opened. And Don invited some of his friends and neighbors to pool our money and invest with him. Together a bunch of us could afford one share. We invested in a Mary Martin show, a Gertrude Berg ("Molly Goldberg") show, each of which never opened due to the star's illness, and a few other money losers. But we did do well with *Oliver Twist* and *Stop The World I Want To Get Off.* Such investors are known as Broadway Angels. As unofficial investors we had to pay full price for tickets -- but we could get tickets for opening week! Often that was closing week, too.

Two brothers lived in two houses near us in Rye Hills and became our friends. They were both lawyers and partners. One was William Kunstler and I have forgotten his brother's first name. They first came to my attention when they put up signs directing people to their homes. Signs that said only "SNCC" with a directional arrow. It seemed mysterious but did not mean anything to me at the time. Later I learned that it was pronounced "snick" and stood for the Students' Non-violent Coordinating Committee. I hadn't heard of it then but soon everyone did: It was really one of the first civil rights organizations for blacks; the other was the NAACP, the National Association for the Advancement of Colored People.

Bill Kunstler became famous as the lead attorney in the Chicago Conspiracy case and he was sentenced to four years in prison for contempt of court. A New York City boy, he had been a gang member but became an A student, earning degrees from Yale and Columbia Law school. The brothers' practice concentrated on civil liberties law and helped create many initial legal battles for Negroes, as African-Americans were called at that time. Bill wrote that he tried to put the American criminal justice system on trial. His clients included Lenny Bruce, H. Rap Brown, Stokely Carmichael, American Indian leaders, Jack Ruby, Martin Luther King, Jr., Malcolm X, and Islamic terrorists. Yes, Islamic terrorists even then!

Later, I was even elected the president of the Rye Hills-Rye Brook Homeowners' Association but I resigned when we moved to Chappaqua and sold our house to a nice black couple, thus integrating the Kunstlers' own neighborhood.

75. Maxwell Sackheim

Max Sackheim became famous with his ad headlined, *Do You Make These Mistakes In English?* in the *100 Best Ads Ever Written* book. It was for one of the first self-help books and one of the first mail-order schemes. Max also started the Inertia Principle, as he called it. It was for the first book-of-the-month club, based on man's inherent laziness or inertia: Sign up for something and then do nothing and you automatically get another item, such as a book or vitamins, month after month. But you have to actually send in a cancellation notice in order <u>not</u> to receive another item. He was a brilliant adman and, with his wife and two sons, owned his own advertising agency. They had an ad in *The New York Times* for a copywriter just when I was looking for a job.

I got it. And it was one of the most important jobs in my career. For it was the Sackheim agency which also taught Maury Lerman, Les Richter, Ronnie Romano, and others I met in the business. It is not a coincidence that we four spent many years at Ted Bates. And all also became Creative Directors at Bates.

It was great training because Mail Order Advertising actually sold the products. So you knew if your ad sold as many as the previous ad. You constantly wrote and tested new ads to keep improving sales. And that was the basis of the kind of advertising Ted Bates was famous for. The only question directed at any ad you wrote was: Did it sell? Did it sell more than the previous ad? More than the competition? More than last year? More than ever before? If so, your client ran that ad again and again until another test ad beat it. At huge agencies, with multi-million-dollar ad budgets, a test ad or commercial would run in a test market area. When it beat the national ad campaign, it became the next campaign. Any ad ran as long as it sold products. My first television commercials, for Pez, had sold a tremendous amount of the candy (or the dispensers, it didn't matter which). The saying was, "sell the sizzle, not the steak," such as the dispenser. <u>Selling</u> was what advertising was all about.

Those were also the initial days of television advertising. And I worked at Maxwell Sackheim only long enough to get the whole idea: An ad *must sell*. Advertising was not an amusement, entertainment, or popularity contest. It was not, in those early days, designed to impress associates or to pump up the company's stock.

But if clients don't come in the door, employees go out. I was let go.

76. Mogul and Kaplan

Now I had a "book" of ads to show, a portfolio of scripts and samples of published writing. My next job was at a medium-sized Manhattan agency, Mogul, Williams & Saylor, then owned by Emil Mogul and his

197

wife. Their agency was a conglomeration of diverse small agencies and many account executives. They had British Motors (I worked on the Morris Minor) as well as Rayco (auto seat covers) and retail accounts like Barney's. I did mostly radio spots and print ads for them.

One of the account execs was Alvin H. Kaplan (and his wife, Betty) who did mail- order advertising, the kind I was becoming an expert in *already!* Their clients included Speedwriting (which ran subway posters headed: "gt a gd jb w mo pa") and such mail-order schools as the Locksmithing Institute and the Newspaper Institute. I shared an office with Mrs. Kaplan.

At MW&S I wrote broadcast and print ads, brochures, car dealer deals, mail order letters, matchbook covers, skywriting -- everything. In what became known as Direct Marketing, a.k.a. Mail Order Advertising, I concentrated primarily on the Kaplans' accounts, going to their clients at times to present the ads I had written. We developed a Speedwriting-based secretarial school that became known as the Nancy Taylor Institute (a totally fictitious name) which was sold to ITT, the conglomerate which I also worked on years later at Ted Bates. I was doing a successful job with the Kaplan accounts in particular and spent most of my time on their business. But I also gained experience in the production of ads, brochures, mailing pieces, radio, everything but TV, which is what I really enjoyed doing most.

It was then that I suffered a slipped disc. One day I reached across my desk for a piece of paper and felt my back "go out." I went to New Rochelle Hospital for tests which included a myelogram. A doctor performed a spinal tap, removed some fluid and replaced it temporarily with a dye in order to diagnose my condition. It was a slipped disc all right. and I was soon bent over so badly that I literally could not move. First they tried bed rest but it actually seemed to get worse. I couldn't get out of bed when Ellen Zilka and her brother from England, Gerald Freeman, came to visit us.

Soon I could only walk all bent over. They had to operate. I had a laminectomy and fusion, in which they took a bit of bone from my hip and put it between the two lumbar vertebrae, L4 and L5, to fuse them. Since it was my own bone, there was no risk of rejection. The operation worked perfectly and I soon had, and still have, complete mobility. I can even touch my toes without bending my knees. But for a while there, while Betty was pregnant, I had been no help at all.

The Kaplans were very solicitous and concerned. I would not say that it was because of me that Alvin H. Kaplan decided to split off from MW&S. But he did ask me to join his agency when he started it. I told him I would, simply and frankly because I wasn't positive I'd still have a job after Kaplan left Mogul, Williams & Saylor.

It was exactly at that time that David was born. Alvin and Betty Kaplan came to visit us and brought a wonderful rocking horse as a gift for the baby. It was a truly generous gesture and showed how much they cared for me.

So it was not easy when I changed my mind and decided not to join their agency. But that's what I did.

77. David Alan Friedman

It was the 4th of July weekend, 1961, and my parents had gone to Atlantic City. There was no reason not to; after all, it was a full six weeks before Betty was due to have a baby. In those days people did not know if it was going to be a boy or a girl.

Betty and I were at home in 3 Jennifer Lane, Town of Rye, in Westchester County, New York. It was Saturday morning. She asked me the time. I told her. A little while later, after some conversation, she asked me the time again. I told her. I wondered what was going on but didn't say anything.

Sweetly, gently, she told me to get the bag we had packed, ready for a trip to the hospital. But the hospital she was booked into was Mt. Sinai in Manhattan. It was more than a half hour away *without traffic*. She thought we'd better go.

We were in the car when she asked me the time again. I said, "You just asked me that about three minutes ago!"

Quite calmly, she said, "<u>About</u> isn't good enough; tell me <u>exactly</u> what time it is."

"You're not timing contractions, are you?"

"That's what I'm doing," she replied quite matter-of-factly.

I stepped on the gas and we got to the hospital in record time. But I felt sure it was a false alarm, after all, it was six weeks early. A full month and a half too soon!

The reason we were headed for Mt. Sinai was because Betty's obstetrician, I'll call him Dr. Klamper, was the same one who had delivered her. A young doctor then, he was now -- twenty-five years later -- the head of obstetrics at famed Mt. Sinai Hospital.

When we got to the hospital I was sent to the "Father's Waiting Room." I tried to phone my parents at their Atlantic City hotel. They were out. I left a message: "Betty's in the hospital." Not the best message I could have left, but I was now an excited, nervous, expectant father. Then I called Betty's parents. Her father said, "I'll be right there!"

Alex Klein came to join me in that waiting room. I don't know where Frieda was. She probably stayed at home, knowing it was too early. Alex said, "It'll be a boy."

I was annoyed by his certainty. It could be a girl. We had boys' and girls' names ready, but I felt sure it would be a girl. Perhaps it was because Alex was so sure about it being a boy. I really thought it was most likely a false alarm! It was *so very* early -- *six weeks early.* The date was July 2, 1961.

I wondered if the baby would survive if he or she was born this early but I didn't say anything to Alex Klein. He was a real worrywart and I surely wasn't going to increase his natural anxieties.

I did not know it then but about one in ten babies at that time were born prematurely. It was defined as at least three weeks early -- and this was six weeks early! Another definition called any baby born weighing less than five pounds a premature baby. Prematurity was, as Christine Gorman put it in *Time*, "a significant cause of blindness, chronic lung problems and birth defects" and, she added, "no incubator -- no matter how high tech -- will ever replace the womb."

There was no one else in the waiting room but the two of us. So we waited for a half hour. We glanced at magazines. An hour passed. I tried to reach my parents again. Now an hour and a half had gone by. Alex phoned Frieda. Two hours. What was going on? Is a long wait good news or not?

We waited nervously. Alex paced the floor like an expectant father. I read one magazine after another without really understanding what I was reading.

Finally, almost two and a half hours after we'd arrived, a doctor came to tell us it was a boy and that Betty was fine ... *but the baby has difficulty breathing.* They had rushed him to an incubator.

Alex acted happy that it was indeed a boy but I was worried. Soon Dr. Klamper came and told us that she had done wonderfully and was resting, but that the baby had hyaline membrane disease! It was a term I remembered.

That was exactly what little Patrick Bouvier Kennedy had! He was the premature baby that Jacqueline Kennedy was pregnant with during the recent presidential campaign. The boy was born soon after Jack became President. But he had died just two days after he was born. The Kennedys certainly must have had the very best of care. He was the president and fabulously wealthy; they must have had the best medical treatment possible! Now the same disease threatened the life of our new baby boy!

Alex and I went to see Betty. I kissed her and told her I was proud of her and loved her so very much. She was exhausted, tired, spent, but wide awake. And, of course, very worried about the baby. We asked to see him. Only the baby's father, not the mother's father, was allowed into the room full of incubators.

David Alan Friedman was so very tiny. Fearfully small and tender-looking. He weighed only four pounds, six ounces! Under five pounds is considered premature and he surely was that. Six full weeks premature!

It was frightening. He was in an incubator with tubes taped to his nose. His breathing seemed irregular. He was fighting for every breath he took! You could see his tiny frame struggling for air. It was heart-wrenchingly sad. I felt sorry for the little guy.

Betty and I had decided upon the name David in one of our early dates; we both liked the name and thought it went perfectly with Friedman. He was middle-named Alan after my father's father Aron, in Jewish custom, naming after a deceased ancestor. We had decided on the simple spelling of Alan because Aron was also the simpler spelling.

Now we learned more about hyaline membrane disease. It was due to premature birth and the lack of surfactant production from the immature lungs. The incubator was essential, for mechanical ventilation was vital for the baby's survival. The tubes were adding liquid -- but not too much for his underdeveloped lungs! I realized that Dr. Sussman had died because he had gotten fluid into his lungs. Could our tiny baby handle what a grown man couldn't? Then we were told that hemorrhages could develop!

The same *Time* magazine article mentioned above said, "Doctors can sustain a tiny baby ... with lungs so fragile that even the gentlest respirator can permanently damage them. But should they?"

We got further scary news: If the baby survived -- and it was a big *if* -- a later complication could be bronchopulmonary dysphasia (BPD) and respiratory distress could continue *for months!* We were also told that hemorrhages could develop "which can be devastating." He could begin to bleed internally! Our fears were, unfortunately, realistic.

It was really touch-and-go; so very frightening for anyone, especially young parents. I kept looking at little David. I was glad we had named him that because David was a strong fighter; he was the little guy who had beaten the giant Goliath. Our little David would have to be a real fighter, too! I watched him fighting for every breath. The machine and the tubes were helping him. Yet hadn't little Patrick Kennedy had all that? He had lived two days with the best care, yet he did not survive.

I was very glad we were at Mt. Sinai and under "the big boss'" care! The baby was not yet assigned to a pediatrician; at this point it was still Betty's obstetrician who was in charge. We did not ever see Dr. Klamper again. But I felt good knowing he was on top of this case.

Later, months later, we heard that he had been one of the first OB/GYN doctors to lose a multimillion dollar lawsuit convicting him of "neglect," a primary cause of rising medical insurance rates.

Betty and I both tried to keep each others' spirits up. Alex was confident. It frightened me, how sure he was. Still, I reassured my wife that little David would be fine.

I kept calling the hotel clerk in Atlantic City who didn't want to give my parents the message that Betty was in the hospital although I didn't know that at the time. When I changed the message to "It's a boy!" she finally did reach them. They got the mixed news: Betty was fine but David was fighting for his life. They cut their vacation short to come back to Manhattan.

Of course I visited my little family, each one separately, every day. The worry was constantly there. After a few days Betty was discharged from the hospital, but tiny David stayed in his incubator. We drove home and went home, with mixed emotions, without our baby. Betty had to pump her breasts to release the milk.

We both visited him every day. Finally, they let us take him out of the incubator for a short time, just so Betty could feed him a bottle of her own milk. That was also when I got to hold him: all of little David fit easily into my one hand. He was that tiny. I fed him, too.

David won the fight and was out of the incubator and out of the hospital. Finally, we had our baby boy home with us at last. We put him in a crib in our bedroom. Now friends and family could come to visit, but we were afraid he might catch cold or some germ from somebody; we wanted to treat him gingerly. However, it didn't take long for Betty to say he was totally OK now; he could be treated like any other baby.

So my parents and Betty's came to visit, as did our friends and neighbors. Now we had a baby we could hold. I was delighted to do just that. A little afraid to do much more. But I must admit I was truly scared of giving him a bath in our bathinette.

You see, before his birth we had both taken the Red Cross classes in caring for a newborn. One of the classes was bathing a baby in a bathinette. We used dolls, of course. And when it was my turn, while I was concentrating on washing the doll's rear end properly, I inadvertently drowned the baby: the doll's head was underwater and I hadn't realized it. Years later I wrote a Pampers commercial in which that was what happened in a new-parents' class.

One day we put our little David into a baby chair in the living room. Our dog, Biff, sniffed and immediately raised a rear leg at the chair. We stopped him in time! He had shown his disapproval of having to share his "parents" with a new baby! Or was it, as David now says, Biff marking his territory?

Now perfectly happy at home, baby David became very active, a noisy, squealing baby -- day and night. We couldn't sleep. When he cried, he cried himself to sleep. But when he was awake, he made noises.

Betty picked him up and sang lullabies to him and that helped him go to sleep. But she got exhausted very easily and asked me to take him and walk around with him and sing to him. I didn't really know any lullabies. So I sang old Army songs - softly - to put him to sleep. Of course, the only Army songs I knew were somewhat risqué, even dirty. Our little baby didn't know the difference; they put him to sleep as easily as lullabies. It worked so well on David, I used it on all three of our sons. By the time Michael was born, however, David may have been old enough to understand the lyrics.

It quickly became apparent that David's prematurity didn't really harm him at all. He had no residual effect whatsoever. He was a normal, healthy boy.

It was not clear at the time, however, that Betty's smoking may have caused David's premature birth. Or both of his brothers' premature births. In fact, Betty's continued smoking also may have caused her early death. Cigarette packs had no warnings whatsoever at that time.

When David was young he pronounced most words, even big words, perfectly. One that he did mispronounce was "butterflies." He called them, "flutterbys," which we thought was a better name for them.

One day, while he was still quite young, Dave wanted a prize from a gumball machine. He put in his nickel or dime, I doubt it was a quarter then, in the hopes of getting what he wanted, it may have been gum. Instead, however, the machine produced a small plastic dolphin. David was so disappointed that he burst into tears. He was almost inconsolable until Betty told him that the dolphin toy was the most valuable thing he could have gotten, it would protect him against all kinds of trouble. He was incredibly lucky and should be delighted to have it. In fact, she told him, she would hang it up in the front of our car as a good-luck charm. That little dolphin went from car to car as we traded them in; today it hangs from my car. The fact is, every car has had good luck!

Another day, while riding on his bike, Dave somehow went head-over-wheels and landed on his face. That broke his two front teeth. So he got false teeth early in life.

As David grew up he was usually among the shorter boys in his class. I don't think that they measured percentiles at that time. When he played baseball, for example, the team uniforms were numbered on the back, the shortest boy got number 1 and so on, up the number and size scale. On his team, the Falcons, Dave wore number 2.

One day, while David was sitting on the team bench along the first base line, he was hit in the mouth with a batted baseball. That added stitches to his upper lip on top of his false teeth.

David Alan Friedman became a boy scout, quickly earning merit badges to gain promotion up the ranks. He created a trail through nearby woods as his major project which earned him the exalted rank of Eagle Scout. His grandparents and parents attended the ceremony and were even prouder than he was. I am still very proud of him.

78. Ted Bates

My friend Maury Lerman phoned me to tell me there was a job open at Ted Bates, that I should apply to his boss, "Bo" Carlaw, and stress my experience with Maxwell Sackheim. I did and was offered the job, starting salary $10,000 a year!

Ted Bates was the major leagues, the 5th largest agency in the world, while Alvin H. Kaplan was a Class D minor league team! I also hadn't talked salary with Kaplan, but I was earning $100 a week -- about half of Bates' offer -- and I guessed that Kaplan wouldn't double my pay. Besides, I now had a family to consider. A no-brainer!

I jumped at the chance to join Ted Bates & Co., Inc. And I stayed there 15 years.

The Bates agency had been started by a group of advertising men who named it for the "front man," the elegant, stylish, white Anglo-Saxon protestant (WASP) who had some Colgate-Palmolive business. I worked with Ted Bates himself on one account: Carter's Little Liver Pills.

The Creative Director was Rosser Reeves. Son of a Southern Baptist preacher, he had a booming voice with a strong Southern drawl. He was known throughout the industry for the hard-hitting, repetitive commercials the agency made famous. He coined the term U.S.P., or Unique Selling Proposition. He demanded that we find the exclusive, or seemingly exclusive, big idea which would conclusively convince a customer to buy the product. And then Bates would pound that U.S.P. home through repetition upon repetition after repetition.

Rosser was also famous as a tough guy who chewed people out and actually was reputed to draw from one victim - not blood - but tears. I was in a meeting with him when he ripped a storyboard off the wall and stomped on it. His copywriters were known for having a *yiddisher kopf* -- a Jewish head or brain.

Many quivered in their boots when they had to present their ideas to Rosser. I was in the meeting when Rosser solicited ideas for a brand new client, a Japanese firm just starting to do business in the U.S.A., called Panasonic. I do not now remember what I suggested. The winning idea was "Just slightly ahead of our time." But the idea submitted by Jerry Della Femina was "From those wonderful folks who brought you Pearl Harbor." For once in his life, Rosser was speechless. Jerry's quip became the title of his memoir, a best seller.

Jerry quit Bates to form his own ad agency which became very successful. He offered to sell me shares of stock in his agency, but I was still at Bates and I thought it unethical to own competitive stock.

Rosser was also known as the owner of the Rosser Reeves Ruby, the world's largest, which he showed me in his handkerchief and, years later, I saw on permanent display in the Smithsonian. Rosser also headed the U.S. chess team in international competition. He was a master in chess, perhaps a Grand Master. Rosser Reeves' brother-in-law was the equally famous adman David Ogilvy.

My first boss or group head under Rosser was Bogart Carlaw, a 60-ish gentleman who was a tough taskmaster and good teacher. "Bo" lived in Chappaqua. Maury was also in his group, which at that time consisted of five copywriters. We were responsible for, among other things, Anacin and Super Anahist. But for starters, I worked on Sleep-Eze, Compound W, Preparation H, Primatene (for asthma), and Carter's Little Liver Pills. It was 100% television commercials. And it was competitive!

I wrote audio-and-video scripts, as I had since my earliest copywriting days. But I learned some new terms: XCU for extreme close-up and MOS -- which "quoted" a German-born director who wanted something shot, "mid oudt sound."

Those thirty- and sixty-second commercials were short, very short stories that I was writing. And they were almost all fiction. Stories I made up.

More and more often, I would write something which Bo approved for me to work on with an art director. Together we would turn the idea into a storyboard, a kind of blueprint for a TV spot, like a comic strip that showed what we wanted to film. I worked with a number of different art directors.

Many years later, when Jeremy Gury had become the Creative Director, copywriters and art directors worked together from the start to come up with ideas. There were many times that a copywriter had the visual idea or the art director came up with a key phrase. Still later we worked at times in a group of three, including a producer who figured out how to do something or suggested a video technique.

But in the beginning, the idea was what the copywriter originated. He had to sell it to his boss. Then collaborate with an art director to draw it up. Then it had to be sold to the account group which was sometimes done by the group head but occasionally by the writer. And finally sold by the account guys or group head or writer, to the client. Only thereafter did we worry about how to produce the commercial.

Yet I did not get a single commercial that I had written produced in my entire first year at Bates! Not one! However Bo Carlaw was once stuck for an opening line for his commercial for Carter's Little Pills. (It had become illegal in America to call them "liver pills" since it was a laxative that had no effect on the liver.) The scene Bo had was a gym being decorated with balloons for a dance. I suggested that we put "Aunt Mary" (the Carter's spokesperson) on a ladder and have her say, "Reach me up a red one, dearie."

That was the only thing of mine to appear on TV in my first year. In a sense, I had earned $10,000 for just that one line! Happily, that's not the way Bates looked at it. I even got a raise at the end of the year. Rosser was happy when the client was happy, especially if he did not change the campaign that was running. He said, "I pay my people to convince the client not to change the campaign." We wrote ads that were tested against the national commercials, which were changed only when or if they were bested.

I wrote a TV commercial for Anacin for a local TV station that happened to be in Cincinnati. Anacin was then the leading headache remedy, ahead of Bufferin and Bayer Aspirin. When my script was approved for production, I was sent to Cin-city to supervise its broadcast, much like I had for Pez TV commercials. Only this time there was videotape for me to take to show my boss and the account group and the client exactly how it came out. Luckily, everybody liked it. But I never got a copy of it.

Commercials that I had written got produced and filmed in 35mm and even on the air nationally. My first was for Sleep-eze, a mild sedative, which had a spring as its key visual. Then Primatene Mist, as asthma remedy, featuring a swimmer. Finally, an Anacin spot with a lady and her baby. And now there was videotape so I could get copies of my work. It took quite a while, but I amassed a reel of TV spots I had written and could show to other agencies to try for a better job. The best one was for Rolaids, the antacid, featuring a jury. I thought I'd be on my way.

But that was just when color television came in and every commercial I had on my reel was black-and-white. So everything I had done looked old-fashioned. Therefore I had to stay at Bates to amass a color reel. That took a few more years.

Every Friday Bo Carlaw told all his copywriters to come in Monday morning with "ten new ideas on Anacin." And we did. Ten new ideas. Every Monday. For fifty weeks a year. I was in his group about three years. So I literally came up with about <u>fifteen hundred</u> ideas on Anacin alone! And that doesn't count the other products we were on, as well as presentations for prospective or new clients. For those, we had a so-called gang bang ... everybody in the entire copy department had to present ideas.

How does anyone keep coming up with so many "new" ideas? First, you recycle old ideas, even other people's old ideas -- but in a new form, a fresh dress. Then I had my old Philosophical Logic list of fallacies, seemingly sensible arguments that are not truly logical. Advertising is full of them. One example is the "just as/so too" fallacy. As in, "just as this protective shield prevents arrows from striking me, so too Colgate toothpaste's shield protects my teeth." Or I think of a sunny beach and give myself the challenge of writing a Wonder Bread spot that would mean shooting at that location. Or what in today's *New York Times* suggests an idea? Or what on last night's TV? Tricks to oneself to come up with ideas.

I always slept with a pad and pencil next to my bed to jot down ideas that came to me in the night. Very often I thought I had had a terrific idea, wrote it down, and then, in the morning, I could not read my own writing. Other times, I had jotted down the same idea that had been in my typewriter when I left the office. All too often, however, I did not have any ideas when I got on the commuter train Monday morning. I read the *New York Times*, did the crossword (Monday's was always the week's easiest), and I always jotted down ten Anacin ideas (not full commercials, just ideas) before the train got to Grand Central Station.

When we got the OK to produce a spot, we had casting sessions to choose the actors. We cast some actors who were unknowns, before they became famous, like James Woods, Swoozie Kurtz, Judd Hirsch, and Henry "Fonzie" Winkler. Later in my career I worked with many famous people, sports and movie stars. Casting sessions were always interesting. I have a video of one and it clearly shows how bad many actors and actresses are and how few aspiring ones are any good.

Sometimes we went on location to shoot commercials, other times we used a studio. Elaborate sets were created for 30-second commercials. We shot scenes of Niagara Falls, Alaska, Chicago, and others all in a New York City studio. And we filmed pilots seemingly inside an airplane cockpit using a Link trainer in Miami. We frequently went to Los Angeles; sometimes Betty came with me, more often not. At times we went to L.A. because the actors or the sets or better weather was there. We usually shot beach scenes I wrote in the hope of getting to the Caribbean, in the Los Angeles area, or on a set.

Once, when Betty was on the set during a shoot, I warned her not to do anything that the director asked to have done. Whatever anyone said, they were not talking to her. I explained that it was a union job; there were specialists who worked with the lighting and other specialists who handled props while others worked only with the cameras. So, although she was sitting at the lunch table, she wisely did not stir when the director yelled, "Somebody get me a half-apple!"

She asked me afterward why she never noticed anyone cut an apple. She never saw anyone give the director what he'd asked for. And she wondered why he had even asked for such a thing. I explained that he'd wanted, and gotten from the props department, a half-size wood crate or applebox for an actor to stand on!

This was all long before computer animation or digitalization. We had to figure out how to shoot the commercials we wrote and not spend a fortune. I did Prudential Insurance spots in which you thought cars crashed (although we returned them to Hertz unscathed); and you'd swear a tree crashed onto a house roof (though both tree and roof were pristine). It certainly was more of a challenge in those good old days! Now effects are created by computers and anything's possible -- and easy to create.

OK, I'll reveal that we often shot a scene backward, for example, lifting a tree from the house with an off-camera crane, then reversing the film and speeding it up. Or we put two cars on giant rubber springs and backed them up to the point that they never really touched, but it looked like they bounced off each other -- with great crashing sound effects added later.

In my 30-plus year career in advertising I must have written about 100,000 TV commercials. Only about 500 were actually produced -- a pretty good batting average.

I never kept any old storyboards, but one of my favorite art directors, Don Michelson, kept many of his and gave me one that we had done together, the Wonder Bread spot that introduced the "fresh guys," which ran, as a campaign, for three years.

A spot I co-wrote to introduce Ocean Spray Cranapple -- and I sold to the client and helped produce -- won the "Clio" (advertising's equivalent of the Oscar) as the best 30-second TV commercial of 1974. It was a take-off on an old Nelson Eddy-Jeanette MacDonald movie using two look-alikes. He says that Cranapple's "sweet, like apples." She says, "tart, like cranberries." They argue back and forth: Sweet. Tart. Sweet. Tart. Then together burst into song, "Sweet-Tart, Sweet-Tart," to the tune of the Eddy-MacDonald song, "Sweetheart." Don Michelson was the art director on that one, too.

When Rosser Reeves retired from Bates I was made a vice-president. When I told my kids, they thought I'd be next in line for the presidency, since that's the way the United States works. What a disappointment it was for them to learn that, while our country has only one, Ted Bates & Co. had at least twenty V.P.'s.

Because the agency was a privately-held corporation, only employees could own its stock and only for as long as they were employed there. Rosser's leaving created lots of stock for sale to other corporate officers. But one had to pay for it. Maury Lerman convinced me to take out a loan that was bigger than my mortgage in order to buy Bates stock: $50,000! I signed notes for more than three times my annual income! And the loan was deducted from my salary. But that stock and subsequent agencies' stocks, made me a lot of money.

I'll never forget my meeting at American Home Products' office as the Creative Group Head on Anacin when a secretary handed Sam Earp, the account exec, a note. He read it then handed it to me. It said: "The Wall Street ticker says 'Ted Bates resigned Anacin.'" It was a $34-million-dollar account!

That was absolutely unheard of! An ad agency doesn't quit a client! What did it mean? The note went around the room and the meeting was immediately suspended. We went back to the office in a daze, not knowing what was happening. Or going to happen.

When I got back to my office I had a message waiting for me from the Creative Director, Jeremy Gury, to come to his office immediately!

It was the only time I was summoned to his office alone. If Bates had indeed resigned the account which was my major responsibility, I'd probably be fired. After all, I'd been fired for agency losses that were not my responsibility. I didn't have time to worry, nor time to call Betty.

Jerry Gury said, "Wally, your job with us is secure." Then he picked up a piece of paper, put his feet on his desk, and read to himself. He had a strange style, but I was glad, a major worry off my mind.

It all came clear about six months later when Bates announced that we had been awarded Bristol-Myers' Bufferin. Gury called on the phone and told me I couldn't legally work on it for six months, but that I would thereafter.

Much later I learned that American Home Products had wanted Bates to earn less than the standard 15% agency commission, in what amounted to asking for a kickback. I do not know if Bates' officers had talked with Bristol-Myers before "firing" A.H.P. That was the first time that an agency switched to a competing client by resigning one, although many clients change ad agencies very often. But copywriters more often changed agencies.

When I did work on Bufferin, I wrote TV commercials that competed with ones I had written for Anacin. One was that Bufferin "goes to work in half the time." Its visual was a half-watch or half-clock. That was the first time -- but not the only time -- that I had two competing ads on the air! Usually it happened when I changed jobs.

I also freelanced jobs while employed by Bates and later agencies. When I was no longer on Wonder or Home Pride breads, I free-lanced spots for Country Hearth breads. I had become a "drug" writer (over-the-counter drugs were the only ones advertised in those years) and a "package goods" writer, which included foods and soaps, altogether the biggest categories on TV at the time.

I moved with Ted Bates when they went from 666 Fifth Avenue to 1414 Broadway. That's when I got my window office, overlooking the famous Camel sign in Times Square. The smoker puffed O-rings right at me.

In the 1970s, 42nd Street was overrun with porn shops, hustlers, pimps, junkies, and homosexuals. When, once every year, Bates had a "bring your kids to work" day, we four took the train to Grand Central Station and then I'd walk the boys around the long way showing them department store window decorations to avoid the worst sightseeing in New York. They never noticed.

Promotions came slowly, but they came. From Junior to Senior Copywriter, to Group Head, to Associate Creative Director. I even became a Creative Director at Bates. But not in the U.S.A.

79. True, Legal and Ethical Ads

Ted Bates & Co. had two lawyers on staff, Larry Johnson and Elhanan ("Elky") Stone. I enjoyed working with them because they were nice guys and very helpful.

There are people who believe that advertising copywriters are in a class with lawyers and politicians as being unethical. But I think it is important to understand the times and circumstances, and then everyone has to decide where, exactly, to draw the ethical line. The lawyers drew the legal lines.

What is right or fair or honest? What is shady or questionable? What is illegal and dishonest? These are important distinctions and you must decide what is best for you -- and your family. If you are, or want to be, a scientist or lawyer or copywriter or businessperson or in practically any job or profession, you must decide such things. I certainly had to.

Let me give you an example of what copywriting was like at Bates in those days. And an example of the ethical questions I mentioned. I was the writer on the product that became Home Pride Buttertop Bread. I introduced it to America.

The butter is not in the batter. Instead, melted butter is applied only on top of every loaf. So we had to call it Buttertop. It was a good name and a legal necessity.

The bread had very little butter in it; about a pat's worth per loaf. We legally had to tell people they should still butter the bread. Also taste is a matter of opinion. When I wrote, "it tastes buttery, even before you butter it," it sounded good but it was also a legalism.

I wrote, "we pour on the butter" and we showed liquid butter being applied to a loaf. To "pour it on" can mean to add a lot. So we filmed the actual amount that is poured on one loaf. We literally revealed how it was applied and how much butter was in each loaf. It was legal.

The copy I wrote was absolutely true even if it implied more than it said. I firmly believe that advertising should tell the truth. But in a 30-second TV spot one cannot possibly tell "the whole truth." Usually a copywriter tells a <u>truth</u> about the product, one that might convince you to buy that brand.

So, to me, what's true is legal and therefore ethical.

Besides, it put bread on my family's table.

When I moved to Chapel Hill recently, I met Jim Pomroy. He had been the president of Rolling Rock Beer and president of Sara Lee. But years earlier he was one of the "junior clients" in the room at ITT-Continental Baking when I presented the first Home Pride Buttertop storyboards and sold them to him and the "senior clients."

The brand became a major multi-million-dollar success story.

80. John Todd Friedman

Since our first baby had been born six weeks prematurely, we wanted to take no chances with our second child. For one thing, we changed obstetricians to one that was closer to home. So, too, was Port Chester Hospital in Westchester County at the Town of Rye near the Connecticut border. This time also, my parents would not go on vacation for at least two months before the baby's due date.

But, sure enough, the baby was premature again. This time we were prepared. Betty felt contractions, started timing them, and we phoned a neighbor to babysit. Then we drove to the nearby hospital.

Even so, there was not enough time for Betty to even be assigned a room. She was rushed right into the labor room and I was left standing outside the door.

I heard a baby scream while I stood there, dumbfounded. Already? Yes, John Todd Friedman was born almost immediately, after a very short labor, four weeks early, on March 4, 1963.

I was still standing outside the door when they brought the baby out of the labor room. He was bloody. And it was Betty's blood.

Now, I have never had a strong stomach. And that bloody sight, as well as the thought that it was Betty's blood, upset me very much. That mingled with the pride in having another son.

I recovered because I was immediately told that both Betty and the baby were fine. She was awake and happy; he was breathing perfectly and was 100% all right. Considering the worries engendered by our firstborn, this was pure pleasure. I was then allowed to go into the labor room to visit with Betty who was glowing with pride and happiness, as I'm sure I was.

We had the name John ready if it was a boy; a girl would have been named Joan. The baby's name was to honor my two grandmothers, both of whom were named Johanna Friedmann. Furthermore, we had previously decided to honor the late Dr. Ted Sussman, by giving John the middle name of Todd.

Betty was taken to "her" room; one that was readied for her. And baby John was brought in almost immediately thereafter. Because David was born so prematurely, Betty was never able to nurse him. But now, even though John was also premature, she was really delighted to be able to do this very intimate act of mothering.

Unlike with our firstborn, we were able to take this newborn home three or four days after Betty gave birth. We had a professional baby nurse lined up to take care of either David or John, as needed. But the woman did not last long, perhaps one week. My mother came up for a week, then Betty's mother for the third week. And by that time Betty was ready to do practically everything herself.

We had been taking care of David for two years already. We certainly did not think that there was any need for a refresher course in baby care, we were confident of our abilities to do whatever needed doing.

It was a bit more than a month after John's birth when I had the task of giving him a bath in the bathinette. Remember that in the prenatal class I had accidentally "drowned" the doll we used as a baby. And that I later wrote a TV commercial for Pampers using that situation. This time I felt sure that I knew what I was doing, how to handle the baby and perhaps I was just a bit overconfident.

What happened was that almost as soon as I put him into the warm bathwater, John urinated on me. I had forgotten to put a washcloth over the offending part. And I'm sorry that I couldn't use that incident in a commercial!

When John was a young boy he rarely had dreams that interrupted his sleep. But one night he did. He had a nightmare that there was a lion in his room and he screamed us awake. I came rushing in to find out what the matter was.

"It's terrible! There's a lion here!" he explained.

"Where?" I wondered.

"Right there: he's twirling above my garbage can!"

I said, "I've got him!" and slapped my hands together. I motioned into the wastepaper basket and told John, "I'm taking him out of here; you can go back to sleep."

I did and he did. I left with the empty garbage can. And that ended that. Except that it entered into Friedman Family Lore.

John's son Alex recently had what may have been his first nightmare and John called me up to tell me, reminding me of the terrible twirling lion.

I told each of my three sons "the facts of life" when I thought each was old enough to understand it. I hadn't explained it when John found "a double-decker frog." So I explained sexual intercourse to John at a young age. His response was: "I don't think I'd like to do that. It's like sticking your finger up someone else's nose!"

215

As I mentioned earlier, my mother would come up to Chappaqua for a week to stay with the boys when Betty and I were on vacation or a business trip or a commercial shoot. Once when we were vacationing on some island and my mother was babysitting, John got poison ivy on his penis. It became swollen, red and blistered. John told his brothers about it but was too embarrassed to tell his grandmother. So Michael went to his Oma and asked her, "Have you ever seen a boy bare?"

She, naturally, thought he meant a male bear cub! Of course their father's mother had seen a naked male child, but never a bear cub, so she said, "No."

Once they got past that confusion, John's grandmother examined him and promptly took him to the hospital. They wondered whether he had inserted something into his penis. They did not think it looked like poison ivy. So, rather than treating him right away, the nurses wondered about what to feed him. Did he want ice cream? That got John mad: why didn't they believe him and treat him?

It took a while in the emergency room, but the reason for his illness became obvious. John had touched poison ivy and had urinated thereafter. It had spread to other parts of his body, but really inflamed and enlarged his penis. After what certainly seemed to him an excruciatingly long time, they finally did treat him for poison ivy. The excitement was over by the time we got back to Chappaqua, but the embarrassment and the tale lingered.

Like his brothers, John went to Horace Greeley High School. A member of his class was Vanessa Williams, the second Miss America I met.

John is our middle child. The contrarian.

He and Michael were in the same Boy Scout troop, different from David's. Both of John's brothers made Eagle Scout. John did something similar. But he stopped one step short, he became a Life Scout.

Both of his brothers went to SUNY-Binghamton. John, just slightly different, selected SUNY-Albany.

The two others became math/computer majors. John did something else; he majored in Communications.

And John went into, not Advertising as I had, but instead, a similar field, Public Relations. The French have only one term, *publicite*, which includes Advertising, Public Relations and Publicity. In the U.S.A. they're three different careers.

My friend and art director Don Michelson helped John get a job with the Advertising Council, the organization that arranges for volunteer ad agencies to create public service campaigns for worthwhile projects and gets volunteer media to contribute time and space. Their ads have been so memorable that most people can recall a dozen such campaigns.

Many years later a past president of the Ad Council, Bob Keim, John's former boss, wrote his memoirs which he entitled, *A Time in Advertising's Camelot.* In the opening paragraph of his "Acknowledgments," Keim names five people who "like a Greek Chorus" urged him to write his memoir. One was John Friedman. John was also mentioned four or five times in Keim's book. But there's one story about the Ad Council that Keim did not tell; I will.

I had worked at Ted Bates for a short while when Ariel Allen, a tall, buxom, single woman had the office next to mine. Later, when I was at Norman Craig & Kummel, Ariel Allen was a client, Assistant Advertising Manager at Colgate-Palmolive. Many years later, when Ariel Allen was introduced to John at the Ad Council, he told her that she had worked with me at Bates and Colgate. She was horrified! "Now I'm working with the children of my contemporaries! Boy, do you make me feel old!"

John never made another public relations mistake like that.

He became the P.R. and public affairs manager at various private and public organizations and associations. John spent many years at Lafarge, the huge international construction materials company, becoming their director of public and government affairs. Now he's with NCQA, the National Committee for Quality Assurance.

81. Chappaqua

When Betty was pregnant for the third time it was clear that the 3-bedroom house at 3 Jennifer Lane in Rye Hills would be too small for our growing family. So we went house hunting for a larger place.

Betty and I looked in the *New York Times'* Real Estate section, the same section that I had written many ads for at the start of my career. We drove around on Sundays, looking at homes for sale. At first Betty and the two boys came with me. But as she became more and more pregnant, I'd often go house hunting with little David on Sunday afternoons while John was asleep and Betty rested. I narrowed down the search and she would only join me when I found a good prospect.

One Sunday's *New York Times* had an ad for a development of new homes in Chappaqua. I had heard a lot about the town because my first boss at Ted Bates & Co., Bo Carlaw, lived in Chappaqua, in Westchester County, New York. He often called it, "a winter wonderland," and boasted of the excellence of the school system. So David and I went to look at it.

Bill and Hillary Clinton live in Chappaqua now, at 33 Old House Lane, but they didn't then.

I liked the area right away. There was going to be a cul-de-sac, a dead-end street where our children could play safely. It was in the woods -- and there was deer spoor there, right on the property. And it was in the famed Chappaqua school district.

The builder was named Hughes but I did not like any of the models they had or were building. They said that there were many plans that we could look at and even alter to our liking. That sounded good.

Betty came and fell in love with it as much as I did. Then we looked at the plans for a split-level house. We altered it into a raised ranch and added a few feet to some rooms. That was easy to do on paper. But would it be practical? Pappy Hughes, as we called him, said he'd price it out.

We had paid $20,000 for our first house on a quarter acre which had a 4¼% mortgage. They wanted $40,000 for this house on two-thirds of an acre with a 5½% 30-year loan. If we could get $30,000 for our Rye Hills house it would be doable!

So we signed a contract for our dream house to be built, with the entire downstairs to be unfinished and with a penalty clause that made Hughes pay for every day's delay beyond the due date. Jerry Deoul was our lawyer. We sold our house for $28,000.

I have a VHS movie of the house-building, showing the progress. On the film the next-door neighbors' daughter, Carol Clapper, came over one day and literally pushed David over onto his back. He was more shocked than hurt. But he never really liked her.

I was still at Ted Bates, but I no longer worked for Bo Carlaw who lived in Chappaqua, but for Maury Lerman, who also lived in Chappaqua. To be fair, I had signed the contract for our house long before Maury bought his. But he bought an existing home on the other side of town and they had moved in before we did. I say that I beat him to town, figuratively if not literally.

Of course Michael Bruce Friedman was born early and equally of course the construction of our new home was not finished on time. So we put Biff in a kennel and put our furniture into storage while we put ourselves into a motel. With it costing him more money every day than it cost me, Pappy Hughes got the job done only ten days late!

When they had completed the upstairs and later, when we ourselves finished the downstairs, the house on 627 Douglas Road had plenty of room in spacious rooms: The main living quarters were all upstairs: living room, dining room, kitchen, four bedrooms and two full baths. Downstairs were a two-car garage, entry foyer, mudroom, large playroom, laundry room, pantry, office, guest room (or two bedrooms), and a third full bathroom.

As Bo Carlaw had said, the Chappaqua school system was then one of the best in the U.S.A. John sent out an email in May, 2005, saying that their high school in Annandale, Virginia, was rated #34 and Horace Greeley High School in Chappaqua was now rated #43.

My parents and Betty's often came up to visit us on a Saturday or Sunday, taking the train from Grand Central Station. My mother especially loved to come on holidays; she often did something special for her grandsons to celebrate the event. Every year she eagerly hid Easter eggs in our backyard, the foil-wrapped chocolate ones, of course. She did that every year. And every year Biff always found them first and we had to stop him from eating them, foil and all! Every year.

Two minor disasters befell our house in Chappy, as Marvelle called it. One was when the concrete slab on which the house was built collapsed. Luckily, it was only in its center, the floor of the family room. It was quickly repaired.

The other was a fire downstairs, in the laundry room which was under the kitchen. Luckily, Michael was home as well as both of us. He had the foresight to close doors that contained the fire, rush us out, and call the local volunteer fire department. They put it out quickly but the whole house smelled of smoke. Insurance paid for the extensive repairs as well as our hotel stay.

Our family lived in that house all through the boys' school years, except for the one year when we rented out our home and lived in Germany. We lived in Chappaqua for 28 years. We sold the house after all three boys had finished college and moved away.

82. Michael Bruce Friedman

When we were first dating, Betty and I talked about having children. We both agreed at that time that we wanted two. We thought that we'd have a boy and a girl, we both just imagined that it would happen that way.

We were not at all disappointed that we had two boys. Quite the contrary, we were as delighted as our parents were. David and John played together nicely sometimes but mostly as little kids do, they ignored each other. All was well. I was working at Ted Bates & Co., Inc., bringing home ever-increasing paychecks.

Betty and I had an excellent relationship, an ideal married life. We complimented each other and complemented each other. What I was good at, she wasn't and her areas of expertise were my downfall. While she undid knots, I did zippers. We did not have real arguments, we had sincere and honest discussions. That is important: we could always talk to each other. We loved and respected each other.

We both took care of the money. But I handled the income and she handled the outgo. She was a numbers person, I was a words person. She did the taxes. Well, we did that together, but she understood it better than I did. We didn't need an accountant.

One year, working on the taxes together, we did the Federal form first, then the New York State form, and finally the New York City one. Since I earned my income mostly in the city, that was a necessary form to fill out. But the city lets you deduct those days that you were out of the city: weekends, holidays, out of town business trips. So you fill out the form and then work the fraction of how many days of the 365 you were earning money outside the city. We thought we understood fractions well, until we figured out that we owed the City of New York something over two million dollars!

Our financial advisor, Wolf Popper, recommended an accountant, Jerry Shafer, who has been our tax man and friend ever since. I have no doubt that he saved us money and not only from that particular miscalculation.

Betty and I were delighted that she was pregnant again. Before the baby's birth, however, Betty and I agonized over names. I do not remember what we came up with if it had been a girl. But we both liked the names Michael and Bruce.

The name Michael was then and for many, many years, the most popular boy's name. But before we two agreed on the name, I checked with my Aunt Thea, my father's brother Paul's widow, the grandmother of the other Michael Friedman. She had no problem with the name.

So if our third child turned out to be a boy, as it did, he was Michael Bruce Friedman. He, too, was born prematurely, on April 7, 1965. After his brothers were born six weeks early and four weeks early, Mike was born only two weeks early. I joked that if we had another baby, he'd be born right on time.

Mike's birth, also in Port Chester Hospital, was normal in every way. Now we had it down pat. So Michael Bruce Friedman came into our lives. A bouncing baby boy.

Each of our three sons is unique and different from his brothers. They all obviously had the same genes, the same upbringing. It is not a question of Nature versus Nurture because they shared all that. Their personalities, their temperaments, everything about each one is different from the others. I still find that amazing. I suppose that if we had had 18 children as Betty's grandmother did, we'd have had 18 different ones. But we did stop at three. My mother put it well. She said, "three boys -- now that's riches!"

We had a simple "house rule": because each boy had his own room and we had ours, everyone knocked on any closed bedroom door before entering. Privacy was important to each of us but being sent to your room was a punishment. It was the equivalent to a "time out".

In his early childhood, Michael had a small speech impediment which gave him a slight lisp that made him seem to have an almost German accent. It was very cute. In the middle of the night one night there was a knock on our door. Little Mike said, "thomething happened in mein bett!"

We started to laugh but discovered that he had thrown up in his bed. In wasn't long thereafter that we sent him to a speech therapist who corrected it quite quickly.

He frequently came home with his shoes full of water because he liked jumping into puddles. We created a mudroom just inside the house from the garage. Even that got too muddy, wet, and dirty just from Mike's shoes and clothes in the winter. So Betty finally insisted that he undress in the garage.

Michael was called to the principal's office in grammar school one day. His left shoe had been found in a classroom with a broken window. He had come to her office with "one shoe off and one shoe on," as in the ditty, "Diddle, diddle dumpling, my son John." But this was Mike. To this day he insists he doesn't know how it got there.

I don't know how Betty handled them. All three were too much for me at times! When I had them outdoors by myself, they often went in three different directions.

They were all healthy, all normal, and definitely all boys. Although not really good at sports, they were very athletic. They often wore me down playing in our own backyard, or bicycling, sledding, fighting. They worked hard and they played hard. But they did not always play well together. Each was truly an individual and an individualist.

Now that we had three sons, I decided to get my own haircutting machine. And because they played in our sandbox so often and got so much sand in their hair, I gave them all crew cuts. At that time, however, ultra short hair was not fashionable. It was just easier on the parents.

Michael did not know that he was breakable. He was a daredevil. A boy who would try anything. Especially if someone dared him to do something, anything. But "unbreakable" Michael split his lip one day while we lived in Germany. He calmly came to us. Betty asked me what was German for plastic surgeon. I had no idea. It wasn't in our handy pocket dictionary. I was not surprised to learn that plastic surgery is *plastisch chirurgie.*

We took Mike to the plastic surgeon's waiting room. It was huge and filled with people and with art. Modern paintings on every wall and statues all around. With all the people and artwork, there literally was no room for anything or anyone else. We thought we'd have to wait forever and the poor little child was bleeding.

I went to the nurse's desk to register. She asked what our insurance company was. I said that I'd pay cash, since I had no idea what insurance we had, if any, that would cover this. With that, she took us to the head of the line and we were next in the doctor's office; next again right into his surgery. It was done in minutes. Mike never had any observable qualms, never seemed worried, just went on as if it were nothing. And never developed a scar. His brothers and I believe he leads a charmed life.

He also never acted like the youngest child. He always tried to keep up with his brothers. And he always did keep up, not only with John, but even with David.

He was, if anything, more daring than either of his brothers. Especially off the high diving board at Chappaqua Pool at a very early age. He took to it like a duck to water. Fearlessly. All three were good swimmers. But only Mike was a daredevil diver. In my 2005 visit there, the pool looked small, the place appeared run-down, and the high diving board was gone!

David set local swimming records, John didn't care, and Michael broke them.

As the boys grew up they helped with the chores around the house. We taught them the value of money by giving them very little allowance. They had to earn "spending money." Each in turn delivered the local newspaper. Each worked for a neighbor to assemble a small mechanical measuring device which he sold. And they were each, in turn, babysitters to neighboring little children.

They each learned a musical instrument. David screeched his notes on a clarinet. John blasted his way on a trumpet. Mike really got into drumming. He is the only one who can still play his specialty. He had a full drum set which was set up in our downstairs family room.

Mike formed a band that rehearsed where the biggest, least transportable instrument was: in our house. They played gigs at the Chappaqua Civic Center and the library and a school dance. They composed original music and lyrics. They even had a girl singer. The band was named "The Plague" because Mike was Jewish and one of the others was Egyptian.

Iman Mubarak played high-brow music on a violin, low-brow on a fiddle, both the same instrument, of course. Iman and his brother Muhammad are the nephews of the president of Egypt, Hosni Mubarak. His brother, the boys' father, was a doctor in Chappaqua. We considered inviting Iman to a Passover Seder because he was a good friend of Mike's and there is a tradition of inviting outsiders. We reconsidered when we remembered that the Egyptians are the villains in the story.

When our three boys were grown and we had five licensed drivers in the family, we had only one car. We did that on purpose since I had to be driven to the railroad station to commute to Manhattan every workday -- and picked up. I almost always made the early train, but often had to take a late one. So the car and at least one licensed driver had to stay home to await my phone call and then pick me up at Chappaqua station.

In high school, Mike saved the life of a girl who wanted to commit suicide. Her mother knitted him a sweater. Naturally, Mike became an Eagle Scout, like David.

Paul Schwartz, who my mother called, "the fourth boy in a house of three sons," was a classmate of David's and thereafter a housemate of John's. So it was natural for Mike to ask, "Do I get Paul Schwartz now?"

Instead, we got Jacques LaPlace. The son of Myriam and Turenne LaPlace from St. Barth's, he had quit the island's high school before graduation and his mother wanted him to have at least a high school diploma. So he came to live with us in Chappaqua and went, not to Horace Greeley High as our sons were, but to Pleasantville High School because they accepted him there.

Jacques was a handsome boy who had posed for ads as a male model and had a delightful French accent. He seems to have slept with every girlfriend every one of our sons had -- and some of their mothers! He bought a car and junked it on a street. Then he quit high school. Jacque was a bit wild. So we got him to live with a priest who had a rehabilitation home. But he left and went back to St. Barth's. Obviously, he was not easy to control. But he was charming.

Back on island, Jacques had a daughter with a Metro French girl and he married a St. Barth's girl who already had a daughter and had another daughter with her. They all now live with his widowed mother. He has been an auto mechanic, male model, radio disc jockey, house painter, roofer, you name it, so we call him a "Jacques of All Trades."

All three of our sons were graduated from Horace Greeley High School. David went to SUNY Binghamton, John to SUNY Albany,

Mike to SUNY Binghamton, of course. Dave worked there for Mario DiCesare, doing computer stuff for his publishing company; so did Mike.

Two things about Mike, however, concerned us. First, he hated to wear clothing of any kind, especially a jacket or tie. He often dressed in jeans and a T-shirt, even in winter. Second, Mike hated to get up early in the morning. Betty and I wondered to each other, how will Michael ever succeed in the business world?

Now we know that they invented "dress down Fridays" and "flextime," just for our son Michael. He has that kind of incredible luck.

His first job after graduating from SUNY-Binghamton with his degree in computer science and math, just like David did, was with Unisys in the Washington, D.C. area, near where David lived. He worked for a temp company for a while, then for a small telecom outfit I had never heard of, called MCI.

MCI was taken over by Worldcom. Then there was a huge financial scandal and Worldcom went bankrupt. But true to Michael's luck, he was never in any trouble. He continues with MCI now that it is a newly acquired part of Verizon. And they offered him a retention bonus if he stays for some months after the merger! Once again, as always, Mike was simply lucky.

Yes, the one son who rarely calls his parents is the one who has been working for a telephone company.

83. The Pool and the Gilberts

If Chappaqua was indeed a Winter Wonderland, it was a Summer Sweatshop even though our home was fully air-conditioned. Besides, we were all swimmers and quickly joined the Chappaqua Swim and Tennis Club, within easy walking distance (for the boys) from our home. None of us ever played tennis.

The boys all learned to swim there and went on to be lifeguards and teach other little kids to swim. Boy, did the boys swim! Each was on the swim team.

Little Mike started off in the kiddie pool but it didn't take him long to move up to the big, Olympic pool. He even took up diving in a big way at a very early age, even off the high board. It really looked scary to me. Betty's father didn't even dare watch him dive. Even after someone was badly hurt diving there, Mike kept on diving there.

Only Chappaqua homeowners could buy a membership and could only sell it either with the house or back to the pool organization. And there were annual dues and fees as well as the expense of the lunch counter there. One really felt a part of the community and recognized one's friends, neighbors, and fellow commuters.

Our three sons competed for the team against local pools. Then they competed in the Westchester County meet. The top swimmers would compete in New York State and those winners would vie for spots on the U.S. Olympic team! I wanted the boys to swim, and to compete, but not to become obsessed with swimming as Olympians must be. So I was delighted when David finished sixth, just out of the running in a State meet. But I couldn't have been prouder!

There were also father-and-son meets which we never won but usually came in a close second. Our boys were all great swimmers, but their Dad wasn't as good.

All three were lifeguards at Chappaqua and other pools. David even taught little children, three years old and up, how to swim.

Betty spent all her time at the pool while the boys were there. One day, early in our membership, John was crying "his head off" for some reason and a kind, thoughtful woman came over to Betty and asked her if that was her son. That is how Betty and Marvelle Gilbert met.

They quickly became the very best of friends; each called the other the sister she had never had. Our two families became the closest, lifelong buddies. It sometimes felt like one big, happy family. And now, with their mother gone, the boys still visit and telephone Marvelle whenever they can.

Marvelle was originally from Ohio, but she's a New Yorker at heart. She and Paul lived in the city and owned one of the first natural foods and natural drugs stores. She "prescribed" the vitamins and minerals twenty-five years ago that I am still taking. I don't know why, other than Marvelle said to. That's still a good enough reason for me.

Paul Gilbert was a "space rep," he sold ads for trade magazines. Paul was in the army at Pearl Harbor when the Japanese bombed it, December 7th, 1941. He was a journalist and wrote a vivid first-person account of the surprise attack.

Marvelle and Paul have two sons, Glenn and Richard, each just a little older than our two older sons. Glenn is an amateur herpetologist and gives demonstrations on television and at parties. His knowledge of snakes is intuitive and thorough; he has rare breeds and often goes to Florida, returning some to the wild as he gathers others. Glenn has a girlfriend I met at Marvelle's 80th birthday party and found to be interesting and intelligent.

His younger bother Richard started a unique business in Manhattan with a friend. Big City Volleyball arranges volleyball leagues, games, competitions. I recognized that it was a great way for guys and gals to meet, in T-shirts and shorts. But, to his mother's consternation, while their customers meet the opposite sex, Richard has not met "the right one!" His business, however, has thrived and earns him a comfortable living.

Marvelle was one of the original organizers of the Chappaqua Drama Group, which put on plays at the Horace Greeley High School auditorium and other venues. She was in many shows, as was Richard, and we attended them all. Especially memorable were *Fiddler on the Roof* and *The King and I*. The group even entered international competitions, winning an award in Korea.

Marvelle still lives in the house she and Paul bought when they moved to Chappaqua. There is a couch in her living room and she traditionally takes a photo of every visitor, posed on that couch.

Betty and Marvelle often went shopping, particularly bargain hunting and yard-sale searching together. They knew what each other's children wanted or needed as well as their own and went shopping with each other and without each other for each other. They bought such things as Christmas cards after the holiday for the next year.

One year a local Chappaqua drug store had a going-out-of-business sale and the owner, knowing Marvelle's shopping habits, thought she might like their stock of greeting cards for all occasions. She said "yes," and was surprised when a big truck pulled up full of cartons of cards. They filled her garage to the exclusion of her car, even after many boxes were shipped to St. Barth's; it took years before the cards were used up.

When we lived in St. Barth's, we would come up to Chappaqua every three or four months. I would visit my mother in her Manhattan nursing home and Betty would go shopping with Marvelle. We'd then get together for dinner.

One time, Betty and Marvelle were driving behind a truck filled with soda, I'm not sure if it was Coke or Pepsi. But the truck accidentally swerved and spilled much of its contents. They stopped the car and went to pick up the cans or plastic bottles. They managed to gather quite a few when a police car arrived. Naturally, they turned the soda over to the cops. Then a local newspaper reporter arrived. He wrote up a story about the goodness of "two Chappaqua ladies" who were so helpful.

Those of us who know both Betty and Marvelle wonder whether they were collecting soda for the truck or from the truck. What would they have done if the cop had not arrived? We will never know for sure. Unless, of course, we're sure we know.

Between our visits, Marvelle would stock up on bargains she found for Betty. She got the stuffed animals and toys that we gave as prizes for the annual Library Fair. For years many local St. Barth's people bought their greeting cards there. Those who could not read English understood the Christmas or Valentine's pictures.

Nowadays Marvelle is striking with her snow-white hair and, usually, a purple outfit. After all these years she knows so many people in town. And she is as friendly as any good politician.

She greeted her new neighbors when they moved in and is truly on a first-name basis with Bill and Hillary Clinton, often meeting him at the local delicatessen or when he takes a walk on her block with his dog. She has met her Senator at the local beauty parlor. Marvelle appeared on New York City's NBC-TV affiliate when they interviewed our ex-president in town. She is still active in an amateur acting group and frequently appears on local television, perhaps more often than Bill or Hillary.

84. Island Vacations

The first vacation that Betty and I took away from the boys was to Bermuda. My mother came up to Chappaqua by train and watched the boys. She insisted that she would only do this for one week at a time, and a school week at that. Our three young hellions were not easy, even for a trained kindergarten teacher who really loved them.

I believe that travel is in my heritage. My mother's parents and my parents were truly world travelers. (I have now been to 67 countries!) Yet Betty had never flown before and her father, afraid to fly, instilled some fear in her. But she overcame it at once. Eventually she loved flying, especially in small "island hoppers" or "puddle jumpers."

Bermuda is not a tropical island; it is in the North Atlantic. But it has lovely pink sand beaches and inviting waters. I am not going to describe this, or any of our vacations, but Bermuda was notable: It was our first true underwater experience.

We took a boat that was fully equipped for the adventure. We each put on a heavy steel diving helmet that had an air hose attached to its top, connected to the pump on the boat that constantly supplied us with air to breathe. We went down to the sea bottom but we couldn't go far, having to stay not only together but directly under the boat.

Betty and I loved it! We saw lots of colorful fish. And we were hooked. It was thereafter that we started watching Jacques Cousteau's underwater films, and both learned scuba-diving. It changed our lives.

For our two weeks of vacation every year, which was all I had at first, we started vacationing on different islands. Over the next ten years we went to twenty different islands in the Caribbean. As I got three and four weeks of holidays, we kept going to a different island every time. We resolved not to talk about the next island vacation until we were coming home from the last, at the earliest. I got a book from National Geographic entitled *Isles of the Caribbees* which told, among other islands, about St. Barthelemy, one we'd never heard of before. So we went there next. It was 1969.

We did not think we were looking for something, but we found it -- the only island we kept coming back to! So Betty and I bought a piece of land in 1970 and built a home on St. Barth's. We had found our place in the sun and resolved to retire to "our" idyllic island someday.

85. Germany, the Third Time

It was the time that all the major American advertising agencies went international. Ted Bates was no different. Some agencies opened their own shops in foreign countries but most of them simply bought an

229

existing place with its staff of experienced, native-language-speakers and -writers.

Maury Lerman was sent to Germany when Bates acquired an ad agency there. He knew Yiddish well enough to understand some German. He made two trips and then told the agency that I spoke German. So I was not surprised when Bates sent me to Germany to help solve a Colgate-Palmolive problem. I went a second time a while later to help on a presentation.

They saw that I was fluent in German and knew a lot about advertising. So they offered me the one- or two-year job as the Creative Director of the Bates office in Frankfurt-am-Main, the place I had been stationed in the army. The agency was the result of Ted Bates & Co. buying into an existing German ad agency owned by Horst Slesina; the agency was renamed Slesina-Bates. (I had mentioned *Herr Slesina* in Chapter 26).

Betty and I agonized over whether it would be good for the children and when I didn't immediately accept the job, they raised their offer. More money -- now it was $40,000 a year -- plus a Mercedes car with all its expenses paid, plus paid schooling for the three boys at the Frankfurt International School, including paid transportation for them to and from school. They'd even pay the realtor to find our choice of rental home.

It was an offer we couldn't refuse. And a wonderful experience for the boys. We rented our Chappaqua home to an IBM executive on a one-year assignment and I accepted Bates' offer for a year or two.

The five of us flew to Germany on August 1, 1975. None of us slept a wink and few of the other passengers did either, since our kids often ran up and down the aisles and generally behaved like teenagers although David was 14, John was 12 and Mike 10.

When we arrived at Frankfurt airport and entered the terminal, the very first thing that the boys saw was a sign they could easily read: "Dr. Mueller's Sex Shop."

We were booked into the *Schlosshotel Kronberg,* the castle that was converted into a hotel in the Frankfurt suburb of Kronberg. It was a real castle and still looked it, inside and out, with stone walls and turrets unchanged from eons ago. There were real knights in armor standing in the corridors; well, empty suits of armor. Authentic antiques from centuries ago and precious artwork were in every nook and cranny. Our room, on an upper floor, had original paintings on its walls and the windows opened to the slate roof with gargoyles at every edge.

The Vice President of the United States, Nelson A. Rockefeller, on an official visit, was also staying at our hotel. The boys asked his driver if they might look into his parked car. He opened the door and they climbed inside! He didn't mind.

Boys will be boys and they played with the knightly armor nightly. Betty and I stopped that. Once in our room they started a normal, American kids' pillow fight -- among the precious antiques! We managed to halt that, too. But the final straw was when his brothers dared Michael to climb out onto the slanted slate roof to get a close look at the gargoyle! That was just too dangerous!

So we moved out of this deluxe palace into an ordinary hotel, the *Viktoria,* in the nearby village of *Oberursel.* That's the town where I was stationed when I first arrived in Germany as a private in the army, twenty years before, in Camp King. It's also where our kids attended the Frankfurt International School for the year we were in Germany.

This accommodation was a more normal setting for our rambunctious boys, a nice hotel which even had white rabbits on its front lawn. Not statues, live ones. Mike enjoyed playing with them upon our arrival.

We checked in happily and tried the hotel's dining room. Since we were going to be eating there often, we decided to each order something different. Mike recognized something he had heard of and ordered it: *hasenpfeffer.* When the food arrived David quickly and quietly took Michael's dish from the waiter and gave Mike what Dave had ordered. The good big brother had suddenly realized that Mike would have been served one of those cute little bunnies he'd played with out front.

As part of my deal with Slesina-Bates, I was to get an "acorn yellow" Mercedes. When it came, the boys called it baby-poop yellow.

The rental agent showed us around and we quickly picked a row house in Kronberg on *Brunnenweg 8.* It had an unusual interior layout, with rooms on six different levels. The rental agent arranged for furniture too, selling us some usable but used items, possibly even antiques. He gave us a painting, too, as a gift. In 2004, when they moved into their new house, Mike and Mary hung that artwork in their kitchen.

There were not that many Americans, outside of the army, in the area. But there were a lot of Brits and many IBMers. So we joined the British club, had many IBM acquaintances, got to know some of the International School's teachers, and went to the American Officers Club for Sunday brunch. Thus we had lots of English-speaking friends. Betty especially had friends for day-time activities and shopping trips.

Our best friends were IBMers Kevin and Carol LaCroix, pronounced "LaCroy." They had two kids, Sean, pronounced "Shawn," and Siobhan, pronounced "Shivon." She became Michael's first girl friend and gave Mike his first kiss.

We and the LaCroix decided go to Nuremberg one weekend and took Sean in our car and they took Mike in theirs. We followed each other all the way, but lost each other just as we hit Nuremberg. Mike told them our Friedman Family Rule: if you get lost, go back to the last place we were together. He almost convinced them to go back a few hundred kilometers to Frankfurt. But we happened to meet just in time.

All the years I was in the army in Frankfurt, I never went to the Officers Club. But now we made it a regular Sunday ritual. Their brunch was fantastic and it was cheap! We really gorged ourselves. We went there every single Sunday that we were in town. Without fail. But we were on a trip the particular Sunday when the radical Bader-Meinhof gang set off a bomb in the place killing many Americans! It was really the first act of terrorism against America.

Of course I showed my family the apartment house on *Henry-Budgestrasse* where I had lived while in the army. In June, 1975, the 65th MP Detachment was relocated there and they reported, "The location required many hours of cleaning and painting as the building was in a bad state of repair."

I also showed my family the local *bierstube* or bar where we used to hang out many evenings. It had been transformed into the Harry S. Truman Post of the American Legion! The PX was still there, but we couldn't shop there.

We took lots of trips and took off every German and every American holiday. Naturally, we traveled together most of the time. On occasion, the boys took class trips or Betty went with her friends. Once, the five of us were in four different countries!

All of us celebrated the U.S's 200th birthday on July 4th, 1976 at Jutland Denmark, along with hundreds of Danes including the Queen. They truly appreciated our country's helping them get rid of the Nazi occupation of their country. So they celebrated freedom and liberty in grand style with fireworks, speeches, drugs, and demonstrations which included arrests.

Many of my absences were business trips. Eventually, I became Bates' European troubleshooter, going to our offices in England and France and Italy, usually on Colgate problems. In Milan on one trip, their Creative Director invited me to his house for dinner. He and his wife spoke English and really wanted me to come. So I went and met her and their little son, possibly three years old. Unfortunately, he did not speak English and I couldn't understand a word of his baby-talk Italian. The kid told his folks he thought I was an idiot!

Slesina-Bates was a very different kind of ad agency. For one thing, the German socialist system had *mitbestimmung,* where labor had a voice in management decisions. So I had trial period before they "elected" me to be the Creative Director.

We did some good advertising and gained some business. I helped a great deal in pitching and winning the M&M Mars candy account for Germany. I did some local ads, even a billboard series for the German Federal Rail System. Some familiar American products were different in Germany. One example was Arid Deodorant. I had worked on it in the U.S. and our claim was that its ingredient, Perstop, "stopped perspiration cold." But German Arid had a different formula, it had no Perstop. They told me, and it was true, that Europeans do not want all underarm odor stopped -- some of it should linger. They thought it was sexy. So Europe's deodorants truly are not as effective as ours. That should explain French people to you!

Many other products were different. Their "nonalcoholic beer," advertised for nursing mothers, actually does contains a little alcohol!

As a copywriter, I often gave myself a challenge in order to come up with a fresh idea. I noticed that German television and advertising had nudes. So I decided to write a TV spot we could shoot with a nude woman. It worked for a fabric softener. I created a demonstration to show just how soft the product made even a scratchy towel: Our naked model took the towel out of the dryer and rubbed it across her nipples. A good ad in many ways. Unfortunately, I don't have a copy of it.

The International President of Ted Bates & Co. was Bob Jacoby. At his request I sent him regular reports on the agency. They also sent him reports on me.

Our agreement said that I would be paid in U.S. dollars. As it happens, the dollar rose in value compared to the *deutchmark* and Slesina-Bates complained that I cost too much.

More important to the German company and all its employees than my Mercedes car was my exclusive parking spot. I still have the metal sign with "Friedman" on it. But parking in downtown Frankfurt was a real nightmare. If you don't have a space with your name on it, you won't find one. When Betty saw she was stuck in a suburb, she suggested that I take the train to town, as I had been accustomed, while she used the car. It was the shortest commute I ever had. The company expected me to drive to work and leave the car in *its* spot so that other employees could use it during the day. When Betty had the car, they could not. I maintained that it was *my* spot, my name was on it. But what really rankled them is that my parking space was unused all day!

Grey was known in New York as a Jewish ad agency; I wondered about their German office. So I interviewed for -- and got the job offer -- as the Creative Director of Gramm & Grey in Dusseldorf, for 100,000 *Deutschmarks!* I declined.

It was toward the end of that year in Germany that I decided to give up smoking. I blame my unusual behavior on that. The agency changed telephone companies and my wife could no longer telephone me directly, but had to go through a switchboard operator. I didn't like that and ripped my phone line from the wall: if she couldn't call me, nobody could! I unfortunately also got mad enough one day to jump onto my desk. But it was a good thing that I gave up smoking!

My agreement had been for a one- or two-year stay. Our whole family had really enjoyed the experience but we never wanted to keep the kids out of Chappaqua's great school system for longer than one year. We had rented our American home and our German home for one year each. So Bates and I easily agreed to make it just one year.

We packed up cartons of excellent wines and labeled the boxes "books." We had contracted for a container, the huge 40-foot type that goes on ships, to transport our stuff from Kronberg all the way to our home in Chappaqua. When our container arrived, however, its only markings, and they were huge, were CCCP -- the Russian language equivalent of USSR -- the Union of Soviet Socialist Republics. It caused quite a stir when it was unloaded on Douglas Road in Chappaqua.

The contract I had with Bates stated that they would pay for our return trip (which they did) and would have a job for me when I returned (which they didn't). On the advice of my investment advisor Wolf Popper, I threatened a lawsuit and we settled for a $25,000 payment. I had to sell my Bates stock back to the company, having made a wonderful profit, so that Bates could sell itself to Saachi & Saachi.

86. Avon and Impress, Inc.

I was unemployed. So, of course, I looked for a job, answered ads, went on interviews, called up friends, and did everything I could to find a job.

Betty, bless her, did what she could, too. She was already working; she had started as a volunteer Teacher Aide only because she could work the exact same hours on the same schedule when our kids were in school. Wisely, she worked in the same school district but not in the same school as any of our boys. Now that I was out of work, she managed to get a paying job as a Teacher's Assistant in the second grade at the new school our district had just built, West Orchard School.

She also started selling Avon cosmetics door-to-door, to our neighbors, to our friends, to strangers. She was never one to wear much makeup of any kind herself but she sold the stuff! She did so well that the company kept rewarding her. They gave her some very good looking costume jewelry.

I also had to do something, anything, that paid. I wasn't getting any real job, so I simply had to create one. I wrote an *eitsis* booklet. That's Yiddish for advice. These days they're called self-help books. It was a very simple, cheap-looking, Xeroxed and folded booklet. But buyers wouldn't know that. I wrote an ad for it, charged a mere $3 although it cost me pennies, and ran classified ads. I ended up writing two booklets, *Hold Onto Your Teeth* and *Save Your Skin*. The first was on good dental hygiene; the second on proper skin care. I hoped my ads would "hype" the booklets better than they did.

This publishing venture was incorporated, by mail, in Delaware. I had to have a company and a name that people could write checks to. So I called my "publishing company" by a name I liked a lot: Impress, Inc. Well, perhaps I'm easily impressed.

The ads sold a few. Very few. One customer even ordered the other booklet after he'd received the first. Impress, Inc. was profitable but not lucrative.

It's a good thing I got a real job after being out of work for the longest time, about eight weeks. With Betty as an Avon lady and me as a publisher, we didn't earn enough to cover expenses. Thank you, President Franklin Delano Roosevelt, for unemployment insurance. That combination kept us above water.

But we never did tell any of our parents when I was out of work. Never.

87. Benton & Bowles, Canada

There was a job possibility, through a "head hunter" or placement specialist, as the Creative Director of Benton & Bowles Canada, part of a major international ad agency. So I flew to Toronto for an interview. When I entered their offices, I instantly saw someone I recognized from Ted Bates' New York office. He had been a copywriter just as I was and now was the retiring Creative Director, going back to New York. He knew me and recommended me for his job.

They paid for Betty to come up. We were taken to Maple Leaf Stadium. The fans went crazy over hockey; Betty didn't. B&B wanted me to move our family to Canada and become Canadian citizens. Privately she said, "no way will we take the kids out of Chappaqua schools again!"

So I told them that I'd commute for a while. My international experience must have impressed them; I mentioned not just Germany but also France and Italy. Since all the Canadian advertising had to be done in English and French, I got the job.

I kept up that commute for an entire year, leaving every Monday and returning every Friday, just as my father had always done. The flight from La Guardia Airport to Toronto took exactly as long as the train from Westchester to Manhattan had: one hour each way. I rented a room near the office which I used four nights every week. There was just one weekend I was snowed in.

Professionally, it was my best year. I assembled a good group of writers, art directors and producers by firing some, keeping most, and hiring others. We made a lot of excellent print ads and commercials, and our clients were mostly international brands like Proctor & Gamble, Phillips, and Vicks. We did presentations that won new clients and the creative group had a terrific spirit. We made many "minute movies" that were potential award winners. And it was fun.

I created many Pampers spots that were particular favorites of mine. For those commercials, we hired a "baby expert" who, we were assured, could make an infant cry at precisely the time we needed one to. I was amazed at how he did it: he stuck a pin into the baby's heel and that innocent little infant cried instantly!

In Canada, I was interviewed by a newspaper columnist and I wrote a "media column" for an issue of *Stimulus*.

Whenever we shot a TV commercial, we got three bids from different production companies; that's normal agency procedure anywhere. An old friend of mine, Nat B. Eisenberg, and his company, N.B.E. Productions, had an arrangement with a Canadian editor. Nat would fly in from New York to direct the spot which the Canadian company edited. They won a lot of bids and produced many excellent spots. I continued to use N.B.E. Productions a few years later in New York when I had my own agency.

We had some purely Canadian clients, too. One made jeans for sale in the U.S. and it gave me another chance to work with a topless model. I insisted that any other clothing would distract from the jeans. It also made for interesting print ads and billboards.

Another Canadian client was a soda-pop private label. I said soda-pop because what I call soda, they call pop. At any rate, I wrote and designed a newspaper print ad that ran often. Here's my layout:

COLASSAL
COLA SALE

We produced more ads -- and more good ads -- in my year in Canada than I had at any time since my year at Pace Advertising. Everything was in English and French. I had done many in German and was soon to do ads in Spanish, too.

I prepared a brochure on our Canadian agency which had a paragraph on each of our principal officers. B&B Canada's president, whom I'll call Dan Borswig, wondered how I would handle my bio, since I was not a Canadian or even in Canada. I started it, "Wally Friedman comes to Canada with lots of international experience."

B&B Canada and I had an ongoing contract dispute. I had been commuting for a year but they wanted my family to move to Toronto and now - incredibly - they wanted me to reimburse them for my travel expenses. That was unacceptable to me. I called it a "kick-back" and walked out of the contract discussion at 5 PM on Friday since I had a plane to catch. On Monday, when I arrived at the office, Dan Borswig fired me.

My Creative Department staff was more upset than I was; some of the guys joined the girls in crying. But I didn't cry, I just flew home and was out of work again.

88. NCK and Tom Land

I was interviewing for many possible jobs when my old pal Maury Lerman suggested I join him at Norman, Craig & Kummel. He was the fellow CCNY graduate who earlier helped me get my job at Ted Bates. Another potential position was as the Creative Director of Warwick & Legler, yet another as an Associate Creative Director at Compton Advertising. W&L asked me back for a third interview after I had gone to work for NCK. I had to decline. And I didn't hear back from Compton for two years.

I joined Norman, Craig at about the time that Betty took a job as a market researcher with Tom Land in Mt. Kisco, the town just north of Chappaqua. She really liked the work, it was very convenient. She kept that job for many years until we left the country. And soon thereafter, Tom Land sold his company.

I was working in NCK's building at 485 Lexington Avenue that had been used in the disaster movie *The Towering Inferno*. While I was there another movie was made in our offices: Meryl Streep and Dustin Hoffman in *Kramer vs. Kramer*, a wonderful film. Some scenes were shot in the office next to mine, my buddy Andy Boncher's office. Other action was filmed in our conference room.

The *New York Times* of June 30, 2006, wrote about a new TV show being filmed in that same building! It's about an ad agency in the 1960's and is titled *Mad Men*. The article says the show shows how the industry has changed.

Downstairs in that building is Michael's Pub, where Woody Allen sometimes played his clarinet. I often met him coming in when I left late.

One of my first assignments was in Puerto Rico on NCK's Colgate business for a couple of weeks. I wrote several commercials that were filmed and recorded while I was there. We actually recorded five different versions because some of the idioms and pronunciations are different in Cuban, Puerto Rican, Mexican, Argentinean, and Castilian Spanish.

While in San Juan I attended a pig roast with some of my local agency colleagues. I turned out to be a guest of honor and thus was awarded the ears. They did not taste kosher. I still do not know if they were honoring me or kidding me.

Shortly after I got back to New York, NCK sent me to Paris for two weeks to work on Colgate-Palmolive there. I worked for that client in the U.S., Germany, France, England, and Italy. And I worked for Procter & Gamble in the U.S. and Canada in between those assignments. With English, German, French, Italian, and Spanish ads, I was truly becoming an international adman.

Back in New York I worked on various brands and attended a lot of Colgate client meetings. Their advertising manager was Reuben Mark, assisted by Ariel Allen. He became Colgate's President and C.E.O. She had once been a copywriter in the office next to mine at Ted Bates. Now she was the client. I had written a commercial for Cold Power detergent involving women dancing with glee in a launderette after their discovery of our product. Ariel and Reuben OK'd it for production and we were ready when a dancers' strike hit New York City. Would you believe that I directed the dancers?

In another Cold Power commercial I worked with a live polar bear. I got very close to him because he was behind an invisible electronic fence.

Messrs. Craig and Kummel were no longer with the NCK agency when I joined; it was entirely in the hands of Norman B. Norman. An interesting character. However, he sold the shop. So, while I was there, none of the names on the door were.

And when Compton did call back, I took that job on Madison Avenue.

89. My Father's Death

My father was hospitalized in April, 1979 with late onset leukemia. His doctors spoke to us about what would later be known as *hospice* care. They assured us that my father was in no imminent danger of dying.

It just happened to be when our house on St. Barth's was completed, a 4-year project we had never mentioned to anyone, not our parents nor our children. The construction supervisor, Prosper Berry, refused to rent it out, insisting that we be the first ones to sleep in it. So Betty and I decided to make it a real family vacation and we bought five nonrefundable plane tickets. It was the first the boys had heard of the house and we all went to see it together.

Prosper welcomed us all at the airport the evening of April 13th and took us to our new home, which was absolutely delightful. He waited until the next day to tell us that he had gotten a phone call the day we arrived that my father had died that day!

David had just recently gotten his New York State driver's license, learning on automatic cars. The only cars on-island were shift and we rented one, a Volkswagen, from Prosper. I gave David one lesson in shifting, told him he could drive the entire island in 2nd gear and reverse, which is true, and took him to the narrowest road with one edge a cliff and had him do K turns. I told him that if he could shift there he could do it anywhere and left my family to shift for themselves. I phoned my mother and flew back to New York.

Hans Henry Friedman died of "Pre-leukemic Pancytopenia, manifested by severe peripheral anemia, leucopoenia, thrombocytopenia in association with marrow infiltration by atypical blast cells." He was 85 years old.

He was buried in the plot he had carefully selected and prepaid in the Cedar Park Cemetery in Westwood, New Jersey. It was near the foot of a large tree. Just my mother and I attended his funeral. And I flew back to St. Barth's the next day.

My mother is now resting in peace beside him.

My Oma's good old friend Klara ("Klaerchen") Caro wrote her
"Thoughts About Hans Friedman" after his passing, which I have
translated from her German: "He was one of the noblest and finest
people I have ever known in my life. He was the truest friend, ready to
give any offering. His loyalty and devotion to others was without equal.
His interest in political and spiritual things remained to the end."

Well, certainly the political things!

90. Compton

I joined Compton Advertising for more vacation time, a good salary,
and stock options as the Associate Creative Director on Tide -- the
major brand of Compton's chief client, Proctor & Gamble -- as well
as Pert Shampoo and new products. I had to go to Cincinnati often,
usually flying up and back the same day. I worked with the President
of P&G and his eventual successor, Jack Pepper, now President of
Disney.

Flights to Cincinnati, Ohio, landed in Kentucky. The account exec
on Tide loved the barbecue they do in Kentucky. So we had lunch
there practically every time. It was pork ribs in tomato sauce and it was
delicious. Now that I live in Chapel Hill, the word "barbecue" has a
totally different meaning. More about that later.

Late in the morning one day, I was told that I had a meeting in
Cincinnati that afternoon. The only airline tickets available were First
Class, so I took that. On the way back to New York, however, I was
seated first in the forward section; then the top brass of our agency,
chairman, president, creative director, all walked by me, heading for the
rear. What a humiliation, but there was nothing I could do about it.

Another client was Johnson & Johnson whose offices were in New
Jersey. One time I happened to meet my buddy Andy Boncher there;
he was with another agency.

The chief art director in my group at Compton was Al Gruswitz
who became a good friend. He got me some free lance business and
later, I got him some, too. Al and his wife Judy had five children --
all boys! One was allergic to milk so Al and Judy started a goat farm
at their New Jersey home, eventually selling goat milk and excellent
cheese. Al is now doing computer animation for advertising.

One of Compton's other Associate Creative Directors told me about a guy he had interviewed for an art director's job. He had no advertising experience but showed a portfolio of his work: every single one was a drawing of a shoe. Nothing but shoes in his whole "book." The guy even gave one of his "artwork" to the ACD. Part of our job was to judge talent, so he quickly threw the drawing away. Out with the garbage. It was not much later that he realized what he had done to an original early Andy Warhol!

I think I did nice work for Compton, but most of my commercials were tested and did not beat the existing national campaigns. Others were for new products that did not work out -- the products didn't, so few of my ads made it on the air.

After about three years at Compton, I quit to join another ad agency. When I left I had to sell my stock, for a nice profit, so Compton could sell itself to Saachi & Saachi, too.

91. The Thompsons and the USSR

This chapter is <u>not</u> about Monica Friedman Thompson <u>or</u> her family. <u>Nor</u> is it about the J. Walter Thompson advertising agency. It <u>is</u> about my next job, working for David Thompson and his wife, Jane.

Those Thompsons had a small advertising agency that specialized in travel. David and Jane were looking for a Creative Director. Bob Ribetti was their art director. They, and then I, hired travel writers; I wrote ads, travel brochures, presentations, house organs and a regular monthly magazine for Howard Johnson Motor Lodges, clients of the Thompson Agency.

They had some other interesting accounts, including Finnair, some Swissair and TWA business, travel tours and programs, some travel publications, the New York-New Jersey Port Authority (which owned the World Trade Center), as well as projects for many others and prospects for much, much more. It seemed to me a good fit, as I was becoming more and more interested in traveling, having done so much of it. They made me a nice offer and I asked for additional vacation time -- hey, I want to travel, too! We agreed, and Jane and I went out to find me a nice new office chair.

I did a lot of writing and created the Superpoints program for HoJo, with awards for the motor lodges that took the winners (and the Thompsons) to the NFL Superbowl. On June 3, 1983, we were working feverishly on a presentation when I got a phone call from Betty. Her mother had had a sudden heart attack and dropped dead! The Thompsons protested but I went right home.

The same funeral parlor that had held a short ceremony and cremation for Alex Klein now did the same for Frieda. She was the ideal mother-in-law, always helpful, never critical; always there for us and her grandsons. I truly loved her. And I miss her.

Then there was a presentation I made to our clients, the NY-NJ Port Authority, on the 86th floor of their World Trade Center. I do not remember if it was the North or South tower, but of course both of them are gone now.

I recall that before either building was erected, when there was just a big hole in the ground where the buildings would be, Betty, a very young John, and I passed the construction site. I told him that they would build two buildings there, each of which would be taller than the then-tallest building in the world, the Empire State Building we visited earlier. John, very concerned, asked, "Does the Empire State know about this?"

The presentation meeting was in a big conference room on the 86th floor of one of the World Trade towers and I, making the pitch, was on one end of a long wood table, looking at everyone seated on both sides. On the far end, a huge window gave me a great view of Manhattan. Suddenly I felt just slightly dizzy. Then I realized that the building was swaying back and forth, back and forth. I interrupted myself to warn everyone that something strange was happening to the building. But those who worked there reassured me that the building had to bend in the breeze, just like a tall tree; they were used to it.

I wondered, after 9/11/01, what some of the people in the World Trade Towers may have thought when the first plane hit the other building: could they have felt a shock wave and believed for just a moment that it was a natural occurrence, like a storm?

It was through our Finnair client that Betty and I flew to Helsinki which we really enjoyed and then we went on to the USSR -- the Union of Soviet Socialist Republics. The airport inspectors upon our arrival there saw some gold-colored costume jewelry that Betty was wearing when we entered the country and asked us to declare it as gold (to be sure we had it when we left Russia). But it was cheap costume jewelry, given to her by Avon as a prize. We said it was junk jewelry. They didn't believe us until Betty took it off and threw it in their garbage can. Then they gave it back to her, for fear that someone might snitch it from the refuse.

Next the inspectors wondered about the secret code they noticed in Betty's notebook. She explained it was the operating instructions for the Leica camera that John had lent her and written down for her.

Leonid Breznev was the Soviet Prime Minister and we traveled, by ourselves, through what was then still called Leningrad. Now it is once again St. Petersburg. While there, we were assigned our own "tour guide," a very well-dressed and coiffed woman who was, we were convinced, a KGB (Soviet Secret Police) agent. She soon realized how innocent and boring we were and left us alone. We were supposed to eat and sleep in the hotel. We did, generally.

But we also went to a local workingman's type restaurant and waited on a line until a table opened up. Then the next six people were seated there, most were strangers and some friends were split up; the next six waited for the next table. I tried to strike up a conversation, trying English, German, French, Spanish -- nobody dared speak to the foreigners in those days of rigid, authoritarian Communist dictatorship.

Our hotel had been the one that Hitler planned for his personal use if the Nazis had won the war. Now it was for special, foreign tourists only. Our room had a "bug" or listening device; they all did. So when the bed was too soft and we put the mattress on the floor, a knock came at our door to suggest a room change. We said no.

Our tap water was brown so we brushed our teeth with Pepsi-Cola and drank vodka. The hotel vodka was clear. Vodka sold on the streets by the shot was brown.

Special stores were open for Americans and those who had "hard currency." I bought a Russian fur hat there, which they told me was mink. Back home, a Russian-speaking friend translated the label: it was rabbit. But I still have the warm hat.

Betty and I walked down the main street and people seemed to stare at her chest. We realized it was the camera John had lent her that was of great interest to all.

I took a flash photo in a large department store. Everyone stopped suddenly. No one dared do that in a public place! Their surprised looks were reprimands to me.

Eight different strangers came up to us to change money; knowing that most if not all would be KGB, we ignored every one of them.

Russians lined up whenever there was a line, not caring what was being sold. It was clearly whatever was available. One day it was oranges, another day, shoes.

So we really felt what living under a totalitarian regime was like.

Through the Thompsons I once again met up with my old army buddy, Art Frommer. He had become a multimillionaire, in an affiliation with KLM, Royal Dutch Airlines, he had KLM-Frommer hotels and his own travel publishing empire.

David Thompson was a member of the prestigious, glamorous, exclusive Manhattan Club and frequently took me to lunch there. He spent money freely, lavishly, insisting on only the finest quality merchandise or most fashionable stores to shop in. He acted rich in every way.

I was glad when David Thompson hired my son John to work on some projects for a few months. A while later I learned that Thompson had previously gone bankrupt. I feared that he might bankrupt himself again.

Soon thereafter I got myself another job. And then John did, too.

92. Sailing, Scuba and Sharks

Jews have been sailors since biblical times. Especially those early pre-Christian Jews living in what is now Israel or Palestine, existing on the trade routes between Europe and Africa and Asia as well as the Mediterranean Sea. Yet my family, on all sides, were never sailors. Oh, many of us sailed across the Atlantic from Europe, but none of us were sailors, if you know what I mean. In fact, when I sailed the Atlantic to Europe (see Chapter 66) I got awfully seasick.

Yet I loved islands and swimming and scuba diving; it seemed almost natural for me to become a sailor. I really wanted to learn to sail. So I took a sailing course from the U.S. Coast Guard. Then I took another from a private sailing school. And then I contacted a fellow Chappaqua resident, Lucien Greif. He taught sailing on Long Island Sound, leaving from Mamaroneck in his own little boat, the Portislef.

That was his sailboat's name. I wonder if you figured out its meaning. I'll give you a paragraph of time before revealing it. Here is a big clue: Lucien named his boat the Portislef because, as he put it, "If you can remember the boat's name, you'll remember the first rule of sailing."

Can you?

Time's up.

Portislef -- and I know you knew it -- stands for "Port is left," which it is, in the direction the boat is going.

Second simple mnemonic sailing lesson: Port wine is red. So a red light on a boat's side is on its port or left side. A green light is on the other side, the right side, the starboard side.

When returning to port, keep the red buoys on your right. There's another simple memory trick for that: red, right, returning.

See how simple Lucien made it? Just a few lessons and I was ready for my first sailboat. And would you believe it, that first sailboat was an inflatable! It was made by Sevilor, a company that is now part of Zodiac but was independent at that time. They made many inflatable boats, but only one with metal rods that attached to its outside plus one metal mast. Its rigging gave the inflatable a main sail and a jib, with two outside boards, called sideboards, instead of a daggerboard or keel. John christened it "The Intrepid" with a stick-on from the famed aircraft carrier of the same name. He even gave me a gold-braided cap emblazoned "USS Intrepid."

The boat was big enough for two so Betty and I sailed it on an upstate lake; John and I sailed it, Dave and I, Mike and I, and I by myself sailed it on that lake. Then I packed it in a suitcase and took it to St. Barth's.

Betty and I sailed it there, going out from Public. One day we met a stranger, a nice young man whose name I have forgotten, in Maya's Restaurant in Public. He had just eaten a very spicy pepper and asked if he could bite Betty's hair. A strange request, but she allowed it. A bite of hair calmed the spiciness in his mouth. That is how we learned a valuable trick I have just passed on to you.

That day we three sailed The Intrepid from Public beach. The young man was so frightened that we had to turn back.

Soon thereafter, the intrepid Intrepid sprung a leak I could not fix with the handy-dandy repair kit that Sevilor supplied. So that was the end of my first so-called sailboat.

Then I took another sailing course with the U.S. Coast Guard, passed it, and bought a real boat. A small 19-foot O'Day Mariner that was originally named the *Arc-en-ciel,* French for rainbow, a name I liked. Even though it was bad luck to change the name of a boat, John decided to name it "Dreamboat." Betty liked that, so that became its new name.

We joined a boat club called Phillipse Manor in a village that was then named North Tarrytown, right at a stop on the New York Central's Hudson Line. It is just north of the Tappan Zee bridge on the Hudson River. I kept a change of clothes, jeans and a shirt, onboard. So, with the boat docked there, I could often take that train right to the boat and go sailing -- solo -- after work. I did that about 25 times every summer. Betty would then pick me up there. More often, however, I drove from Chappaqua and went sailing with Betty or one of the boys, mostly John.

I frequently sailed up the Hudson, past Ossining, home of the famous Sing Sing Prison. One could see the men in the exercise yard and they often waved to me. And I sailed in the other direction, under the Tappan Zee Bridge, toward Manhattan. I went by the then-Ford factory and by a small lighthouse. John and I sailed upriver past the Atomic Energy plant in New Paltz. Once we went on to Croton to see Pete Seeger in an open-air concert to benefit the Friends of the Hudson (which I joined) and we saw his boat, the *Sojourner Truth.* That group actually helped clean up the Hudson to make it swimable. It is strange, I think, that we actually swam in the river closer to New York City while it was still fouled further upstate. And only the truly intrepid fished in those waters.

I even got a trailer-hitch for the back of the car and so actually managed to drive the boat to its winter storage in our Chappaqua garage. It wasn't easy and our friend Heinz Buell helped a lot but I am proud to say that I did that for a few years.

On September 7, 1987, I wrote a letter to my wife and my sons, which began, "There I was, all alone on my little 19-footer in the middle of the Hudson River's shipping lanes, out of wind and out of gas -- with a huge tanker heading for one side of me and a tug pulling eight barges heading for the other side, about two miles from home port, with my wife out of the country and all my sons out of the area, too."

It was somewhat treacherous, sailing where big boats and barges as well as sightseeing-passenger ships all took precedence over a tiny sailboat. The large vessels could not change course as easily as a little sailboat. The winds generally were such that the so-called New Jersey side (actually still New York State) with its Palisades created back winds that literally suddenly came from the opposite direction. Of course, when the winds died and I had trouble starting the motor, it was a bit tricky. And running out of gas was sheer foolishness on my part. It only happened that once. Obviously, I survived. But only because a large sailboat towed me back to port.

Our first underwater experience was in Bermuda but that was with an old-fashioned hard hat and air hose. It did turn us onto really experiencing the fish first hand. Next we went snorkeling and bought masks and fins. But we soon graduated to scuba, or self-contained underwater breathing apparatus, invented by Jacques Cousteau.

Betty and I met him when he lectured in Westchester and we discovered that he was a true Frenchman, that is, a sexist. Nevertheless we were forever grateful for his invention and the films of his we saw on television that enticed us underwater.

I took classes at a pool and Betty did in a lake. And we both learned to love it. We got certified -- which is vital -- and then went places just to dive. One was New York harbor under the Statue of Liberty! And we bought more than wet suits and a prescription mask for Betty; we got a compressor and scuba tanks and took courses in equipment repair. We had all that in St. Barth's.

There was a wreck just off St. Barth's which we often visited. It was a luxury yacht, the *Non-stop*, and its somewhat mysterious owner, suspected of drug involvement, had disappeared, his pregnant girlfriend was still on-island, and the boat's captain was found dead on board. A major local mystery.

The truly interesting part to us divers, however, was that the *Nonstop* was upside-down at the bottom of the sea, only about fifty feet down. Once Betty and I dived into the boat, swam along its corridors, entered various luxurious upside-down rooms. Then we swam into a huge empty room, difficult to identify at first. When we swam upward inside that room, we reached air and suddenly recognized that we were in an upside-down swimming pool! We took off our regulators to breathe normally and immediately realized that the air was foul. It was, in fact, not good air but the exhalations of previous scuba divers which had risen upward and been trapped in the bottom of the pool -- which was now on top!

Betty and I enjoyed diving in the Red Sea until our Egyptian boat captain turned on his engines (and their propeller blades) before everyone was aboard! That experience convinced us that there was too much to scuba diving beyond our control. But it didn't stop us -- not yet.

Avid swimmers, all our sons took scuba in college, got certified, and we became what a dive master in St. Barth's called us, "the scuba-diving family." They even used a picture of the five of us diving off their boat in their advertising.

We have all seen many sharks in our many hours underwater. Once Betty was the first in our dive group to jump into the sea and immediately reported that we had chosen a large group of sharks to jump on top of. So we all did.

Another time John and I were diving off St. Barth's and clearly saw -- and annoyed or perhaps even frightened -- three nurse sharks at the bottom of the sea, at least one of which was so much larger than either of us, it must have been at least eight feet long! By the way, the French name for nurse sharks translates as "sleeping sharks."

On a trip to the Monterey Aquarium, we Friedmans -- David, Debbie, Sarah, Rachel, Nicole, and I -- saw a great white shark in their huge tank, swimming with other fish. It had survived far longer in captivity than any other of its kind, a record-breaking 195 days at that time, and had put on more than 100 pounds. The previous in-captivity record had been 16 days. Just three days after we saw her, and photographed her, she was released into the wild because she had nibbled a few other fish and, the day we saw her, "was starting to exhibit true hunting behavior," according to the official news release. I "swum" with dolphins in Islamorada on the Florida Keys whereas the whole rest of our family (except Mary and Rachel) swam with dolphins in Mexico.

Famed professional underwater photographer Cathy Church was on one of our Cayman Islands trips and took three excellent photographs of us underwater, one with Betty tickling a grouper's belly.

Off Grand Cayman there is "Sting Ray City," which Betty and I dove. We fed them octopus. As I did so, one of the rays sucked my thumb into his mouth. Cathy Church caught that on film, too. In his college dorm, John kept her photo of us underwater as his "Mom and Dad" picture.

On one night dive, an octopus attached itself to my mask and kind of spread-eagled itself across my face. We've also had ink squirted into our faces by squids. On another night dive we saw sea horses. It is mostly on night dives that we've seen lobsters; they are nocturnal and only come out of their caves at night. And we saw a rare blenny off the coast of Dominica. We've done night dives, wall dives, drift dives, and wreck dives. We dived 100 feet and more. About 40 dives each.

Our equipment included twin or duplicate regulators called "octopuses" (not octopi, the plural for the animal) for each of us, so that in case of a "blown" regulator we did not have to "buddy breathe" but each had an extra source of air. It came in handy only once, when one of my regulators broke while we were deep underwater. Luckily, Betty had that extra regulator on her equipment. But it was that experience -- as well as aging -- that made us give up scuba diving.

93. My Mother's 80th Birthday

Betty and I gave my mother, my *Mutti,* an 80th birthday party in March of 1986 at the Roosevelt Hotel in New York City and invited all the relatives from both sides of the family and from far and wide. Many of them came. We asked them all to give us any photos they could spare of my mother in her younger days and with that, and our own collection, we created an album to celebrate the affair. It was a great party and the album has kept the memory of it fresh in our minds

Everyone who came signed a register, so I have the names of all 55 guests, but I can't read every signature! Among those there from my mother's side of the family were Heddy Friedman and her daughter Ruth and Robert Bruckner from England; Fritz Wolff from Israel; Alfred and Denise Altman and their children Jacque and David from Canada; Gerald and his son Martin Freeman from England; Donald and Linda, Peter and Rosie Silversmith; Eva and Howard Posener, Vera and Sal Marshall and their children, Linda, Gary, and David; Sam and Ellen Zilka and their children, Jeff and Ivy Stern, Annette and Diane; Ilsa and Eric Goldberg; Bernie and Thea Simon and his mother, Selma; plus, from my father's side, Inge and her son Paul Friedman; Hilde and Walter Levy and their daughters, Evelyn Garson and Ray Lipson, Dede and Brian Dorney; Martin Oppenheimer and Hannah Fink; Ted and Bunny Rubin and their children, Jefferson, Steven, and Marjorie; plus Paul Schwartz, Heidi Henle; and, of course, Betty and I and our three sons.

We also created the first official Friedman family trees and had all the members of the family put themselves into their proper places. Our son David has kept it going with all the new additions over the years. He created 21 descendancy charts!

Among the few who could not come because his wife, Erika, was sick, was Friedrich Buchholz from Arnheim, Holland. He wrote that he was eleven days younger than my mother. (David and I visited him in Arnheim in 2004 when he was 98!)

In a 1985 letter, Friedrich wrote of "a legendary celebration on *Kaiser Wilhelmstrasse 8*, Breslau, at the home of Clara and Ludwig Friedmann, where we possibly have seen each other [my mother and he] as children. Our real acquaintance with the Friedmann Family at Bielefeld took place September, 1931, for me and about a year later for Erika.

"That was a secret appointment in the garden of Café Lindenhof, only Lotte and the two of us, where we exchanged information about our prospective plans for marriage (in) a few weeks, in the autumn of 1932.

"It was rainy weather, but much bigger clouds of tempest were already visible at that time, threatening our future."

Friedrich also wrote of his daughter Gaby and her husband Jan Carel going to clinical pharmacists gatherings. David and I met them, too, in 2004, and they were kind enough to let us shower and sleep at their home the day we arrived in Europe.

94. Hakuhodo and Sammy

Hakuhodo was then the second largest Japanese advertising agency in the world. They wanted a Creative Director for the United States. And I was their man.

After a series of interviews with others, I was invited to lunch with the agency's president whom I was to meet at the Nippon Club, of which he was a member. I was used to a fancy eating club from many lunches with David Thompson, but this was different. Luckily, I can handle chopsticks very well, and so probably passed the first test.

In the previous interviews I had asked for more than they were planning to pay and for four weeks' vacation which was more than they wanted to give. But there was no negotiation; they had listened to my requests but were inscrutable. I wondered if I should press the point with the obvious final authority, the boss, Mr. Masui.

We spoke very little at the table across from each other, just ate our sushi slowly, sipped our saki, and mostly nodded to each other. At long, long last he said, "It is usually the American who breaks the silence."

I did not immediately answer. Then, after a while, I nodded.

He nodded in response.

"You know something about Japan," he said.

"I had the pleasure of visiting Japan," I replied.

"Ah, so."

Then silence.

We finished our meal and went outside. As we shook hands, I finally asked, "What about my salary and vacation requests?"

"That will be acceptable."

I wondered, when would I start. But I said, "It has been a pleasure to meet you," and I bowed at the waist.

"Can you begin on Monday?"

I said, "That will be acceptable." I offered my hand, we shook, and we parted company until Monday.

Hakuhodo had major clients as well as little ones. Canon, Ricoh, NEC, Ban Dai, and Star Electronics. But also some Japanese food merchants and gimmick makers, such as hand warmers (which I now use to play winter golf).

Their offices were on 52nd Street near Carnegie Hall and the Plaza Hotel. A nice neighborhood. There is a hotel and bar next door to the agency. I often had a drink there and frequently saw the acting couple, Hume Cronyn and Jessica Tandy, who lived there.

Years later, on stage at Playmakers in Chapel Hill, I've often seen Tandy Cronyn, their daughter.

The agency had only Japanese clients doing business in America. I am reminded of the movie *Lost in Translation* for which Bill Murray won the Academy Award.

One client, Canon Cameras, had an arrangement with Sammy Davis, Jr. He was very popular in Japan; a pal of Frank Sinatra's and member of The Rat Pack, they knew him as an actor and singer in his own right. They recognize true talent.

I had the pleasure of working with Sammy for three years, doing one print ad a year. We created it together, although I came ready with some ideas. He made me feel that he liked working with me and enjoyed my company as much as I did his! And he was always "on," always funny, excited, on the go until all hours of the night. Even when I met him the next day for breakfasts.

The first time I met Sammy was on March 25, 1984 in Las Vegas, at the hotel where he was appearing, the star of his show. It was the fabulous Flamingo, THE nightspot on the famous strip at that time.

It was my first trip there and Betty came with me. We flew out and checked into our room. That evening there was a message: "Come to Sammy's dressing room tonight after the show. There are seats reserved for you and your wife at the show."

Prior to the trip I read Sammy's two autobiographies, *Yes I Can* and *Why Me?* but not the more recent *In Black and White*, by Wil Haygood, or *Gonna Do Great Things*, by Gary Fishgall. On October 20, 2003, *Time* wrote "it would take at least a dozen volumes to capture his life." Yet I thought I knew the man.

I knew of the automobile accident which caused him to lose his left eye and convert to Judaism. Sammy was in the back seat with a Jewish man whose Star of David Sammy was admiring when the accident happened. Sammy woke up in the hospital, barely alive, with the Star of David imprinted in his palm. He took that as an omen.

He told me many stories about Frank Sinatra, how much he admired Frank and whose generosity Sammy believed was boundless. Only he'd have phrased it better.

Little Sammy (he was very short) started in show business in 1928, at the age of 3, wandering on stage while his father and uncle were performing. He has hardly been off since.

He was THE STAR of his show, his name, SAMMY, up in lights. He no longer needed, "Davis" or "Jr." any more than he needed the old "Will Mastin Trio, starring Sammy Davis, Jr.," which had been his original and long-time billing.

Betty and I were given great ringside seats that evening and we loved the show. She went up to our room as soon as it was over and I went to Sammy's dressing room. He had his valet pour me a drink. Others on his staff Sammy included a white bodyguard, a bandleader, and an entourage of hangers-on, almost all black. Sammy was still very "up" after the show and I personally do not think it was drugs. But it might have been.

He said that his mother was born in San Juan, so, he joked, "I'm Puerto Rican, Jewish, colored, and married to a white woman. When I move into a neighborhood, people start running four ways at the same time!"

Sammy was married to May Britt, a beautiful blonde actress, but she wasn't there. After a while, a bunch of long-legged, white Las Vegas showgirls from some other show came in. That's when Sammy turned to me and said, "Go up to your wife now, Wally, these girls are for the brothers."

I have now seen three of his shows, different each year, in different cities: Las Vegas, Phoenix, and Hartford. Each was sensational. He had absolutely amazing talents: singing, dancing, telling jokes -- with racial and religious humor -- playing up to guests, never ignoring the "little people." He told me, quite rightly, that he dealt in nostalgia.

When he later had me pay a breakfast bill for him and his entourage of maybe ten people, he said, "Wally, remember, I'm a big tipper."

So I tipped big, really big. About as much as the bill itself. But he said, "I'm a bigger tipper than that!"

I tipped double the actual bill! I paid in hundred-dollar bills. For breakfast! He noticed and smiled, approvingly.

For lunch he insisted upon one of three choices: hot dogs, hamburgers, or Southern deep-fat fried chicken. None of the "fancy foods" for him.

When I caught up with him at the "Canon/Sammy Davis, Jr./ Greater Hartford Open," in Connecticut one year, he pulled me up from the sidelines while he was on local television, and said, "Here's my friend Wally Friedman."

He had his valet send photos of us to my Hakuhodo office. He stayed in touch with me!

It was in more than mere gestures that he was truly kind, thoughtful, and very considerate. He might have said, "a *mensch*." Sammy was a pleasure to work with, even when he disagreed with me. Sammy most often invited me to his hotel suite, usually the Presidential Suite or the equivalent, where we would work together. I came prepared with copy and layouts. He always had other ideas of his own. So we talked, we worked it out. I knew what the Canon client wanted, Sammy knew what he wanted. He clearly cared about his image and he knew what people thought of him. Sometimes he liked what I had done, more often I made his changes. He did it with humor, kindness, thoughtfulness, and consideration. I can't say that about many clients, much less many of the great and near-great stars I worked with.

The only thing wrong with the job at Hakuhodo was that the Japanese do not consider the Creative Director as the decision maker. They prefer a consensus. Also, they are definitely sexist; women are servants, only men should be bosses.

When a female copywriter became pregnant, they asked me to fire her. Was it because they had no respect for her or because, as an American, she might want maternity leave? I will never know. But I knew my place and fired her.

Then they really put me in my place. The same president, Mr. Masui, who had hired me, hired a free-lance writer to kind of compete with me. He did whatever they wanted. Their consensus decided that his ad was better than mine on one job. So they decided to give him my job.

I was out of work again.

95. Isabella

In February, 1981, two years after my father's death, my mother wrote a letter to Martin Oppenheimer, my cousin who grew up on the chicken farm. She made a carbon copy, which I have. In it she conveyed her life as a widow and her continuing activities:

"I am going on with my life, filling it with my interest for art, theater and opera and can take advantage of what New York City has to offer. Most recently I saw an exhibition in Columbia University - your old Alma Mater - in the rotunda of Low Memorial Library, entitled 'Dizzy and Beaconsfield' showing books, manuscripts and memorabilia of Benjamin Disraeli, whose life and accomplishments have interested us for years. It is the centenary of his death on April 19, 1881. Also, I have as many friends as I have time for, to telephone with or visit."

She continued to live in Apartment 4B at 44 Bennett Avenue. But two things began to limit her, her memory and the Manhattan winters. She had dementia but not Alzheimer's. She knew who she was and where she was, but her short-term memory was not what it once was. One example: She paid her quarterly federal income tax by check and mailed it. Then she wrote the next check to pay the same tax again if I hadn't stopped her.

Bennett Avenue was also a slight hill; not so bad that it really mattered -- except in the winter when the sidewalk was slippery with snow or ice. Although she still telephoned the Kosher Butcher who delivered to our door, as she had when my Oma was doing the cooking, my mother was still in the European habit of shopping almost daily for fresh fruits and vegetables. And it had gotten dangerous in the winter, although she had not yet fallen.

So I managed to convince her that it was time to go into an "old age home," as they were then called. There was no question about which one. It would be Isabella Home, right next to good old George Washington High School. My parents had known a few people who were there and had visited them a number of times. My father had often said that someday they would end up there. So, because Hans had said so, she agreed to go there.

Isabella is located on the highest point in Manhattan and she had a corner apartment on the 13th floor, the next to the highest. It had a truly magnificent view -- all Manhattan, and I do mean all, was at her feet. On a clear day, and there were many, one could see all the way to the Statue of Liberty, the Bronx, and enough of Long Island to see planes going into LaGuardia and sometimes even Kennedy airports!

She had a living room and dining room with a small kitchenette. I bought her a TV set and she was quite happy there, especially when she met her next door neighbor who became a good friend right away. She showed *Mutti* around.

But that neighbor passed away and my mother seemed lonely. We had the great good luck to hire a perfect nursemaid, Terry Lambiase.

She was also an immigrant to the U.S., but from Ireland. I honestly do not know how they understood each other's accents, but they did. They understood each other perfectly. Terry came to take care of her, help her get up and get around, first with a cane and later with a walker. She saw to it that my mother did not miss a meal.

Mutti even liked the food very much, which I thought was standard institutional fare. This Irish-Catholic lady even made sure that my German-Jewish mother got to all the ceremonies at every Sabbath and all the Jewish holidays, something my mother was delighted with.

I visited her often in Isabella Home and I handled all her money. She had inherited everything from my father and received checks monthly from Germany. Her expenses were minimal, mostly to Isabella and to Terry plus "incidentals." I took care of her TV set when she needed a new one, etc.

96. Wally Friedman, Inc.

I had been doing some freelance work almost since I began writing ad copy. I had written mail-order copy for Ed Axel and others. Ed paid me in cash, often meeting me on Times Square and peeling hundred-dollar bills off his bankroll in payment.

Another "client" whose name I do not remember took the booklet I wrote for him and never paid me more than the "good faith" money I had demanded in advance.

I tried two parallel career paths. First, to get a job. And, at the same time, to get more clients for my ad agency. I had some small clients, however, for whom I had to not only create but also place ads in print and broadcast media. They were a mail-order jewelry retailer and Betty's alma mater, Manhattan Medical School. So I had to have "agency recognition." And for that I needed to incorporate. I did it in Delaware, by mail. I named my ad agency simply Wally Friedman, Inc., and issued shares of stock. I was president, Betty was treasurer, and David John Michaelson, the VP.

Once I had a real ad agency, I got two client through my friend Alan H. Taylor. One was for a rejuvenating skin cream. Unhappily, our small ads did not get enough responses. Another was a realtor for whom I placed ads. Unfortunately, it was a bad time for Manhattan apartment rentals or sales.

My biggest client at that time was the Sibarth real estate and house-rental agency, the only one then on the island of St. Barth's. It was run by Roger (pronounced the French way, "Rojay") and Brook Lacour. Roger sold real estate and Brook did house rentals. She had been an account executive on Procter & Gamble at Compton Advertising before I ever got there. She had discovered "our" island, met and married the handsome, young ex-Guadeloupean (or *Bequi*) and settled there, opening a boutique which offered fashionable clothing. I even brought down from New York some T-shirts imprinted with "St. Barth's. Sorry no telephones" a true statement at that time. Later a few people, very few, got phones. They included Eugene Camille Bernier, a friend and neighbor, who took our calls for us.

Wally Friedman, Inc. placed ads for years in the *New York Times* and some travel magazines for Sibarth and for the island of St. Barth's. We even did national ads in American magazines for a restaurant on island. It lasted until Brook had her brother run the growing U.S. side of the business, including other islands' properties. He, under the name of Wilco, was perennially late in paying my bills -- for which I had to lay out the money to the media! When I tried to charge him interest on his late payments for the *New York Times*, we came to a parting of the ways.

I had a few job interviews with New York City agencies that did not pan out. I tried for one in Philadelphia, another in Kansas City. Neither materialized.

97. The March of Dimes

Through a headhunter I applied to the March of Dimes for a job in their Mamaroneck, N.Y. national headquarters, a short drive from our home in Chappaqua. It would have been an easy commute. We realized that they would not pay me enough to live on.

I then opened an office for Wally Friedman, Inc. at 185 Madison Avenue, yes, the Madison Avenue, subletting from another ad agency, doing some ads for them, mostly for Yonkers Raceway, in lieu of rental payments. Both Betty and I appeared in our TV commercials which were shot by Nat B. Eisenberg and his NBE Productions. I did not forget my old friends. Another of their clients I did commercials for was the Catskill Hotel Association.

Finally, many months after my previous interview, when the person who had initially interviewed me was no longer with them, I pitched the March of Dimes as an independent contractor advertising agency. They hired Wally Friedman, Inc.

We started on an excellent arrangement. Excellent for them, I believe, in the print, radio, and TV spots I created for them. Excellent for me as far as remuneration was concerned. I was put on a retainer, getting a monthly income. I even made more money, as all agencies do, by marking up the production bills. The March of Dimes alone paid me more than $125,000 per year. Their agency of record was Ogilvy & Mather, who handled their solicitations and WalkAmerica campaigns, but I believe we produced more TV spots, PSA's or public service announcements, for the March.

I should tell you that the March of Dimes was initially created by President Franklin Delano Roosevelt, who had polio, as a way to get millions to contribute funds to find a cure. It funded Dr. Jonas Salk, whom I had the pleasure of meeting, along with his wife, Jacqueline, an ex-wife of Pablo Picasso's. Salk, a fellow CCNY graduate, developed the vaccine that virtually ended the dread disease.

Now the March of Dimes was positioning itself as working toward the cure for prenatal and early childhood diseases. They wanted an anti-sexually transmitted diseases campaign, which they called STDs. One such disease, AIDS, auto-immune deficiency syndrome, was just then recognized as passing from a pregnant mother to her fetus.

My first assignment for them was on AIDS, to publicize that prenatal fact. I did real research, going to hospitals, clinics, and discussing experimental procedures with doctors and scientists. I met some people who had AIDS, including many babies. I attended the second annual AIDS conference in Washington, D.C. I was in the third row to hear the keynote speaker, the then Vice President, George H. W. Bush.

I did a slide-show presentation on AIDS (which I still retain) to about twenty March of Dimes staffers that resulted in my "Marionette" PSA's -- 30-, 20-, and 10-second announcements with English and Spanish voice-overs, as well as radio and print ads.

Next came celebrity endorsement spots, using stars they lined up for me, those who would work for free, discussing AIDS and other STDs. I wrote and produced pre-natal care spots, on anti-smoking and drinking while pregnant campaigns, on low birth weight, on infant mortality and crib death, and more.

Through the March of Dimes I had the pleasure of working with the comedian Bob Hope (we shot his spot in his home) and the basketball star "Dr. J," Julius Irving (shot on a court) as well as the golf great Arnold Palmer (filmed on a golf course), movie stars like Ricardo Montalba (in a hotel room) and Hal Linden (in a park), comedian Paul Rodriguez, Elizabeth Pena, Jill Eikenberry, Michael Tucker, boxing champion Ray "Boom Boom" Mancini (all filmed in their homes), Jayne Kennedy, Steve Kanaly, Michael and Marissa Pare, Mary-Ann Mobley (the third Miss America I met) and TV host Gary Collins (filmed on sets), among others.

My ad agency, which was really just me and the art directors, producers, and directors I hired as freelancers -- guys I had previously worked with: Al Gruswitz, Don Michelson, Nat B. Eisenberg, and Andy Boncher -- created a few dozen additional public service announcements for the MOD. For some of those projects I cast announcers and actors, purchased the use of National Geographic photos, selected footage from the Bettmann Archives, even film taken of a fetus inside a woman, and used some of the March's historical footage.

The March of Dimes and I were talking about a fascinating new project that I had started on. It was explaining to the public the benefits of genetic manipulation. The potential was just coming into public notice now that the DNA double helix had been discovered. The March felt it vital that people understand why scientists were identifying and mapping human genes on our chromosomes. And, most important, that the potential benefits be explained to ordinary citizens.

It was a complex concept that needed careful depiction. There were religious issues, abortion questions, and potential stem-cell use factors. What did a gene for, say Tay-Sachs disease, really mean and what could be done about it? I was just getting involved, enough to realize that our genes could give us a propensity toward a disease (lung cancer, for example) which did not guarantee it would afflict an individual -- unless some other, outside factor (such as smoking) also was present. Nature and nurture questions. These were ideas that demanded public understanding and discussion if we could get the concepts across clearly and succinctly. I believed that the right public service announcements could communicate such complex ideas to the general public as quickly, painlessly, and simply as possible.

It was a project I really enjoyed working on. I was doing well and doing good.

98. North Tarrytown or Sleepy Hollow

All three of our children had finished college, earned their own living, and definitely moved out of our large home in Chappaqua. So we sold it and moved to a year-by-year rental in a condominium at 327 Martling Ave., in North Tarrytown.

It was the area in which Washington Irving had lived. His home is still a local tourist attraction. He even wrote about the town in his story, *The Headless Horseman,* which is often re-read at Thanksgiving time. He fictionalized the town by calling it "Sleepy Hollow." I did not think it was a compliment. Yet recently, long after we moved away, the area has officially renamed itself with its fictional name.

When we put our Chappaqua home up for sale we had a buyer who was interested in both the house and the boat but he eventually only bought the boat and we sold the house to someone else. We had paid $40,000 for the house in Chappaqua when we built it in 1965 and we got $440,000 for it when we sold it in 1988. (Since Bill and Hillary Clinton moved to the area, real estate prices have soared much higher.)

We lived in the apartment exactly one year. Betty never would have said this because she only half believed it, but I honestly think I moved there partly to be closer to our boat, the *Dreamboat*, which was moored on the Hudson River just north of the Tappan Zee Bridge, at Phillipse Manor.

Shortly <u>after</u> we moved there, the major client of Wally Friedman, Inc., the March of Dimes, temporarily moved their national headquarters from Mamaroneck, N.Y., to North Tarrytown! I had not known that they would. It was so that they could renovate their building and they moved back to it when the work was done. But it was certainly convenient for me.

Our rental apartment was perfect: it had an L-shaped living-dining room and two bedrooms plus a den which became my office. Of course I deducted part of the rent from my taxes as well as other legitimate business expenses. Our first and only accountant, Jerry Shafer, suggested that I buy a second car and call it "the company car," which I did.

99. An Accident and Lyme Disease

My "company car" was the Nissan in which I had an accident near our new home in 1988. The collision was not my fault, as was quickly established by several witnesses. The police took me to the hospital and the car was towed away, to be declared "totaled."

I felt fine after the accident, not hurt in the least, and the emergency-room physicians agreed. Betty came to pick me up in "her" car, a Toyota.

The morning after the accident, however, I felt a tingling in my left leg. I went to our doctor to have it checked out. He did tests, some which I thought were unnecessary. When the results came in he said that what I felt was not due to the auto accident. Rather, I had Lyme disease! I hardly believed it, but confirmation came thereafter.

Lyme disease was named after the town in Connecticut where it was first identified. It is transmitted by a tiny tick the size of the period at the end of a sentence. Its bite usually creates a ring-shaped red rash, which I never saw on me. The most common is the deer tick. In Chappaqua and North Tarrytown, in all of Westchester County, there were plenty of deer and a rising number of cases of Lyme Disease. It

262

was a relatively new condition and the treatment was debated by doctors and scientists. Samples of my blood were sent to different labs. I went to an expert on Long Island.

I joined a Lyme Disease Support Group with about fifty people. We made up a list of 43 possible symptoms which many of us had. It included headache, sleeplessness, itching, dizziness, falling down stairs, biting one's tongue, losing one's balance, things like that. I had at least twenty of the listed symptoms at that time.

The most-agreed-upon treatment was a series of intravenous drips of penicillin. I have been allergic to penicillin ever since I had an operation as a boy in Boston. I reacted to the drug -- my fingers became swollen. Now they were suggesting a penicillin-derivative called Rosephin. Before I dared try that treatment, I had a skin-patch test done by a dermatologist. It determined that Rosephin was tolerable.

So I started a scheduled twice-a-week intravenous flow for a projected ten weeks. After three and a half weeks or seven treatments, Betty noticed that I had developed a rash on my face. By the time I got to the hospital, the red rash had spread over my entire body. They quickly isolated me. Doctor after doctor came to look at me. They decreed that I should stop all Rosephin treatments. I had no other treatment.

I often bite my tongue and I frequently stumble and fall going up stairs. Those symptoms convince me that I had chronic Lyme disease. Perhaps I still do. If so, it doesn't slow me down a bit.

100. A Classic Mistake

Wally Friedman, Inc. had one major client and a few very small ones. And since I had no time for anything else, I wasn't even trying to drum up any new business. That's a classic mistake but I just couldn't help making it.

Then the president of the March of Dimes retired and a new president came into office, the woman who had been head of the New York Chapter. She said she liked my work but that she needed to show that there was a regime change. So she decided to use her advertising agency instead of Wally Friedman, Inc.

I was given the contractual 90-day notice. I was left with too little income to live on and no unemployment insurance. My long-time financial advisor, Wolf Popper, suggested that I team up with two other people and we formed U.S.Advertising. In the next year we made 17 presentations to prospects that I uncovered. I hired my old pal Maury Lerman to help in a pitch at American Express. Not one of the 17 worked out.

During that year I also tried to get a job, as copywriter, copy chief, creative director, anything, in ad agencies and corporations, through headhunters and by answering ads. But I was 55 years old (although my resume said 50) and I could not get any employment anywhere. I had always known that advertising was what we then called a young man's business.

If nobody was going to pay me to do my job, I decided and Betty agreed, that I might as well retire. Happily our retirement plans had been made more than ten years earlier. We just had to settle our affairs and wait until the right moment to announce our retirement to ... no surprise ... our home on St. Barth's.

X. OUR KIDS' FAMILIES
(1989 - 2006)

101. A Very Good Kach

When my son David asked me what I thought was the right kind of girl for him to marry, I told him to do what I did: find a woman who was similar in background to himself. A like-minded person with much the same kind of upbringing, education, and life experience. Someone with whom he had a great deal in common. The same religious, political, and economic past. The same social attitudes. The same values. And the same ideas for the future. I thought I gave him good advice because what I did led to a very happy and successful marriage.

David graduated from the State University of New York or SUNY Binghampton, with a degree in math and computers. He was offered a teaching assistant's job at Pennsylvania State University, which effectively paid him for getting his Master's Degree.

When David had his Master's in computers, IBM offered him a job in Gaithersburg, near Rockville, Maryland. One day on the volleyball court of a Jewish organization, David met Debbie Kach. They started dating. While Michael followed David by also finding his future wife on a volleyball court, David was the only son of mine to take my marriage advice so literally.

Deborah Lynn Kach's parents, Peter and Barbara, had both come from German-Jewish stock. Debbie's parents even went to Germany to work there with the U.S. military. In fact, Debbie was born in Wiesbaden, Germany, in an Army hospital, on January 16, 1963, six minutes before midnight, after a twelve-hour labor, weighing 7 pounds 8½ ounces Her father told his mother on the phone that day that "it wasn't too difficult" and that she was born two weeks late. Deborah was named after her great-grandmother, Dora Jacobson.

Peter, Barbara, and Debbie Kach returned to the U.S. and settled outside Washington, D.C., in Rockville, Maryland.

Like our son David, Deborah was the oldest of three children. Her sister Lori was the middle child, her brother Randy, the youngest. At three, Debbie asked, "Can I play with Lori on the floor? I promise I won't push her."

She went to high school, started college but didn't finish and then took up medical assistant's training, all just as Betty had done. She even worked in a doctor's office, exactly as Betty had. David was struck not only by how similar her background was to his but also by how cute and clever Debbie was, and still is.

She lived close enough to Dave's workplace that they got together as often as they could and quickly fell in love with each other. They did, however, have two major disagreements. He did not want to have any children; she wanted children very much. They worked that one out very easily: he came around to her way of thinking. So she went along with him on the other point: she would maintain a kosher home and give their children a Jewish education.

D & D had one engagement party in Chappaqua, at the Kittle House, and another in Rockville. Our oldest son married the oldest Kach daughter on September 10, 1989. It was a wonderful wedding with a "rehearsal dinner" the evening before. There, in what is a Friedmann family tradition, I read my poem about the bride and groom. By the next day their best man, Brian Kretch, had rewritten his own remarks into a wonderful poem! Part of his rhyming remarks told of how he met David. At work one day they passed each other in the corridor and he noticed Dave's identification card and realized that there was another Jew at IBM!

The wedding was a blast. I have a VHS video of it. It was a traditional Jewish wedding with the Chair Dance and Handkerchief Dance, the getting of the garter and the throwing of the bouquet. Maybe it was a put-up job, but David's brother John got the garter and Debbie's sister Lori got the bouquet.

The very next day after the wedding I announced to my entire family that I was retiring, and that Betty and I were moving to St. Barth's. No one was surprised.

Peter and Barbara Kach continued to live in Rockville. When each of their children, Lori and Randy, got married, they visited us in St. Barth's on their honeymoons and they and their children live near their parents.

Barbara took up playing the organ in a big way and with her lovely singing voice, often led sing-alongs. Retired, Peter started raising hosta lilies, more than 20 varieties, in their back yard which has extensive woods (and deer) beyond it. Peter has also come up with dozens of money-making ideas. He's a licensed travel agent but doesn't work for a travel agency. He has recommended his ideas for second careers to me but I continue to believe that retirement beats work, every day of the week.

Very unfortunately and very suddenly, Barbara passed away in March, 2006. Her funeral was attended by friends and family from near and far, including my entire family with Nicole Friedman and me.

When they got married, David and Debbie lived at 9422 Fern Hollow Way in Gaithersburg, Maryland. Even then they insisted that visitors take off their shoes. And already then they had a 55-gallon fish tank.

Pretty soon Michael and later John also moved to that area, both of them to Virginia, just outside Washington, DC. And Michael also had a tropical fish tank in his apartment. John didn't get his until later.

When the four members of our family got together they made an unusual video (VHS) together. It is entitled, "D&D&J&M Visit the Mall," and it's the funniest things this family has ever done. They did it to show Betty what a modern mall was like, what bargains there were in the up-to-date USA as opposed to the out-of-date island we were on. It stars all four of them, with camerawork, direction, and plot by all. It's a completely impromptu documentary. At one point a saleslady, told that they were making a tape for their mother, addressed the camera: "Mom, your family is crazy!"

102. Sarah Tamar Friedman

IBM transferred David to Springfield, Illinois, Abe Lincoln's birthplace, so their first child, Sarah Tamar Friedman, was born on there on September 9, 1992, three years minus one day after Dave and Deb's wedding.

Soon thereafter Betty and I came to visit and help the new parents. As an unprejudiced observer, I found little Sarah to be absolutely beautiful. She was certainly not premature like her father, but a healthy and robust baby. A friendly, smiley baby.

One day when David and Betty were out shopping together, a deliveryman came to the house with a package. He congratulated Debbie and me on our baby! I suppose it was a natural assumption on his part since we were the only ones home. I, on my part, was flattered. And Debbie laughed. As did David and Betty when they heard about it.

IBM next moved them to California. I have a VHS videotape of Sarah entitled "The Pumpkin Bear," because that is what David first called his firstborn child. Later he called her just "Bear." The tape shows a chubby-cheeked, close-cropped brown-haired little girl at Gymboree where Debbie reported that after 12 weeks there, Sarah had learned how to crawl, clap, and wave.

They lived in Orangevale where I helped David put in the in-ground sprinkler system. The video also shows Sarah being introduced to her backyard kiddie pool by Betty and Debbie. Many years later Sarah did not want to move from Orangevale so that she could keep that small kiddie wading pool. She didn't understand that Roseville included a big backyard in-ground swimming pool!

Sarah has taken to swimming in a big way. When she was about six, her family visited us in St. Barth's and she really enjoyed our pool. And when we took her to Cul-de-Sac Beach, the one that is so shallow we call it a "kiddy wading pool," she walked out pretty far and, still only waist deep, said, "I want to swim in the deep end."

I told her that the deep end was France, about 3,000 miles away.

Sarah has quickly grown up to be a highly intelligent girl who is doing fantastically well in school. She gets all A's, like her father. She plays the flute beautifully, unlike her father on the clarinet. I told her that a flute player is called a flautist in an orchestra and a flutist if in a band. Now she also plays a bassoon.

Sarah has long said that she wants to become a marine biologist. Long before she could possibly comprehend what a marine biologist does. Our trip to the Monterey Aquarium did not change her mind, and I was able to realize that she now clearly understands what marine biologists do. I wish her well if that remains her ambition.

She loves indoor rock climbing which looked awfully dangerous to me. I couldn't do it when I tried. And Sarah is constantly plugged into her iPod and cell phone.

Nicole and I went to Sarah's wonderful *bat-mitzvah* in September, 2005, which was a glorious affair. We attended the Friday evening services, in which Sarah had a small role, and the Saturday morning service, in which she did so much so well! She chanted the Hebrew perfectly from the Torah scroll, which is entirely without vowels or musical notation. Her superb speech in English was about her commitment to Judaism and what it has meant to her.

Absolutely grown up, 13-year-old Sarah Tamar Friedman did everything perfectly with aplomb and delight. She is indeed a delightful young lady, self-assured, sophisticated, responsible, and also beautiful!

At the party that evening, dressed in a white gown, she looked like a bride. So much so that the band performed the traditional wedding music as we lifted Sarah up on a chair. They played a hora and much youthful dance music. It was truly a fantastic affair. David spared no expense for more than 200 people.

It was Debbie's wonderful idea for the party that, instead of having tables numbered 1, 2, 3, and so on, the tables were named for islands. For example, I was at "St. Barth's" and the Solomon family was placed at the "Solomon Islands," etc.

Best of all, the children's table was named the "Virgin Islands."

103. Rachel Eliana Friedman

Dave and Debbie moved to northern California when IBM transferred him there. The company's name is now just IBM. But it originally was International Business Machines, although its employees said IBM stood for I've Been Moved.

At first David, Deborah, and Sarah lived in Orangevale. They moved when David joined O.S.I., Objective Systems Integrators, in nearby Folsom, site of the famous prison and Folsom dam which contains Folsom Lake.

Their second daughter, Rachel Eliana Friedman, was born May 11, 1994. Betty and I came up from St. Barth's once again, very glad to help in any way we could. Right from the start of her life, Rachel was cute. That's truly the best word to describe her, cute. Some say cute as a button, an old expression. Or a cutie-pie. I say Kewpie-doll cute, another outdated expression. But that's what Rachel was, right from Day One, and that's what she still is. Cute. A real doll-face. But a live and lively doll.

Nowadays Rachel has taken to electronics in a big way, online with her NeoPets or playing GameBoy games, yet she and her sister both love to read.

Rachel is also very intelligent, with a mind of her own. After a trying time, with her independence, obstinacy, and resentment of strict rules, Rachel is now doing very well in school.

The family moved from Orangevale to Roseville, both near Citrus Grove, all suburbs of Sacramento, the capital of California. What's in a name? None of them ever had oranges, roses, or citrus groves; their names where created by copywriters for housing developers, akin to what I did in my first advertising job. My cousins Walter and Hilde Levy lived in Olivenhain, California, and olives were grown there. But not any more.. Now Orangevale, Roseville, Citrus Grove, and Olivenhain all have strawberry farms!

David then switched to a small upstart company, Cerent Corp., in Petaluma, which was subsequently bought by Cisco Systems, one of the largest companies in the world. David commuted from Roseville to Petaluma, about 100 miles from his house. He drove there on Tuesdays and home on Thursdays, telecommuting the rest of the week.

As a Group Product Manager for Cisco, David has international responsibilities. The year in Europe was certainly beneficial and he continues to amaze me with how well he can still speak German. He travels often, far and wide, recently including Hong Kong, Italy, and India. In fact, Cisco had him take a seminar in Spain for potential managers. Cisco has its eye on him.

But David also has his eye on the Las Vegas area, investing with his friend David Shapiro, making loans banks won't make, for much higher returns. So far, so good.

Although our little Rachel is indeed a California Girl, she is not quite everything that implies. She is very intelligent as well as very cute. She does not talk like a "valley girl," perhaps because she lives far from L.A.'s San Fernando Valley, relatively closer to the foothills of the Sierra Nevada Mountains, but she doesn't talk like a "mountain girl," either. She talks like Rachel. There is no one quite like her, except, of course, in some ways her sister is like her. They do look a lot alike. Well, like sisters.

Rachel was amazingly quick to learn computer skills. Seemingly obsessed with computer games, she is not easily distracted from them, especially when riding in a car. She has started playing the trumpet and does so very well. There just aren't too many compositions for flute and trumpet, so we have not had a combined concert recital.

Our California family visited Betty and me when we lived in St. Barth's and stayed in a neighbor's rental home. They all swam in our pool and clearly showed everyone how very well the two daughters of "Fish" could swim. Both girls played pool games, easily diving and finding numbered pool "eggs."

Back in the USA, both girls started taking Karate lessons, as did their mother who, I believe, achieved a Black Belt. The sisters are also Girl Scouts and so Debbie has become a scout leader.

I recently took up golf and played a 9-hole game with David and his daughters. I won. On another visit we all played miniature golf. I lost. Rachel maintained that miniature golf is harder than real golf because it's easier to get the ball into a hole surrounded by grass than to get the ball through a windmill, over a bridge, into a dragon's mouth, and then into the hole! Looking at it that way, she has a point. And I do appreciate her making excuses for her old *grandpere.*

I think that golf is harder than baseball. In golf, you have to play your foul balls!

Nicole, David, Debbie, Sarah, Rachel, and I, Friedmans all, recently took a trip together. On the way to Monterey we witnessed a horrible automobile accident. Debbie took charge and David immediately telephoned 911 to call for an ambulance and the police. That evening we learned from the local TV that three people had been killed and one hospitalized.

That experience caused David to quickly buy a safer and brand new Toyota van rather than the one we were riding in which had more than 100,000 miles on it. He had been touting the advantages of buying a used, off-lease vehicle rather than a new one; but now he had a reason to buy a new van: the increased safety of multiple air bags.

As I write this at Carol Woods, I am eating my lunch. It is something I never heard of before, a Rachel Sandwich. It's a kind of Reuben Sandwich, with turkey and coleslaw, on rye toast. And like its namesake, a Rachel is very good indeed.

104. Some Riddles

John has many friends. He makes friends easily and keeps them. That is true of his high-school, college, and job-related friends. His old friends are still friends.

One of his many friends, David Henn, was living in a shared-rental home in the Washington, DC, area. It was a house in which each renter had his or her own room and they all shared such things as the kitchen and downstairs laundry room. One day when John came to visit, the front door was unlocked. John entered and jokingly yelled, "Hi, honey, I'm home!"

A female voice from the basement replied, "I'm down here doing laundry."

That is how John met Karen Marie Riddle. And why Dave Henn was the best man at their wedding.

Our middle son married the Riddles' middle child -- they had seven kids! And it was a glorious affair. John and Karen danced a mean tango, surprising their guests, but not really those who knew them well.

You could say that it was typical of their relationship: unique, different, surprising, but definitely THEM.

They complement and compliment each other perfectly. She's basically shy and quiet, John's talkative and outgoing. He does words, she does math. She is great with her hands, cooking, baking, sewing, creating stuff. He is terrific with his mind, talking, writing, selling, creating ideas. While she's a Catholic and he's a Jew, they both agree on being neither, yet celebrating both Chanukah and Christmas with their son Alex.

Karen taught school in Burke Center, Virginia, for five years and then went to work for the famed Washington Opera. Her boss was the General Director, Placido Domingo, a temperamental tenor. She made costumes, re-sized some, created others and became the head of the Opera's Costuming Department.

Many of those costumes have to be made to come off almost instantly for a quick change of clothes. Or twenty of the same costumes must be made, but in almost 20 different sizes. Once Domingo had "last year's costume" waiting for him at final dress rehearsal. That's when they discovered that his waist had grown four inches! Karen fixed his costume incredibly quickly and well.

One year Karen and John attended the Opera's gala opening-night performance and were almost seated on the stage! They were in box seats at the back of the stage, facing the audience, and their picture appeared on the front page of a Washington newspaper with the cast!

Her ability with a sewing machine has brought her many interesting freelance jobs, including costumes for Wolf Trap. She even gets some part-time jobs she cannot and will not talk about. It makes me wonder what costumes CIA or FBI or NSA agents could be wearing when they go undercover.

Karen's parents, Marvin and Helen Riddle, live in what Betty used to call No-Place, Pennsylvania. It's actually the largest city in PA, as Marvin is quick to point out. St. Mary's is now bigger than Philadelphia or Pittsburgh or any city in the state. Bigger in area, that is. And that's only now, after St. Mary's recently incorporated some neighboring towns into itself and became a widespread city.

But it started small, in 1842, as *Marienstadt*, when North German Catholics left their native land because it had become predominantly

Protestant. German Protestants later moved to a different part of the state and they are known as Pennsylvania Dutch. "Dutch" is really the German word for German, *Deutsch.*

St. Marys -- which recently lost its apostrophe to the U.S. Post Office -- is located in the upper northwest of the state in rolling mountainous country, very picturesque. It is always snowed in for the winter, starting before Thanksgiving and often lasting until Forever. I know, because Betty and I have attended the Riddle's annual Thanksgiving Dinner, an extended-family affair. It really is very pretty in the snow.

This year Nicole and I were invited to come up when it wasn't snow-covered, in July, 2005, when Marvin and Helen celebrated their 50th anniversary. The area looks great in green instead of white. It was a delightful affair and a pleasure for us to get to know these hard-working, deeply religious, very resourceful and self-sufficient, truly kind and thoughtful people who seem to me to live the way our farming ancestors did.

Marvin had purchased the 12½ acre mountaintop property when he got engaged to Helen. Then he built what became their basement but was their home until he had finished the entire house. And finish it he did! Almost all the wood was homegrown, cut from his trees. He did a fantastic job: The wood floors are absolutely perfect, the wood paneling incredible, but the wood kitchen cabinets are really something. The grain of the wood matches all the way around, not a millimeter of wood is missing; every piece's grain fits its neighbor absolutely perfectly because they originally were of a piece. Marvin also makes matching bowls and other wooden items which he sells at craft fairs.

He was in the honey business, first building wooden boxes into queen-bee homes that keep the bees in their place while their honey flows to Marvin. The side product the bees make is beeswax, so Helen makes all kinds of candles and she sells them at craft fairs, too. When the postal authorities decided to name the road on which the Riddles and a few others live, it was christened "Honey Lane."

Now that the house is finished, the Riddles do upholstery and re-upholstery, working on old-fashioned chairs, for example, the old-fashioned way. One recent job was to re-upholster all the pews in a local church.

Most of Marvin's and Helen's families live in the area. A sister of Marvin's, now deceased, was a Sister, that is, a nun, Sister Valentina, who was known as Teeny. She danced at John and Karen's wedding. Years ago when Betty and I were invited to her convent, I read the Old German inscriptions on the decorated windows which, they told me, none of them could read. I translated them. To no one's surprise, they were biblical passages.

At John and Karen's wedding, I pointed out to Marvin that we were now *mechutten* --a word in Yiddish for which there is no single word in English. I can say that Marvin is my son's father-in-law, or my daughter-in-law's father, or that we share a grandson, but there is no one English word for our relationship.

Perhaps that made him think of us as family, that we have a closer relationship in Yiddish than in English. I'm delighted that they have invited us to their family affairs. But you'd think there'd be enough of them for a party without us. For Karen is one of seven children and both sides of both Marvin and Helen's families are from St. Mary's. Well, actually, it's not accurate to say "from" St. Mary's. Their four sons all married local girls and stayed but the three daughters left and only come back for visits.

Marvin and Helen sold their bee-keeping business to their son Michael and his wife Theresa. He still works nights in a factory because the bees can't support his family yet. Sons David and Marty work in factories, too, but also do regular farming.

Marty and his wife Janine have built a home out of logs which is a wooden marvel although you don't wonder where he learned woodworking. Marty also has an ingenious farming sideline: He raises chickens and grows peppers to sell eggs and peppers in the local farmers' market. He has built wooden boxes on wheels for his chickens instead of chicken coops. He places these bottomless boxes between the rows of peppers. By rolling them slowly down the row, he lets the pecking chickens weed his garden! Unfortunately the Riddles' son Christopher drowned in Lake Erie in a boating accident. His widow, Anne, lives in town with her two sons.

Marvin's youngest brother, Jerry, owns a tortilla factory in town, about as far from Mexico as you can get. He sells his tortillas -- red, white, and blue ones -- among other places, in Yankee Stadium.

105. Alexander Henry Friedman

He had not been easy to conceive and his parents and grandparents were all absolutely delighted when our only grandson was born at 2:56 PM on May 4, 2001 and named after Betty's father and mine, Alexander Henry Friedman.

Karen quit her job as the head of the Washington Opera's costume department to spend full time with her son. Naturally, they became very close.

Alex was a perfect bouncing baby boy and his parents certainly bounced him around. John took to turning him upside down and swinging him around in ways that scared me -- but not Alex. He loved it and wanted more.

Little Alex loves to follow his father around and do what he does. So they got him a toy lawn mower, for example, to use when John mows the lawn. And they even have him using a computer -- but his is not a toy!

His parents also never talked "baby talk" to him, but rather conversed in adult language that few children three times his age understood. But he always did.

That proved wise when Alex started talking, speaking in sentences rather than just words, with complex thoughts I doubted he understood. But, again, he always did.

In the shower with his father one day, Alex clearly announced that, "Alex has a small penis; Daddy has a big penis!"

A short while later, after John had quoted that to Karen, John asked his son, "What do Daddy and Alex have that Mommy doesn't have?"

Alex thought for a moment and answered, "Lawn mowers!"

He is clearly a happy child who knows he is loved and who enjoys himself. He is also very much a boy. Because his father often jokingly threatened David that he, John, would buy Sarah and Rachel a pony, I gave Alex a pony. All right, it was a stuffed toy. But Alex totally ignored this doll-like creature in favor of machines, trucks and trains.

He was only two when his *grandmere* passed away. Happily, I have a wonderful photograph of Betty in her hospital bed, looking on and beaming as Alex and I kissed.

JK&A come to visit me in Carol Woods now, but the first time they came I was not prepared in the morning with appropriate breakfast food. So I served what I had and we all enjoyed cake for breakfast. The next time they came, Alex, not yet three years old, reminded me that, "We have cake for breakfast here." So that became a tradition.

Already at age two, while his father was working for the construction-materials company Lafarge, Alex knew the proper names of all kinds of construction equipment, from earthmovers to concrete mixers ("not 'cement mixers,' *grandpere*!"). Then Alex got into trains, correctly naming more different kinds of engines than I knew existed.

In preschool at Christmastime, the teacher asked 3½-year-old Alex the name of the man with the big belly and white beard who comes to your house and brings you toys. He quickly and correctly answered, "*grandpere*."

Alex has a way with words, like his father and father's father before him. One example: When we were walking and talking in the woods, 3½-year-old Alex heard an echo and said, "There's an ecosystem here!"

Another example: It was at Nicole's house one day when 4½-year-old Alex picked up her large triton trumpet shell, put it to his ear, and announced it was, "My shellphone."

I could tell you more but I'll let John write the book of Alex's sayings.

106. A Pattajoe

One time when Betty and I came from St. Barth's to Washington, D.C., to see our sons, Mike did not show up. He went, instead, to a volleyball game. When we did get together, I asked if his team had won. No, he said he wasn't playing, he just went to watch a game. This surprised me: he had not come to see his parents but rather to watch volleyball? What was so special about the game?

It turned out that he had played volleyball a week earlier and noticed a woman on the opposing team. Now he went to the game that team was playing to observe and actually talk to her. Our good friend Richard Gilbert had created a business of friendly, neighborhood volleyball games, primarily because it was a wonderful way to meet members of the opposite sex, especially when they were wearing little clothing.

Mary Wright had not noticed him at the previous game, but now they met and made a date.

She was born Marylu Pattajoe on June 14, 1953, in Tampa, Florida, the fourth child of abusive, addictive, alcoholic parents. Her parents divorced when she was young. Steve, Barbara, and Larry all left but little Mary was sent to live with her grandparents. When they wanted to send her to a Catholic school, she ran away from home. She threw away her school books and knocked on the door of the nearby home of a school friend -- not even a very close friend -- and was welcomed. She simply did not leave.

Later she telephoned the police to find out the age of majority. It was 17. So, the day she turned 17, she went out on her own. Her independent nature was obvious to all who knew her. For a while she lived on a boat. She didn't sail anywhere, the boat remained docked.

Her father remarried and fathered a girl but Mary did not know she had a half-sister named Jenapher (not Jennifer) for many, many years. Jenapher found Mary only because of their original unusual last name. There aren't any unrelated Pattajoes.

But Mary changed her name when she married a military man who she thought was Mr. Right since his name was Glenn Wright. Mere days after the wedding, he was transferred to England. She had to prove that they were married to be allowed to follow him there. They stayed a year but it became an abusive, addictive, alcoholic relationship. She didn't like the military or England or the man who turned out to be Mr. Wrong. They divorced.

Mary was working for a golf course developer when she met Michael. She quit to become a real estate agent, joined the largest such agency in their area, and became the "rookie of the year" her first year, a "million-dollar seller" her second year, earned more money than Mike her third year, and became a "multimillion-dollar seller!"

Mike had often proposed marriage but Mary said she did not want to hear "the M word." He gave her a diamond engagement ring but she traded it in for earrings -- which did not signify engagement -- because she didn't want to get m.....d!

No one was more surprised then I when, after more than eight years of living together, splitting up, then living together again, they did decide to get married. I asked each of them, separately, why they were getting married now. Mike said that the time was right. Mary said it was because she "always wanted a beach wedding, but a small wedding, with as little ceremony as possible." So that's what they arranged.

On income tax day, April 15, 2004, our youngest son married the girl who had thought she was the youngest Pattajoe. I was delighted to be there especially since there were only two other witnesses to their wedding: Mary's newly discovered half-sister Jenapher S. Carpenter and Jen's partner's daughter, Kayla. I only wish Betty could have been there.

It was held at Paradise Point Resort & Spa, an island off Mission Bay, north of San Diego. It was literally a beach wedding: we stood on the sand, the waves lapping at the shore right behind us. We all wore bathing suits, and Mike and Mary both wore Hawaiian leis like large necklaces around their necks. They did not exchange rings; they switched their necklaces and Mike said, "With this lei, I thee wed."

Mary Wright, being Mary quite contrary and of very independent mind, kept the name she was known by in the real estate business. And I think that's only right.

Mike and Mary are DINKS, Double Income No Kids. They have, however, given me two granddogs, two grandcats, and lots of grandfish. Their new home is grand also, with, according to the builder's brochure, "arch-topped windows, multiple turned gables, an elegant recessed Palladian entry, stunning two-story foyer, private first floor study, family room with built-in entertainment niche, 4 bedrooms, 3½ baths, sunlit breakfast area." Their mansion has more than 4,000 square feet plus a full basement that is as yet -- temporarily, if I know my son -- unfinished. The house literally has two grand staircases, like in *Fiddler On The Roof,* "one going up, the other going down." It is really grand!

Mike has already created a small pond with a small fountain in his backyard and a dramatic fountain in the front. He has moved some of the trees and shrubbery that came with the house and planted new ones. M&M imported a huge truckload of dirt (I know, I helped shovel some of it) and created wonderful gardens around the house and around their backyard fence. They also have made an indoor garden to keep tender warm-weather plants alive through the winter.

Mike is the Senior Manager of Provisions Workflow Systems for the bankrupt MCI, which has just become a division of Verizon. He earned a nice bonus for staying with MCI through the transition.

And Mary is now, finally, for the first time in her life, enjoying the fruits of her labor. She bought herself a brand new orange two-seater Mini-Cooper convertible sports car. It's not for work, but just for fun. So the two of them have three vehicles. And a boat.

Ever the Floridian, Mary says she wants to retire there someday. I think they will. Lots of people do. But I told her that many Floridian "snowbirds" now have a second home in North Carolina for the summers. And she does have experience with the aftermath of a hurricane. See Chapter 113, Luis.

Mike and Mary went to Iceland in September, 2005. He reported that they saw waterfalls, whales, ponies, a few glaciers, and puffins, including one puffin they saw "while whale-watching who just wanted us to watch him being a puffin."

As that may imply, Mike is a birder. He has joined a birding club and often goes to various places to spot and count different birds. The *Washington Post* even quoted Michael correcting his group leader in identifying a bird. In fact, Mike is never wrong about anything he says. And he's got a good eye. Well, the British slang for a girl is a bird. Mike really spotted his bird early on. And he was right about Mary Wright.

XI. RETIREMENT
(1989-1999)

107. St. Barthelemy

There are two reasons why I was able to retire to St. Barth's at age 55. They are Terry Lambiase and Ellen Zilka. And I owe them my sincere gratitude. Terry took care of my mother in the Isabella Home and Ellen visited her monthly and handled her finances.

At first I had charge of her checkbook and got the four checks she received from Germany (for restitution, pension, insurance policy, and widow's benefits). With that income, she was easily able to live and pay for all her needs, expenses, as well as small luxuries and even all the cards she wrote and gifts she gave.

My cousin Ellen Zilka always called my mother, "Oma New York," and really felt as close to her as to a grandmother. Perhaps it was in thanks for my mother arranging for her and her brother to escape the Nazis on the *kindertransport.* Ellen visited my mother every month religiously and took over my mother's checking account, paying Terry along with all other expenses. I will be forever indebted to her and Sam.

We lived on St. Barth's full time, it was our only home. But my wife and I came to New York four or more times a year. We went to our doctors in Westchester because medical care in St. Barth's was what Betty called "abysmal."

When Betty went to Chappaqua to visit Marvelle and go shopping with her, I went to Manhattan to visit my mother. Then I drove back north to have dinner with Betty and Marvelle. And to a hotel in Westchester thereafter.

We lived on St. Barth's by our own careful choice after having visited more than twenty different islands in the Caribbean. St. Barth's was unique.

But I believe that every island is unique. Each has a different combination of geology, geography, history, population, politics, economics, even climate, etc. So what is it about St. Barth's that was so attractive to us (and lots of tourists)?

Most of the answers begin with "s." It's the sun, sand, shore, sea, shells, swimming, sailing, snorkeling, scuba-diving, scenery, sex, sensuality, sensations, sensibility, seeing skies full of stars, and special sightings of movie stars!

The climate is much the same all year round: dry, breezy, mostly between 75 and 90 degrees Fahrenheit; it is classified as a desert. We also lived on the windward side of the island, with almost constant trade winds giving us a nice, comfortable breeze. While we had air conditioning in all our other homes, we only had ceiling fans in St. Barth's.

Much of its appeal is because it is French, with all the good (food, wine and nude beaches) and none of the bad (the island is tax-free!) The former food critic of the *New York Times,* Craig Claiborne, wrote that "some of the best restaurants in the Western Hemisphere are on St. Barth's." St. Barth's has the largest wine cellar in the Caribbean, at in-France prices.

When we first discovered St. Barth's in 1969, it was "undiscovered;" now it is *tres chic,* a playground for the rich and famous.

But best of all, the natives are very friendly, white, good natured, trusting, open, and amazingly honest. They're descendents of twenty families from Brittany and Normandy who colonized the uninhabited island in 1673.

Let me give you the island's earlier history. Archeologists proved that its first inhabitants were Arawak Indians. Carib Indians living on neighboring isles came to our little island and ate the inhabitants! Nobody was left when the French families arrived.

Now a little geology. During middle Eocene time it was beneath the water. Then volcanoes arose. Our house on Morne Vitet is on a dormant volcano. Dormant, not dead.

I found more than a hundred perfectly round rocks, balled-up volcanic ash or pisoliths, on our property. Think about it: one perfectly round ball of a rock is a very rare find.

A word on the island's name. Christopher Columbus named it for his brother when he saw it on his second voyage to the West Indies in 1493. St. Barthelemy is called "St. Bart's" but spelled the French way, St. Barth's.

108. What Did We Do All Day?

We retired to the home on St. Barth's we'd built ten years earlier and had spent every vacation there. Then we lived there another ten years with no other home. "What did you do all day," many friends asked us, some adding, "after the beach?"

Well, we seldom went to the beach, rarely snorkeled or scuba'd, never sat around just sunning or tanning ourselves. We had two cars on an 8½-square mile island but didn't tour without visiting tourists. As full-time residents we didn't have time.

So, what did we do? Betty did the things she had always done as a housewife, only they were considerably harder here. She cleaned the house even though you could never tell what the wind would blow into the place: dirt, dust, drifting volcanic ash. She had to shop at all three "supermarkets" to find -- not a sale -- but what was on sale. What was available. Which one had tomatoes, for example, although she really resented paying a dollar or more each. Or she had to go to the pier and buy fruits and vegetables right off the boat, depending on what came in from where. Our lovely little island had no commercial agriculture, everything was imported. Some things from the USA, some from France, others from other islands. Betty never planned a menu until she was at all the stores and saw what was available that day.

I did things I had never done before: plumbing, electrical work, painting, car maintenance -- I even changed the cars' oil regularly myself. And lots of gardening. Our property was 2,000 square meters -- about three-fourths of an acre.

Our lovely property was three-quarters of the way up the highest mountain, Morne Vitet. We had a 270-degree view -- the valley beneath us, the beach in front of us, and the ocean around us. We watched whales migrate every January and observed around-the-island sailboat races. Truly breathtaking, our view was pictured on the cover of *Tropical St. Barth's* magazine. But while we admired it often, we didn't just stare at it.

I re-graded our steep slope, terraced it, built rock walls, shoveled dirt around, and created level surfaces with rock steps to ascend the terraces. Seven terraces. This sounds like hard physical labor, which it was, but I usually only worked for an hour or so, wearing only a bathing suit, and then jumped into our pool to cool off. Then I'd put in another hour before swimming again. I took afternoon naps. And that's how I spent most of my days.

We entertained a lot and partied often evenings and weekends. We usually ate at a restaurant once a week, went to friends' houses once a week, had guests at home once a week. We had lots of friends who had boats and airplanes. So we went off-island often. Betty would go shopping by plane to St. Martin and St. Croix. I'd pleasure-sail often. We also traveled the world.

We had television, sometimes, with a dish antenna for a while. And we listened to the radio a lot, (even got WCBS from New York City as well as Radio Moscow sometimes), but mostly to track hurricanes in season. One day in late 1983, I heard Radio Grenada calling for help, appealing to anyone listening, saying they were being invaded by the U.S.A., with planes attacking their airfield and parachutists landing. I thought it was a joke, a local island version of Orson Wells' *War of the Worlds* broadcast. It wasn't.

Most of all, we gardened. We had lots of flowers and cross-pollinated hibiscus to create multi-colored varieties. We had a cacti and succulents garden, varieties of palms (some grown from seeds I got in Israel) and lots of native trees. We had eleven different fruit trees: mango, papaya, key lime, orange, mandarin, tangerine, passion fruit, ganip, cherimoya, banana, and sapodilla.

I planted so many papaya trees and distributed enough fruit that I became known as "Papa Papaya." Whenever papayas were ripe, lots of them were ripe. So I gave many away freely. It was an unofficial barter system. When some neighbor slaughtered a goat, for example, we'd get a leg. Or a rabbit. Or part of a boar. I even traded papayas for lobsters.

We had *citron* trees which bore lots of key limes or lemon-limes. I made a wonderful drink using this native recipe: "One sour, two sweet, three strong, four weak." Translation: one part key lime juice, two parts liquid sugar, three parts vodka or gin, four parts water. Deliciously refreshing

I constructed a watering system on this desert island, an Israeli drip system. It involved PVC pipes and thin rubber drip lines at each plant with different irrigation lines on different terraced levels, each on a timer which shut off the water automatically.

What else did we do? I was invited to join the Lions Club and did. There were two Lions Club meetings and one dinner every month. I even became the *chef de protocol,* which I translate as Master of Ceremonies, and was elected 3rd Vice President. There were many Lions projects, usually cleaning beaches or helping people fix their roof, things like that. Our Lions Club made "friendly raids" and relief missions to nearby islands. Betty and I even went to three international Lions meetings, in Hong Kong, Montreal, and Philadelphia.

I helped create a Marine Reserve around parts of the island that was recognized internationally and the mayor appointed me to its Board of Directors. I was also on the Board and Secretary of FEMUR, an acronym in French for the organization that helped obtain equipment for the local hospital.

Betty and I helped organize a library in Lorient, created a fund-raising annual Library Fair, obtained most of its prizes, and Betty became the library's treasurer. I even took an advertising job with a magazine publisher which took both of us to neighboring islands. We were retired, but we worked. Just not hard. Nor for money.

Then there were always Bastille Day and *Mardi-Gras*, after all, this is a French island. Some friends, spurred on by Lu Chassin, prepared different elaborate costumes every year. One year the local newspaper pictured me dancing with Lu on its front page.

Finally, we partied a lot. There have often been many reasons for a great party, but none as glorious as the year that *Le Select* -- a local bar and restaurant -- celebrated its fiftieth birthday while its owner, Marius Stakelborough, celebrated his seventieth and his mother's ninetieth birthdays. Who came to the party? Everybody, and I do mean everybody on island was there, as well as Jimmy Buffett. He had lived on St. Barth's and had owned a hotel-restaurant called *Autour du Rochet* in partnership with Larry Gray, Captain Groovy in Buffett's book, *Tales From Margaritaville,* which is partly about St. Barth's. The reason Jimmy Buffett came to the party is because he had written his big hit, "Cheeseburger in Paradise,"about *Le Select.*

109. Tropical Magazines

One member of St. Barth's Lions Club was a magazine publisher. His name was Jean-Claude and he did not speak English, or dare to, although I think he understood it. His two magazines were *Tropical St. Barth's,* about "our" island, and *Tropical West Indies* about ten islands in the immediate area: Anguilla, Dominica, Dominican Republic, Guadeloupe, Nevis, Saba, St. Barth's, St. Eustatius ("Statia"), St. Kitts, and St. Martin. Seven of them were English-speaking.

Jean-Claude had five employees. One was a British woman who covered the English-speaking islands. When she discovered a lump in her breast she immediately flew home and Jean-Claude was left without someone to do her job. It involved the only phase of the advertising business that I had never done before: selling space, that is, convincing someone to advertise in the magazine. I did it under the condition that he would pay for Betty to travel with me: airfare, hotels, meals, taxis, everything, instead of any salary. He gladly agreed.

So we went to seven islands, all of which we had visited before, but this time to sell space. I would create their ad and give them free editorial mention. In fact, the magazine was actually a "puff piece" whose content did little more than extol the virtues of its advertisers. Just as in my very first publishing job, with Commercial Circular Co. (see chapter 68) I also had to write the editorial content of the magazine. I enjoyed it, sold lots of ads, and Betty was delighted to go island hopping and shopping.

I also wrote many feature articles about other islands. I met with government officers, ministers of tourism, local museum officials, artists, musicians, hotel and restaurant owners or managers, and I interviewed local characters. I did this for two issues of *Tropical West Indies*, until the British woman returned to her job.

One of my articles was reprinted word for word in another magazine, *Island Hopper*, three years after it had first appeared. I got no money for that, either.

Unfortunately I also had to collect unpaid invoices and payment for ads I sold. Sometimes we got services instead of money in exchange for the advertising. It was the barter system. All our flights were funded by ads in the magazine for Windward Island Airways (Winair). Our hotels and restaurants were advertisers. We had to take certain taxis whose drivers owed money for previous ads.

Another example is the painting I have of a beached blue boat. The artist sold it to me for much more than the cost of the ad and write-up he had previously received.

110. Joe Ledee and Eugene Bernier

When our house in St. Barth's was built, we vacationed nowhere else. Friends and family went and we often rented it out whenever we could. Betty usually went a week before me. Then I'd join her for a week and we'd come back to New York together.

One of the first times she did that, Betty met our up-the-hill neighbor, who introduced himself as Joe Ledee, (pronounced "lay-day,") a native St. Barth. Later we met another native, our down-the-hill neighbor, Eugene Bernier. The island's natives are white, descended from twenty original French families, and all have three names. But they call each other by their middle names.

Josef Irenee Ledee was known by natives as Irenee -- except that Americans pronounced his name as Irene. So he became Joe. Eugene's really Eugene Camille Bernier, so they call him Camille. Americans call him Eugene. Lots of locals' names are confusing: Not just Irenee and Camille, but Jean-Marie, Florimond, Turenne, and Lulu are males, and Lu is a female.

When Betty met Joe, a week before I arrived, the only available rental cars on island, like all the cars on island, were shift cars, not automatics. Betty had gotten her New York driver's license having learned on automatics only. I gave her a few lessons, but that was it. She was game to try, but fearful about driving those narrow, curvy, dangerous roads, the only roads St. Barth's has.

Joe, on the other hand, knew how to drive a shift car but didn't have one at the time. So the instant friendship they started -- and it lasted all her life, even to the very end -- began by her renting a shift car and him driving it.

From that beginning, Joe became the little brother neither Betty nor I had ever had, and, at the same time, he, like Paul Schwartz before him, was like another brother to our boys. There are so many Joe Ledee stories that I could write another book just about him. I'm afraid I can't do him justice in our family saga.

Joseph Irenee Ledee is the eighth of nine children. They all grew up in a *petite case,* the small stone native house that has only one or two rooms. All nine never slept there at the same time and those who were present usually slept in hammocks outdoors.

He came to America as a teenager, went home to marry "the prettiest girl in the school," Christiana Ledee, and they had one daughter, Nicole. Every relative on her family tree is named Ledee. Joe is street smart, kind, understanding, decent, honorable, deeply religious, truly intelligent, with "native intuition." Aside from all that, he's a great guy! And he gives great parties!

On just eight square miles Joe has had more than eight careers: chef, hotel manager, real estate salesman, rental home manager, vending machines operator, library president, construction manager, rabbit breeder, etc. It was John who wisely called Joe, "a failure at everything except life."

Joe gets people involved in his projects. He has done a great deal for the local church and nuns. He got us to help him start and maintain a library, including creating an annual money-raising fair. He is now trying to create an old-age or retirement home.

I nominated Joe for the Lions Club. When I was elected 3rd Vice President and subsequently resigned to go back to America, he took my place. So he became the Lions' President in three years instead of me.

Eugene Bernier was one of the very first to get a phone on St. Barth's. He used bugle calls to call neighbors when a call was for us. Eugene escaped from a German prisoner-of-war camp, was a semi-pro boxer, a raconteur who led a fabulous life.

He mixed a Planter's Punch with three fruit juices and three rums. It tasted great but one drink got people "knee-walking drunk." We often crawled home, slowly, uphill. John got Eugene's "secret" recipe.

And it was Eugene's 1968 Ford Mustang that John drove down the St. Barth's airport runway and bought and brought home to America.

111. Montserrat

Montserrat, one of the nearby Caribbean islands south of St. Barth's, exploded on July 18, 1995, with a tremendous volcanic eruption. We did not know it at the time but soon saw and felt the fallout: a dusting of ash that covered everything on our island.

The St. Barth's Lions Club was quick to organize relief efforts. We collected contributions from our citizenry and merchants. They donated everything imaginable. And our Lions Club picked everything up, brought it to the dock, loaded it on a boat, and steamed off to provide aid and comfort. Since Montserrat was English-speaking, I was among the volunteers to sail there and distribute the contributions.

The "serrated mountain" of Montserrat was covered with greenery that gave the island the nickname, "the Emerald Island," not to be confused with "the Emerald Isle," Ireland. This 39-square-mile, teardrop-shaped Caribbean emerald had a population of about 11,000 people before the volcano exploded. The British had established an observation post and seismographic center on-island which we had visited earlier.

Betty and I had been to Montserrat with the Lions Club about a year before. We went on a "friendly raid," which we often did to neighboring island Lions Clubs. At that time we went up to the crater of Mt. Soufriere. The foul-smelling, sulfurous crater felt decidedly warmer than the surrounding warmth. Soufriere steamed and smoked for more than a year before it exploded.

We had previously smelled such a pervasive odor at Vesuvius in Naples and Sulfatara, Italy, but Pompeii no longer had that odor. We had smelled it as well at a volcano we visited in Japan, near Mt. Fujiyama. That one smelled of rotten eggs. To follow the Japanese tradition, we bought a fresh egg, put it gently into the liquid lava for just seconds and watched its shell turn black almost instantly. Then we ate the instantly-hard-boiled egg for good luck.

Soufriere emitted a worse stink, the like of which I didn't smell again until I returned to Montserrat a second and third time. The cataclysmic explosion had blown away most of the crater we had visited the year before.

Scientists estimated its temperature at 1500 degrees Fahrenheit! The intense heat produced hot ash that rained down on two-thirds of the island, including Montserrat's capital city, Plymouth, some of which burned the tin roofs of many buildings. People described black, red, and white curls of ashy smoke in the air. Some said the lava flow from the mountainside came at 90 to 200 miles per hour. Nineteen people were killed that day. Lava incinerated all wooden structures, porches, doors, and entire homes.

At our visit Soufriere was still emitting ash, pulverized rock, and red pyroplastic flows of lava. On our evening sail outside of Plymouth harbor we clearly saw red lava flowing down the dark mountainside.

Sixty-five thousand people were killed by pyroplastic flows in this millennium. Mount Pele on Martinique, which Betty and I had visited years earlier, suffered 30,000 deaths in two minutes! The only inhabitant to escape death was a prisoner locked in his cell.

Now, 160 miles north of Martinique, Montserrat's capital city, Plymouth, lost half its population. Those who remained moved to the north end of the island where public housing was rapidly erected, thanks to the British government, under the direction of the Royal Governor whom I met on a later trip.

A member of the local Lions Club, Basil Walters, was a former Colonel in the British army and he still had that military bearing, tall and strong and straight. Basil was Montserrat's Director of Emergencies, in charge of the police, fire department, and the evacuations off the island and to the North end of the island.

Basil drove us to places on-island that even native homeowners could not go. I reported in St. Barth's newspaper and in the International Lions magazine that we left our footprints in the ash just like the astronauts did on the moon.

About five thousand inhabitants, half the population, fled the island. But Basil was very clear. He said quite firmly, "I'm not leaving!" Betty and our three boys met Basil at a Lions Club convention years later in Philadelphia.

Scientists say that Montserrat originally rose from the sea about four million years ago. Evidently its shape had not changed until now, when about one square kilometer of new beach -- hot, ashy beach, not sandy at all -- was added to the island's eastern shore. From the safety of our boat, we saw some of that still happening. More than a thousand metric tons of ash per day have fallen on Montserrat through mid-2004! Every so often St. Barth's got another light dusting.

I returned with the St. Barth's Lions to play Santa Claus that Christmas, distributing toys our citizenry had contributed to the children of Montserrat. Another year I went to another island, Dominica, to play Santa to the Carib Indian kids living on their reservation there. Yes, this tone-deaf grandson of a cantor, this New York Jew in a Santa suit, led little Black and Indian kids in singing Christmas carols and religious songs!

112. Why We Left St. Barth's

There are two reasons why we left our wonderful, idyllic island of St. Barthelemy. One was the medical care. Not that the doctors on St. Barth's weren't nice and amiable. But none of them came there to practice medicine; they came to enjoy the island.

What was wrong with the medical care was politics. St. Barth's is part of the *department* or State of Guadeloupe. We were like one of Hawaii's out islands and the only real hospital was on the Big

Island. French law said everyone living within one hour of a major hospital cannot go to any other and we were within one hour's <u>flying time</u> of Guadeloupe's hospital. The law forbade us to permit any non-French-licensed doctors or nurses to volunteer their help at our local so-called hospital. Nor could any babies be born on our island! Besides, Guadeloupe earned lots of money when St. Barthians came, often with a relative. An expectant mother or seriously ill patient had to have someone accompany them to the hospital; that person stayed in a hotel and ate at local restaurants. Their hospital was a boon to Guadeloupe's economy.

St. Barth's *Hopital de Bruyn* is more like an old age home, some "patients" had literally been there for years. We Lions Club members came every Christmas, bringing gifts and singing carols to the same people year after year, plus a few aged newcomers.

Betty and I had evacuation insurance, in case of an emergency. But the airport was not open at night. We returned to the U.S.A. at least four times a year, to visit my mother, our children, Marvelle Gilbert, and, importantly, our doctors and specialists.

The local X-ray machine and radiologist did not recognize a broken ankle when I had one. They had no material to make a cast nor even any ordinary Band-Aids until Betty and I bought some. They would not -- and could not legally -- accept American-made products or supplies. We went to the States when Betty had a shoulder problem that needed arthroscopic surgery. Her surgeon did her left shoulder the same day he did Reuben Sierra's right. Hers was fine and his obviously is, too. Because he was, in 2005, still an outfielder for the New York Yankees!

When we discovered that Betty had heart problems and the only cardiologist had left St. Barth's, we decided to return to the U.S.A. (It's ironic that cancer killed her.)

The second reason we left St. Barth's was because of Luis.

113. Luis

The hurricane that devastated New Orleans on September 2, 2005, "the worst natural disaster to ever hit the U.S.A.," was a Category 4 storm named Katrina.

The hurricane that hit St. Barths on September 4, 5, and 6, 1995 was a Category 4 storm named Luis. It was bad enough. Yet no one on our island was killed and no one was seriously injured. It did result in an injury to me and hurt Betty psychologically.

Luis was an awesome hurricane: <u>250</u> miles across, with fierce, raw, sustained winds whipping the island at <u>150</u> miles per hour, delivering wave upon wave after wave of torrential rain, day after day after day.

Our home, like almost all on the island, was sturdily built, according to the strict building codes which I had not appreciated up until then. For example, I had wanted to have a truly large front window with a fabulous view of the ocean. But the then mayor of St. Barth's would not allow it. (The present mayor, Bruno Magras, does.)

The house was made of poured concrete and cinder blocks reinforced with steel rebars. Our many as-large-as-possible windows, some almost 4-feet across, had sturdy wooden hurricane shutters built by a boat builder, constructed to be easily and firmly shut by a woman alone, if necessary.

We had been listening to coordinates over the radio and carefully tracking every storm on detailed maps as they approached year after year. Each took its own path. We had lived through some that delivered a great deal of rain as they passed near the island. But Luis was different. A meteorologist described it in advance succinctly, "This is a large, powerful, and dangerous storm."

We could not leave the island. By the time Luis was close enough to really threaten us, there were no seats left on the few small planes and boats that had already evacuated the early birds. But we prepared. We stocked up on supplies, brought things up from downstairs (we had no interior stairs) and stayed upstairs, just the two of us.

As reported on the Internet, "On Monday night, as the first fringes of Hurricane Luis were approaching the island, before communications had been cut, a local girl telephoned a friend in New York to share her anxiety and excitement. 'I'm going to be in a hurricane! It's starting now!' There was a pause to consider the matter, and finally her friend asked, 'What are you going to wear?'"

We were there, all alone, for three days and three nights, listening to the wind, hearing things, we knew not what, scrape against our house and across our roof. Monday night, the 4th of September, the water came in through the bottom of our doors and flooded the entire upstairs (as well as downstairs, of course). We could not stop the water with towels at every door stile. We tried to sop it up but needed every pail and container to put under the drips pouring from the leaks in the roof in a few places.

That first night the electricity went off. Therefore we had no water either. The refrigerator and freezer (as well as the downstairs freezer) all defrosted and much food was spoiled. Happily, it wasn't cold on island. Although it wasn't really warm either.

The same Internet reported: "Throughout Tuesday, the heart of the tempest pounded and pounded and pounded St. Barth's, the eye, by mid-afternoon, passing less than twenty miles to the northeast."

Yet we thought we were in the eye itself when, Tuesday afternoon and evening, everything was still and quiet for hours. We told each other that we were halfway through the storm, or, rather, it was halfway through us.

We were in telephone-touch with our three sons; one after another they called us every half hour as long as the lines were working. John reported to us the track of the hurricane as he saw it on his TV. He described it as looking like a buzz saw and that St. Barth's appeared, "between the Black and the Decker."

The last phone call was with Michael and he told both his brothers what I had said. It was: "I can see light between the wall and the ceiling so I think we're going to lose the roof!"

I quote the Internet report again: "For the unlucky few, defenses failed: roofs disappeared into the howling, swirling blast, door and window covers were ripped away admitting wind, water, and shredded vegetation, sucking precious possessions into oblivion. For most, encapsulated in small, dark, damp cubicles, without electricity or running water ... silenced by the buffeting roar just outside a thin skin of protection, powerless to do anything but take what was given, it was a long, fretful, and indelibly memorable day."

Three days and three nights is an awfully long time. Especially when all that time we really did not know what was going on outside. Of course the phone was out, too. And we weren't sure of what was happening or what might happen to us!

By the third evening it seemed that the worst was over. And, although the wind was still raging dangerously outside, we slept soundly, knowing we had survived. Most of our roof remained but there were a few holes.

Thirty-six hours after we had locked ourselves in, we both opened our door to the greatest shock of our lives: Our garden was gone! Toto, we were transported to an unfamiliar landscape! The flowers, plants, cacti, trees, everything had been swept away. A few strange things had replaced our garden: someone else's roof tiles, gutters, a strange door, wood planks, unidentifiable chunks of stuff, parts of a chair, what might have been a pillow, other material. But for the most part there was nothing where our bountiful garden had been. What had been green was brown. It was a painfully unfamiliar landscape. Our beautiful garden -- ruined, absolutely ruined.

Looking around, we were surprised to see that our pool had sprouted trees! Many tiles were missing, but trees and gutters were in the pool. They weren't our trees but they might have been our gutters. We met some neighbors but they seemed to be in as much of a daze as we were. Joe Ledee came downhill to check on us. One afternoon a kind neighbor even brought ice cubes, for he had an emergency generator, and we had our accustomed vodka or, in Betty's case, "vodka tonique." Everyone had indeed survived.

We drove around the island and saw that a massive cleanup was underway already. French armed forces arrived to clear the airfield and other government offices and they stayed to do additional cleanup work. Insurance investigators came and agreed to send a check, which they did. Much of the beachfront property in St. Jean, Flamand, Anse de Cayes, the southeast side of the island, was devastated by the sea surge. Among the worst, the seaside Bai de Flammands Hotel was undermined, its swimming pool and buildings toppled onto the beach. But, for the most part, the island didn't suffer too badly.

So our cleanup began, even though we still didn't have any electricity or running water. A pail on a rope reached down into our very full cistern, however, to supply us with enough water and we had a sufficient supply of food.

One of our first outdoor priorities was to clean up the branches and junk that littered our garden. I had built rock walls that terraced our

293

property, making it much easier to do the gardening. One of those walls was about three feet high and had lots of branches up there. So I easily climbed up, stood on the wall, and tugged at a branch. Before I knew it, I had fallen off the wall and badly twisted my ankle.

X-Rays at the hospital revealed, they said, that the ankle was not broken. But I had to buy a "walking cast." I had done enough damage to myself to limit my activity.

Betty managed to telephone Mike and Mary. They were scheduled to go to the Grand Canyon and camp out there. But they immediately cancelled that trip and came to our rescue. I will never forget how much they gave up and how much they helped us. I don't know what we would have done without them.

Mike brought a chain saw, hand saw, an outdoor shower, and lots of other necessary tools and supplies. Mary had never been to St. Barth's before and this was the worst kind of introduction one could have to such a magnificent (normally) place. The two of them worked like teamsters, cutting up trees and burning what they could. All over the island there were fires as people all did what they had to do.

M&M also showed us how the outdoor or camping shower worked. They put cistern water into the bag, let it warm up in the sunlight, and we showered, individually, in the evening. For them, it just wasn't the same as camping in the Grand Canyon, but it was a lifesaver for us. I am forever indebted to Mike and Mary for their vital aid to us disaster victims.

Our roof and pool had leaked in places and our insurance paid for a completely new roof and an improved swimming pool. Insurance did not cover the garden at all.

Luis had discouraged Betty considerably; she felt as if nature had turned against us. Somewhat reluctantly, she helped restore the garden to a semblance of its former glory. It wasn't the same; it couldn't have been. The original garden resulted from almost 20 years of labor.

When the phone line came back on, Betty said to John, "I don't think I've got another hurricane in me."

Then a lesser hurricane, Marilyn, came just three days later, while Mike and Mary were still there. We literally laughed at it. We said that Luis was more wind than rain while Marilyn was more rain than wind.

Years later, in 1998, after another, considerably lesser hurricane named Klaus, hit St. Barth's squarely, Betty found it all but impossible to re-re-create the beauty that had been our garden. We did it, but she definitely had had it with St. Barth's. Her discouragement was now total. She was sick of hurricanes, period.

For her, Luis was a bigger reason than the lack of medical care for us to leave.

XII. BACK TO THE USA
(1999 - 2006)

114. Chapel Hill

Once we decided to return to the U.S.A. we had to decide where to go.

Money Magazine listed the ten best places to retire to in the U.S. We had been to many and nixed some. Ones I liked, Betty didn't; others she favored, I did not. There was Rochester, Minnesota, which neither of us knew but both vetoed. That left one place we didn't know: Chapel Hill, North Carolina.

We decided to spend a week there and take a look. Marvelle had a friend who lived there and she recommended a real estate agent, Marie Eldridge. She showed us around and we liked what we saw. John said we bought a condo as an impulse purchase.

Marie also introduced us to the Newcomers Club, the Carolina Club, Playmakers, the Duke medical facilities and other organizations in this University town. It was primarily through the Newcomers that we made so many friends so very quickly.

The Carolina Club has been a delight. I enjoy it just for the food: it has two restaurants. One is the informal bar-like grill. After a member has consumed 40 different beers he gets a pewter mug with his initials on it. Mine, of course, says WEF. The other restaurant is the main, formal dining room where there are many elegant touches. We were both on the Club's Membership Committee and Welcoming Committee.

And we enjoyed both Duke's and the University of North Carolina's courses for retired folks. This Triangle area (Raleigh-Durham-Chapel

Hill) has many excellent restaurants, the North Carolina Symphony, various theater companies, and lots of spectator sports.

115. My Mother's Death

Thanks to Terry and Ellen, my mother was very happy where she was and we were able to live on "our" island for many years. Mutti had a picture of her husband by her keys which were on a menorah near the front door. She would always say "good morning" and "good night" to him. She enjoyed her routine for years.

My visits and those of many family members delighted her, especially her great-grandchildren, Sarah and Rachel. The dementia she had did not bother her. She didn't care what day or month it was, one was like the next. But David put it well: by the time she repeated the same question for the third time, it was hard to stay with her.

She kept up her correspondences as long as she could with all kinds of friends and relatives all over the world. There could not possibly be anyone more family-oriented than she was. For example, after her brother Karl divorced his first wife, Miriam, my mother welcomed into the family the son of the first marriage of the man Miriam married!

So many former Camp Edgewood campers called her "Aunt Lotte," for she felt herself related to many of the people who lives she definitely enhanced by her presence and, quite often, her presents.

But now my dear mother was forgetting the names of much closer relatives. She was clearly deteriorating mentally. The physical aging was also evident, of course.

The Isabella administration had been after me for some time to transfer her from the independent living she had enjoyed all those years to the building next door where there were nurses on duty 24/7. They insisted that the time had come. I discussed it with Terry and Ellen and we finally agreed to do it.

Lotte Friedman certainly realized what was happening when Terry and I helped move her. She agreed it was for the best but I got the impression that she went along with the move much like a child doing what she is told to do. She understood that this was the last move she would make.

Now she was watched over by strangers instead of Terry. Without Terry helping her get up out of bed, with nurses just looking in on her, she stayed in bed until someone came to help her into a wheelchair and push her into a TV room, lunchroom, or activity center. She no longer went where Terry had taken her. So, more and more, she spent her time in bed.

In this building there were facilities and recreational activities, game rooms and TV rooms. But these activities did not interest her any more. This most caring of people no longer seemed to care about her own life. Most of all, she seemed tired almost all of the time. My visits may have tired her more than they pleased her.

She didn't last long there, just a couple of weeks. She passed away peacefully in her sleep on February 12, 2001, just a month short of her 95th birthday.

My mother, who had so much family feeling, always carried on a tremendous correspondence with family and friends, keeping up old contacts, remembering birthdays, being considerate, kind, cheerful, and loving. After her passing, we received calls, cards, letters, telegrams, Email from all over the world. She is surely missed by many in her extended family.

I had prearranged for her funeral through the familiar facilities that we had used for my Oma and my father. Both of those had been very private affairs, but now many family members and friends came and we had wonderful speeches and remembrances of this warm, caring, and very family-loving woman.

She was laid to rest next to her husband, but by now the tree was no longer there. I was glad that she didn't know that. Everyone who came to the burial threw a yellow rose, her favorite, atop her coffin.

Lotte Friedman will be sorely missed by her extended family all over the world.

116. The Drs. Silversmith

Both Donald and Peter Silversmith, the sons of Fred and Else, became doctors, but with very different expertise.

Dr. Donald, PhD, the older one, a graduate of the Massachusetts Institute of Technology, was a professor and associate dean of electrical and computer engineering at Wayne State University, Michigan. He joined the Institute of Electrical and Electronics Engineers, the IEEE, the world's leading professional association for the advancement of technology with members in more than 150 countries.

In 2003, IEEE-USA launched a new fellowship program and placed Donald in the U.S. State Department, as their first Engineering and Diplomacy Fellow, to help the Secretary of State, then Colin Powell, better understand the science and technology implications of foreign policy issues.

In early April, 2006, Donald was in Vienna, Austria, for the State Department's Office of Export Control and Conventional Arms Nonproliferation Policy, participating in international negotiations with more than 30 other nations seeking to coordinate "dual use" systems and technologies, which sought, unsuccessfully, to reach any agreement on controlling advanced weapons. Donald left after Dr. Condoleeza Rice became the Secretary of State.

Donald J. Silversmith got divorced from his wife Linda, the mother of their children, and married Karen Cantor, a documentary film maker. Her first movie, *The Danish Solution*, was cowritten, codirected and coproduced by her and narrated by Garrison Keillor. Karen is now working on another documentary, to premiere in 2007, called *Dr. Death or Angel of Mercy*, the saga of Dr. Kervokian.

Dr. Peter Silversmith, MD, the younger one, became a medical doctor at the hospital where his father was the head electrician, Mass General, and became an expert hand surgeon. Peter and his delightful and charming wife Rosie built themselves a huge new home in the very chi-chi McLean, Virginia, outside Washington, DC. It has a huge 2-storey library and literally one set of stairs going up and another going down. They display some wonderful sculptures made by the boys' father, my Uncle Fred. Truly a lovely and very livable home, it is one that a skilled hand surgeon deserves and has really earned.

Hand surgery is obviously a highly specialized field, expertly sewing together very delicate nerves, complicated tissues, tender tendons, usually after an awful accident. It is skilled and complex work, demanding true expertise. I have learned that plastic surgeons now actually earn more for each operation than the more complicated, more delicate, more expert heart or hand surgeon; they can charge more for what is generally a simpler, easier, shorter, more scheduled operation. Peter expanded his practice to include plastic surgery and I can only guess why. Peter and Rosie even did a major renovation to their new home.

The Silversmiths gave their daughter Elana a wonderful, absolutely first-class wedding, a black-tie affair. I rented a tux, which I had never thought I'd do again, once all my sons were married. She married Josh Friedson, so now she's almost a Friedman!

117. A Philadelphia Lawyer

Diane Zilka is Sam and Ellen Zilka's youngest child. This lady lawyer has been admitted to the bar in Delaware, Pennsylvania and New York as well as U.S. District courts in Delaware and New York Districts, but she and her partner make their home in Philadelphia.

Diane has been called integral to her law firm Grant & Eisenhofer's success in prosecuting securities fraud and corporate governance cases on behalf of public and private funds in class and individual actions. She played a key role in recovering money on behalf Wisconsin and defended Connecticut before the SEC in a challenge by the Disney Corp. She also was a key member of the team that won a $200,000,000 judgment in federal court in South Carolina. And she co-authored *The Role of Foreign Investors in Federal Securities Class Actions*.

Diane has concentrated her career in securities, corporate and complex commercial litigation, with experience in securities fraud, corporate governance, mergers and acquisitions, proxy disclosure and contests, limited partnership issues, and bankruptcy matters. She has also represented investors in proceedings before the New York Stock Exchange and the American Arbitration Association.

If that weren't enough, she also volunteers with Literacy Volunteers Serving Adults in Delaware and has enjoyed being a "Big Sister" with the Big Brothers Big Sisters Association of Philadelphia.

Beside all that, she's an excellent dancer!

118. Cancer!

Betty and I visited our children in the Washington, D.C., area for the weekend starting Friday the Thirteenth (an unlucky date) of June,

2003. Betty felt a shortness of breath when we walked with Mike, Mary, and their dogs in their nearby woods. John and Karen noticed that Betty seemed more tired than usual and we discussed it briefly but there was absolutely no indication that something serious was wrong.

She had had a minor operation on her left thumb but had driven part of the way and that surely seemed all right. In an email to a friend, Betty wrote, "First drive of any length since surgery and I did okay."

On Sunday, June 22nd, we drove home and really did not suspect anything other than a cold. Betty thought she had an allergy or a persistent cough, or a cold that might be turning into bronchitis or even pneumonia. She mentioned a pain in her back, too, but thought that might have come from coughing. After all, she was the former Medical Assistant who knew about illnesses. Since she belittled it, I did not worry at all.

But that was reason enough to go our family doctor, Rob Paterson. We had gotten to know him well in these five years, as a doctor and a friend.

We got an immediate appointment for the next day, Monday, June 23, 2003. Betty had had a chest X-ray in mid-April -- *just two months earlier* -- which had given her a clean bill of health. That was so recent that I was surprised he'd ordered another one. Dr. Paterson read the X-Ray himself immediately and did not like something he saw, so he ordered a CAT scan that same day. He told us that he wrote "to rule out mass" on the form only so that insurance would pay for it. So I truly didn't worry.

Betty wrote an email to Marvelle Gilbert, "Just to complicate life further, they think I may have pneumonia. CT scan today; results Thursday. Keep your fingers crossed. I know I'd rather have pneumonia than some of the other things suggested. No fair!!" I believe it was the last email she would ever write.

If she suspected worse news, she didn't let on to me.

The result led to an MRI the next day.

And that led to immediate hospitalization for a biopsy.

Even before she entered Duke Hospital, Betty knew it was cancer. I only suspected that's what they were looking for.

On Thursday June 26th, my father's birthday, her liver was biopsied. It was *adenocarcinoma,* an untreatable form of fast-growing cancer. It was already in her lungs, liver, spine, spleen, and lymph system. The next test showed that it was not in her brain. They did not know where it may have started but we all suspected her lungs. She had been a smoker for almost fifty years. And her father had died of lung cancer.

For Betty, there was no possible cure, only palliative treatment to prevent pain plus radiation aimed at her T-7 spine to prevent paralysis. She was given heavy narcotics, from Morphine to OxyContin, so she literally never felt any pain whatsoever.

Betty was always a realist. She understood completely exactly what her fate would be. Mean life expectancy was three months without treatment, six with aggressive chemo and radiation. So she quoted Shakespeare's Macbeth, "if it were done, when 'tis done, then t'were well it be done quickly."

She did not want to hang around too long, waiting for the inevitable result. I can only say that she took the horrendous news bravely. We talked of suicide but quickly came to realize that Hospice was there to ease her way out of this world as painlessly and as humanely as possible. That knowledge eased both of us and our understanding of the situation.

John recorded a telephone conversation Betty had with his family on July 1, 2003 and I quote it verbatim. They had heard some fireworks in the distance and Alex said, "Hear big noise."

Betty responded, "Yes, I know it's a noise."

Karen, trying to prod her not-quite-two-year-old son, said, "What did we draw today?"

Alex answered what sounded like, "A big hard on."

Betty, surprised, asked, "You had a hard on?"

Karen said, "Alex now has the phone."

So Betty asked, "What did he say?"

John replied, "It sounded like he said he had a hard on."

Alex answered his way: "I got ... a dry ... digger."

I am amazed that no one burst into laughter! As John explained it later, Alex was talking about drawing with chalk on the driveway. He may have said that he drew with something hard on the driveway. Betty misunderstood it, obviously, and clearly enjoyed her mishearing of the words.

Alex seemed wise enough to bring the proper subject back: "Hear big noise."

John said, "We're going to take a walk after the phone call to look for the fireworks."

Alex understood perfectly, saying, "After phone call, go walk, see noise."

Betty understood as well, "Good, you go for a walk and look for the fireworks."

Alex: "Noise. See noise."

John ended the conversation with, "Alex, can you say 'I love you' and 'good night'? (pause) Say, 'I love you.'"

So Alex said, "Love you!"

Betty: "I love you, too."

Alex: "And good night!"

Betty: "Night, honey. Have a good walk. May you see many lights. Love you."

Luckily, John has this CD of Betty's last conversation with her only grandson.

119. Betty's Last Days

My wife was obviously delighted by visits from all of her immediate family and a few others. John, Karen and Alex as well as Michael and Mary came to the hospital right away. David had his company, Cisco Systems, temporarily transfer him to their Research Triangle Park office. He came with his whole family and they all stayed for a month in a nearby hotel and visited with Betty at Duke Hospital and all saw our Priestly Creek home.

Unbeknownst to me at that time, John and Michael arranged with David that the visiting Californians would get and set up fireworks on the 4th of July directly across the street from Betty's hospital room's window. She and I could see them and with their cell phone communicating with her room's telephone, we all could hear them, too! The sound and light show was amazing. It made her feel so great about her loving family. When a cop came to see what was going on, they explained it and he showed them where to set up the next firecrackers!

It was not an easy task communicating the inevitability of Betty's early death to our two granddaughters. Sarah was ten, Rachel only eight. But I explained it as best I could by telling them about my prostate operation. That was a cancer that was caught and completely removed before it could spread. But Betty's was a cancer already so wide-spread that nothing could be done but keep her free of any pain.

We also discussed Betty's 3-in-1 ring. It had been fused together, combining the diamond engagement ring I had purchased in the Army PX in Germany with her plain gold wedding ring and the diamond ring I gave her on our 25th wedding anniversary. The three were now one fused ring that our granddaughters admired. But to which girl should it be given?

Betty came up with the ideal answer: Each girl will probably be given a ring by some boy. But our grandson, Alex, would need a ring to give to a girl. So Betty's ring was given to Karen to give to Alex at the appropriate time. If this writing is the first he hears about it, so be it.

John, Karen and Alex as well as Mike and Mary commuted back and forth. One brother sometimes drove the other's car so at least one of the four of them was always with Betty. She and I were never alone, for my sake as well as Betty's. I am forever grateful to all of them for showing their love in such a constant and meaningful way.

A nurse put quotes up in Betty's room. John added others over the days: "I want a new drug -- Huey Lewis," and "If we weren't all crazy, we'd go insane -- Jimmy Buffet," and "The trick is to die young as late as possible -- Ashley Montague," and "Humor is mankind's greatest blessing -- Mark Twain."

John brought the completed video of our family vacation in Mexico and we were all able to look at it. (I have a VHS copy). Unfortunately, unthinkingly, I made the comment that "You've gotten a lot grayer in the last year, my love."

To which Betty immediately replied, "Thanks a lot. It's not as if I don't have enough problems!" Her quick humor set everyone laughing.

Myrna Dawson and Else Bolotin came to see her at the hospital, the hospice, and at home and she was delighted that they did. Her soul-sister, Marvelle Gilbert, could not travel but they spoke on the phone. Her soul-brother, Joe Ledee, immediately came to the U.S. from St.

Barth's to see her when he got the horrible news. (I am still Betty's soul-mate though neither of us believe in the existence of a soul).

Joe had just previously dealt with the death of our good friend and Betty's successor as the library treasurer, Bobbie Olesky. He felt that he had to see his "adopted sister." She was thrilled that he did. Especially since we wondered how he could possibly afford it. We knew, however, that emotionally he couldn't afford not to see her.

Joe Ledee offered his unique perspective on dying and on life. For one thing, he wanted to light a candle in Betty's room, "so her spirit can rise and leave with it." Unfortunately, the oxygen in her room prevented that.

He believes in a life after death, a Catholic concept, saying, "if you believe in God, life is simple." But Joe also believes in reincarnation, not a Catholic concept. He talked about Turrene LaPlace's last moments. He had prayed and said, "I'll be there soon," just before he died.

Joe toasted us at dinner: "lots of strength, lots of courage, lots of love."

John noted, "This quiet and introspective man has been a great comfort to us all during his days here. He has done a wonderful job getting Dad out of the house for hours at a time -- something none of us have been able to do."

I hadn't realized that; I thought that I showed Joe around the area.

Betty was in the hospital for 22 days and had 18 radiation treatments to her spine. Then she was sent home, by ambulance, and put under hospice care. They were excellent. They supplied us with a hospital-type bed with side restraints, a wheel chair, a woman to bathe her in bed, a nurse to assist us, a social worker to aid us, and plenty of heavy narcotics to keep Betty totally pain-free.

We put Betty into the hospital bed in the front room or office. Either John or Mike (with or without Mary) was in the guest room. Someone was always on a mattress on the floor of the front room with Betty. And Joe Ledee slept next to me, in Betty's bed.

When Joe left, on Friday, August 1st, he said quietly to her, "Goodbye Betty. I will miss you."

We gave her the narcotics, as prescribed by the hospice nurses, so she was totally pain-free. She had mood swings of elation but never any depression. Betty remained a realist throughout.

Towards the end we recognized that we could not keep her at home so she was taken, again by ambulance, to a hospice facility. It was while she was there that John had visited her and found her progressively weaker, but, of course, he had to go back to work. In fact, she had told him to go home. So he was very surprised by her clear voice when, a day or two later, on August 7, 2003, she asked him to come back. She asked, so he did.

Betty told him that she wanted to concentrate on living the life that she has left as well as she can. So John mentioned quotes from a movie he had seen, *Here on Earth*. In it, a young girl is dying and a young man says, "So that's it? You're just gonna die?"

"No," she replies, "I'm going to live … just not as long as you."

It was not long thereafter that Betty was transferred by ambulance to the section of the Carol Woods Continuing Care Center that has a nurse on duty 24/7. We strung all the many cards she had received across three walls of her room. We got her everything she craved which was, at various times, Chinese egg-drop soup, vanilla ice cream, and bar-b-cue (pulled pork, actually) from Allen & Son. Surprisingly she was in amazingly good spirits. I now think she was actually being incredibly considerate of me, of us all.

My beloved Betty passed away quietly in her sleep on August 18, 2003 with Mary Wright at her side. She was only 66 years old. We had been married for 45 years and I had known her and truly loved her for 50 long, wonderful, delightful, truly happy years.

She never cried.

I did.

I still do.

There can never be another like her for me. She completed me, made me whole, she was everything to me, and without her, I am not my true self any more. I still love her. I will always be in love with her. And now I always miss her -- more than I can say, but it is something I always feel. I am truly alone without her, alone while in a crowd of people, alone even when I am with another person. I am not myself, my true self, without my Betty. And I miss her. So very much.

I mourn her in my own way: a big part of that is by simply going on with my life.

But I am, just as Betty was, a realist. And an atheist. I am totally convinced that there is no God. And I am as certain as Betty was that there is no heaven or hell. No life after death. Death is final. She is dead and gone forever. She did not exist before her birth, she was very much alive when she was alive, and now she no longer exists -- except in the memory of all those who loved her and think of her. In that sense, she is still very much with me. She always will be.

I hope to help keep her memory alive. I will not forget her and I cannot ever replace her. I definitely will not try to.

All I want by writing this is for our grandchildren to remember their *grandmere*.

There was no funeral. We had long ago made the arrangements for both of us. Babette Klein Friedman's body was cremated and the ashes scattered in a rose garden, as she had wished. I sent out a death announcement and a letter trying to explain her early demise to a long list of friends and relatives. Everyone was shocked.

120. A Remembrance of Betty

We recorded a CD of A Remembrance of Betty held at Carol Woods. But many of our friends and family were unable to attend. Some who were there and others who were not wrote condolence cards and letters, 84 of them, that I have.

It was not a Memorial Service since there was absolutely nothing religious about it. But a Remembrance of Betty, celebrating her life, and those who spoke were asked to keep to one theme: more laughter than tears. No speeches ... just stories. That is how she wanted it. That is how it was.

Many friends and acquaintances came, from the Chapel Hill Newcomers, the Carolina Club, League of Women Voters, United Nations Association, and our French language lunch table. Others came from far away, from New York, Virginia, but mostly from North Carolina. Many could not make it on such short notice or were traveling.

We put a tropical flower arrangement up front with a wonderful photo of Betty. Carol Woods prepared a buffet of cheeses, dips and nibbles.

I started it off by telling everyone how I met Betty, the story in Chapter 60. Then each of our sons had their say.

David led off by saying that his mother never liked saying 'good bye.' "She would say, 'I love you. I'll see you soon.' But not good bye."

So, he asked, how could he now say that to her? "Perhaps saying 'good bye' is not appropriate. So what can we say? Is it enough to say that she died without pain, at peace, and in her sleep, after a short fight with cancer?"

He said that when she found out she had terminal cancer, "her first concern was that my father be taken care of. Is it enough to tell her that things have worked out so that he'll be okay?" He added, "And we'll make sure he is."

"My mother made new friends everywhere. From Mike DeAnzeris, who delivered the cleaning; to the Brazewells who came up from Georgia to deliver trees and then asked my mother's advice on their daughter's marriage; Ann Sweet, the dentist's receptionist, and Dr. DellAngelo, her gynecologist. She'd go to dinner with him after an appointment and then ask him if he'd washed his hands!

"And if you know my mother, you know that's true!"

Our oldest son spoke of how easily Betty "adopted" siblings from everywhere. "My 4th brother, Paul Schwartz, thank you for being here. My sister, Heidi Henle, who couldn't be here. My older brother from another mother, Joe Ledee. She also adopted Debbie ... Karen ... and Mary."

David went on to say that "part of her is in all of us. All of us who were touched by her love, her life, and her laughter. Her extended family and network of friends, we are the answer to how we can say 'good bye.' We don't!"

He explained, "It is enough to think of her when you have a good belly laugh, gaze out at the ocean, have a great meal, find a great bargain in a store, or see a beautiful sunset; that's how she would have wanted us to do it."

Then David read what his wife Debbie had written: "When I was dating David, I heard all kinds of horror stories about his mom before I actually met her."

It was Michael who interrupted to ask David from whom. He answered, "From me! Okay? She chewed on a couple of my girl-friends, it's true."

Dave continued Deb's letter: "I was so nervous about meeting 'the Dragon Lady,' that I couldn't sleep the night before." David interjected that Mike was the one who had jokingly coined that term for his mother.

The letter continued, "However the next day I found Betty to be nothing like I had imagined. Both she and David's Dad were very friendly to me and tried to make me feel welcome. I enjoyed their company and felt very comfortable visiting with them on several occasions after that. So much so, that if I could have picked parents, I would have picked being part of the Friedman family growing up.

"I always felt like the ugly duckling in my family; I felt like a swan around David's. So it felt only natural for me to call Betty and Wally, 'Mom' and 'Dad' when David asked me to marry him.

"Over time it became evident that Mom and I had a lot in common. We love to travel, eat good food, feed animals that are hungry, and didn't like our pictures taken, to name a few. In fact, there were so many things that John and Mike used to tease David that he'd married his mother. Although David got a little red around the ears upon hearing this, I took it as a compliment. I really felt connected to her in a way I had not been with my own mother. And I think she saw a bit of herself in me, too.

"She was a very special lady with a wonderful spirit. Mom was someone I could always turn to for advice, call when I needed a friendly voice, and looked up to in so many ways. She had exuberance for living life and touched many people's hearts. I feel very fortunate to have had Mom in my life for more than a third of it. I regret not having the opportunity to make new memories with her. However, I will treasure the ones I have. And I will miss her very much. Debbie."

John started by saying, "We're Friedmans, so we correct each other or continue on from each other. That story about my mother and father meeting is true, but what I always heard was that her mother's response when my mother told her she'd met the man she was going to marry, was, 'poor devil, does he know it yet?'"

Then John defined himself as the middle son, husband of Karen, father of Alex. He began by saying that "one of the joys through this terrible summer is our family; the way we've come together and going through it with them, and all of you, has made it marginally less awful. And that's incredible.

"Humor, Mark Twain once said, is mankind's greatest blessing. If that's true, then we have all been blessed by Betty's greatest gift. Jimmy Buffet, who shared a love of St. Barth's, and alcohol, but mostly the Caribbean, with my mother, said 'if we couldn't laugh, we would all go insane.'

"So I think it's appropriate that we laugh. In the hospital when my mother said to me, 'No speeches! ... But when you do ... I hope you laugh.'

"My mother taught us to laugh to make the bad times easier and the good times better. And anyone who has experienced Betty has experienced the rapier wit, the devastating humor, that she often leveled at the absurdities, the ironies, the pretensions of the Republican Party.

"If there's anyone here from the Republican Party, feel free to try to rebut!"

John said that he didn't have many 'Betty stories' because they were always Betty-and-Wally or Betty-David or Betty-Michael stories. But he had one:

"In 1985, I had saved up my money when I graduated college, I was going to buy a car. A stick-shift, 4-door, economical and practical car. But I went to visit my parents in the Caribbean and bought their next-door neighbor's 1968 Ford Mustang!"

He said that his mother always loved that car because it had what she called, "get up and go. Anyone here ever ride with my mother driving? I see some nods. My mother always did the speed limit -- once on the way up, once on the way down!"

He told of his mother doing 85 on the Saw Mill River Parkway, then a 55-mph zone. She was pulled over by a New Castle cop. And he asked the immortal police question, 'do you know how fast you were going?'

"My mother, with that murderous innocence that she could muster, said, 'well, I'm not exactly sure, officer.'

"I don't think he expected that and said, 'what do you mean?'

"My son, here, imported this car from the Caribbean. Show him the papers, John. In the Caribbean, they have kilometers-per-hour. And I know that 88 kph is 55 mph. So I kept the needle at 85 so I'd be a little bit under."

The cop looked, noticed only one set of numbers, and explained that back in 1968 cars only had one set of numbers. John continued: "As we drove away -- without a speeding ticket -- I said to my mother, 'and you taught me not to lie!'

"She said, 'that's because you don't do it well!'"

John then showed off his favorite picture of his parents, saying, "it's like a typical portrait of your parents, except they're 50 feet underwater, wearing scuba gear." When people asked him who that was, John explained that he did not have parents like most people do. His folks lived life to the fullest and did it all their own way.

He remembered that we insisted that our kids phone home if they were going to be later than ten or eleven, whatever that son's deadline was. And that, when we lived on an island and traveled a great deal, he had to pay our credit card bill every month for us. "One time they were in Spain and I get a phone call, 'we have some unusual activity on your wife's credit card.'"

There were some charges in Tangiers. John checked. It's in Africa. He knew his parents were in Europe. So John cancelled Betty's credit card but kept mine active, figuring only one had been stolen. We telephoned him when we noticed, checking out of a hotel, that Betty's credit card had been cancelled. He said we explained that it was a sunny day and we decided to cross the Strait of Gibraltar; we were indeed in Africa. John quoted me as saying, 'if we have to use my credit card, we don't get the airline mileage!'

"So," John said, "the people who worried if I was out at 11:01 on a weekend in New York, I asked them please to let us know if they were going to change continents!"

John concluded with, "laughing through the good times; laughing more through the bad times, and embracing and enjoying your life, those are the lessons I learned from my mother, your friend, Betty. If we can take that lesson and go forward I think our mother has given us the secret of how to get through these days, and through the rest of our lives."

Mike started off telling about his parents' retirement to St. Barth's fifteen years ago. "People who didn't really know my parents would think that they moved there for the beach, the sand, the ocean, the fish, and it's true, those are all good things about St. Barth's. But the real reason they moved there was the food.

"People who truly know my parents know that was the reason they picked that island, with its wide variety of delightful restaurants, all kinds of different cuisines. And they lived there happily for ten years.

"Five years ago, those of us who knew them were surprised that they were moving to Chapel Hill. A place not widely known for its cuisine."

When he came to visit he saw that his parents had indeed found a place with a lot of delightful restaurants. "The Carolina Club would be at the head of that list. But there's a long and varied list of restaurants in the area, a variety of types. Yet if you ask my mother where she would want to go for dinner, not elegant, not formal, not expensive, just some casual, drop-in kind of place, where you could have a good meal, cheap, she would probably pick Allen & Son barbecue."

Michael talked about their barbecue, which is pulled pork with vinegar sauce. But his was not a story about Betty. He spoke, instead, of just three days ago, when the three brothers and I went there without her, while she was in the hospice place.

Mike marveled that we went there at all, since David keeps kosher; but he pointed out that they do serve chicken. He spoke of the eclectic décor there, which he more accurately called "random." He said that there was, among the antlers, stuffed animals and fish, pigs in funny poses, various placards and posters, surprisingly, a map of the Caribbean on the wall there. He said it was interesting "to see a map of a place my mother loved, at a place my mother loved. And just to the left of it, one of the next random things, is a paragraph by that famous author of quoted paragraphs, anonymous."

He said it had no title, but its last line could act as one: "This is to have succeeded."

It read: "To laugh often and much,
To win the respect of intelligent people
And the affection of children.
To earn the appreciation of honest critics,
To appreciate beauty,
To find the best in others,
To leave the world a little better,
Whether by a healthy child, a garden patch,
Or a redeemed social condition.

311

To know that even one life
has breathed easier because you lived,
This is to have succeeded."
Michael concluded, "So I suppose she succeeded."
The applause that followed signaled the gathering's agreement.

Next, Mark Goldhaber, who said he's John's best friend, told how he got adopted into our family. He was a college roommate of John's who first met Betty and me when we came up to Albany to visit our son. The next time he saw us was when Mark came to visit John in Chappaqua. He saw Betty in the kitchen and said, "Hi, Mrs. Friedman."

She answered, "Call me Mom."

So he said, "O.K., hi, Mom."

To which she replied, "Take out the garbage!" And she waited until he did.

He said that she was the kind of mother that everybody wished they had. That she always knew how to put everybody at ease. She always knew the right thing to say.

Mark said that Betty sent a poster up to them but it was not for their dorm room. It showed how to resuscitate a lizard and it should be put up in the college cafeteria next to the Heimlich Maneuver poster! So they did. And he said it took the authorities a few weeks before they took it down.

She crocheted Mark a computer! It's now over 20 years old and he still has it.

Prior to Mark's marriage to Hope he had argued with his parents to the extent that they threatened to boycott the wedding. Betty assured him that if they did, we, his adopted parents, would walk down the aisle with him. She may have shamed them into doing the right thing.

Paul Schwartz, whom my mother called the fourth boy in a home that had three sons, was next. He had been a friend of David's since they were 8, then they were in the same class in Horace Greeley High School. Then Paul was John's roommate. So when Mike graduated he asked if it was now his turn to get Paul Schwartz.

Paul is now an Assistant Principal in a Poughkeepsie, NY, high school. Paul told a story of his dog Charley who kept following him to Chappaqua Pool where dogs were not allowed. Betty plotted to get the dog into the water while she sat there, looking totally innocent. Betty taught him, by her own example, to do what you want to do, that it doesn't matter what other people think.

Else Bolotin spoke next. She said that she and Betty, from very different backgrounds and experiences, had lots in common. Else, who was from Holland, said that Betty could have been Dutch, "especially the thrifty part." They both loved a good bargain. They laughed and joked a lot. It was easy, she said, with Betty's quick wit and sense of humor.

Else admired the courage with which she had accepted her fate. "I am not ready for this," Else quoted her as saying, yet, Else went on, "Betty faced it without complaining and with deep insight into the reality of an ending."

Rita Berman told that she met us about five years ago, referring to our mutual long-time friend, Joe Taormina, who insisted that we get together. She said that Betty, with her humor, helped Rita get over a very difficult recovery from an operation.

Myrna Dawson said that she and Jim only met us about a year ago. She told about the move to Carol Woods that was being discussed during Betty's illness. Myrna said that it was Betty's only concern now that Wally be taken care of.

She continued by telling about a chance encounter she and a friend had with me and my three sons outside Chapel Hill's Caribou Coffee Shop just a day or two before this Remembrance of Betty. One of the boys asked Myrna if she had answered the Caribou trivia question. He added, "You get ten cents off your coffee it you do." She said she hadn't noticed it.

Then Myrna quoted me to the audience as saying, "Betty would have wanted you to." That got a big laugh from all those who knew Betty's coupon-cutting thriftiness.

Rita Weimer said that she had met us through Newcomers and DILR but she told of a time when we were at Wildacres, the DILR retreat in the Blue Ridge Mountains of western North Carolina. She had come with us, in our car, as I drove to the Craft School. There were complicated directions to get there but we followed another car. Later, having taken a lot of time at the gift shop, we had no other car to follow and so I drove from memory, reversing what we had done to get there.

She said, "Betty and Wally were doing this string of one-liners and zingers, and pretty soon we realized that we didn't know where we were. A lot of couples at that point would have stopped, but Betty and Wally just kept on going and an hour or so later, when we got back to Wildacres, we had had the most delightful trip, driving the mountains of North Carolina.

"Afterwards," Rita Weimer continued, "I thought about it and said that theirs was a really great relationship; to really enjoy each other's company and to be able to laugh in a situation that some of us would have gotten up tight about.

"So, it has been a joy knowing Betty and her humor. And I'm sure I'll see you, Wally, at a lot of other DILR things." Rita later became the president of DILR's Board of Directors while I was on it.

While Vickie Hoffmann was in New York City, her husband Lorenz, known as Larry, got up next to speak. He is about 6'6" tall and his experience has been as a negotiator, presenting drug company research results to the Food & Drug Administration. He is a man who towered over Betty, and whose accomplishments and responsibilities might humble others.

"Every time, over dinner or parties, Betty -- God love her -- her one-upsmanship, always, always, with love and affection" seemed to him to have gotten the best of him!

Larry went on, "All the friends here, we will all keep memories of her in mind."

Carol Epstein was next, saying that "to be able to relive and appreciate all of these memories is wonderful and helpful for all of us."

She told about a program the League of Women Voters held at Carol Woods which she and Betty attended. On the way out she suggested they stop at the gift shop. "So we went and did all this shopping and found great bargains and left saying, 'the program was good but the best thing was the gift shop and buying all these things!'"

Carol Epstein also said that she appreciated "Betty's uniqueness" at a party we all attended with David and Else Bolotin and Carol and her husband Stan at their neighbor's house. "It is those wonderful things about our lives that we will cherish."

Bette Wofford said that when she "first met Betty, I really liked her -- which is very unusual for me because I don't like too many women! But I really liked Betty. She was so funny and thoughtful."

She felt a kinship explaining that perhaps it was because they were both from New York. Bette was in a DILR class with us last year, taught by Billy Yeargin. She said, "Billy was going into the hospital for an operation and Betty had immediately jumped up and said that we should take up a collection and get something for him.

"I said that I don't really know what we can get for him. But Betty knew right away: she knew the music he liked, the type of liquor he liked, I couldn't believe the stuff she came up with! She and Wally got these wonderful gifts for him, everybody in the class was just open-mouthed because it was all so special. That was very typical of Betty to do something like that."

Bette started weeping, repeating, "I never met a lot of women that I liked, but she was really outstanding. She really was."

I added that "we all agree on what she was. But for sure she was <u>not</u> phony!"

Dr. Rob Paterson got up next. "I was Betty's doctor. I had the privilege. Betty brought so much to my life. She brought so much to everybody's life, but in just the few moments that we had in the exam room, with HMOs now, it used to be 5 minutes, but it's now 3 minutes. But she had that capacity to really engage people and really bring the best out of me as a physician. It was remarkable what this woman really was. In a very short period of time that I got to know her, clearly, she gave a lot more to me than I ever gave to her. And I just want to say thank you, Wally, for remembering me and telling me about this.

"I still have a lot of feelings for Betty. It was so very sudden, what happened, she just...it was very unexpected for all of us I think, but for me, as a physician of course, it was very hard to lose a patient. But somebody like Betty, who was, as we've heard, just such an extraordinary, unforgettable, just no artifice, a very real person, of course, her wit is unforgettable. That's a good word for it, she truly was unforgettable. And there'll be a place in my heart always for Betty. And my life is so much better, really, because of my knowledge of Betty and her friendship.

"I just want to say 'thank you' to everybody for allowing me to say just those few words and achieve some closure here. Closure is what is difficult at times, no question. So I thank you, thank you, Wally."

I added to Rob at that time: "I think you knew her well."

Then I thanked everyone and said, "I think we did have more laughter than tears. I think we did have some of each. I hope it is closure. But this won't close for me."

There was some applause.

An old army buddy, Bob Luoma, recently published his autobiography which included many references to my wife whom he called "my good friend," although they met only once. He devoted a chapter to her and our comrade in Military Intelligence, Joe Taormina.

"Betty's sudden death in 2003 hit me like a freight train," Bob wrote. "She and I kept up email exchanges. Jokes came like spam from her almost every day." Many friends could say the same about her.

Bob quoted some of her jokes and then wrote, "Betty was a dear, witty, eccentric soul whom I came to think of as a beloved aunt, even though she was younger than I. Her given name, Babette, suited her well. It seemed to say: cute, petite, funny, endearing, French!"

The next thing on the CD was a recording from my telephone-answering machine by Dr. Bob DelAngelo, Betty's gynecologist and our good friend. He said our son John, "who is a real super guy, took the time and trouble to give me a message on my tape.

"I just want to call and see how you're doing, how the whole family's doing, and tell you how sorry Grace-Marie and I are on the whole situation. I don't want to bother you; give me a call at home whenever you'd like to talk. Talk to you soon."

The final recording is also from the phone-answering machine:

"Marvelle here. Richard and I are sitting in front of 627 Douglas Road, it is 10 o'clock Saturday morning. Although we're not there with you physically, we're with you in spirit. Sitting here, we're having our own little Remembrance of Betty. I just wanted to share with you that we are there with you although we aren't. Richard and I are just sitting here, looking at the house, the lawn, and just sharing thoughts of Betty and reliving stories about Betty. So we wanted to tell you. Thank you. Good bye."

We could hear one last word on the tape from Richard Gilbert: "Good."

Ever since Paul passed away, Marvelle has been keeping his ashes in an urn on her fireplace mantle. Every time she comes in the front door, she tells Paul what she has just done, where she has gone, whom she saw, everything. Since Betty's passing, Marvelle keeps her photo and memorabilia, such as a stuffed animal Betty crocheted, on the mantle, too. She misses her as much as I do and that's saying a lot.

On the second anniversary of Betty's death, her *Jahrzeit,* August 18, 2005, Marvelle Gilbert Emailed me: "I still miss her every day when I go to Shoprite, the Kisco Diner, the Thornwood Diner, White Plains, Armonk, etc. ... I miss our talks, our solving problems, our running around, our lunching out, our trips to Javits Center, our bout with pecans, distributing free greeting cards, rummage sales, garage sales, etc., etc.

"Enough -- you can see what a big part of my life she was."

To which I replied: "I miss her more now, somehow, than before. I even think that I love her more now than ever. I can't explain it or understand it.

"Yes, I have a lady-friend now and without her it would be unbearable -- but it is no way the same. Betty was everything to me, a part of me, the most important part, and that is missing. Gone. I think that only you may understand: you miss your Paul and you miss Betty. But I miss my one and only one."

121. Carol Woods

When Betty and I returned to the U.S. on 1998, we investigated five different retirement communities in the Chapel Hill area, as well as long-term care insurance, thinking of our future need for increased medical care as we grew older. Each of the five was truly different from every other one. In February, 1999, we decided that Carol Woods would eventually be our last home. We planned ahead.

And just as my retirement to St. Barth's happened years earlier than we had expected, so too moving into a CCRC -- Continuing Care Retirement Community -- has come to me far, far sooner than either of us had thought it would.

In April, 2002, we checked with Carol Woods and found that we were 47th on the list for the choice of accommodation we had signed up for and that there were only 30 such units. We figured it would still be years until someone died or moved out to make room for us. So we moved from the condominium on Ellsworth Road to the house at the cul-de-sac of Priestly Creek, still in Chapel Hill, North Carolina.

It is certainly true, as Betty had pointed out, that I retired in 1989 but she had not retired. She still was doing what she always had done as a "housewife!"

Carol Woods, in the meantime, had built only 12 new houses. But they also renovated some of their apartments and some residents moved within the Carol Woods community. So, much to our surprise, our number came up sooner than we expected.

We had just heard a speech by the executive director of Carol Woods, Mrs. Pat Sprigg, who said it was better to get into a CCRC a few years early rather than a day too late. She wasn't referring to death, she meant when one would be unable to meet their strict financial and medical and mental requirements for entry.

But I had not planned to go there so soon.

Betty convinced me when she knew she had terminal cancer that I should go to Carol Woods. Our home on the cul-de-sac of Priestly Creek was so completely in the woods that I, all alone, would feel terribly lonely. Carol Woods would take care of me.

Carol Woods is unique. It has been rated in the top ten CCRC's nationally every year since 1992. It's a nonprofit organization, run by its residents through elected representatives, virtually as a cooperative (much like a co-op building in New York City or a *kibbutz* in Israel.) For example, you have four separate interviews and then a committee of eight (half of whom never met you) votes you in or not.

It is very civic-minded, having recently built a daycare center not only for the children of its employees but also for other kids -- instead of adding new retiree housing. Carol Woods now has about 340 residents on its 120 acres, 34% of whom are out-of-staters, 59% singles, 41% couples. And there are four two-generational residents! [I am now counted among the 66% who came to Carol Woods from North Carolina].

Betty and I chose a "garden cottage," #218, for me. It's a brick building attached to another one, on the edge of the woods, on a winding road of similar houses which loops into Carol Woods' main road. It's a one bedroom with den accommodation, with a large L-shaped living-dining room called a Great Room, and 1½ baths. I use the den as a guest/computer room; Carol Woods also has four guest rooms for visitors.

There was an entry fee and a monthly charge, both based on the square footage of one's selected home. I get one meal a day, all utilities including phone and TV cable, complete linen and housekeeping service, plus a full staff of gardeners, maintenance, medical services and on-staff doctors and nurses as well as various types of hospital-medical-assisted living accommodations. There's a pool, fitness center, hobby and game rooms and courts, etc., with lots of activities and events.

I continue to do all the many things I have been doing in the area, going to the theater, concerts, movies, restaurants, Elderhostels, lectures, as well as golfing and my usual and frequent traveling.

I have been taking five DILR classes a semester, usually once a week each. And I go to DILR's summer and winter retreats. I am also taking some weekend seminars in UNC's "Adventures in Learning" plus lectures at CCLL, the Carolina College for Lifetime Learning at UNC.

Last year I was co-chair of two DILR committees which put me on the DILR Board of Directors and we approved joining the Osher Foundation which gave us $100,000 a year for a couple of years. So this year I'm spending some of that money to advertise DILR. I wrote an ad for this worthwhile organization:

DUKE WITH NO TESTS OR GRADES
for anyone 50 or over.

This year DILR, after getting a million-dollar grant from the Osher Foundation, changed its name to OLLI, Osher Lifetime Learning Institute at Duke. Wouldn't you change your name for $1,000,000?

A friend of mine, a retired ambassador, Mike Cotter, recommended me for membership on the Advisory Council of RSVP, which does not stand for what you think it does. It is the Retired and Senior Volunteer Program, and I'm now vice-chairman.

As a subscriber to the North Carolina Symphony, Playmakers, the Deep Dish Theater, Man Bites Dog Theater, Theater in the Park, and the NCSU Theater program, I cannot say that I watch much TV or go to the movies very often, but I do!

I have taken up playing golf. Actually, I play *at* golf. My good friend David Bolotin got me started and sold me his good golf clubs very cheaply. I have joined a group of retired guys who meet Tuesday mornings and play one of 12 or 15 different courses in this area. I enjoy the camaraderie. Once a month the Newcomers and Alumni also have a golf game at various courses. So I get to play a round all around.

This is also a wonderful area for spectator sports on the college level and also the Durham Bulls, the AAA farm club of the Tampa Bay Devil Rays. Many of the ballplayers we've seen here have gone up to, or come down from, the major leagues.

I regularly attend monthly luncheons with an informal group of guys ("the lunch bunch") and we go to a different restaurant each time -- there are so many good ones in the area. And I enjoy the Newcomers & Alumni monthly men's lunch at the Chapel Hill Country Club. About fifty men and women attend.

I also have been going on Elderhostels frequently, sometimes combining one with a trip somewhere or doing two Elderhostels back-to-back. I particularly enjoyed one of my golfing Elderhostels in Georgia. Because they were nearby, I visited both Franklin Delano Roosevelt's Little White House in Warm Springs (where he died) and Jimmy Carter's home in Plains. He was in town that weekend so I got up early and went to church! Since most folks came in couples or groups, I found an empty seat in the 4th row center. The ex-President and Nobel Prize winner taught Sunday School and I really enjoyed his lecture, his sincerity, honesty, openness, and directness. It was uplifting.

And I do travel a lot. I put about 20,000 miles on my car each year, not counting the mileage added by rental cars. By travel I include national and international trips as well as short overnights and weekend voyages. I especially delight in traveling with Nicole. I enjoy her company and companionship wherever we go. We went to Montreal, California twice, New York, and Paris in just six months last year! And we're going to London this year.

The reason Betty and I came here was for the expert medical care. And I do have regular check-ups and exams. But the reason I stay here is simply that I am very busily happy here. And very happily busy here.

122. The Walter and Herbie Partnership

Here's my view on what became a controversial issue in our family. My big first cousin Herbert Friedman, the son of my father's brother Paul, fell in love with California. He wanted his closest family to share what he felt was the Golden State of Opportunity. So he convinced his sister Hilde and her husband Walter Levy (with their daughter Evelyn) to leave cold, wet London and join him in California. Herbie and Hilde are the ones who introduced my parents to each other, Walter is the Dunkirk survivor.

To avoid any confusion with two Walters in the family, I was *Walterchen*; Levy, *Walterle*. Both are diminutives meaning Little Walter. But please call <u>me</u> "Wally."

The Levys came to America in time for my *bar-mitzvah*. And in April 1947, the two brothers-in-law went into a 50/50 partnership in the metal business, the business my Uncle Paul had been in. Their company extruded aluminum.

The partnership worked perfectly. Herbert was the "outside" man -- the salesman; totally essential for the success of any business. And Walter was the "inside" man -- equally necessary because he was responsible for the manufacturing process, quality control, hiring and training of all personnel, labor relations, office, paperwork, payroll et al.

Naturally, it took a while to build up a new business. Herbie, the salesman, got some orders. Walter, the engineer, got the "bugs" out of the extrusion process and kept it working properly. The partnership was just beginning to become profitable when Inge became pregnant with their third child. That was also when the young couple realized that the only life insurance that Herbert had was his old $10,000 army policy. It was high time to get more.

Inge says, "I'll never forget that day. A guy came to the house and explained that the insurance policy demanded a physical. But Herbie did not feel well that day and said he would schedule it later."

Inge remembers telling the salesman, "Don't worry; he's not going to kick the bucket!"

But the next day Herbie felt even worse; he was extremely tired and went to a doctor at Inge's insistence.

She said, "We thought he had a bad flu. So he went for tests, from doctor to doctor, to the hospital for tests. They couldn't find anything wrong with him -- except that his liver was enlarged."

Herbie said, "It can't be anything serious. Because if it were something serious, they would have already found it."

Yet he was getting weaker so they kept him in the hospital to do more extensive tests. One day the doctor called Inge into his office and told her, "The only thing we can do now is a liver biopsy, it looks like there could be a growth in the liver."

Inge revealed that the next thing he said was, "This could be cancer. And if it is, then it's already too late."

Her reaction was: "What!?! Already too late?!?"

She immediately called Herbie's best friend, a dentist, John Haas. He was in his office, she was in the hospital, but he came instantly and took her home. The first thing she said was, "We have to explore other remedies; this just cannot be the end. However, Herbie must never know."

After the biopsy, Inge said, Herbie turned "deathly ill." It was indeed cancer.

Inge recognized that if he realized he was going to die, leaving her with two little children and one on the way, "It would have been real anguish for him."

She told the doctors and nurses, "Nobody is allowed to tell him the truth."

Inge told her husband, "You have a very bad infection. The doctor assured me that you're going to get well. It will be cured, however you have to be very patient."

He was given pain medicine so that he would not suffer.

In those days they didn't let children in just to visit. To 4-year-old Michael and 2-year-old Paul, Inge said, "Your daddy's very sick in the hospital but he is going to make it, he's going to be all right."

Herbie's mother, my Aunt Thea, came to the house to help Inge take care of the children and stayed with them when Inge went to the hospital. When she came home she lied, saying that Herbie was a little better every day.

The doctor said it could be two weeks, it could be two years. Then one day he told Inge that they had something new. It might have been radiation. So she went home and told the children there was a new thing that could really help.

"The next morning I was there at eight," Inge told me, "he had just died."

A nurse told Inge that he had said to her, "I'm sinking, I'm sinking," and it was over. Inge had kept his fate from him and her mother-in-law and the children. She says that today she would have handled it differently, but then she felt she could not explain to a 2-year-old or a 4-year-old what dying means.

She brought the children presents and pretended it was a party. Then, little by little, she told them that Daddy wasn't coming home.

There was a funeral that the children did not attend; my mother did. Walter Levy handled the whole thing. But the bill came to Inge. She remembers it was about $6,000 and all she had was the $10,000 G.I. life insurance policy! And she had no idea how she was going to manage financially.

Herbie's death was a horrible shock for everyone in our family. My big cousin was only 34 years old! But it was horrendous for Inge.

All the men in her life, gone! First her father's suicide. Then her first husband died. And now the same, unbelievably impossible situation happened to her again. This time, however, she was pregnant!

Now Inge was all alone with what would soon be three little children! And their business was suddenly in big trouble, having lost its star salesman! What could she do?

Walter immediately offered to help, to do what he possibly could, that is, to keep up the 50/50 arrangement, to keep paying Herbie's full share to Inge although, of course, there was nothing she could do to bring in any income for the business.

Walter's wife Hilde wondered if he was giving away too much; that he would be one man supporting two families. But Walter Levy thought he could do no more and he would do no less. In fact, he could be considered more than generous.

While Inge, in shock and despair, alone, pregnant, and in great financial difficulty, demanded that Walter sell the business and give her the 50% right away!

Inge Friedman did not think that Walter could be both the inside and outside man, and that he could not hire a salesman anywhere as good as Herbert. But even if he could, she believed that such a salesman would be tremendously expensive, leaving too little profit for the 4-person Levy and soon to be 4-person Friedman families. Plus the 9th one, Paul's widow, Thea. Walter did not know it, but he was to become a widower.

Inge offered to work at the plant which Walter did not want. He thought that she would be a constant critic, a thorn in his side at work. Besides, what could she do? She was a mother with little babies to care for.

The young widow insisted upon her full share immediately. There was nothing Walter could do but sell. A somewhat distress sale; the business was barely profitable. Walter and Inge each got half the money.

Inge was not just tough, having been hardened by a life that was incredibly difficult. She was very smart and extremely capable. She invested the money wisely and went to work, opening a tennis shop at the Brentwood Country Club. She created that business and built it up quickly and well. When he was old enough, her eldest son Michael became the club's tennis pro.

And Inge bought a house for herself and her three little ones. It was a good investment as well as a fine home in Laurel Canyon on Roscomere Road, in Bel Air. And she bought the entire library from the Oscar Homolka estate. He had been a noted character actor and had built an impressive wall of books. The children grew up there and then Inge sold the house for a million dollars to the actor Alan Alda.

She took the children to Israel for her sons' *bar-mitzvahs* and then Inge retired and devoted herself to volunteer and charity work. She moved into a condominium in Venice, at Marina del Rey, where she has a truly magnificent home, filled with artwork of all kinds.

And Walter quickly proved his intelligence, versatility, and capabilities; he was indeed an excellent businessman. He was both the inside man and the outside man. The firm he created, which he called Lyndee by combining parts of his daughters' names, Evelyn and Dee Dee, went into the aluminum storm door and window business. And, by dint of hard work and ability, it succeeded very nicely indeed.

When, about thirty years later, Walter finally sold out and retired, he was able to continue with his volunteer charity work at the nursing home which he and Hilde had supported for years.

Herbert and Hilde and their mother, Thea, died of cancer and Inge had a cancerous breast removed. Walter Levy, in his 80's, is still living at home.

The forced sale left both sides angry at each other. Inge, Walter and most of their families, now three generations, didn't see or speak to each other for almost <u>forty years!</u>

123. A Memorable Party

On January 2, 2004, I wrote a letter to Inge and Walter:

"Three things happened recently that make me write to you both now. First was Betty's passing. That made me realize that you both and I are the oldest generation; you two knew it, but it has hit me lately. And her death made me aware how fragile life is.

"Second was the recent wedding in Washington, DC, of Peter and Rosie Silversmith's daughter Elena, which 27 members of my mother's side of the family attended. That was a great party!

"And yesterday I returned from London where 38 members of our family on my mother's side came to Heddy Friedman's 95th and Robert Bruckner's 60th birthday party. [My Aunt Heddy is the one who took me to my mother's parents when my parents were both arrested by the Gestapo.] Family members came from Canada, Australia, South Africa, California, Boston, New York, and North Carolina, and, of course, England."

So I asked Inge and Walter to help me create a family party on my father's side, to each invite their children and grandchildren, and I would invite mine. It was my only wish for my 70th birthday.

The Friedman Family Reunion on Saturday evening, April 17, 2004, at the Pacific Room of the Holiday Inn Costa Mesa, CA, near Orange County Airport, found 35 members of our family all happily together, some meeting others for the very first time. We had, as I had advertised, "cousins by the dozens." And if I say so myself, it came off beautifully, happily, and perfectly, ending any family feud. Everything was more than just friendly, it was truly a joyous and exuberant reunion.

Inge Friedman, Herbie's widow, and Walter Levy, Hilde's widower, were both delighted to see each other again after so many years and they got along famously, as if they had been apart for only a short time. Some of their children and grandchildren, cousins to each other and living in California, were introduced to each other.

I was also particularly thrilled to be able to announce the marriage of my son Michael Bruce Friedman to Mary Wright (nee Pattajoe) just two days before, on income tax day, April 15th. None of the California families had ever met Mary, most hadn't even met Mike. And we even had Mary's half-sister, Janipher S. Carpenter, and her partner's daughter Kayla at our family party.

Inge and Herbie's three children, Michael and his wife Beth Miller, Paul Robert Friedman, and Monica Friedman Thompson as well as Monica's children, Inge's only grandchildren, partied with Hilde and Walter's two daughters, Evelyn and Diana (formerly "DeeDee," now only "Dee") and their spouses and progeny.

Of course my family was all there, too. David, Debbie, Sarah age 11, and Rachel, 9, DDSR as we call them; John, Karen, and Alexander Henry Friedman, almost 3 years old already, or JK&A; plus Mike and Mary, our own M&M's.

We all regretted that Betty and Herbie and Hilde were no longer with us, especially at this happy event.

With all the loving reunions, it was indeed a memorable party.

124. A Plea from Hilde

In the 1960's, my first cousin, Hilde Levy, nee Friedman, discovered a lump in her breast and went to Kaiser Permanente Hospital. The doctors refused to do a simple biopsy of the suspect lump and literally said, "We cannot biopsy every little suspicious lump in every woman who comes here."

After an extended period of time she had a mastectomy. Years later, another lump and the other mastectomy. But the cancer continued to spread. When she got weaker, she virtually lived in a wheelchair. All in all, Hilde suffered for about twenty years with cancer. Except for a letter she wrote on July 13, 1984, she suffered in silence.

She wrote that she was "totally resigned to having cancer" but she blamed the misjudgment of her doctors for her and her husband, Walter Levy, to have to go through "the next 18 to 24 months carrying the physical and mental burden of having to fight through every painful inch of this ordeal."

Hilde wrote, "Biopsy! Biopsy! Biopsy! What can it hurt?

"We have now arrived at the twilight years of our lives, having taken care of our own responsibilities of looking after our parents up into their 90's, and our children having found happy family lives. Now should have been our time. Time we truly deserved."

Hilde Levy wrote the above remarks when she was 61. She passed away when she was 73.

Others might have sued the doctors or the hospital or Kaiser or all of them. But she and Walter -- who nursed and cared for her throughout -- both suffered in silence. That letter is as loud as she ever raised her voice.

Since then great strides have been made -- mammograms, self-examination, biopsies, etc. Let Hilde's plea remind women to get tested, get second opinions, get biopsies, and get attention from their physicians.

And let Betty's premature death from cancer urge everyone not to smoke.

125. The Traveling Man Mystery

My father truly enjoyed Lee J. Cobb's award-winning performance in Arthur Miller's *Death of a Salesman*. He really identified with the lead role, not only because he knew that the star (whose real name was Lee Jacob) and the playwright were both Jewish. My Old Man was a traveling salesman, but even more than that, he was a traveling man.

What's the difference? I'm glad you asked.

H. H. Friedman, as his business card named him, spent five days a week "on the road" as a salesman. That was how he earned a living. My mother said that he was never happy if he didn't have wheels under him.

Saturdays in the summer he traveled, first by car and later by subway, to Jones Beach. There, with or without me and/or my mother, he parked in Lot 4, walked through the tunnel to the beach, and put his stuff down at a familiar spot. Then he swam out far past the lifeguard's vision, turned, and -- doing breaststroke with his face out of the water -- swam almost the length of the beach, a mile, mile and a half, probably more. Then he would get out of the water and walk back to where his towel and clothing (and sometimes his family) were. He always swam alone.

Saturdays in cooler weather, he'd travel by subway to the Metropolitan Opera. When Sam Zilka "married into" the family, he might meet him there. And subway home.

What did he do on Sundays? He traveled. Most often my mother and father came up to visit us, usually taking a subway to Grand Central Station and then the New Haven train to New Rochelle, then Rye, and later Chappaqua. He'd bring the Sunday *New York Times* and read it in our backyard, occasionally keeping an eye on his grandsons.

And what did he do on his vacation? He traveled! He actually went to Europe three or even four times a year! Of course my parents visited us when we were in Germany. But he hardly spent much time at home or with his family. Did I ever really know him as a father other than when he disciplined me?

I wrote a poem to him on his 80th birthday, June 26, 1974, when I was 40. It was entitled, "The Traveler." It began,

This is the story of a traveling man,
One who went as far as anyone can.
A tale of a particular person who
Epitomizes the famed Wandering Jew.

In 42 such quatrains of bad poetry I used a form of the word *travel* 36 times, citing his business, pleasure, and European as well as Russian trips. His grandson David expressed it better in an English composition dated April 7, 1977, when David was 16 and Hans 83: "He is still as active as most people in their early twenties. Opa goes to classes with college students during the week … he runs with them to all of his classes. He even has a scheduling problem. Two of his classes meet at the same time. He solved this problem by sending his wife with a tape recorder to one while he goes to the other … Opa goes to the opera every weekend and to every show that opens on as well as off Broadway. He also goes to Europe three times a year. If eighty is old, imagine what he did when he was younger!"

I wondered what he did in Europe. Where did he go? Whom did he see?

As a former Military Intelligence Analyst, I should have foreseen the possibility that I can merely theorize about. Only now can I come up with a possible answer to the traveling man mystery.

I realize that my father was actually cold and distant from my mother and me. Just as his father had been to his children. Aron had concerned himself with religion and music, not family. And Hans, why did he leave his family so often, what did he do when he was not with us? He traveled to earn his living but he also traveled on his free time; he never vacationed with his wife and child! He took us both to Camp Edgewood in late June to prepare the camp and picked us up in September when we helped close it.

I hadn't really understood my father at all until I read some old letters and I went to Germany twenty-five years after his death, in December, 2004! On that trip I learned that he met with his first cousin Curt Bois in East Berlin and with my mother's cousin Klaus Kochmann in West Berlin. David and I also met Klaus and his family there. After our visit, he wrote a *Remembrance of Hans* which he sent to me.

Klaus wrote that my father went to Russia before the Second World War, which I had not known. After the war, my father often went to Germany and Russia, that they often met in Berlin, once at a leftist demonstration, that they went to Aron Friedmann's grave in East Berlin and to the Berlin Museum. He wrote that my father went to the Russian Sector of Berlin to meet his cousin Curt Bois and friends "who held high positions in the economic department."

Klaus wrote of my father, "When he saw me in Berlin, he often gave me the impression that visiting in Europe was his 'only' life ... that his present trips had the function of his previous politics.

"Uncle Hans had unbelievable charm, to which Brigitte {his wife} can testify; it showed with his invitations to meals in Berlin ... he could get theater tickets which were absolutely unavailable ... ordinary theater he compared with the incendiary shows of Max Reinhardt, which he had been a part of."

Klaus Kochmann had an anxiety attack when he realized that I was Hans and Lotte Friedman's son; Klaus actually felt closer to my father than he thought I did! That he should have been Hans' son, not me! That really mystified me at the time.

A probable answer to the mystery may possibly turn out to be politics -- my father's undying dedication to the Communist Party! It wasn't, as I had previously thought, his anti-Nazism but his pro-Communism. I have lately come to realize that probability.

So only now may I potentially understand my father. I have now, in September, 2005, found and translated handwritten letters which my father wrote to Ernst Simon and carbon-copied. One, dated October 10, 1996, clearly states, "I have always been an atheist. Already as the smallest schoolboy, and at the time of my bar-mitzvah, a Socialist. I have remained both ... I feel myself to be unhappy over the role that my fellow Jews played in the Hitler time ... Jews could have done more and I have not spoken to any Jew in America who did not mention how successfully he got out of Germany yet never gave it a thought that someone had to stay and fight against Hitler."

This Ernst Simon was not related to the Simons in my mother's family. He was a Professor, Zionist, writer on German Jewry, and lecturer in Manhattan's New School for Social Research, the Leo Baeck Institute, and a temple. My father sent him checks, asking him to make anonymous contributions to specified leftist causes, so that the money would not be traced back to my father.

But Hans did travel to the South to march for Negro Civil Rights, to Chicago to demonstrate at the Democratic National Convention in 1968, and to Washington, D.C. for Martin Luther King, Jr.'s "I have a dream" speech. Ted Rubin recently revealed that when my father was in that huge D.C. protest he held his hat on the side of his face to avoid recognition. Hans Friedman was nonplussed when David told him that he spotted him in a TV film of the demonstration.

My father and I have marched in separate anti-Vietnam War and anti-Nixon demonstrations. David has marched for Russian Jews and for Women's Rights (ERA). I am sure that I was photographed by (I think) the F.B.I. Still, my father was afraid of being photographed at a demonstration.

In another letter to Ernst Simon my father revealed even more: "I cannot talk about this to anyone. The few times I begin, people become very sensitive, perhaps because it presses on their conscience. That includes my few leftist friends. I can talk about it with you because I did my part, carefully and consciously, until the Gestapo caught me. My family, during my absence, arranged for our emigration to the U.S.A."

Had he not wanted to leave but to stay and continue the fight against Nazism? If he had stayed in Nazi Germany as a convicted

330

Communist, could he possibly have avoided imprisonment again or worse, deportation to a concentration camp or extermination camp? I don't think so and he was intelligent enough not to think so.

Yet his devotion to Communism could possibly explain his frequent trips to Russia and East Germany, the so-called "German Democratic Republic." I think my father went to Germany to see his cousin Curt Bois more often than to London to see his brother Paul!

If Hans Friedman was a secret courier or messenger or money-carrier for Communists then visiting his first cousin Curt Bois would be a good "cover story." Did my father's trips, as Klaus Kochmann wrote, "have the function of his previous politics," that is, a Communist function? Was my father still an actor, playing a role? Did Curt Bois return to East Berlin, "surprising his Hollywood friends" (as his biographer had put it) because he too, like his boyhood acting buddy, was an active Communist? Were my father's trips really made to visit his old Adler & Oppenheimer co-worker and Communist cell chief Kurt Bachmann? If so, he might indeed have been a secret agent.

Could that explain the secrets my father kept from me? His not wanting me to know of his actual political activities? His fear of Alex Klein's pal, the undercover cop? Hans hiding his face in political demonstrations?

Now I add the fact that my father, while predicting Harry Truman's victory in 1948, actually voted for Henry Wallace of the Progressive Party. Later my father voted for Earl Browder for President of the United States on the Communist Party ticket.

Hans Friedman supported Communism all his life because it fought the Nazis! Yet it took a war to defeat the Nazis, not a political movement or secret plots by small cells. Even when some German generals conspired against Hitler, they were unsuccessful. Perhaps my father's pro-Communism grew after the Nazis were defeated.

In America Hans may have feared discovery by the U.S. government as he had the German one. He knew what it was like to oppose the legal authorities and the legitimate police force. He had been tortured, he was imprisoned, he missed two years with his wife and only son. Hans Friedman thought he knew what would happen if his true political feelings had been discovered. So he never told me of his imprisonment by the Gestapo. His financial contributions were always secret. He hid his activities. And he remained cautious and vigilant. He never told me about his Berlin or Russian trips. I don't know what he told his wife.

The young idealist who trained for two years before going to Palestine and then saw that Zionism was not what it purported to be and actually became an anti-Zionist was the middle-aged idealist who did not see "the evil empire" for what it turned out to be! My father, who clearly but secretly identified himself as a Communist from pre-war times, saw Senator McCarthy as a personal threat. Hans Friedman had to keep his affiliation secret, lest the legal U.S. government do to him what the legal German government had done to him. He had to keep his opinions pretty much to himself yet he wanted to act -- as he felt too few Jews in Germany ever did -- against a real threat. He knew what a legitimate government could do when civil liberties are ignored!

If Joe McCarthy or J. Edgar Hoover were looking for him, they never found him. Hans Friedman might have been the kind of man they were indeed looking for!

But perhaps not; I may be completely wrong about him. It is also possible that he had a lady-friend although I doubt it.

In 2006 my cousin Gerald Freeman, Ellen Zilka's brother who had been on the *Kindertransport*, put a different perspective on my father's visits to Russia. He told Nicole and me that he remembered a letter he had received from my father revealing his travel plans to help a Jewish woman in Russia get her family to Israel. He asked Gerald, who had been involved in similar activities, not to mention it to anyone!

But his possible commitment to the Communist cause seems to me a logical explanation for his coldness toward me. He may have been like his own father who thought music and religion more important than family. My father's distancing himself might be due to his single-minded dedication to political activism.

Long after my father's death, Betty and I visited the Soviet Union while it was still under Communism. We saw the fear in people's faces, the lack of trust of strangers, the police presence everywhere, the intimidation of the citizenry, the long lines of silent people patiently waiting for whatever might be available to them. This was not Marxist idealism, it was Stalinist realism. We both saw a police state; we were sure that Communism was not the answer. The Soviet collapse and the end of the Cold War proved it. I remain a Capitalist and a Democrat.

My father must have seen what we saw when he went there. He was disillusioned only once, by Zionism. Amazingly to me, my father stuck to his Socialist-Communist ideals. Hans Friedman kept his feelings a secret he took to his grave.

126. Three Sons, Daughters and Grandchildren

I have been incredibly lucky. I have three wonderful sons who have given me three great daughters and three terrific grandchildren.

David is now a deeply religious Jew, a leader in his reform synagogue, the co-president of the congregation. He has seen to it that his wife and children have a complete Jewish education and keep a kosher home.

He is also following my mother's familial interest by making contact and keeping up with far-flung members of the family, creating incredible descendancy charts, meeting relatives, celebrating family events and occasions.

David also stays in excellent physical condition, watching what he eats, exercising, and getting up very early to run, even running in half-marathons.

In addition, David has held two responsible jobs, one with Cisco which has taken him to distant California cities as well as far-flung corners of the globe. And, at the same time, he and a friend created a very successful investing business.

Debbie handles the household, including an active dog named Casey and those two even more active girls! She is involved in girl scouts, practices judo, contributes a lot of her time to the temple, and keeps up a great social life. How does she do it all? I honestly don't know, but she does it all very well!

John has so many friends -- he keeps on collecting more and more people -- and actually does more than just keep in touch. He sees them, gets together with them, goes places with them. He retains friends from childhood, from jobs he's had, from places he has gone, and friends of friends. Old friends, new friends, tried and true friends. It must be his personable personality. He is a faithful friend, one that one can always count on. He is also empathetic and sympathetic, very verbal and understanding, too.

John and Karen were visiting her parents in St. Marys at Christmastime. Her father, Marvin, had fallen off a scaffold about a month earlier, while working on his son Michael's house, and hit his head. Everyone noticed that he wasn't quite himself. Only John would call Marvin's doctor on Christmas day to detail his condition. Marvin was immediately helicoptered to a Pittsburgh hospital for emergency surgery. Now Marvin correctly credits John with saving his life.

Karen's creativity comes from her good, old-fashioned, self-sufficient parents. She is incredibly able, handy, efficient, and proficient at just about everything. Among the many amazing things that she has truly created, I must say, her greatest is Alex.

Michael is a take-charge guy. At the time of a summer blackout in the Northeastern United States, Mike was nowhere near the problem physically. But he stayed in telephone touch with the problem locations in his MCI telephone company. It was quickly determined that their primary difficulty was in the Cleveland, Ohio, area. The loss of electricity severely affected that particular place.

Without any notes, just from memory, Mike directed the shutting down of certain specific switching stations, concentrating their efforts on other ones, in a sequence that he determined. The MCI machinery needed to be kept cool but air-conditioning was out. There was a lake nearby which Mike ordered to be drained and water used to cool the vital locations, yet even that water was not cool enough. So he kept the facilities that were most vital working while cutting off the less essential ones, regardless of the other consequences.

Mike now modestly says that he was but one small factor; there were many others. But I realized just how important he -- and some others -- were to MCI when he was among those rewarded for those efforts with gift certificates good for live lobsters. He was also good enough to share his reward with appreciative members of his family.

My M&M's have given me two granddogs, Casey and Willow, two grandcats, Punkin and Missy, and lots of grandfish, gold and koi.

Through her determination, perseverance, and dedication, Mary is now a very successful real estate agent. So much so that she bought a Morris Minor and a 25-foot boat.

And my three grandchildren, well, I can only express my complete pride and delight, my pleasure and enchantment, my absolute love of all of them. The three of you are truly special!

127. Some More Friedmans

Fortunate Gagnon, a woman whose name means "fortunate winner," married Lucien Richard in Montreal, Province of Quebec, Canada. Their first child was born on March 3rd, 1939 -- 3/3/39 -- lucky numbers -- and named Nicole.

She was the oldest of six children -- all girls. A photo of the six Richard sisters shows how much alike they look. Nicole actually said, "I always thought of us as a litter."

Nicole is the mother of two children -- both girls. And she is the grandmother of four children -- all girls. Girls don't just run in her family, they congregate. Ten children in a row and not one boy!

Nicole left school at fifteen when her father arranged a job with a *notaire* as a clerk. Next she became a "robotypist," taking dictation from a kind of Dictaphone machine. She had to turn her pay over to help support the family.

She left home when she was twenty. Nicole had her eye on coming to America, but it took one thousand U.S. dollars! So she became a typist at an American Army base on the Canadian East Coast -- Goose Bay, Labrador. After a year she was able to go to San Francisco and stayed three years.

Then she was off to New York City. She met Leonard Friedman, converted to Judaism, and married him. Lenny told me that his Friedman family came to America in the 1880's from Russia. After their two girls were born, they moved to New Jersey. Then Nicole and Lenny got divorced.

Nicole worked for a pharmaceutical company in New Jersey as a medical copy editor for seventeen years, retiring in 1997. She continued as a freelancer, until her second retirement in 2005.

Lenny and Nicole's first daughter, Francoise Friedman, married Steve Mosteiro, a Managing Director at Bear Stearns investment advisors; they live in New Jersey. Their second daughter, Joelle, married Edward Cantu III but retained her maiden name of Friedman. Already as a young boy, Ed dreamed of becoming an open-heart surgeon. He went to Harvard, got his M.D. from Columbia, interned at Duke University Medical Center and moved his family to Durham, North Carolina. Now a Chief Resident, Ed has performed heart and lung transplants and other delicate surgeries.

After living close to Francoise's family for years, Nicole decided to move near Joelle's family in Durham. Why? Because, when Nicole came for a visit, Joelle's license plate had the letters NRF, Nicole Richard Friedman's initials. A believer in serendipity, she took that as a good omen and now lives in the Woodcroft section of Durham about 15 minutes away from me in Chapel Hill.

Nicole and I enjoy living here for the various educational opportunities. One of them is The French Table. An outgrowth of DILR, its participants meet weekly for a French language lunch. Betty and I went there to maintain our French and met Nicole.

One day Nicole mentioned Dr. Frank Netter, a noted medical illustrator whose books she had edited. I was familiar with those books from my years of working on TV advertising for drug companies. She was surprised and amazed. I think she gained some admiration for my wide ranging interests and my memory through that incident. The coincidence of our last name was instantly apparent, as was a liking for each other. Speaking the same languages, we understood each other very well.

After Betty's untimely death, I was comforted by Nicole's understanding, genuine warmth and companionship. Our first get-together other than the French Table was after a DILR class, for lunch at the Spartacus Restaurant in Durham on January 16, 2004. Our first real date, for dinner at the Provence Restaurant in Carrboro, was January 21st. Our first trip together, to Sanford, N.C., was March 20th.

Nicole is fun to be with. We have traveled together along the East Coast, West Coast, North to Canada and to Paris. We are clearly compatible and enjoy each other's company very much. She's a wonderful traveling companion. We get along so very well. She laughs at my jokes. She even thinks they're funny! So much so that she is compiling a list of "Wallyisms," not to be confused with witticisms.

She is very different from Betty. Although they both grew up in poverty, Nicole is certainly no coupon-clipping bargain-hunter, preferring prestigious brand-names and high-quality retail stores instead of sales and discount factory outlets. What could be more different? Nicole also believes in fate, karma, kismet, luck. She goes out of her way to avoid making left turns on 4-lane roads, keeps to the right lane on highways and drives the speed limit. Indeed, who could be different?

She is very warm, considerate, and loving -- when she really like something she says, "I <u>love</u> that!" And when Nicole really loves someone, her love is expressed through loyalty, kindness, and true caring. She calls many different women (Margaret, Norma, Maria-Rosa, Myrna) her best friends.

Nicole also has an instant attraction to children of all ages which is quickly reciprocated. My three grandchildren immediately fell in love with her as she did with them. My six sons and daughters and Nicole love each other, too.

After receiving a gift from Nicole, my then-10-year-old granddaughter Rachel, already a very perceptive girl, wrote her this thank-you note: "I have never seen a nicer person than you. You are constantly thinking about doing nice things for other people. And I want to thank you for giving me the chance to meet you."

On June 2, 2004, Nicole wrote me a note which said, "Wally, I do not ever foresee a time when I will get angry at you."

A year later, on June 5, 2005, Nicole wrote a poem, "To my Wally," which detailed the many things she loved about me and ends, "But I love you most because you never, ever say 'no.'"

All I can add is that I love her!

We two have decided that there is no reason to get married or to move in with each other. She is a wonderful lady-friend and companion. I believe that I am good for her and I know that she is very good for me. And to me. I really do love her.

So I have followed both of my grandmothers, my father, my mother, my wife, and all three of my daughters-in-law in our family tradition of falling in love with a Friedman.

128. Biblical Creation and Evolution

On March 28, 1981, the day I turned 47, I wrote a letter to Isaac Asimov, the noted science fiction writer. I had just finished reading his latest book, *In The Beginning*. In it he tried to reconcile the bible and modern science. And I actually attempted to interpret a

...o make the creation story compatible with modern
...ice!

... you Mr. Asimov's response to me, written on May
... he most ingenious interpretation of *Genesis 1:25-26*
... I have never seen it before, nor have I ever thought
... myself. I hope you won't mind if I make use of it at some time in
the future."

Perhaps my thoughts then are still novel today. In my letter to him
I quoted this biblical translation, undoubtedly a Jewish version: *And
God made the beasts of the earth ... And God said, Let us make man in
our image, after our likeness.*

And I wrote, "Could it be that God was speaking <u>to</u> the beasts
of the earth that He had just created? If so, it would account for His
use of the 'us' and 'our' form. His meaning could then be considered
to suggest that God, through the 'beasts of the earth,' would create
man. This might then be interpreted to mean, as Science has found
in evolution, that man was created with, by, and through the 'beasts
of the earth.' It would seem to me to be as if God were saying, let us
make man together.

"As further confirmation of this particular theory, I suggest the
passage continues with God's words, 'after our likeness.' If one considers
this to mean that man would be made in 'our' (i.e., God's and the beasts
of the earth's likeness), it could imply evolution...Man did evolve on
earth in the likeness of the beasts of the earth!

"Perhaps it would indeed have been clearer if there had been
quotation marks around God's words. He might then more likely be
addressing the beasts. For, indeed, who else could there have been for
Him to talk to?"

That's what I wrote to Isaac Asimov.

Yet I do not believe in God nor the bible. I believe in science and
the scientific method rather than any religion. There need not be an
intelligent design; there may only be natural forces we do not yet fully
comprehend. I find evolution a much more reasonable assumption that
has almost been proven. Einstein's *Theory of Relativity* does explain a
great deal. And the Unified String Theory explains even more. I do not
pretend to understand it, but that does not matter. There are intelligent

ideas in the scientific community that explain many things that human beings had not previously understood.

My heritage is Judaism; it is an important part of me. Yet I am an atheist; I have no doubt that God does not exist, that there is no Heaven or Hell.

I believe that God was created by man in his own image. Heaven was invented by the educated class to convince the uneducated masses, in the extreme poverty and misery of feudalism, that there is a better world ahead. Karl Marx was right: religion is the opiate of the masses. More wars have been fought, more people have been killed, in the name of various religions than for any other reason, including a leader's ego, economic gain, political advantage, territorial capture, or racial reasons. Richard Dawkins in *The Selfish Gene* said, "Faith is one of the world's great evils."

When Durham Rabbi John Friedman, no relation, delivered the DILR convocation, on September 11th (!) 2005, he began by asking how many in the audience, which I estimated at 250, believed that God wrote the Torah, the bible's first "Five Books of Moses." Or that God inspired Moses to write the Torah, or that one human wrote it at once, or that many people wrote it over a period of time. The rabbi himself came out for five authors over a few centuries. I accept that and certainly don't believe that Moses wrote about things that happened after his own death.

I think that God does not watch over us. If he did he could not have allowed the Holocaust! Prayer is useless. It is preposterous that prayers are answered when both opposing football teams pray to the same One True God for their team's victory. I do not believe in a trinity of god, man, and spirit. Nor in resurrection, reincarnation, or an afterlife. And I cannot conceive of a virgin birth.

I believe in the scientific method, in science, not Scientology. I am convinced that it is utter foolishness to think that whoever or whatever created our planet is also guiding its future as well as our individual futures. That simply does not make sense to me. I think that Jesus Christ was a Jewish rabbi. That he prayed to his "father" as many people call their god. Greek and Roman myths had a god fathering an earthling. I doubt that Jesus himself believed anyone but Joseph was his father. He said, "I am the son of man." As a Jew, Jesus undoubtedly believed in the first commandment: *Thou shalt have no other God before me.* Therefore I think it would not make sense to him, as it does not make sense to me, to pray to an intermediary, as many Christians do, to Jesus or Mary or a saint. Jews, like Tevye in *Fiddler on the Roof,* speak directly to God. So, if you want a religion, if you feel a need to pray instead of merely wishing for something, I suppose Judaism is as good as any and better than most. It is your heritage, too.

What is terribly wrong in our world is *fundamentalism in any religion,* Muslim, Christian, or Jewish. Take science literally, not nonscience or religious nonsense, not Creationism nor Imagined Design.

129. Your Future

I would like to make some predictions about the future, your future, my grandchildren, a time that I will not live to see.

Early man thought that the sun and the planets revolved around our Earth. He assigned Heaven upward and Hell downward. But man soon learned that those things are not literally true. I think that there is no heaven or hell.

Christopher Columbus discovered that the world is round. Yet *New York Times* columnist Thomas L. Friedman, no relation, has written a book entitled, *The World is Flat.* He means that we are on a level playing field, that India, China, and the Far East have caught up with the U.S. in technology, that ideas can come from anywhere, from anyone. Competition is international.

On July 5, 2005, a NASA spacecraft called Deep Impact crashed into the comet, Tempel 1, with a force equal to 4½ tons of dynamite. A *New York Times* editorial said, "With luck … the deeper debris (will) shed light on the evolution of the solar system and on the possible role of comets in carrying elements and perhaps even precursors of life to Earth." If that did not reveal enough information, a future such mission may.

Mankind is now exploring four broad but distinct scientific pursuits that I believe will be most important for the future and which may well change the future of civilization in my personal opinion.

1. We are exploring Outer Space and finding not only many new planets but more and more galaxies. We will discover that the universe is expanding outward constantly and that may or may not prove the

Big Bang theory of creation. That alone does not prove or disprove the existence of a Creator but it may well show how it was done!

Scientists are not only sending rockets into the universe, ordinary citizens are doing so. Some are sending up a craft, launched by a submarine and propelled by sunlight or starlight, with giant triangular solar sails. Others are experimenting with a plasma-magnetic-powered rocket to inflate "invisible sails" tens of miles wide.

It probably will be possible to discover what "natural forces" created life elsewhere and, by deduction, on Earth. And we will learn if there is any form of life on other planets, inside and outside of our own Milky Way galaxy. We may come to understand whatever it is that created life on Earth, and I think it will not be a God-like thing but a scientific occurrence.

As of this writing, scientists are not able to reconcile the Big Bang Theory with String Theory. But that is just my point: there is so much left to be understood by man. An experiment reported in *USA Today* on April 20, 2005, revealed that, Dan Thanh Son of the University of Washington said, "will help us uncover a deep connection between the real world and string theory. That would be fantastic."

Scientists are attempting to replicate in the laboratory the conditions, as we discover them, existing on other planets. Someone may figure out a way to create life! That will not make the scientist a god. But it may downgrade our idea of God. (I am, you must remember, an atheist at heart.)

I learned in school that there were nine planets. In my lifetime literally *hundreds* of planets have been discovered. Infrared Light, indicating radiating heat, has been detected recently from planets orbiting relatively close stars. Hundreds of thousands of comparatively young stars have been detected recently, also in our galaxy, some with a brilliance of almost a million suns and about 2,000 times larger than our own sun. New discoveries about the universe are coming, more and more than ever before, as we continue to send up scientific rockets.

There is also a project, initially funded by the U.S. government, but whose financing has recently been severely cut, called SETI -- the Search for Extra-Terrestrial Intelligence. Dr. Frank Drake, who serves on SETI's board, created the Drake Equation which estimates the number of technologically advanced civilizations that might exist in our galaxy. Dr. Drake's estimate is 10,000 communicative civilizations in the Milky Way. So "someone" may contact <u>us</u>! Thousands of SETI's volunteers are listening.

2. We are exploring Inner Space, that is, the depths of the land as well as the oceans on our planet. This so-called Earth is about 70% water, so "earth" is a misnomer. J. Craig Venter of the Human Genome Project is now identifying the unique mixes of microbes in different soils and "some new type of light-driven biology" in the oceans. I believe that we will find more creatures that live on this planet which do not breathe oxygen or drink water or eat vegetation. Recently we learned of nonoxygen-based life on our own planet, creatures that live at great depths in the oceans. Our exploration of new life forms may also come from microscopic discoveries, living creatures which exist utilizing chemical forms previously unknown or even anathema to us. So we will have to expand our definition of "life" to include some things that may exist on our -- and on other -- planets. And we might figure out how some other life forms came into existence.

The *New York Times* printed an editorial by Paul Davies on April 10, 2005, entitled, "Goodbye Mars, Hello Earth." I quote selected sections:

"... in the 1960's, anyone who believed that there might be life on other planets was considered a crackpot. Now all that has changed. ... NASA is spending billions of dollars to search for life on Mars ... but we may not need to go all the way to Mars to find another sample of life. It could be lurking under our very noses ... It's possible that pockets of microbes could have survived ... opening up the tantalizing prospect of two or more different forms of life co-existing on the same planet ... Our planet could be seething with alien bugs without anyone suspecting it.... Even if alien life has not endured to the present day [on Earth] it may still have left its mark ... A form of biology that is unrelated to familiar life.

"... Nobody knows how life began. ... Our ignorance of this process is so great that scientists can't even agree ... a Nobel Prize-winning biologist was adamant that life is a bizarre accident confined to Earth ... another Nobel laureate declares life ... bound to occur wherever Earth-like conditions prevail. ... Are we alone?"

3. We are exploring other forms of life that do or did exist on our planet as well as on other planets. *Falcarius utahensis,* the recently discovered fossil of a small, agile meat eater, was an interim stage that led to huge, dinosaurian vegetarians. *Repenonumus robustus* is a newly found fossil of a dinosaur-eating mammal, much larger than any previously known. We may soon find other "missing links" and prove evolution as fact.

Surely we will someday decode the language of other creatures, starting perhaps with dolphins or whales. Or a recently found creature that seems to cross those two species, as we categorize them now. We "discovered" radar by understanding how bats fly in the dark. I think we will find that many forms of communication exist, even on our planet. For example, how do flocks of birds or schools of fish travel in tight formations, change directions suddenly, and never bump into each other? It must be some form of communication. How do elephants communicate over distances of many miles? How do Monarch butterflies know where to go in the winter; how do salmon know their upriver spawning sites or birthplaces? How instinctive is motherhood? For sea turtles, for birds, for humans? And what is instinct? Will we settle the age-old question of Nature versus Nurture? I think so.

Scientists from Georgia State University are studying the language of bonobos, the apes most like humans, in the Great Ape Trust of Iowa's Des Moines campus. Bonobos vocalize as though they are conversing and often walk upright. What will they teach us about us? A lot.

Dutch scientists, testing a European chickadee, found that some birds are shy and others bold, broad personality differences that have a genetic foundation. We humans do not like to think of ourselves as animals. Nor do we think that behavior may have genetic or evolutionary roots. But we are coming to terms with all forms of life.

I believe that humans are animals, nothing more. We normally eat, sleep, and reproduce much as other animals do, hopefully with better manners. We may have better-developed brains than any other species but some "animals" can do things we cannot. A bat's radar, dolphins' sonar, reptilian tissue regrowth, are but a few examples.

The definition of intelligence will have to expand beyond present human understanding. I predict we will discover we are not the only intelligent creatures, on this planet or elsewhere. Many animals do communicate within their species; some convey varied messages. Many chimps have learned to type as a form of intelligent communication. A famous chimpanzee named Koko has mastered a sign language well enough to carry on arguments with humans!

4. Finally, we are exploring ourselves, making tremendous medical strides in the understanding of DNA, the true building blocks of life. I believe that the similarities of human and chimpanzee or bonobo DNA will show that we are indeed descended from apes, proving Darwinian evolution. DNA will, in time, show the true relationship of humans to animals and even reveal the "blood line" of all species, detailing the evolutionary lineages. The rare discovery of eggs inside a dinosaur supports the theory that birds evolved from dinosaurs in addition to the evidence of winged, even feathered, reptilian dinosaurs.

The recently discovered fact that chimpanzees have 24 chromosomes and humans 23 created cause for wonder. Then it was determined that two chimp chromosomes have merged into our one. I think that almost proves evolution!

On May 11, 2005, the *New York Times* editorialized that, "We are already partly down the path of mixing human and animal cells or organs. Although it once seemed odd and unsettling, no one worries much anymore about transplanting pig valves into human hearts or human fetal tissue into mice ... (scientists) want to put lots of human-brain stem cells into mice to see how they perform in a real body as opposed to laboratory ... If stem cell therapies pan out, the Food and Drug Administration will almost certainly require animal experiments before they can be approved for the public. Research that some consider scary today may be required by regulators tomorrow."

When my father was a boy he learned in school that man could not fly. Yet in his lifetime, he flew in airplanes. I learned in school that we could not escape the gravitational pull of this planet. Yet in my lifetime, men from Earth walked on the moon. What are you learning that science will prove to be untrue?

Scientists at Purdue University recently announced that plants, yes, plants, sometimes select better bits of DNA in order to develop normally even when their predecessors carried genetic flaws. This completely contradicts Mendel's Laws of Genetics which go back to the mid-1800s. The implications are astounding -- some species may be able to repair their deficiencies.

Many lizards, geckos are but one example, shed their tails when attacked. That independent appendage then wriggles around to distract the predator. And the lizard grows a new tail! What those stupid creatures can do, mere humans cannot -- yet.

Nearby Duke University Medical Center used stem cells taken from umbilical cords (and therefore legal in the U.S.) to actually prevent Krabbe's disease in babies.

We have already created new creatures -- there are, for example, ligers and tiglons, the mixtures of lions and tigers that nature never created. Mules are a mix of horse and donkey. A rare female "wholphin" or whale-dolphin mix was born in captivity. How many other new combinations can we create? As we understand more of DNA, we will probably learn new possibilities. Mankind might master its own evolution some day (well, maybe or maybe not), but some Science Fiction has already become Scientific Fact. And who knows what a human mind can think of? Will we make a mixture of different species' DNA in a laboratory to create entirely new creatures? That's neither cloning nor clowning.

There is also so-called junk DNA, unidentifiable, un-understandable DNA. Who knows what we will discover about those molecular structures.

I recommend any of those four broad scientific studies as worthwhile careers to my grandchildren. Any of these fields should make for an interesting and richly rewarding life's work. Go for it. You can do whatever you want to do.

I know that Sarah has wanted to be a marine biologist ever since she was five years old. There can be nothing more important and worthwhile than a career that is really looking for new knowledge, conceiving new ideas, exploring new possibilities. Do whatever you want, my dears. In any field of activity you choose.

What all of this means to me is that any individual's life on Earth is the only life he or she will ever have. And when a human being is dead, that's it. So, my darling grandchildren, make the best of it.

Have a good life.

I have.

Printed in the United States
65176LVS00003B/1-81